To understand the emergence of
tual written text in ancient Greek
to trace the history of Homeric pe
beginning of alphabetic literacy in
the way through the critical era ot ᴄᴇᴛᴜᴀᴌ canonizations in
the Hellenistic and Roman periods. In making this argument, the author applies the comparative evidence of oral
poetic traditions, including those that survived in literate
societies, such as the Provençal troubadour tradition. From
such evidence it appears that a song cannot be fixed as a
final written text so long as the oral poetic tradition in
which it was created stays alive, potentially re-creating ever
new versions of the 'same' song. So also with Homeric poetry, it is argued that no single definitive text could evolve
until the oral traditions in which the epic was grounded
became obsolete. In the watershed era of Aristarchus,
around 150 BC, the gradual movement from relatively more
fluid to more rigid stages of Homeric transmission reached
a near-final point of textualization.

Poetry as performance

Poetry as performance
Homer and beyond

GREGORY NAGY

Francis Jones Professor of Classical Greek Literature
and Professor of Comparative Literature, Harvard University

CAMBRIDGE
UNIVERSITY PRESS

Published by the Press Syndicate of the University of Cambridge
The Pitt Building, Trumpington Street, Cambridge CB2 1RP
40 West 20th Street, New York, NY 10011-4211, USA
10 Stamford Road, Oakleigh, Melbourne 3166, Australia

First published 1996
Reprinted 1996

A catalogue record for this book is available from the British Library

Library of Congress cataloguing in publication data
Nagy, Gregory.
Poetry as performance : Homer and beyond / Gregory Nagy.
p. cm.
Includes bibliographical references and index.
ISBN 0 521 55135 8 (hardback) ISBN 0 521 55848 4 (paperback)
1. Homer–Criticism, Textual. 2. Epic poetry, Greek–History and
criticism–Theory, etc. 3. Epic poetry, Greek–Criticism, Textual.
4. Oral interpretation of poetry–History. 5. Performing arts–
Greece–History. 6. Oral tradition–Greece–History.
7. Transmission of texts. 8. Homer–Technique. I. Title.
PA4037.N35 1996
883'.01–dc20 95-13248 CIP

ISBN 0 521 55135 8 hardback
ISBN 0 521 55848 4 paperback

Transferred to digital printing 2000

A O

Contents

Preface

This book grew out of the J. H. Gray Lectures that I gave for the
Faculty of Classics at the University of Cambridge on 10, 12, and
14 May 1993. I am very grateful to the faculty, students, and
friends of the Faculty, many of whom are singled out below, for
the happy memories of my visit.

A shorter version of Chapter 5 was read as a paper at an international conference organized by Françoise Létoublon, the
"Colloque Milman Parry," held at the University of Grenoble on
14, 15, and 16 September 1993.

This book took a long time to write, and I was fortunate
to get the advice of many people along the way. These include:
Elizabeth Adkins-Regan, Robert Albis, Margaret Alexiou, Nancy
Andrews, Ernst Badian, Ann Batchelder, Victor Bers, Graeme
Bird, David Blank, Timothy Boyd, P. G. McC. Brown, Myles
Burnyeat, Paul Cartledge, Matthew Clark, R. G. G. Coleman,
Derek Collins, Gregory Crane, Olga M. Davidson, Laurence de
Looze, Marian Demos, Carol Dougherty, Peter Dronke, Ursula
Dronke, Andrew Dyck, Andrew Ford, Patrick K. Ford, Philip M.
Freeman, Marjorie Garber, Simon Goldhill, John Hamilton,
Michael Haslam, Albert Henrichs, Carolyn Higbie, Geneviève
Husson, Barbara Johnson, C. P. Jones, Pierre Judet de La Combe,
Charles de Lamberterie, André Lardinois, Françoise Létoublon,
Geoffrey Lloyd, Janet Lloyd, Anthony A. Long, Nicole Loraux,
Mary Louise Lord, Deborah Lyons, Richard P. Martin, Michael
Messersmith, Steven Meyer, Elisabeth Mitchell, Stephen A.
Mitchell, John Morgan, Kenneth Morrell, Oswyn Murray, Blaise
Nagy, Joseph Nagy, Robin Osborne, George Pepe, Ann Perkins,
Rupert T. Pickens, M. D. Reeve, Panagiotis Roilos, Philippe

Preface

Rousseau, Ian Rutherford, William Sale, Albert Schachter, Elizabeth Scharffenberger, David Schur, Charles Segal, Kathryn Slanski, Laura Slatkin, Christiane Sourvinou-Inwood, Richard Tarrant, Richard Thomas, Thomas du Toit, S. V. Tracy, Roger Travis, Emily Vermeule, Dimitrios Yatromanolakis, Jenny Wallace, Calvert Watkins, Heather Williams, Dan Wiley, James Zetzel, Jan Ziolkowski, Bella Zweig. To anyone whose name I may have forgotten in this list, I apologize. Also, I assume responsibility for whatever mistakes may remain.

The title of the book is an indirect tribute to the pioneering anthropological insights of Richard Bauman, *Verbal Art as Performance* (Prospect Heights, Ill. 1977).

On 7, 13, and 17 January 1994, I had a chance to "repeat" my Gray Lectures, this time in French, at the Ecole des Hautes Etudes en Sciences Sociales in Paris, thanks to the initiative of my friend Nicole Loraux. She has always been the most supportive of colleagues, but I particularly appreciated her encouragement as I was struggling with the final phases of this book. In the fall of 1994, just as I was about to write to her to announce jokingly that the ordeal was finally over, I learned, to my shock, that Nicole had suddenly become very ill. As I write this, she continues a gallant struggle against the effects of her illness, living out the heroic meaning of an ancient Greek word for 'ordeal' that she herself has understood better than any other Hellenist, *pónos*. I dedicate this book to her in recognition of her heroic courage, and in fond hopes that she will prevail yet again, as she has always prevailed before.

x

Introduction: a brief survey of concepts and aims

The two central concepts of this book can be summed up in the words *performance* and *composition*, which are to be taken as two different aspects of one process in oral poetics. The emphasis here is on performance, as the title of the book indicates. The basic work on the interaction of performance and composition continues to be Albert Lord's *The Singer of Tales*.[1] Since we will be concentrating here on the oral poetics of ancient Greece, it is important to stress, from the very start, the importance of Lord's book for Hellenists.[2] Though it is cited by many who offer various arguments about "oral poetry," the book is often treated only superficially, and there are even instances where those who agree or disagree with it have evidently not read it at all.

The complementarity of *performance* and *composition*, as observed by Lord, parallels that of *parole* and *langue*, as formulated by Ferdinand de Saussure in the field of linguistics.[3] The present book places the emphasis on *parole*, parallel to the emphasis on *performance*.[4]

The English noun *song*, along with the verb *sing*, expresses admirably the coexistence of performance and composition as a

[1] Lord 1960.
[2] Cf. N 1992a.26.
[3] Saussure 1916. A critical summary in Ducrot and Todorov 1979.118–120.
[4] See for example the implications of *parole* in my preface (pp. ix–xi) to the inaugural volume of the "Myth and Poetics" series, Martin 1989, *The Language of Heroes*. See also Dronke 1977.13–31, the Introduction, which is entitled "Performers and Performance." Eric Havelock remarks in *The Muse Learns to Write* (1986.93) that "surviving orality also explains why Greek literature to Euripides is composed as a performance, and in the language of performance." The term *orality*, however, can lead to many misunderstandings, some of which I survey in N 1992a.

1

continuum. Further, the idea of performance inherent in *song*, which is absent from the word *poetry*, makes it more useful to apply the word *song* rather than *poetry* to archaic Greek traditions, which do not explicitly distinguish song from poetry. The resonance of *performance* led Albert Lord to describe the medium of the South Slavic *guslar* – and of Homer – as *song* rather than *poetry*. The same idea figures prominently in the title of his pathfinding book, *The Singer of Tales*.[5]

The background for applying the linguistic terms *langue* and *parole*, especially with reference to other linguistic terms such as *synchronic* and *diachronic*, *unmarked* and *marked*, has been worked out in *Pindar's Homer*, a compendium of over ten years of research,[6] and in the essay "Early Greek Views of Poetry and Poets" in volume I of the *Cambridge History of Literary Criticism*, which can serve as an epitome of that compendium.[7] Another essay, "Homeric Questions," offers a general outline of comparative linguistic as well as ethnographic approaches, summing up in this way the task at hand: "The essence of *performing* song and poetry, an essence permanently lost from the *paideía* that we have inherited from the ancient Greeks, is for me the primary question."[8]

A qualification is needed concerning the term *comparative*, which in linguistics can be used in two senses, one more specific and the other more general. The first is represented by the *méthode comparative*, perfected by linguists like Antoine Meillet, where comparison entails the study of cognate forms and meanings within the discipline of historical linguistics.[9] The second sense is more general, referring to the study of typological parallels, that is, of analogies between historically unrelated languages.[10] While

[5] Lord 1960.
[6] N 1990a.
[7] N 1989. One additional set of terms introduced in the present work involves the distinction that needs to be made, in analyzing oral poetics, between a *syntagmatic* or "horizontal" *axis of combination* and a *paradigmatic* or "vertical" *axis of selection*. Cf. Ducrot and Todorov 1979.111: "Thus the meaning of a word is determined both by the influence of those that surround it in discourse and by the memory of those that could have taken its place."
[8] N 1992a.23.
[9] Meillet 1925.
[10] A classic example is the study of Benveniste 1946 on the function of the third person in the verb-systems of a wide variety of unrelated languages.

the establishing of cognates or borrowings is a matter of empirically proving a historical connection between the languages compared, the adducing of typological parallels need not be taken as proof for a given argument, but only as an intuitive reinforcement. The "beyond" in the subtitle of this book refers to both senses of comparison, applied to the study of song and poetry in performance.

Suffice it for the moment to offer one example each of the two senses of the term *comparative*. To start with the more specific sense: if we compare the meters of Song 44 of Sappho with those of Homeric hexameter, we are dealing with forms that are arguably cognate, that is, derivable from a common source.[11] The more general sense of the term comes into play if we compare, for example, the conventions of a performer's switching from second person to first person in Song 1 of Sappho with similar conventions in the female initiation songs of Athapascan language groups like the Apache and Navajo.[12] Such a comparison is not a matter of proving something outright, since the ancient Greek and the contemporary Athapascan traditions are obviously unrelated to each other historically. What is achieved, rather, is simply the enhanced likelihood that parallel lines of interpretation might lead to a deeper understanding of the individual traditions being compared.

One long-range comparative inference reached in previous work extends into the present book, which is, that group dynamics in performance help explain solo dynamics more effectively than the other way around.[13] This inference leads to a new emphasis on the distinction between *group* and *audience*, which in turn leads to refinements of the Greek concept of mimesis. Ultimately, these questions converge on a more specific question, that is, the relationship of *lyric* and *epic*.

Epic is more difficult to define diachronically than lyric. The eventual form of ancient Greek epic is more complex than that of "lyric," despite the fact that epic happens to be the earliest-attested body of literature in Greek history.[14] "Epic" is also more

---

[11] Such a comparison is the main topic of N 1974 ch. 4.
[12] See ch. 4 in this book.
[13] Cf. N 1990a ch. 12.
[14] N 1974, 1990a.439–464.

difficult to define synchronically, because it is even more de-
ceptive than "lyric" when we apply the distinction between what
Plato and Aristotle call diegesis and mimesis. While the first of
these two terms is easily understood as 'narrative', the second is
much more difficult to pin down. It will be argued at length that
the primary meaning of mimesis is 'dramatic re-enactment'. Suffice it to stress for now a central conclusion reached in this book,
that the diegesis of epic is subsumed by mimesis. We may recall
the perceptive wording of Stephen Halliwell, who considers the
possibility that "Aristotle's guiding notion of mimesis is implicitly
that of enactment: poetry proper (which may include some works
in prose) does not describe, narrate or offer argument, but
dramatises and embodies human speech and action."[15] Such a
formulation of Aristotle's notion can apply even to the "I" who
narrates Homeric song.[16]

The ultimate aim, then, is to show that both epic and lyric in
ancient Greece were fundamentally a medium of mimesis, which
we can understand only if we keep asking how, when, where, and
why these two kinds of verbal art were *performed*.

---

[15] Halliwell 1986.128.
[16] There is a key formulation in Martin 1989.87–88.

PART I

Mimesis and the making of identity in poetic performance

I

The Homeric nightingale and the poetics of variation in the art of a troubadour

Let us begin with a passage from epic, where the epic is representing lyric, not epic. Specifically the lyric form is a song of lament. Penelope is at the moment comparing herself to a nightingale, the typical songbird of lament in ancient Greek traditions, who in a previous life had been a woman who suffered the ultimate grief of "inadvertently" killing her own child:

ὡς δ᾽ ὅτε Πανδαρέου κούρη, χλωρηῒς ἀηδών,
καλὸν ἀείδῃσιν ἔαρος νέον ἱσταμένοιο,
δενδρέων ἐν πετάλοισι καθεζομένη πυκινοῖσιν,
ἥ τε θαμὰ τρωπῶσα χέει πολυηχέα φωνήν,
παῖδ᾽ ὀλοφυρομένη Ἴτυλον φίλον, ὅν ποτε χαλκῷ
κτεῖνε δι᾽ ἀφραδίας, κοῦρον Ζήθοιο ἄνακτος.   520

As when the daughter of Pandareos, the nightingale [aēdōn]
    in the green[1]
sings beautifully at the onset anew of springtime,
perched in the dense foliage of trees,
and she pours forth, changing it around thick and fast, a
voice with many resoundings,

---

[1] On the identification of the aēdōn, here apparently personified as Aedon, with what we know as the nightingale (*Luscinia megarhynchos*), see Thompson 1936.16–22; cf. Pischinger 1901.15–16 and Schmid 1904.3–4. For the moment, *khlōrēis* (χλωρηΐς) is rendered as 'in the green'. Cf. Irwin 1974.72–75, who points out that the usage of *khlōrēis* must be related to that of *khlōraukhēn* (χλωραύχην), conventionally translated as 'green-throated', which serves as epithet of the nightingale in Simonides PMG 586.2 (ἀηδόνες … χλωραύχενες). The visual characteristics of *khlōros*, even if we translate it imperfectly as 'green', are linked metaphorically with the auditory characteristics of the nightingale's voice: see p. 59n1.

7

lamenting her child, the dear Itylos,[2] whom once upon a
time with weapon of bronze she killed inadvertently, the
son of Zethos the king.

Odyssey 19.518-523

This form of the story, where the unfortunate woman is
daughter of Pandareos and wife of Zethos, is different from the
better-known variant native to Athens, where Procne the daughter of Pandion and wife of Tereus deliberately kills her child Itys.[3]
For now, however, the focus is on the variations not in the myth
but rather in the actual wording of the passage. At verse 521, a
variant reading πολυδευκέα (*poludeukéa*), the meaning of which is
unclear, is reported by Aelian *De natura animalium* 5.38, in place of
what we see in the text as quoted, πολυηχέα (*poluēkhéa*) 'with
many resoundings'.

In a book about the textual history of the Homeric poems, one
critic notes that *poludeukḗs* (the nominative) is "rarer" than *poluēkhḗs*, adding: "we have seen, however, that many conjectures
were introduced by the ancients into Homer and that sometimes
the *original* was replaced by a rarer and more difficult word."[4] In
his footnotes, he offers this opinion: "in a poet such as Homer
the simpler and less sophisticated expression is likely to be the
original one."[5]

Let us juxtapose this opinion with a general formulation
offered by Albert Lord in response to modern cultural precon-
ceptions about oral poetry:

[2] On the onomatopoeia implicit in the name Itylos = *Itulos*, as derivative of *Itus*,
see p.41n7. In the ancient Greek lyric traditions, as we will see, this name apparently
mimics the birdsong of the nightingale.
[3] Cf. Apollodorus 3.14.8. Van der Valk 1949.203 argues that the *Odyssey* version is
an Ionic myth. On the pertinence of the nightingale simile, and of the implied myth of
Aedon/Procne, to the situation of Penelope in this narrative context, see Papadopoulou-Belmehdi 1994.135–147; cf. Austin 1975.228–229 and Seaford 1994.56.
[4] Van der Valk p. 83. My emphasis. He points out, however, that the variant πολυδευκέα (*poludeukéa*) of *Odyssey* 19.521 is attested not only in Aelian but also in Hesychius, where πολυδευκέα φωνήν is glossed as τὴν πολλοῖς ἐοικυῖαν '[the voice]
similar to many' (on the basis of the arguments assembled in ch.2, we will see that this
gloss is perhaps not far off the mark). In Hesychius we also find, besides πολυδευκέα
φωνήν, the variant that prevailed in the Homer text as it has come down to us: πολυηχέα φωνήν.
[5] Van der Valk 1949.83n4. My emphasis.

8

The poetics of variation

Our real difficulty arises from the fact that, unlike the oral poet, we are not accustomed to thinking in terms of fluidity. We find it difficult to grasp something that is *multiform*. It seems to us necessary to construct an ideal text or to seek an *original*, and we remain dissatisfied with an ever-changing phenomenon. I believe that once we know the facts of oral composition we must cease trying to find an *original* of any traditional song. From one point of view each performance is an *original*.[6]

If we apply this line of thinking to the passage about the nightingale, we may ask whether the variant readings *poluēkhḗs* and *poludeukḗs* may *both* be "original," if indeed they stem ultimately from variant performances in oral poetry. But how do we square variation in performance with variation in text? This question brings me to consider two concepts, *mouvance* and *variance*. As we will see, neither of these concepts provides an immediate answer to the question at hand, but together they help shape an ultimate answer.

The term *mouvance* was suggested by Paul Zumthor as a way of coming to terms with his perception that a medieval literary production like the *Chanson de Roland* is not so much a finished product, *un achèvement*, as it is a text in progress, *un texte en train de se faire*.[7] Viewing *mouvance* as a widespread phenomenon in medieval manuscript transmission, Zumthor defines it as a quasi-abstraction that becomes a reality in the interplay of variant readings in different manuscripts of a given work; he pictures *mouvance* as a kind of "incessant vibration," a fundamental process of instability.[8] He links *mouvance* with the workings of oral tradition: for example, he suggests that certain textual variations in the *Carmina Burana* reflect the potential for actual variations in performance.[9]

---

[6] Lord 1960.100. My emphases.

[7] Zumthor 1972.73.

[8] Zumthor 1972.507: "le caractère de l'oeuvre qui, comme telle, avant l'âge du livre, ressort d'une quasi-abstraction, les textes concrets qui la réalisent présentant, par le jeu des variantes et remaniements, comme une incessante vibration et une instabilité fondamentale." Cf. Zumthor pp. 43–47, 65–75. (In N 1992a.44, another discussion of *mouvance* is cited, Zumthor 1984.160; this citation should be corrected to 1987.160.) On the notion of a "transitional text," as applied to the *Chanson de Roland* in Curschmann 1967, see the critique of Zwettler 1978.21.

[9] Zumthor 1987.160–161.

Zumthor's idea of *mouvance* is not far removed from the idea of *variance*, which is a second concept that I apply to the general question of variation in performance and variation in text. This term *variance* was formulated by Bernard Cerquiglini in his influential *Eloge de la variante*.[10] For Cerquiglini, "medieval writing does not produce variants; it *is* variance."[11] Unlike *mouvance*, however, Cerquiglini's model of *variance* is not to be viewed in terms of oral tradition as reflected in written tradition: his definition insists that the written tradition itself is a matter of variance.[12]

While there is much to be learned from Cerquiglini's far-reaching insights concerning the fact of variation in medieval manuscript traditions, it is more useful for now to pursue the implications of Zumthor's term *mouvance*. There are two reasons.

First, since the term *mouvance* is predicated on a link with oral traditions, it seems apt for describing a wide variety of situations where we do indeed observe a distinct degree and even a distinct kind of textual variation: there is a genuine distinction, it can be argued, between variant manuscript readings stemming from errors or deliberate changes in the mechanical process of writing copies of previous manuscripts on the one hand and, on the other, variant manuscript readings reflecting a performance tradition that is still alive in a given culture. This observation about the writing down of poetic wording extends also to the writing down of melodic patterns that may accompany the wording, as the research of musicologists has suggested: in the case of the medieval French *chansonniers*, for example, "there was not only a scriptless culture next to a literate one, but also a notationless culture side by side with a very small notated one."[13] It has even

---

[10] Cerquiglini 1989; cf. Vance 1987.xxvi–xxvii.

[11] Cerquiglini 1989.111: "Or l'écriture médiévale ne produit pas de variantes, elle est variance." Cf. Nichols 1990.1, with reference to "new" philology; as he points out at p. 3, "editors of the 'old' philological persuasion sought to limit variation, not reproduce it." In the same volume edited by Nichols, we may note the remarks on Cerquiglini by Fleischman 1990.19 and Bloch 1990.46. Pickens 1994 offers a critique of the "new" philology in medieval studies.

[12] See Cerquiglini 1989.120n19, where he distances himself from Zumthor's idea of *mouvance*. Other important works on the question of approaches to variation in the editing of texts include McGann 1983 (cf. also 1991) and Gabler 1984 (cf. 1993); see in general Greetham 1993. Thanks to Jenny Wallace for introducing me to the pioneering studies of McGann.

[13] Van der Werf 1993.173.

been argued that "for each *chanson* there existed probably as many versions as there were *jongleurs* who performed that particular *chanson*."[14]

Second, *mouvance* is not just a word coined by Zumthor: we are about to see a word meaning 'to move' which actually designates the process of *mouvance* and which is being used by a given song-making tradition in referring to its own capacity for variation. Moreover, this word meaning 'to move' is used in this given tradition to refer to the song of both the nightingale and the poet.

It should be noted in advance that the tradition in question – even the culture in question – differs in many ways from that of the ancient Greeks. We must therefore recognize from the start that any parallels we may find between the two traditions about to be compared are merely typological ones, and the implications of such parallelisms will have to be re-examined at length in terms of the available Greek evidence – to which we will turn in the two chapters that follow this one. Still, the poetic and even philological problems that we are about to see are in some respects strikingly similar to those faced by specialists in the ancient Greek Classics.

The key word in question is Provençal *mover*, the equivalent of French *mouvoir* and meaning, like the French word, 'to move'. The textual tradition in question involves the medieval Provençal *chansonniers* – in this case a sub-set of songs or lyric poems attributed to a twelfth-century *troubadour* named Jaufré Rudel, prince of Blaye. The edition in question is a 1978 publication by Rupert

---

[14] Van der Werf 1967.232. There will be more below concerning the convergences as well as divergences between *jongleur* as "performer" and *trouvère* as "composer." For instances where the scribe may have copied from memory what was *heard* in formal performance – or even in his own informal unit-by-unit reperformance – rather than what was *seen* in an earlier copy, see van der Werf 1965.65–66. Though there are isolated instances where the musical notation may have been affected by the copyist's adherence to principles of theory rather than praxis (van der Werf p. 66), it can be said in general that "the *chansons* of the *trouvères* originated and circulated in a *notationless* musical culture in which notation and theory exercised little or no influence" (p. 67, with his highlighting). Surveying the textual variants in the musical notations of medieval French *chansons*, he notes that "only an infinitesimally small number of them" are mechanical errors of the scribe. This formulation differs from that of earlier editors who "seem to have been guided by the principle that most of the discrepancies in the sources are deteriorations caused by scribal inaccuracy or by inadequacies of the oral tradition" (van der Werf 1965.62).

T. Pickens. The methodology that is adopted in this edition, as we will see, is particularly relevant to the questions at hand.

Pickens, as editor of Jaufré Rudel, is candid in telling his readers that he had originally undertaken his project in hopes of improving on an earlier edition of this *troubadour* by Alfred Jeanroy (1924):

> In the beginning stages of this project, I thought simply that it was possible to determine what Jaufré's "authentic" texts were by adopting a more dispassionate regard for the poems than Jeanroy was apparently able to do. The arrogant assumption was that Jeanroy's edition could be "improved upon" by rigorous application of Lachmannian principles.... It soon became apparent, however, that not only can "authentic" texts not be discovered, much less "established" with a sufficient degree of certainty, but that, given the condition of the manuscripts and the esthetic principles involving textual integrity affirmed by Jaufré himself as well as by his transmitters, the question of "authenticity," insofar as the meaning of the texts was concerned, was largely irrelevant. The conventions and traditions of the courtly lyric have conspired to efface the author and to create at least as many Jaufré Rudels as there are medieval anthologies.[15]

In abandoning one solution, where the goal is to reconstruct a given manuscript tradition back to one textual archetype, following methods established by Karl Lachmann,[16] this particular editor adopts an alternative solution by invoking the concept of *mouvance* as formulated by Zumthor,[17] and he explicitly connects "the poetics of *mouvance*" with the factor of "performance" in oral tradition.[18] More than that, this editor has discovered a remark-

---

[15] Pickens 1978.40. My underlines, to be explained further below.

[16] The case in point is Lachmann's 1850 work on the manuscript tradition of Lucretius. For a critique of Lachmann's methodology, see Pasquali 1952.3–12, Timpanaro 1981, Zetzel 1993.101–103; for background, see Reynolds and Wilson 1991.209–211.

[17] Pickens 1978.34; also in his article, Pickens 1977, which is actually entitled "Jaufré Rudel et la poétique de la mouvance."

[18] Pickens 1977.323. In this article, written as it is in French, the author puts "performance" in quotation marks in view of the fact that the word is considered by native speakers of French to be a borrowing from English. It goes without saying that Pickens' reference to Provençal songmaking as *oral tradition* should not be taken to

able detail, to which I have just now drawn attention: that the Provençal word *mover* in the sense of French *mouvoir* and English *move* is actually used in Provençal songmaking to express an idea of *mouvance*. The passage in question is the ending of Jaufré Rudel's Song VI, version 1a:[19]

> *bos es le sons s'ieu non menti*
> *e tot qant i a, ben ista;*
> *e cel qi de mi l'apenra*
> *gard si non mueva ni camgi,*
> *qar si l'auson en Caerzi;*
> *le coms de Tolsa l'entendra. a. a.*

The melody is good, if I have not lied,
and all there is in it goes well;
and the one who will learn it from me,
beware lest it move or change,
for if they hear it in Quercy,
the count of Toulouse will understand it. Ha! Ha!

In other attested manuscript versions of Song VI of Jaufré Rudel, it is made clear by the composer that the intermediary transmitter of the song, described in the passage just quoted as "the one who will learn it from me," must deliver it unchanged to two noblemen, who must in turn hear it. In version 1a of Song VI, the composition ends as just quoted. In other versions, however, the references to the destined audiences are followed by further references, resulting in a longer song. Of these other available versions, let us take as one example the last eight lines of Song VI version 1 (as distinct from 1a):[20]

> *bos es lo vers s'ieu no.y falhi,*
> *ni tot so que.y es, ben esta;*
> *e selh que de mi l'apenra,*
> *guart si que res no mi cambi,*
> *que si l'auzon en Caerci*
> *lo vescoms ni.l coms en Tolza.*

mean that the Provençal and the ancient Greek poetic traditions are the "same." On the dangers of trying to universalize the features of oral and written traditions, see N 1990a.35.

[19] As edited by Pickens 1978.232; here as elsewhere, I follow closely his translations of Jaufré Rudel. The underlines are mine.

[20] Pickens 1978.224.

bos es lo sos, e faran hi
quas que don most chans gensara

Good is the poem if I did not fail in it
and all there is in it goes well;
and the one who will learn it from me,
let him beware lest he change anything for me,[21]
for thus may they hear it in Quercy,
the viscount and the count in the Toulousain.

The melody is good, and they will do there
whatever things from which my song will grow more noble.

As another example, let us take the last eight lines of Song VI
version 1b:[22]

bos es lo vers can no.i falhi,
e tot so que.i es, ben esta,
e sel que de mi l'apenra
gart se no.i falha ni.l pessi,
qu[e] si l'auzo en Lemozi
e Bertrans e.l coms el Tolza.

bons er lo vers e faran y
calsque motz que hom chantara

The poem is good, since I did not fail in it,
and all there is in it goes well,
and the one who will learn it from me,
let him beware lest he fail in it and <u>break</u> it up,
for thus may they hear it in the Limousin,
both Bertran and the count in the Toulousain.

The poem will be good, and they will make there [the
     Limousin or the Toulousain] (for it)
whatever words someone will sing.

Whereas according to Pickens the intermediary must deliver
the song unchanged to two noblemen, "those who are destined
to receive it must, on the contrary, introduce changes."[23] It is

---

[21] For this interpretation, see Pickens 1978.225n40, which seems preferable to "let
him beware lest anything changes me," as Pickens 1978.225n40 renders *guart si que res
no mi cambi* at p. 225. On this point, I have benefited from the generous advice of
Ursula Dronke and Peter Dronke.
[22] Pickens 1978.236.
[23] Pickens 1978.36.

probably enough to say that the destined audience *may* "move" the song while the intermediary *must* not.

As we see from the wording of the variations in Song VI, the chance to *move* the song is equivalent to the chance to *change* it into a version different from that of the composer, even though the intermediary must keep the composer's version the same until it reaches the destined audience. The noblemen who are to be the song's audience are in turn to become the song's new performers – and thereby the song's recomposers.

The remarkable thing, moreover, is that *mover* 'move' can designate not only the recomposing of a song through reperformance but even its archetypal composition through its archetypal performance. As Pickens also notices, *mover* 'move' can refer not only to the *changing* of the song, as here, but also to the actual *singing* of the song, even to the actual *beginning of the singing*, as when the poet starts his song by picturing a nightingale as it sings, that is, as it *moves* its song.[24] Here is the beginning, for example, of Jaufré Rudel's Song I version 1:[25]

> *quant lo rosignols el fuoillos*
> *dona d'amor e.n quier e.n pren*
> *e mou so chant jauzen joios*
> *e remira sa par soven,*
> *e.ill riu son clar e.ill prat son gen,*
> *pel novel deport que reingna,*
> *me ven al cor grans jois jacer.*

> When the nightingale in the leafy wood
> gives of love, asks for it and takes of it
> and composes (moves) his song rejoicing and joyous
> and beholds (reflects) his equal often,
> and the streams are clear and the fields are pleasant,
> through the new sense of pleasure that reigns,
> great joy comes to lie in my heart.

Here in Song I of Jaufré Rudel, the symbol of the singing nightingale is drawn into a parallel with the singer who is the

---

[24] Pickens 1978.36. In the Provençal tradition, the nightingale is a he not a she, as in the ancient Greek. Pliny *Natural History* 11.268 tells us that the female nightingale has the same song repertoire as the male. On the topic of the nightingale in medieval literature in general, see Pfeffer 1985.

[25] Pickens 1978.70.

poet. Just as the nightingale *moves* his song by singing – that is, by performing – so also the poet implicitly *moves* his own song by composing it.[26] This symbol provides an opportunity to compare the model of Parry and Lord centering on composition-in-performance with the model of Zumthor centering on *mouvance*. The symbol of the nightingale, deployed as it is to launch the poet's composition, superimposes the medium of performance on the act, the fact, of composition. By comparing himself to the nightingale, the poet presents himself as one who performs as he composes. Just as the nightingale goes about his performance, so also the poet goes about his composition by performing it, by *moving* it. Just as the poet composes his song, so too his model, the nightingale: in Pickens' translation, the songbird "composes (moves) his song rejoicing and joyous" (*e mou so chant jauzen joios*). We may recall the image in Aeschylus *Suppliants* 60–67 of the mythical figure Procne, who has been transformed by the gods into a nightingale (*aēdón*, verse 62: ἀηδόνος): the songbird is pictured as literally "composing" (*sun-títhēmi*, verse 65: ξυντίθησι) the sad song of her murdered child's fate (verse 65: παιδὸς μόρον).[27]

Just as the nightingale's song in Song I of Jaufré Rudel is an implicit model for the poet who hears him and makes his own song, so also the poet is the model for the noblemen who in turn hear him and make their own song by performing the song of the poet. To perform the song, however, is to recompose it, to change it, that is, to *move* it. In this light, *mouvance* is the same thing as recomposition-in-performance. The nightingale who is "composing" his song in Song I of Jaufré Rudel may serve as the model, the archetype, for the song of the poet, but even the songbird is in fact recomposing his own song by virtue of performing it. So it is apt for the nightingale to *move* his song, which is "original" for the poet but which is at the same time inherently recurrent and recomposed, much as every new season of spring is

---

[26] For another attestation of this theme in the *troubadour* traditions, see for example Bernard de Ventadour, Song 20 verse 4, where the nightingale *mou so chan* 'moves his song'.
[27] Cf. Loraux 1990.145n138, who points out that the same word *sun-títhēmi* is used by Thucydides in referring to the process of composing history (1.21.1: ὡς λογογράφοι ξυνέθεσαν; cf. 1.97.2).

a joyous event of inherent recurrence and recomposition, even re-creation.

In applying the idea of a "poetics of *mouvance*" to his edition of the songs of Jaufré Rudel, Pickens confronts a set of problems. Even without a single holograph, to be reconstructed according to the principles of Lachmann,[28] the question remains whether it is possible to explain the variations in Jaufré Rudel's manuscript tradition simply in terms of the poet's own lifetime activity: "a stemma," Pickens explains, "could represent the career of a poet just as easily as a two-hundred-year tradition of manuscript transmission."[29] It is in any case impossible to exclude the author himself from the process of varying his own composition.[30] Accordingly, in considering all the variations attested in the manuscript tradition of Song V, Pickens is willing for the moment to entertain the idea that all these variations may be "by" Jaufré Rudel; after all, Jaufré "was a *troubadour* who constantly reworked his material."[31] Pursuing the question, Pickens concludes after an intensive analysis of the manuscript variations in both Songs I and V of Jaufré Rudel:

> Jaufré's authorship of at least two formally and linguistically distinct versions of the former [Song I] and two of the latter [Song V] cannot be disproved; the poems have equal claims for authenticity and there is no reason to suppose that Jaufré did not compose them. If he could have produced two or three versions of the same song, then why could he not also have produced six or ten or fifteen? Corollary to the theory is the assumption that Jaufré was a *troubadour*-performer creating his works in an atmosphere heavy with the esthetics of oral composition. As epic criticism has suggested, orality and mutation, not writing and fixity, were the compositional medium and consequent destiny of *chanson de geste* texts. The courtly lyric is also an oral genre, performed orally and heard, not read. It is not

---

[28] Pickens 1978.23, with references to studies arguing for such a hypothetical holograph.
[29] Ibid.
[30] Pickens 1978.24.
[31] Pickens 1978.32. Pickens at p. 26 sets up a useful distinction between palaeographically significant or non-significant variants, while all along insisting that "no variant is poetically non-significant."

unreasonable to suppose, therefore, that Jaufré altered his works frequently in conformity with the practices of oral tradition and that, in concert with all poetic practice, he strove to "perfect" his poetry by reworking, adding and casting out (but, like all who publish, the person who changes must still ever be confronted by what has previously been released to the public).[32]

Even allowing for this much participation by the author himself in the process of variation, we are reminded of his own references to other participants, such as the noblemen in Song VI who are imagined as not only hearing the song in performance but also reperforming it themselves afterwards and thereby recomposing it. Pickens explicitly argues for the reality of such participation by invoking "the dynamic condition of the medieval poem," with specific reference to Zumthor's idea of *mouvance*.[33] Here he links his observations about the medieval Provençal *troubadour* with those of Harry H. Lucas about the medieval French *trouvère*: the song, Lucas argues, is not only created by the *trouvère* but also re-created by any number of fellow *trouvères*, as well as amateurs, before it is ever incorporated into the manuscript tradition of the *chansonnier*, and most likely even afterward, so that the song of a *trouvère* can truly be said to be a work of *collaboration*.[34]

By now, Pickens has brought into play two "solutions": according to the first, Jaufré Rudel is the only contributor to the "creative acts"; according to the second, these creative acts "are seen as operating in transmission as well."[35] Moreover, "Jaufré himself affirms the principle of change as esthetically proper to his genre, so that it might be said that *mouvance* is an aspect of the intention of his songs."[36] Precisely in this context Pickens introduces the passage

---

[32] Pickens 1978.32–33.
[33] Pickens 1978.34.
[34] Lucas 1965.701, quoted by Pickens 1978.34–35: "Toutefois, une chanson de trouvère n'est pas qu'un document historique; et le trouvère, bien qu'il ait joué le rôle prépondérant dans sa création, n'a pas été seul à contribuer. Telle chanson, "trouvée" par tel ou tel poète, mais qui a eu du succès, qui a été chantée, modifiée, améliorée parfois, par des douzaines de confrères et d'amateurs, avant d'être incorporée dans la tradition des chansonniers – et encore après, sans doute – est, en un sens très réel, une oeuvre de collaboration." The underlines are mine. This formulation by Lucas is comparable with the term "collaborative interpolation" suggested by Tarrant 1989.
[35] Pickens 1978.35.
[36] Ibid.

from Song VI where the poet urges that the noblemen must hear and then reperform the song of Jaufré Rudel, with the implicit assumption that they will thereby recompose it as well.[37] In this same context we have seen the poet urging the intermediary transmitter not to "move" the poem, that is, not to recompose it. This detail is essential for coming to terms with questions of authorship in this culture. If indeed Jaufré Rudel is not the only contributor to the "creative acts," then how exactly is he an author? Here we may recall the striking formulation of Rupert Pickens: "The conventions and traditions of the courtly lyric have conspired to <u>efface the author</u> and to create at least <u>as many Jaufré Rudels as there are medieval anthologies.</u>"[38]

Let us go beyond the problems raised by this particular example in this particular culture and ask a more general question: what is it, in any case, to be an author in any tradition where performance is needed to make a song come to life?[39] Applying the observation of Parry and Lord that composition and performance are aspects of the same process in oral traditions, I suggest that *authority* in performance is a key to the very concept of *authorship* in composition.[40] In the present example from Jaufré Rudel as well, it is authority in performance that is crucial: the poet's song does not become *authoritative* until it is performed in an *authorized* setting. Only then does the song become real, authentic. Thus the intermediary transmitter is enjoined not to "move" the song of Jaufré Rudel *because he is as yet unauthorized to do so.* This injunction by the poet is presented not as a statement of fact so much as a stylized gesture to his intended audience. Thus I doubt that this unnamed intermediary is really understood by the poet to be a "mechanical" transmitter who is not a "recreative" singer.[41] I propose instead that the authorization of the composer is implicitly not enough *because the transmitter as performer must also be authorized by his audience*, who are presumed to be authoritative members of the song culture.[42]

---

[37] Ibid.

[38] Pickens 1978.40. My underlines.

[39] This discussion has a bearing on the broader question posed by Foucault 1969: "Qu'est-ce qu'un auteur?"

[40] N 1990a.339–381, ch.12: "Authority and authorship in the lyric tradition."

[41] To use the wording of Pickens 1978.36.

[42] On the term *song culture*, see Herington 1985.3–5.

The intermediate transmitter of the *troubadour*, who is potentially a *jongleur*, becomes an authoritative performer through the dual authorization of composer and audience.[43] It would be misleading, though, to generalize the *jongleur* as a mechanical performer who repeats the song of the authoritative composer, the *troubadour*; it would also be misleading to set up a strict dichotomy between a "creative" *troubadour* and a "re-creative" *jongleur*.[44] In the *troubadour* traditions, the transmitter of song becomes a potential *troubadour* by virtue of reperforming the song. It all depends on the circumstances of reception: in Jaufré's song, for example, it is implied that the transmitter of his song must have approval from both the composer and the audience which is to hear the transmitter's performance. The transmitter is to be authorized on the grounds that both the composer and the audience of noblemen are authoritative. The noblemen may reperform and thereby recompose the song precisely *because they are presumed, by the song, to be authoritative*. So also the nightingale "moves" the song because he has the authority to do so. Only in this case, the authority is not social but elemental – even archetypal.

We see another example of performative intermediacy in Song II of Jaufré Rudel, where the song is pictured as being transmitted from the *troubadour* to a nobleman through an intermediary, named Fillol or "Godson" in some versions.[45] Here is the text of Song II, version 1, strophe v:[46]

> *senes breu de pargamina,*
> *tramet lo vers en chantan*
> *plan et en lenga romana*
> *a.n Hugon Brun per Fillol.*

---

[43] On the relationship between *troubadour* = *trobador* and *jongleur* = *joglar*, the remarks of Dronke 1977.20–21 are most helpful. Of special interest is his observation, p. 20, with reference to patterns of social difference between higher-class *trobadors* and lower-class *joglars*, that "the *joglar* tends to adopt a 'stage-name', a name that is striking, piquant, witty, or self-mocking: Alegret, Esperdut, Falconet, Brisepot, Mal Quarrel, Quatre-oeufs." Dronke's use of the term "stage" here is pertinent to the concept of mimesis as interpreted in ch.3 and following. The *jongleur* is represented as a nightingale in the poetry of Elias Cairel, Song 13.49–53 (cf. Pfeffer 1985.110–111).

[44] N 1990a.55.

[45] For more on the nobleman and on the "godson," see Pickens 1978.103n.

[46] As edited by Pickens 1978.102.

bon m'es, car gens Peitavina,
de Beiriu et de Bretaigna
s'esgau per lui, e Guianna.

Without any writing on parchment,
I transmit the poem in singing,
plainly and in the vernacular language,
to Lord Hugh the Swarthy, by Godson.[47]
I am glad, since the people of Poitou,
of Berry, and of Brittany
are delighted by him; and of Guyenne.[48]

The song, as its poet stresses, is not fixed by writing on parchment (*senes breu de pargamina*), so that the intermediary is not a text but a live performer. Moreover, this performer is cherished by the poet, so that the composer implies authorization on his own part while all along presuming a reciprocal authorization on the part of his intended audience. Although we may agree that the poet's song is here being "released to the hazards of oral transmission"[49] in terms of the reality of its historical setting, it is at the same time imagined to be safe and intact in terms of its own rhetoric. Here the composer is implying his certainty that the setting for the performance is to be authoritative, as surely as if it were written down on parchment, thanks to his confidence in both the performer and the intended audience.

Even in the sort of situation where the composer allows himself to express a concern that his song may be exposed to unauthorized performance, as if there were a danger that someone will "move" it in a negative sense, this concern turns out to be a rhetorical way of seeking reassurance from the audience that the performance really is authoritative, so that those who heard the song and learned to perform it can thus implicitly "move" it in a positive sense, much as the nightingale "moves" his own song.

[47] I have added the comma before *by*.
[48] Pickens 1978.103 points out that the wording can also mean *it*, that is, the song; the *him* could be either Hugh or Fillol the "godson." Pickens p. 103n compares the godfather-godson relationship that is evoked at Song V strophes vii–viii; on the basis of this comparison, we may infer that the "godson," in his role as "messenger" of the song (so Pickens ibid.), is the poetic apprentice. If indeed Fillol is to be the *jongleur*, whose authorization depends on both the *troubadour* and the audience, and if indeed Hugh represents an authoritative audience, then the *him* could refer to both.
[49] To use the wording of Pickens 1978.35.

We come back to the case of Song VI, which is predicated on the poet's satisfaction with his composition: *bos es lo vers can no.i falhi* 'the poem is good, since I did not fail in it' (version 1b strophe v). The anonymous transmitter is enjoined to learn the song from the poet exactly as it was composed: in the different versions of the song, we hear that the transmitter must therefore "beware lest he fail in it and break it up" (*gart se no.i falha ni.l pessi,* version 1b strophe v) or "beware lest he fracture it or break it up" (*gart no.l fran[ha] ni [no.]l peʒi,* version 2a strophe vii) or "beware lest it move or change" (*gard si non mueva ni camgi,* version 1a strophe iv) or even perhaps "beware lest anything changes me" (*guart si que res no mi cambi,* version 1 strophe vii).[50]

The fact that even this poetic injunction against variation survives by way of variants is a striking example of a paradox that is characteristic of a wide variety of oral traditions: a tradition may claim unchangeability as a founding principle while at the same time it keeps itself alive through change. Outsiders who are looking in, as it were, on a given tradition can be objective about any change that they do observe. Insiders, however, are apt to be subjective. Participants in a given tradition may of course choose to ignore any change whatsoever.[51] If they do recognize change, however, either it must be negative or, if it is to be positive, it must not really be change after all. In other words, positive change must be a "movement" that leads back to something that is known, just as negative change leads forward to something that is unknown, uncertain, unpredictable. And yet, even if positive change is a moving back toward whatever is known, certain, and predictable, all the more will it be deemed to be an ongoing process of improvement, not deterioration, by those who participate in the tradition. In fact, it will be an improvement precisely because such positive "movement" aims at the traditional, even the archetypal.

From this point of view, the noblemen who are to hear the song of the poet are described in Song VI of Jaufré Rudel as

---

[50] Cf. Pickens 1978.35. But see p. 14n21 above. In a late twelfth-century poem entitled *Donnei des Amants,* Tristan secretly woos Iseut by imitating birdsong: he "disguises his human language" (*humain language deguisa* verse 463), "like one who had learned to break it up" (*cum cil que l'aprist de pec[e]a* 464), and he "counterfeits" a series of song-birds, the first of which is a nightingale (*il cuntrefit le russinol* 465); hearing Tristan's sound, Iseut leaves the bed where King Mark is sleeping. Cf. Pfeffer 1985.155.

[51] See pp. 221–222 on Theognis.

destined to improve that song by way of a presumed author-itativeness inherent in their reperformances. To quote from one of the variants that we have already seen, "The melody is good, and they will do there/whatever things from which my song will grow more noble."[52] When the nightingale "moves" his song, it is a matter of positive change because tradition is reactivated. If, however, a *jongleur* "moves" the song of a *troubadour* in an un-authorized situation, it is a matter of negative change because tradition breaks down. For a performer of a song to "move" it in a negative sense is to "change" it, even to "break" it.

Just as the idea of "moving" a song can be turned from a negative to a positive sense, however, even the idea of "breaking" a song can be made positive in the poetics of *mouvance*. The neg-ative poetics of the verb *franhar* 'break', as deployed in the poet's injunction to the transmitter not to "break" the song, are echoed by the positive poetics of the verb *refranhar*, to be interpreted in another poem of Jaufré Rudel as "refract" in referring specifically to the singing of the nightingale and, in response, of the poet.[53] Before we reflect on the meaning of the metaphor inherent in the image of "refraction," let us consider its precise context in Song II version 1 strophe i:[54]

> *qan lo rius de la fontana*
> *s'esclarzis si cum far sol,*
> *e par la flors aiglentina,*
> *e.l rossignoletz el ram*
> *volf e refraing et aplana*
> *son doutz chantar et afina*
> *dreitz es q'ieu lo mieu refraigna*

When the stream from the spring
runs clear as it is wont to do,
and the sweetbrier flower appears,
and the little nightingale on the branch
turns and <u>refracts</u> and polishes
his sweet singing and refines it (brings it to an end),
it is right that I should <u>refract</u> my own.

---

[52] Song VI version 1 strophe vii. For this and other examples of the theme of im-provement by way of reperformance in a noble context, see Pickens 1978.36.

[53] Pickens 1977.330–331.

[54] As edited by Pickens 1978.100; I follow his translation at p. 101, except for my substitution of the working translation 'refract' in the sense of 'modulate'.

The metaphor inherent in the Provençal verb *refranhar* can be explained as an auditory equivalent of a visual metaphor, the "refracting" of light (as in Latin *re-fringere*). The driving image of *refraction* also accounts for two Provençal nouns: *refrins*, meaning 'echo' (as a part of sound that repeats itself), and *refrim*, meaning 'birdsong, sound, refrain'.[55] The verb *refranhar* can also refer to the musical process of *modulation* in song: much as light is refracted through glass or a prism, so also the musical sound of song is modulated.[56] When the nightingale "turns and *refracts* and polishes" his song, the songbird is being envisaged as a craftsman who is constantly engaged in the process of *improving* the work of his craftsmanship, in principle coming ever nearer to the finished product. The poet echoes the songbird as he reaches the end of the strophe just quoted, and so also by implication the other singers must echo the poet, as they too must "turn and refract and polish" the song, refining it and "bringing it to an end." The end of one singer's "refinement," however, is the beginning of another's, and each beginning, each new "movement," is a return to tradition. In this theme of "refinement," we see the ultimate image of improvement as an eternal return to the traditional, which is envisaged as an eternal musical modulation.

Let us return here once again to the *troubadour*'s image of the songbird, with one more example of the word *mover* 'move' in the archetypal sense of referring to birdsong. In the sole extant version of Song IV, the first four verses of the last strophe run as follows:[57]

> *el mes d'abril e de Pascor,*
> *can l'auzel movon lurs dous critz,*
> *adoncs vueill mon chas si' auzitz;*
> *et aprendetz lo, cantador . . .*

---

[55] Extended discussion in Pickens 1977.331n20. For an archaic Greek parallel to the idea of "breaking" a song in a positive rather than negative sense, see p. 58n67 below, with reference to the expression περὶ δέ σφισιν ἄγνυτο ἠχώ in the Hesiodic *Shield*, verse 279, which could be translated 'and the sound [*ēkhō*] was refracted all around them'. The word *ēkhō* in this context applies to the 'sound' of choral voices accompanied by herdsmen's pipes.

[56] Pickens, ibid. See N 1990a.91–103 for a discussion of ancient notions of *mode* as a system of intervals in pitch and of *modulation* as a process of switching from one given system to another. Pliny *Natural History* 10.85 refers to the *vox* 'voice' of the nightingale as *modulata* 'modulated' and *varia* 'varied' – qualities that he says become diminished in the birdsong as the summer wears on.

[57] As edited by Pickens 1978.148.

In the month of April, and of Easter,
when birds <u>compose</u> (<u>move</u>) their sweet cries,
then I wish my song to be heard:
and learn it, singers ...

It is time to propose a reformulation of the idea of *mouvance*, supplementing it with the usage of *mover* as we have seen it operate in a *troubadour*'s poetics — and in light of one given editor's detailed and patient work on the texts attributed to Jaufré Rudel. I propose, then, that *mouvance* is the process of recomposition-in-performance as actually recognized by a living oral tradition, where the recognition implies the paradox of immediate change without ultimate change.

On the basis of his editorial experience, Rupert Pickens concludes that "at least in the case of Jaufré Rudel, mutation is appropriate to the lyric genre."[58] According to this line of thinking, the courtly lyric of Jaufré is not "authoritative" in the same sense as Scripture, in that the work *is* freed to be "re-created and regenerated."[59] I agree, though I stress that the authoritativeness of Jaufré's tradition is as real as that of Scripture, with the basic difference being that the *troubadour*'s words do not insist on the idea of unchangeability, typical of the claims of scriptures in a wide variety of cultures. At a later point, we will consider in further detail the very notion of "scripture."

Pickens observes about the patterns of mutation in the lyrics of Jaufré Rudel that "it is impossible to determine at what points his personal interventions ceased and his transmitters continued the process of perfecting beyond his personal intentions."[60] Which leads to this conclusion: "Given these conditions, under which it is impossible to rediscover Jaufré's intentions (i.e., the extent of his personal involvement in the creation and regeneration of his works), each manifestation of a song must be considered to be, in its own right, as valid a whole, complete poem as any other versions."[61] In light of these findings, this editor of medieval texts differs from the approach of previous

---

[58] Pickens 1978.38.
[59] Pickens 1978.36.
[60] Pickens 1978.38.
[61] Pickens 1978.39.

scholars like Gaston Paris and Alfred Jeanroy, whose goal was to recover a given author's archetypal text.[62] But he also differs from the approach of other editors like Joseph Bédier, whose own findings about textual variation led him to abandon the idea of recovering the archetypal text, but whose goal remained nevertheless the idea of recovering at least the closest thing to an archetype.[63] Pickens offers the following critique:

> ... the Bédier method forces the editor to ignore what the poem has acquired through *mouvance* (making what is not in the base manuscript become, in Gaston Paris's phrase, "les oubliettes de l'appareil critique," whatever their literary worth); moreover, it might be added that Bédier's methodology tends to falsify the historical question by giving only the "best" version of a song the stamp of authority.[64]

While offering his own adjustments in line with the hermeneutic principle of *mouvance*, Pickens has this to say about the criteria of editing proposed by Lucas: "to my knowledge, they have never been observed in an edition of medieval lyric poetry."[65] In a retrospective work, Pickens with good reason describes his own 1978 edition of Jaufré Rudel, with its "multitext format," as "the first widely recognized edition attempting to incorporate a procedure to account for re-creative textual change."[66]

The need for a multitext format in editing texts is most evident in the case of manuscript traditions where the phenomenon of phraseological variation seems to reach all-pervasive proportions. A striking example is the textual transmission of the medieval French epic, the *Chanson de Roland*.[67] As Ramón Menéndez Pidal observes, three of the earliest manuscript versions of the *Chanson*

[62] Paris 1893, Jeanroy 1934.

[63] Bédier 1928. See the critique by Nichols 1990.5–6; also Cerquiglini 1989.122.

[64] Pickens 1978.41.

[65] Pickens 1978.42.

[66] Pickens 1994.61. Here he refers also to other editorial projects in multi-text format that take into account the factor of *mouvance*, most prominently the complete edition of the *fabliaux* by Noomen and van der Boogaard 1983/1984/1986 (with reference to Zumthor at 1983.ix); this format is also used by editors for whom "textual change is regarded as a hindrance to our perception of medieval textuality rather than its essence." Cerquiglini 1989.112 mentions some of these editors, along with Noomen and van der Boogaard, but he does not stress the differences in their methodologies.

[67] A key work on the subject is Duggan 1973.

The poetics of variation

have not a single identical verse in common with each other.[68] He concludes that such a degree of textual variation is symptomatic of an ongoing oral tradition, and that in fact an oral tradition stays alive through its variations and reworkings.[69] Following Menéndez Pidal, Michael Zwettler has concluded that early Arabic poetry is likewise the product of a vigorous oral tradition, as reflected in the extraordinary wealth of variants transmitted in the textual tradition:

> We are doubly fortunate in Arabic, in that we often have not only two or more recensions of many poems ... but also a mass of additional variants presented in the scholia to the poems or in various supplementary philological and literary–historical sources where poetry held a paramount position. And nowhere does the inherent instability or, better, fluidity of the early Arabic poem – its essential multiformity – emerge with greater clarity than through consideration of the body of those *lectiones variae* that the textual tradition has preserved.[70]

Following Lord, Zwettler emphasizes not only the *multiformity* inherent in the oral tradition, as in the observation just quoted, but also the futility of attempting to establish an "original" text on the basis of attested variants. If indeed oral poetry lives through its variants, then it is ironic, Zwettler finds, "that scholars of Arabic poetry have so often cast doubt upon the 'authenticity' or 'genuineness' of this or that verse, poem, or body of poems or, sometimes, of pre-Islamic poetry in general, because they have found it impossible to establish an 'original version'."[71] Following Zwettler, Olga Davidson argues that the degree of textual variation in the medieval Persian manuscript transmission of the epic *Shāhnāma* of Ferdowsi likewise reveals the product of an oral tradition.[72] Using as a test-case a randomly-selected passage from the *Shāhnāma*, Davidson shows that "every word in this

---

[68] Menéndez Pidal 1960.60–63, the importance of whose discussion is emphasized by Zwettler 1978.207 and Davidson 1985.134.
[69] Menéndez Pidal 1960.67–68
[70] Zwettler 1978.206. He stresses, ibid., that scribal mistakes "do not constitute a major source of variation."
[71] Zwettler 1978.189.
[72] Davidson 1994.54–72.

27

given passage can be generated on the basis of parallel phraseology expressing parallel themes."[73] She finds, moreover, that "the degree of regularity and economy in the arrangement of phraseology" is "suggestive of formulaic language."[74] She advocates the need for a monumental new edition of the *Shāhnāma* that would account for all attested variants except for verifiable instances of scribal error, in order to come to grips with "the full creative range of the *Shāhnāma* tradition."[75]

Davidson too, like Zwettler before her, stresses the futility of trying to recover the archetypal fixed text from a mass of textual variants that can all be judged "genuine" in terms of the poetic tradition that had generated these variants. There are many other studies that focus on variation in textual transmission as a mark of oral tradition, but it will suffice for the moment to mention just one more example, the work of Joseph Nagy on medieval Irish traditions: he concludes that "the bewildering proliferation of variants which often characterizes the medieval literary transmission of Irish narrative takes on new meaning when viewed as the imprint of an ongoing oral tradition."[76]

In all three of these studies just mentioned, as also in the study of *troubadour* poetry that we had considered in detail earlier, it is the degree of multiformity in the textual tradition that leads to the conclusion that an oral tradition is at work backstage, as it were. In each case, the nature of the given oral tradition may be quite different, but the *effect* of variation may be strikingly similar. The question arises, then, whether we can find cases of a comparable degree of variation in ancient Greek – or for that matter in Latin – textual traditions.

From a survey of Martin West's handbook on textual criticism, we see from the precise wording of his descriptions that the most likely candidates are (1) Greek tragedies, "which suffered extensively from interpolations by actors (or at any rate for their use), probably more in the fourth century BC than at any later

---

[73] Davidson 1994.63–64.
[74] Davidson 1994.64. On the concepts of "economy" and "formula," cf. N 1992a.26–31.
[75] Davidson 1985.139.
[76] [J.] Nagy 1986.288, who in turn cites the work of Melia 1975.37 and Slotkin 1977–79.450.

time,"[77] (2) the comedies of Plautus, "which may have undergone something of the sort on a smaller scale in the second century,"[78] and (3) the Homeric poems, through the "embellishment" of *rhapsōidoí* 'rhapsodes' as reflected in quotations by authors of the fourth century and in the attested papyri, especially those dated before the middle of the second century.[79]

In West's descriptions here, as also in most accounts written by Classicists, the textual traditions of ancient tragedy, comedy, and epic are not organically related to the performance traditions of these three forms. It is as if the performance traditions were impositions on the text, rather than historical antecedents of the text. Thus textual variations are explained in terms of textual rather than performative conditions even when the medium in question is overtly performative. It is not the performance itself that is held accountable for textual variation, but the text that is used by the performer. Thus the so-called "actors' interpolations" are invoked to explain textual change in drama. Where epic, too, is concerned, West explains the existing patterns of textual variation in terms of textual causes: the "embellishment" of rhapsodes, he notes, is primarily characterized by "additional lines of an inorganic nature (often borrowed from other contexts)."[80]

Where the Classical text stems not so much from performance traditions as from "practical learning," the role of ongoing re-composition as a direct cause of textual variation is more easily understood.[81] With reference to works of practical learning, West makes the remark that "commentaries, lexica and other works of a grammatical nature were rightly regarded as collections of material to be pruned, adapted or added to, rather than as sacrosanct literary entities."[82] A similar description applies to more exalted compositions such as treatises on rhetoric, perhaps even to such canonical works as the essay on style attributed, rightly or wrongly, to Demetrius of Phalerum. An ideal example of a literary

---

[77] West 1973.16, citing Page 1934.
[78] West 1973.16.
[79] West, ibid., citing [S.] West 1967. In ch.3, I propose to re-examine the concept of *rhapsōidoí* 'rhapsodes'.
[80] West 1973.16.
[81] For applications of the term "practical learning," see Zetzel 1993.111.
[82] West 1973.16.

form in which massive textual variation results from active ongoing recomposition is the Hippocratic corpus: as West puts it,
parts of this corpus "were subject to revision or rearrange-
ment."[83] James Zetzel is exceptional among contemporary Classicists in
comparing explicitly the textual variations resulting from traditions of practical learning with those resulting from traditions of
performance.[84] Zetzel's list of "works that provide practical
learning," subject to "wholesale alteration," includes such other
diverse examples as the cookbook of Apicius, magical pre-
scriptions, and the *Digest* of Roman Law.[85] Adopting for all such
works the operative metaphor of the cookbook, Zetzel goes on
to describe them as "unprotected texts."[86] By contrast, he notes
that "wholesale alteration of the sort just described rarely oc-
curred in the transmission of standard texts of the school curric-
ulum ..., precisely because they generally stayed out of the
kitchen."[87] A notable exception among standard works, however,
is a text that stems from a performance tradition: Zetzel cites
Plautus' comedies, "the only major Latin literary text that I know
in which wholesale alteration has taken place, precisely because
our manuscripts largely descend from actors' versions."[88]

Zetzel makes clear his sense that the ultimate sources of textual variation in such cases as Plautine comedy are the traditions
of performance, even if we posit the texts of the performers as an
intermediate source. Zetzel's emphasis on performance is subtle
but clear, as we see in his assessment of textual variations in
Greek tragedy: "similarly, our texts of Greek tragedy incorporate
actors' interpolations that must have been added at a time when
the plays were still being performed."[89]

Where textual variations stem from outright performance traditions, as in the case of drama, it seems justified to compare the
phenomenon of *mouvance*. In cases of textual variations stemming
from the vicissitudes of practical learning, as in the case of, say, a

---

[83] West 1973.17.
[84] Zetzel 1993.
[85] Zetzel 1993.110–111.
[86] Zetzel 1993.111.
[87] *Ibid.*
[88] Zetzel 1993.111–112.
[89] Zetzel 1993.112.

cookbook, the broader term *variance*, as coined by Cerquiglini, seems a more appropriate point of comparison. It must be recognized, however, that the prescriptive traditions of a cookbook may also be to some extent "performative." As for instances of textual transmission following the schoolbook mentality, in sharp contrast with the "cookbook" mentality, we may expect the minimum degrees of variation.[90] In such instances, it seems unnecessary to insist on any point of comparison with either *mouvance* or *variance*.

Let us focus on the subject of variations in the textual traditions of Greek drama and epic. Unfortunately, historical circumstances have prevented our access to an ample range of attested variants in the performance traditions of drama. As for epic, there is relatively more attested evidence, but the history of Homeric transmission is in any case far more complicated than what we have seen so far in the case of medieval traditions. If indeed a multitext format is needed for editing medieval texts like the songs of Jaufré Rudel, then perhaps the need is even greater in the case of ancient Greek drama and epic. But the difficulties are greater as well.

Here we must confront a major intellectual and aesthetic obstacle for Classicists. It is clear to us that the actor in a Sophoclean drama is not another Sophocles, the rhapsode of epic is not another Homer. How, then, could an actor's so-called "interpolation" or a rhapsode's "embellishment" be comparable to the *ipsissima verba* of a Sophocles, of a Homer? Any answer must be formulated in relative terms, and varying degrees of comparison are to be applied. To start at one extreme of the spectrum, we might say that the compositions attributed to, say, Sophocles, are relatively less adaptable to the process of recomposition because the phraseology itself is less capable of variation in the first place. At the other extreme, the compositions attributed to Homer were in the earliest recoverable periods doubtless far more adaptable to

[90] In the transmission of the medieval English text known as Cædmon's *Hymn*, there is noticeable difference between the Latin and the vernacular environments, as noted by O'Keeffe 1990.46: "when the *Hymn* travels as 'gloss' to the *Historia ecclesiastica*, the text is subject to little variation, while those records of the *Hymn* which are integrated in the West Saxon translation of the *History* show a high degree of freedom in transmission." In general, we may expect the Latin environment to foster the schoolbook mentality in medieval textual traditions.

ongoing recomposition because the phraseology traditionally operated on the very principle of variation. In the later periods of Homeric transmission, however, this adaptability becomes drastically reduced, for reasons that we will later on examine in some detail. Concentrating on the principle of variation in earlier phases of Homeric transmission, let us return to the passage with which we started this chapter, the Homeric image of the *aēdṓn* 'nightingale' in *Odyssey* 19.518–523, who is pictured as singing her beautiful song at the onset of yet another new season of springtime (ἔαρος νέον ἱσταμένοιο 519), perched in the dense foliage (520) and pouring forth her voice as she keeps *changing it around* (τρωπῶσα 521), thick and fast (θαμά 521) – a voice that is described as *poluēkhḗs* 'with many resoundings' (πολυηχέα 521) or, according to the variant reported by Aelian (*De natura animalium* 5.38), as *poludeukḗs* (πολυδευκέα 521), the meaning of which word we have not yet examined. Here, then, is Aelian's report:

Χάρμιδος ἀκούω τοῦ Μασσαλιώτου λέγοντος φιλόμου-
σον μὲν εἶναι τὴν ἀηδόνα, ἤδη δὲ καὶ φιλόδοξον. ἐν γοῦν
ταῖς ἐρημίαις ὅταν ᾄδῃ πρὸς ἑαυτήν, ἁπλοῦν τὸ μέλος
καὶ ἄνευ κατασκευῆς τὴν ὄρνιν ᾄδειν· ὅταν δὲ ἁλῷ καὶ
τῶν ἀκουόντων μὴ διαμαρτάνῃ, ποικίλα τε ἀναμέλπειν
καὶ τακερῶς ἑλίττειν τὸ μέλος. καὶ Ὅμηρος δὲ τοῦτό μοι
δοκεῖ ὑπαινίττεσθαι λέγων

[*Odyssey* 19.518–523, with πολυηχέα at verse 521]

ἤδη μέντοι τινὲς καὶ πολυδευκέα φωνὴν γράφουσι τὴν
ποικίλως μεμιμημένην, ὡς τὴν ἀδευκέα τὴν μηδ᾽ ὅλως ἐς
μίμησιν παρατραπεῖσαν.

I hear tell from Charmis of Massalia that the nightingale is a creature who is a lover of the Muses and even a lover of fame. He [= Charmis] goes on to say, in any case, that when she is singing to herself in desolate places, her melody is simple, and that the bird sings without preparation. But when she is captured and has no lack of an audience, he says that she strikes up her melody in a varied [*poikíla*] way and meltingly changes the song around. And Homer seems to me to be referring to this enigmatically when he says:

[Here Aelian quotes *Odyssey* 19.518–523, with *poluēkhḗs* at verse 521]

But there are even those who write πολυδευκέα φωνὴν [a voice that is *poludeukḗs*], that is, "making imitation [*mímēsis*] in a varied [*poikílos*] way," just as ἀδευκέα [*adeukḗs*] means "not at all adapted for imitation [*mímēsis*]."

Aelian *De natura animalium* 5.38

In considering these two variants *poluēkhḗs* and *poludeukḗs* at *Odyssey* 19.521, I am ready to argue that both are legitimate, both ultimately generated from the multiform performance tradition of Homer. I will also argue that the variant reported by Aelian has an archaic meaning that even he could not fully understand. This meaning, as we will see in the next chapter, captures the very essence of continuity in variation.

We have already considered one critic's analysis of these two variants.[91] His view is that, although *poludeukḗs* is "rarer" than *poluēkhḗs*, the editorial principle of *lectio difficilior* should not be applied in this case: "we have seen ... that many conjectures were introduced by the ancients into Homer and that sometimes the original was replaced by a rarer and more difficult word."[92] Arguing that the other reading could not be "original," this critic goes on to say: "If this reading were original, it would be very surprising that the leading critics of antiquity ignored it, while it was preserved by a later author like [Aelian], who had far fewer resources at his disposal."[93]

Let us contemplate for a moment the resources at Aelian's disposal. Born in the third quarter of the second century AD, he seems to typify the kind of scholars who populate the compendium that we know as Athenaeus' *Deipnosophistai*. As for his specific source in this case, Aelian says that he "had heard tell" – that is to say, that he "had read" or had someone read to him – about the nightingale, and that his source was a man called Charmis of Massalia.[94] At the very mention of Massalia, a question may arise

---

[91] Van der Valk 1949.82–89.

[92] Van der Valk 1949.83. See also p. 8 above for a further statement about the "original" reading.

[93] Van der Valk 1949.83.

[94] On the idiom ἀκούω + genitive of name X + λέγοντος, see Schenkeveld 1992.132, context type iii: "the hearer himself read, or listened to a public reading by his slave, from a text written by X." At p. 133, Schenkeveld cites Aelian *De natura animalium* 7.7: Ἀριστοτέλους ἀκούω λέγοντος ὅτι ἄρα γέρανοι 'I hear tell from Aristotle that the cranes ...'.

in our minds whether this man from Marseille may also have
been Aelian's actual source for the variant reading in the Homeric
passage about the nightingale – and whether this variant may
even have stemmed from the so-called *Massaliōtikḗ*, the city text
of Homer that was often cited by the Homer critic Aristarchus.[95]
While we cannot with any certainty answer such a question, we
can say at least this much: that Aelian in *De natura animalium* 5.38
uses the report of Charmis about nightingales as a pretext for
offering what he implies is his own scholarly interpretation of the
Homeric variant *poludeukéa* describing the sound the nightingale
makes.

"I hear tell," says Aelian, "from Charmis of Massalia" (Χάρμιδος ἀκούω τοῦ Μασσαλιώτου λέγοντος ...) that the nightingale is a creature that loves the tradition of the Muses: it is
philómouson. It also loves the fame that songmaking brings with it:
it is *philódoxon*. When the nightingale sings in the wilderness, as
Charmis reports, her song is simple and unvaried; when she sings
in captivity, however, she becomes aware that she now has an
audience, and so she now shifts to a different style, that is, ποικίλα ... ἀναμέλπειν καὶ τακερῶς ἑλίττειν τὸ μέλος 'she sings in
a varied [*poikíla*] way and meltingly changes the song around'.
Then Aelian quotes the passage from the *Odyssey*, 19. 518–521 in
the same form that we have in our latter-day editions, featuring
poluēkhéa 'with many resoundings' as epithet of *phōnḗn* 'voice' at
verse 521.

It would seem at first sight that the reading *poluēkhéa* 'with
many resoundings' has already aptly illustrated the report of
Charmis about the more patterned voice of the nightingale who
has become aware that she has an audience. It is only as if it were
an afterthought that Aelian adds at this point the scholarly observation that "some even write" (ἤδη μέντοι τινὲς ... γράφουσι) not *poluēkhéa* but *poludeukéa*, which he glosses as τὴν
ποικίλως μεμιμημένην 'making imitation [*mímēsis*] in a varied
[*poikílōs*] way', and he compares the formation *poludeukéa* with the
negative *adeukéa* (ἀδευκέα), which he glosses as μηδ' ὅλως παρατραπεῖσαν ἐς μίμησιν 'not at all adapted for imitation'. The use
of the word *mímēsis*, which can be translated for the moment as

95 More on Aristarchus and the Marseille "edition" of Homer in ch.5.

'imitation', is crucial for the interpretation of the variant reading *poludeukéa*, as we will see in Chapter 2.

Whether this variant reading is Aelian's own additional piece of information or, as is more likely, it stems ultimately from Charmis of Massalia, it seems that Aelian's own interpretation does not do full justice to the archaic meaning of *poludeukéa*. Aelian is interested mainly in the nightingale's versatility as an imitator, whereas the epithet *poludeukéa* draws attention also to the continuity of the singer's performance, as we will see in the next chapter. We may be dissatisfied also with other facets of Aelian's interpretation. He seems to be saying that the expanded variety of the songbird's repertoire as a musician (*philómouson*) is a singer's desire for fame (*philódoxon*) before an expanded audience, now that she finds herself in captivity. We may note the fact that the nightingale in the ancient Greek songmaking traditions is generically female, singing a song of lament, unlike the male nightingale of the medieval *troubadour* traditions, which is conventionally singing a love-song.[96] This is not to say that songs of lament and songs of love are incompatible: they are in fact regularly interchangeable in Greek traditions, for example.[97] The point is, rather, that the nightingale sings from the heart, as it were, the afflictions of love or death. As a captive, the nightingale may sing her heart out not only because of any pride in her songmaking virtuosity but also, more basically, because of her sorrows.[98] In light of the

[96] I recall the *viva voce* remark made by Nicole Loraux (7 January 1994) when she first heard my arguments about Aelian's interpretation of the Homeric nightingale: Aelian forgets that the nightingale *is* a lamenting woman. In other words, he forgets about the metaphorical world that constitutes the habitat, as it were, of this Homeric songbird. On the nightingale as a singer of lament (*thrênos*): *Homeric Hymn to Pan* 18. On the association of the nightingale with love-songs and even with eroticism in medieval European traditions, see especially Pfeffer 1985 ch.7, "Sex and the Single Nightingale."

[97] Alexiou 1974.56.

[98] Again, the evidence of Greek traditions in the performance of lament shows that the expression of pride in one's songmaking virtuosity – *even the element of intense competition* – is not incompatible with the expression of one's sorrows: see Alexiou 1974.40 (cf. Herzfeld 1993). For a zoömusicological perspective on the competitiveness of the nightingale as singer, see Mâche 1991.156; see also in general his discussion, pp. 155–157, of the musical *duel* as a functional equivalent of a *duet*. In the same discussion, he reviews some salient ethnomusicological examples of "*duel* as *duet*," including the *sfide* traditions of latter-day Sicily, analogous to such stylized amoebaean compositions as Theocritus 5, 8, 9, and so on. When one *troubadour* competes with another, as when

tragic story underlying the nightingale's lament in the Greek traditions, we may wish to reinterpret the variety of the songbird's song not only as a performer's response to an ever-widening audience but also as a victim's response to an ever-widening threshold of pain and suffering. We may note in passing the title of the autobiography of the poet Maya Angelou, *I Know Why the Caged Bird Sings*.[99] Surely the nightingale in the *Odyssey* sings her beautiful song of lament about the fact of her own suffering. The woman who had killed her own child – inadvertently, the *Odyssey* claims – had suffered much, but now she suffers more, transformed into a songbird singing her own mournful song. Of course the song is as beautifully varied as it is mournful, and then it can become even more so with her new misfortune, her loss of freedom and her new identity as a captive singer. We may recall the words in Toni Morrison's *Beloved*, a novel centering on the twin tragedies of slavery and infanticide: "it was not a story to pass on."[100] And yet, as we will see in the next chapter, the song of the nightingale has a continuousness, a continuity. It is indeed passed on.

The continuity is implicit in the variety. We may note the meaning of *trōpôsa* (τρωπῶσα) at *Odyssey* 19.521, describing the nightingale as she *changes around* or literally *turns* the sound of her beautiful song. Let us recall the song of the he-nightingale in Song I of Jaufré Rudel, where birdsong serves as model for the song of the poet, and where the model itself is that of re-composition, not just composition, in that even the songbird is in fact recomposing his own song by virtue of performing it. The nightingale *moves* his song, which as we have seen is inherently both recurrent and recomposed, much as every new season of spring is a joyous event of inherent recurrence and recomposi-

---

Peire d'Alvernha in Song 28.1–7 challenges Bernard de Ventadour by name (verse 1), the challenge can take the form of a comparison with nightingales: in this case, Bernard is told that the nightingale understands love better than he does (verse 7, *melhs s'enten que vos en amor*).

[99] Angelou 1969. Thanks to Marjorie Garber and Barbara Johnson for their helping me think through the "caged bird" conventions.

[100] Morrison 1987.274. In Ovid's version of the tragic story of Procne, Philomela, and Tereus, *Metamorphoses* 6.412–674, the pain felt by Procne – as a woman – is beyond verbal expression: *silet: dolor ora repressit* 'she is silent: the pain has repressed word of mouth' (verse 583). Segal 1994.267 remarks: "what she finds is a tale whose pain lies beyond the power of words." On the expression of this pain *as a text*, see p. 65n25.

tion, even re-creation. To the extent that *mouvance* in the poetics of the *troubadour* conveys the idea of continuity through variation, we can see in the usage of the word *trōpôsa* (τρωπῶσα) at *Odyssey* 19.521 the first attestation of this idea in European traditions.

The usage of the root *trep- as in *trōpôsa*, with the basic meaning of 'turn' or 'change around' and with the implied meaning of continuity through variation, lives on in the song-making traditions of ancient Greece, taking on the form of the noun-derivative *trópos*. This word refers in practical terms to a given pattern of modulation in the singing voice, corresponding to a given pattern of *accordatura* or tuning of the accompanying lyre (an ideal example is Pindar *Olympian* 14.17). More generally and theoretically, *trópos* is a 'style' of melody ("Aristotle" *Problems* 19.38). Such a 'style', in the usage of ancient Greek music theory, "may be determined by any combination of scale-structure, pitch, and melodic shape."[101] Eventually, *trópos* becomes a word for 'style' in general, especially rhetorical style (Plato *Republic* 400d). In the technical language of rhetoric, it takes on the meaning of 'trope, figure of speech', and it is at this stage of semantic development that Greek *trópos* is borrowed into Latin as *tropus* (Quintilian *Institutio oratoria* 8.6). From the high language of the schools, the noun *tropus* is borrowed into the popular language, which creates on its own a derivative verb *tropāre. This "Vulgar Latin" verb *tropāre is actually attested in late Latin authors as the compound verb *contropāre* (also *adtropāre*),[102] and it lived on as an inherited form in the Romance languages or as a borrowed form in the Celtic languages, witness modern French *trouver* and medieval Irish *trop*.[103] Most important for now, *tropāre also lived on as the medieval Provençal verb *trobar*, meaning 'find, invent' or 'compose poetry', and in the noun-derivative *trobador*, later spelled as *troubadour*. This meaning is pertinent, as we shall see, even to the modern French verb *trouver*, in the everyday sense of 'find, invent, discover'.

This is not the time to attempt a systematic retracing of the semantic route of continuity in meaning from *tropāre to *trobar* in

---

[101] Barker 1984.199n68.
[102] Ernout/Meillet *DELL* 704.
[103] Meyer-Lübke 1935 entry no. 8936 a.

the language of the *troubadours*. We may simply review the intuitive summary of Peter Dronke concerning medieval musical traditions during the century and a half following the death of Notker in the year 912:

> Sequences become more and more abundant throughout this period, especially at the established musical centres such as Saint-Gall and Saint-Martial, but also in England. Gradually syllabic parallelism in the sequence is embellished by regular stresses and rhymes, giving more obvious – and less subtle – harmonies than any that the ninth century had known. Alongside the sequences were composed *tropes*, that is, poetic and musical amplifications of liturgical texts, some of which, probably under the influence of vigorous popular oral traditions of drama and dramatic song, become lyrical dialogues.[104]

The concept of lyrical dialogues, which we may picture in ancient Greek terms as the *mímēsis* – let us translate the word for now as 'imitation' – of speech by way of song, lies at the heart of the medieval *troubadour* traditions, where one side of a dialogue, the side of the lover, is highlighted as if it were a monologue. As a performance, such a monologue is of course implicitly a dialogue with the audience who is being addressed, as also with the beloved, real or imaginary.

Here the chapter comes to a halt. But the subject of the nightingale's song, sung again and again in all its varieties through time, from the *aoidoí* of ancient Greece to the *troubadours* of medieval Provence, will continue.

---

[104] Dronke 1977.44. At p. 103 below, I suggest that the technical metaphor of "trope" leads to the everyday meaning of "find," as in Provençal *trobar*. For an alternative explanation of *trobar* in the sense of "compose poetry," see Menocal 1982, who posits a borrowing from Arabic.

2

Mimesis, models of singers, and the meaning of a Homeric epithet

Let us continue where we left off, with the song of the nightingale. In the previous chapter, we noted that the idea of variation is implicit in the epithet *poludeukés* describing the voice (*phōnḗ*) of the songbird at *Odyssey* 19.521, but the task remains to formulate the precise meaning of this epithet, which will be pertinent to the meaning of the elusive word *mímēsis* (henceforth spelled simply as "mimesis"). We will see that mimesis, ordinarily translated as 'imitation', can have a deeper sense, 'reenactment'. To make a re-enactment is to pattern something on a *model*, and the idea of such patterning is inherent, as we will see, in the meaning of the Homeric epithet of the nightingale. This idea will prove to be essential for understanding poetry as performance.

Let us look again at the context of the epithet for the nightingale. We have seen that Aelian in *De natura animalium* 5.38, who says that *poludeukés* is an alternative to *poluēkhḗs* 'with many resoundings' at *Odyssey* 19.521, interprets the first of these two variant epithets to mean τὴν ποικίλως μεμιμημένην 'making imitation [mimesis] in a varied [*poikílōs*] way'. If he is right, then this variant epithet *poludeukés* points to the songbird's capacity for variety, that is, the capacity to perform *poikílōs* 'in a varied way'.[1] The idea of variety is reinforced by the meaning of the participle *trōpôsa* (τρωπῶσα) at *Odyssey* 19.521, describing the

---

[1] The semantics of *poikílos* 'varied' are illuminated by the context of the epithet of the nightingale in Hesiod *Works and Days* 203, *poikilódeiros*, which is interpreted as 'having a varied[-sounding] throat' at p. 59n1 below; also by the context of the epithet of Aphrodite in Sappho 1.1, *poikilóthronos*, which is interpreted in the sense of 'with varied embroidered flowers' at p. 101n40.

39

nightingale as she 'changes around' or literally 'turns' the sound of her beautiful song.[2] The nightingale's distinctive capacity for variety – for "turning" as it were – is empirically verifiable. In his "zoömusicological" description of patterns inherent in the singing of the nightingale, specifically the *Luscinia megarhynchos*, François-Bernard Mâche actually uses the term "strophe," deliberately evocative of the idea of "turning," to denote a distinctive sequence of sound-units – let us call them "notes" – in the bird's song.[3] Moreover, the melodic patterning of the nightingale's song, as opposed to that of the lark, for example, involves the operation of a paradigmatic or "vertical" axis of selection, not only a syntagmatic or "horizontal" axis of combination.[4]

Such a patterning is made clear in Mâche's study of a "corpus" of 165 strophes produced by four individual nightingales, two of the singers recorded in Hungary and two in France.[5] According to one formulation, each strophe is divisible into three parts: an opening, a middle, and a closing or coda.[6] The opening consists of different notes and different numbers of these notes, averaging between five and six; the middle consists of a series of repeated notes, with an average of two-thirds being in *staccato* format, that is, where one note is being rapidly repeated between extremely short pauses, and the other third being in *trill* format, that is, where the alternation of two notes – one of them simplex in timbre and the other, complex – is likewise being rapidly re-

---

[2] Pliny *Natural History* 10.85 refers to the *vox* 'voice' of the nightingale as *modulata* 'modulated' and *varia* 'varied' (where *modulated* is to be understood in the ancient, not modern, sense: see p. 24n56).

[3] Mâche 1991.119, with reference to the *Luscinia megarhynchos*. A "phrase" in birdsong, according to the descriptive scheme developed by Mâche, is a sequence or "suite" of sounds framed by intervals of silence; wherever such a sequence or "suite" begins with a repeated pattern of sounds, it is a "strophe" (p. 112). On the functioning of such strophes in situations where we find no explicit framing by pauses or intervals of silence, see Mâche p. 144.

[4] Mâche 1991.119. On the concept of an opposition between an axis of combination and an axis of selection, see p. 2n7. On the sequencing of the "strophes" themselves in the case of the nightingale's singing, Mâche p. 121n14 refers to Todt 1971, whose work raises – at least implicitly, in my opinion – important questions concerning the opposition of *langue* and *parole* in the performance of an individual nightingale.

[5] Mâche 1991.119–123.

[6] Mâche 1991.121. What follows in the rest of this paragraph is a close paraphrase of his formulation. We may note in passing the implications of many of these formulations for the diachronic analysis of Greek lyric meters, as in N 1990a.439–464.

peated; and the coda, finally, consists of a single note in general, uniquely different from all the other notes in the strophe. There exists an option to insert – at a point that comes before the coda and after the middle, with its cluster of repetitions – transitional notes and even one or several clusters of further repetitions; moreover, the actual linking of such clusters of repetitions generally causes an abrupt change in tempo.

We may compare this description with the onomatopoeia that represents the nightingale's song in the *Birds* of Aristophanes: τιὸ τιὸ τιὸ τιοτίγξ = *tiò tiò tiò tiotínx* (738, 741, 743, 751) and τὸ τὸ τὸ τὸ τὸ τὸ τὸ τοτίγξ = *tò tò tò tò tò tò tò tò totínx* (748).[7] In the first instance of *tiò tiò tiò tiotínx* (738), the birdcall is framed by the vocative of "Muse in the thickets" (Μοῦσα λοχμαία 737) and by her epithet, *poikíle* 'varied' (ποικίλη 739). Also, the music of the *aulós* 'reed' fulfills the representation of the nightingale's song, as indicated in the manuscript tradition of the *Birds* by the notation αὐλεῖ 'plays the *aulós*' at verse 222.

To return to the description by Mâche, what emerges is a pattern of interplay between combination and selection in the song of the nightingale. In other words, it is not just a matter of the songbird's capacity to combine sounds into given sequences. More than that, each combination of sounds can be selected – or, better, re-selected – to create further combinations. The idea of re-selecting, that is, selecting again the same combination in order to make another combination, fits the image of coming around, turning, returning.

In this light, let us return to Aelian's interpretation of the epithet *poludeukés* describing the voice of the songbird at *Odyssey* 19.521. To repeat, if indeed *poludeukés* implies that the nightingale

---

[7] There is an analogous onomatopoeia implicit in the form *Itus* ("Ἴτυς), a name of the son of the unfortunate mythical woman who was turned into a nightingale, in contexts where *Itus* is doubled, as in Aeschylus *Agamemnon* 1144: "Ἴτυν Ἴτυν στένουσ' '[the nightingale] mourning "*Itun Itun*"'; also Sophocles *Electra* 148: Ἴτυν αἰὲν Ἴτυν ὀλοφύρεται 'who keeps on mourning "*Itun Itun*"'. As Ian Rutherford points out to me, the refrain ἴτω ἴτω χορός = *ítō ítō khorós* 'let the chorus get under way!' in SLG S 460.13/15/17 represents not only the song of the nightingale (ἀηδονὶς ὧδε λέλακε 'thus the nightingale spoke' at line 8) but also the *sound* of the song, by way of onomatopoeia; in this context, the songbird signals the inception of choral song and dance in springtime (cf. ἐν ὥραις at line 12). In the song of Tereus at Aristophanes *Birds* 228–229, the onomatopoeia of *ítō* is made explicit by the purely onomatopoeic sequence that precedes it: ἰὼ ἰὼ ἰτὼ ἰτὼ ἰτὼ ἰτὼ | ἴτω ὧδε τῶν ἐμῶν ὁμοπτέρων '*iò iò itò itò itò* | *ítō* [let come] all my fellow feathered-ones'.

is τὴν ποικίλως μεμιμημένην 'the one who makes imitation [mimesis] in a varied [*poikílos*] way', then this variant epithet *poludeukés* points to the songbird's capacity for variety. But the argument goes beyond establishing the idea of variety in the word *poludeukés*. There is even more to Aelian's description of the nightingale's birdsong, since he insists on the notion of mimesis in his definition: τὴν ποικίλως <u>μεμιμημένην</u> 'the one who <u>makes imitation [mimesis]</u> in a varied [*poikílos*] way'. If Aelian is right, then the variant epithet *poludeukés* conveys not only variety but also the very idea of mimesis, which is translated here as 'imitation'. If he is right, then *poludeukés* is closely parallel in meaning to *poluēkhés* 'with many resoundings', since *ēkhō* 'resounding, echo' likewise conveys the idea of mimesis. As we will now see, moreover, there is a deeper meaning of mimesis, which can be understood by discovering the deeper meaning of the epithet *poludeukés*.

Let us pursue the argument that *poludeukés*, once we examine its usage and its etymology, is indeed parallel in meaning to *poluēkhés* as an epithet of the Homeric nightingale's song. Let us begin with the first component, *polu-*, of both *poluēkhés* 'with many resoundings' and *poludeukés*, the variant epithets describing the voice of the nightingale in *Odyssey* 19.521. In the case of the compound *poluēkhés*, which has been translated up to now simply as 'with many resoundings', that is, 'having many resoundings', the idea of variety is inherent even in the semantic combination of *polu-* 'much, many' with *ēkhō* 'echo, resounding', to the extent that we may interpret the meaning of this compound not only as 'having resoundings/echoes many times' but also as 'having resoundings/echoes in many ways'.[8] In the case of *poludeukés*, however, the idea of variety is revealed by its etymology, in the second component as well, *-deukés*. Also inherent in the etymology is the idea of mimesis.

---

[8] The scholia V at *Odyssey* 19.521 explain *poluēkhéa* as *pollàs metabolàs poiouménēn* 'making many changes'. The same word *poluēkhés* occurs at *Iliad* 4.422, epithet of *aigialós* 'beach'. Applying the interpretation of the scholia, we may translate either 'resounding many times' or 'resounding in many ways'. To emphasize the idea of variety, we may translate hereafter: 'resounding in many different ways'. For other compounds where the combination of *polu-* 'much, many' with a given noun yields a meaning that can be approximated by 'in many different ways', see below.

The strong sense of variety, even multiformity, in *poludeukḗs* is evident in its application to the word *morphḗ* 'form' in Nicander *Theriaka* 209, in a zoological description of vipers as a sub-set of the snake family. The combination of the words *poludeukḗs* and *morphḗ* with the genitive of the word for 'vipers' has aptly been translated by the editors of Nicander as "the various forms of the viper."[9] In the next verse of Nicander (210), we are in fact told by the poet that vipers are to be found in a wide variety of shapes and sizes. We have in this attestation, then, a convenient point of departure for surveying the ideas of variety and polymorphism inherent in the rare epithet *poludeukḗs*. But the question remains to be pursued: is there an idea of mimesis as well as variety in *poludeukḗs?*

Let us for a moment turn to matters of etymology. Pierre Chantraine in his *Dictionnaire étymologique de la langue grecque* and Ernst Risch in his *Wortbildung der homerischen Sprache* are both uncertain about how to explain the meaning of the root *deuk-/ *duk- in *poludeukḗs*, but they are both quite certain about the morphological relationship of this word with two other words, the negative *adeukḗs* and the adverb *endukéōs*.[10] We have seen in the previous chapter that Aelian as well, in his discussion of *poludeukḗs* as an epithet of the nightingale, treats *adeukḗs* as the negative of *poludeukḗs*. He thinks that *adeukḗs* means 'incapable of mimesis'. As we will see, mimesis in such a context means more than 'imitation': it conveys also a deeper sense of *continuity*.

Let us start, however, not with the negative adjective *adeukḗs* but rather with the adverb *endukéōs*. From a survey of its contexts, I infer that this word *endukéōs* is associated with the notion of an *uninterrupted sequence*, as for example in contexts like *Odyssey* 14.337 involving the action of sending or accompanying someone on a journey (verb *pémpō* at 333, 334, 338). There are sinister implications here concerning any interruption of the journey as a sequence, a continuum. Similarly at *Iliad* 24.438, a disguised Hermes tells Priam that he will accompany him *endukéōs*, whether

---

[9] Gow and Scholfield 1953.43. In the scholia to Nicander *Theriaka* 209, *poludeukḗs* is glossed as *poikílos* 'varied' in *morphḗ* 'shape'.

[10] Chantraine *DELG* 19 (cf. already Frisk *GEW* 20) and Risch 1974.81–83 (cf. also Bader 1986, whose explanation differs from the one presented here).

on ship or on foot: as your *pompós* or 'conductor' (437), he continues, I would journey with you even as far as Argos itself, and no one will dare stand up to you so long as I am your 'conductor' (again, *pompós*, 439). Again, a successful journey is pictured as a sequence, a continuum.

Conversely, the negative *adeukés* occurs in contexts referring to an *interrupted sequence*, as in a quoted question about the Achaeans coming home from Troy at *Odyssey* 4.489: did any of them, Menelaos is asking the Old Man of the Sea, perish while on a ship at sea, destroyed by a doom (*ólethros*) that is *adeukés*?[11] At *Odyssey* 10.245, Eurylokhos puzzles over how to announce the bad news that Odysseus' companions have just been turned into swine, which is a fate (*pótmos*) that is *adeukés*. At *Odyssey* 6.273, Nausikaa is worrying about bad things that the Phaeacians may say about her: they may, she fears, make the kind of utterance (*phêmis*) that is *adeukés* for her reputation. It is as if one's good reputation were a steady stream of positive speech, the interruption of which threatens to produce a bad reputation.

Returning to the adverb *endukéōs*, we may say that its contexts of an *uninterrupted sequence* imply a ritualized continuity or consistency, as in descriptions of a host's treatment of a guest. At *Odyssey* 15.305, for example, Odysseus is testing the swineherd Eumaios, who is, unwittingly, playing host to his disguised master, whether he *philéoi* 'loves' him *endukéōs* or whether he will suddenly switch, turning against him. At *Odyssey* 15.491, *endukéōs* refers to the steady flow of food and drink provided by the master of the household to his dependent, in this case Eumaios, without ever cutting off the supply; Eumaios is not aware that he is being told all this by his own long-lost master, the disguised Odysseus. At *Odyssey* 14.111, a disguised Odysseus as guest is eating, in a way that is described as *endukéōs*, the meal that Eumaios, *philéōn* 'loving' host that he is, is offering him. At *Odyssey* 17.111, Telemakhos says that Nestor as host *ephílei* 'loved' him *endukéōs*, treating him as if he had been a son who had just returned after an absence: here the status of the child as dependent

---

[11] On the possibility of a variant reading involving *adeukés* at *Odyssey* 1.46, with reference to the death of Aegisthus, see Dyck 1993.11–12, especially p. 12n26. In Apollonius of Rhodes we find *adeukés* as epithet of *átē* 'doom' (1.1037), *aîsa* 'fate' (4.1503), *háls* 'sea' (2.388), *áellai* 'gusts of wind' (2.267).

has been interrupted, but the love of the father has not.[12] This is how, continues Telemakhos at 17.113, Nestor *took care of* me (*ekómize*), along with his own sons. At *Odyssey* 14.390, the old woman *endukéōs takes care of (koméesken)* the old man.[13] At *Homeric Hymn* 26.4, the Nymphs *endukéōs* raised (*atítallon*) the infant Dionysus in Nysa.[14]

At *Odyssey* 10.65 there is a combination of both sending and hosting contexts: Aeolus the god of winds is telling Odysseus that he had sent him off *endukéōs, so that the hero could reach home*, but now the journey has been interrupted and the hero's home-coming is utterly ruined because the bag of winds has been opened. We see here an ultimate interruption not only in the journey of the hero but in the epic narrative as well.

It is worth the effort to go to such lengths in examining the contexts of *endukéōs* and the morphologically related *adeukés* because their positive and negative associations respectively with the notions of *uninterrupted* and *interrupted* sequences makes it clear that these words, and *poludeukés* also, as we will see presently, are all derived from the same root *deuk-/*duk- that we find in Latin *dúcere, dux*. The arguments that follow are intended as proof of an etymological connection of *endukéōs/adeukés/poludeukés* with Latin *dúcere, dux* on the basis of the inherited contexts that we are about to find for these Latin words.[15]

In their etymological dictionary of Latin, Ernout and Meillet explain *dúcere* as an old pastoral word conveying the basic idea of *pull* rather than *push* (*agere*): the herdsman or *dux* is "pulling" or *leading* (*dúcere*) the herd when he goes in front, while he is "pushing" or *driving* (*agere*) when he is coming up from behind.[16] Going beyond this formulation of Ernout and Meillet, Emile Benveniste adds the notion of a *continuum*, so that the *dux* who

[12] We may compare the collocation of verse-initial *épios* and verse-initial *endukéōs* at *Odyssey* 15.490/491, the earlier Eumaios passage. On the semantics of *épios*, see Edmunds 1990.98: "The typically *épios* figure is mature, gives good advice, understands justice, and promotes social cohesion."
[13] At *Odyssey* 10.450, Circe *endukéōs* washes and anoints the companions.
[14] For the moment, let us simply note in passing the combinations of *endukéōs* with *tréphō* 'raise' at *Iliad* 23.90, *Odyssey* 7.256. These combinations turn out to be valuable evidence in the discussion that follows.
[15] In the discussion that follows, I have benefited from the valuable advice of Richard P. Martin.
[16] Ernout/Meillet *DELL* 185.

marches in front of the aggregate is necessarily connected, as the prime linking force, as it were, to the train that follows.[17] We may compare the semantics of Latin *prae*, which means not simply 'in front of' but 'in front of and connected to what follows'. When someone falls *praeceps* or 'head-first', for example, the body follows the head *because it is connected to it*.[18] We can understand the semantics of *dūcere* more clearly if we substitute for the translation *pull* the English synonym *draw*, the richly varied compound patterns of which, such as *draw up, draw out, draw in, draw back*, and so on are comparable to the ones that we are about to see in the Latin compounds of *dūcere*.[19]

As we will now see, the idea behind *dūcere*, and *draw*, for that matter, is not only an uninterrupted sequence but also one that draws toward a definite goal. Benveniste's most telling example is the Latin expression *rationem dūcere*, which means 'add up' or 'add up the account' and which we may translate more literally as 'draw up', as in the expression *draw up the account*.[20] When you add, you are following an uninterrupted sequence from the bottom up, with the definite goal of a *summa* or summit, that is, a sum. The direction of sequence in a *sum* is likewise from bottom to top, as in the idiom *to sum up*. There is a similar set of semantics, with the same visualization of movement from bottom to top, in the Greek verb *ekkoruphóō* (as in Hesiod *Works and Days* 106).[21]

Another instance of this idea of an uninterrupted sequence drawing toward a definite goal is the Latin expression *dūcere aquam/aquas* 'conduct water'. As we may infer from the derivative *aquae ductus*, an aqueduct must ultimately have a destination.[22] As we look back at the contexts where the Greek adverb *endukéōs* is associated with the idea of raising a child, we can now see a basic semantic connection with the Latin compound verb *ēducāre*,

[17] Benveniste 1973.121–130. Cf. Ernout/Meillet *DELL* 185, who stress the correlation of *dūcō* 'lead' with *sequor* 'follow' – the verb conveying the very idea of sequence.
[18] Benveniste 1949.
[19] Besides the English combinations, we may consider the vast variety of nuances in the Gothic compounds, as noted by Benveniste 1973.125. On the implications of German *ziehen* and *Zug*, see Schur 1994.
[20] Benveniste 1973.122.
[21] Cf. West 1978.178.
[22] See *OLD* 578 as marked. Ernout/Meillet *DELL* point out that Cicero uses *ductus aquarum* where Vitruvius has *ductio aquarum*.

which conveys the idea of raising a child, or a plant, toward the definite goal of maturity.[23] Having a set sequence and a set goal by no means precludes the idea of variety. We may consider Benveniste's examples of Latin expressions combining the verb *dūcere* with a direct object indicating the shape of a letter of the alphabet: hence the *ductus* of a letter is the *drawing* or *tracing* of a letter, and of course each different letter has its own different *ductus*. Thus the sequence or pattern of *drawing*, the pattern of *dūcere*, is itself a matter of variety. Even the English word *pattern* provides a striking illustration of this idea: a basic meaning of *pattern* is 'model', as in the world of dress-making. Etymologically, a pattern is a model. And yet, pattern *is* variety, as we can see even from the current sense of the word.

The idea of pattern as variety comes to life in the rich variety of compound patterns built from Latin *dūcere*, such as *condūcere*, *dēdūcere*, *ēdūcere/ēducāre*, *indūcere*, and so on, as also the corresponding compounds in the Germanic languages.[24] And there is a rich variety of meaning and application even within each one of the compounds. In the case of *indūcere*, for example, let us consider some of the categories of definition in the *Oxford Latin Dictionary*: meaning 5 is 'introduce a custom or law'; meaning 6, in the legal sense, is 'sanction, give grounds for'; meaning 7 is 'apply a rule'; meaning 1, again in a legal sense, is 'bring in', as for example a witness; meaning 8 is 'initiate, install into a position'; meaning 3 is 'put on stage', that is, introduce a performer into the action of the drama, or alternatively, to introduce a character into a narrative by presenting him or her to the mind's eye, as it were; and the list goes on. Then there is the abstract noun derivative, *inductiō*, meaning (1) bringing in a performer, (2) initiation, (3) prompting to a *course* of action, focusing the mind, (4), reasoning by analogy – which translates the Greek philosophical concept of *epagōgḗ*. In Cicero's *De inventione* 1.51, we read the following definition: *inductio est oratio quae rebus non dubiis captat assen-*

---

[23] Contexts of *ēducāre* with plant as object include Columella 4.29.17 (human agent; other contexts listed in OLD 588 s.v., section c); we may compare the correlation, as noted above, of the Homeric adverb *endukéōs* with contexts of *tréphō* and *atitállō*, where the object of the verb may be a child or a plant.

[24] See p. 46n19. For an illuminating analysis of the poetics of German *ziehen*, see Schur 1994.

*sionem eius quicum instituta est; quibus assensionibus facit ut illi dubia quae-
dam res propter similitudinem earum rerum, quibus assensit, probetur* 'induction is a form of speaking that seeks, in matters that are not open
to doubt, the assent of the person with whom this form of speaking
has been undertaken; by way of these assents the speaker makes
credible to this person some matter that *is* open to doubt, because of
its likeness to those things to which he has already given assent'.[25]

This definition of induction can also serve as a definition of
the root *deuk-/*duk- itself, as we focus our attention on the notion of *similitūdō* as a key to the process. In terms of Cicero's
definition of induction, we may view the root *deuk-/*duk- as
'draw continuously toward a definite goal', where continuity is
established through the mental process of connecting like with
like. Moreover, the continuum is achieved through variety. The
notion of "continuum through variety" may be pictured as a
game of "connect the dots," where the object of the game is to
keep on moving from one dot to the closest dot: the thicker the
clustering of dots along the way, the easier is the movement.[26]

The Alexandrian dictionary tradition that goes under the name
of Hesychius helps confirm this interpretation with a series of
glosses. The otherwise unattested adjective *endeukéa* is glossed in
Hesychius as *empherê, hómoia*. The Greek adjectives *empherés* and
hómoios mean 'similar, resembling'. Also in Hesychius, *endeukés* is
glossed as *hómoion* 'similar, resembling', and the first gloss for *endukés* is *sunekhés* 'continuous'.[27] In Nicander *Theriaka* 263, *endukés*
is attested in the sense of 'continuous'.[28]

---

[25] The notion of *captat assensionem* 'seeks assent' is analogous to the implications of
assent in Aristotle's description of mimesis in terms of the formula οὗτος ἐκεῖνος 'this
is that' in *Poetics* 1448b17 as discussed in N 1990a.44, especially n134; further discussion of this formula below.

[26] Cf. the formulation offered by Mâche 1991.125 concerning the "art" of birdsong
in particular and music in general: virtuosity is a matter of finding an equilibrium between *recurrence* and *novelty*.

[27] The other glosses given in Hesychius for *endukés* are *sunetón* 'aware, understanding', *apbelés* 'even', *asphalés* 'steady', *glukú* 'sweet', *próthumon* 'cooperative', *eúnoun*
'kindly disposed', *pistón* 'reliable', *epimelés* 'caring'. Most of these interpretations suit the
contexts of the Homeric adverb *endukéōs* as surveyed above. I see as a common semantic
thread the idea of *attentiveness to proper procedure*. The glosses in Hesychius for *endúkion* are
pistón 'reliable', *phílon* 'near and dear', *empherés* 'similar', *bébaion* 'certain', and *apókruphon*
'obscure'; perhaps the last of these is meant as a comment on the meaning; the gloss for
deukés is *hómoion* 'similar' (in Latte's 1953 edition of Hesychius vol. 1, the other gloss
lamprón 'shining, visible' is removed and transposed under the entry *deikés*).

[28] This *endukés* is also apparently attested as an adverb in Apollonius of Rhodes
1.883: as bees are *ekkhúmenai* 'pouring forth' from their hive (880), so also the women,

The word *sunekhés* 'continuous' is actually used in ["Aristotle"] *Historia animalium* 632b21 to describe the singing of the nightingale: ἀηδὼν ᾄδει μὲν συνεχῶς 'the nightingale sings in a *sunekhés* way'. Likewise Pliny *Natural History* 10.81 describes this birdsong as *garrulus sine intermissu cantus* 'a talkative song without interruption'.

As we approach the end of this sequence of examples for the idea of continuity in the root *deuk-/*duk-, we reach perhaps the most striking example in the Latin expression *filum dēdūcere* 'draw out a thread [in spinning]' (e.g. Ovid *Metamorphoses* 4.36; cf. Tibullus 1.3.86). There are comparable expressions where the verb *dūcere* or *dēdūcere* is metaphorically combined with objects like *carmen* 'song' to mean 'compose the song' (e.g. Propertius 4.6.13, Ovid *Metamorphoses* 1.4).

The association of the root *deuk-/*duk- with the idea of songmaking takes us back to the meaning of *poludeukés*, variant epithet for the nightingale's song in *Odyssey* 19.521, which we may now interpret as meaning 'having much continuity' or 'having continuity in many different ways' or even 'patterning in many ways' (or 'many times').[29] The translation 'patterning' highlights the idea of *continuity* through *variety*. And the patterns of continuity and variety are conceived as the distinctly poetic skills of songmaking in performance. From the discussion that follows, moreover, it will be clear that the idea of 'many different ways' (or 'many times') is an inherently agonistic one, with each new

in an *endukés* manner, *prokhéonto* 'poured forth' (883), lamenting, around the men. We may note that the nightingale in *Odyssey* 19.521 *khéei* 'pours forth' her *poludeukéa* (or *poluékhéa*) sound. Recalling the adverb *endukéōs*, derivative of this adjective *endukés*, we may note some additional attestations beyond the Homeric ones already surveyed. In Bacchylides 5.125 *endukéōs* refers to the steady fighting of warriors over the hide of the Calydonian Boar, and at 5.112 *endukéōs* is used correlatively with *sunekhéōs* 'continuously' with reference to the warriors' fight against the Boar itself. Chantraine *DELG* 346 emphasizes the idea of continuity and perseverance in this passage. In the Hesiodic *Shield* 427, *endukéōs* refers to a lion's tearing away at the flesh of its prey: in today's idiom, we would say that the lion is systematically or methodically devouring its prey. At Pindar *Pythian* 5.85, hosts are described as receiving their guest *endukéōs* with *thusíai* 'sacrifices'.

[29] On the semantics of *polu-* in the sense of 'many different', not just 'many' or 'much', cf. *polu-ēgerées* 'assembled from many different places', a variant reading reported by Aristarchus for *tēle-kleitoí* at *Iliad* 11.564, and *polu-sperés* 'much-dispersed', referring at *Iliad* 2.804 to peoples who are dispersed throughout many different places. Further morphological parallels for this kind of compounding with *es*-stems: *polu-tharsés* 'having much audacity', as at *Iliad* 17.156, etc., and *polu-kankés* 'much-burning', epithet of thirst at *Iliad* 11.642.

performance ever competing against previous performances. Thus we will find that *poludeukḗs* in the sense of 'patterning in many different ways' (or 'many times') is an apt description of oral tradition itself.

As Lord observes about the dynamics of oral tradition, "there is a pull in two directions: one is toward the song being sung and the other is toward the previous uses of the same theme."[30] If we reformulate this insight in terms of Prague School linguistics, we may say that the poetic process of referring to anything involves, simultaneously, a "horizontal" *axis of combination* and a "vertical" *axis of selection*.[31] Lord himself implies such an interaction between combination and selection when he says:

> Where the association is not linear, it seems to me that we are dealing with a force or 'tension' that might be termed 'submerged.' The habit is hidden, but felt. It arises from the depths of the tradition through the workings of the traditional processes to inevitable expression. And to be numb to an awareness of this kind of association is to miss the meaning not only of the oral method of composition and transmission, but even of epic itself. Without such an awareness the overtones from the past, which give tradition the richness of diapason of full organ, cannot be sensed by the reader of oral epic. The singer's natural audience appreciates it because they are as much part of the tradition as the singer himself.[32]

From this point of view each occurrence of a theme (on the level of content) or of a formula (on the level of form) in a given composition-in-performance refers not only to its immediate context but also to all other analogous contexts remembered by the performer or by any member of the audience.[33]

Pursuing the argument that the Homeric epithet *poludeukḗs* conveys a distinctly poetic idea, we may use as evidence the formulaic system of Homeric diction. There is a striking parallelism, both morphological and semantic, between *poludeukḗs* 'having

---

[30] Lord 1960.94; cf. also pp. 66, 94–97.
[31] See p. 2n7.
[32] Lord 1960.97.
[33] Cf. Foley 1991, who invokes the term *immanencé* to argue that the immediate reference in oral poetics is but a *part* of the *totality* of meaning.

much continuity [*es*-stem **deúkos*]' or 'having continuity in many different ways' (or 'many times'), epithet of the *aēdōn* 'nightingale' as a lamenting songbird on the one hand and, on the other, *polupenthḗs* 'having much grief [*es*-stem *pénthos*]' or 'having grief in many different ways' (or 'many times'), epithet of the *(h)alkúōn*, another lamenting songbird, in *Iliad* 9.563.[34] In Homeric diction, both *pénthos* and *ákhos* mean not only 'grief' but also 'song about grief', that is, a ritual song of lament.[35]

Also pertinent is the name of one of the two Divine Twins, *Poludeúkēs* (*Iliad* 3.237, *Odyssey* 11.300). The noun itself is straightforwardly related to the adjective *poludeukḗs*, in that the recessive accent of the name is typical of the naming function, as we see from such morphologically related formations as *Poluneíkēs* 'having many quarrels [*es*-stem *neîkos*]' or 'having quarrels in many different ways' (or 'many times').[36] In the mythological functions of the divine figure *Poludeúkēs*, the idea of continuity seems as evident as that of variety, since the Divine Twins are models of consistency, perseverance, reliability (as in *Homeric Hymn* 33).[37] In an astrological sense, we could say that *Poludeúkēs*, in the role of Morning Star, is 'repeating many times', the symbol of many happy returns.[38] And the repetition can be visualized as a cyclical one – a pattern of eternal return. There is a striking semantic and morphological parallel in *poluderkḗs* 'seeing in many different ways' (or 'many times'), epithet of the dawn-goddess Eos in Hesiod *Theogony* 451.

The multiple repetition of the same, each repetition being different, is an idea encapsulated in the very identity of *Poludeúkēs* as a twin, one of the Divine Twins. The very idea of a twin conveys both sameness and difference. Here we may consider in general

---

[34] On the explicit connections of the *(h)alkúōn* with songs of lamentation, see N 1979.111.

[35] N 1979.94–117, especially pp. 99–100 on *Odyssey* 4.220.

[36] Cf. also *Polupheídēs* at *Odyssey* 15.249, which could mean 'having parsimony in many different ways' (or 'many times'). On the poetics of naming as an aspect of a poetic system, see N 1990a.206–207 and Higbie 1995.189.

[37] In light of the close association of *endukéōs*, as surveyed above, with the ritualistic performance of one's duties as *xénos*, 'host' or 'guest', we may note the traditional characterization of the Divine Twins as *philóxe(i)noi* 'dear to *xénoi*', as in Pindar *Olympian* 3.1.

[38] On the mythological model of the Divine Twins as alternating Morning Star/ Evening Star, see N 1990b.258–259.

the semantic function of the Homeric epithet: each time the epithet is repeated, it is both same and different in meaning.[39] With
each of its countless returns, the epithet refers to the same thing,
but to a new instance of the same old thing.

The word *repetition* has been introduced in this context in order
to evoke a 1843 work of Kierkegaard, entitled *Repetition*. Just as
ancient Greek philosophy teaches, it is claimed, "that all knowledge is a recollecting," so also "modern philosophy will teach
that all life is a repetition."[40] To quote further: "repetition and
recollection are the same movement, except in opposite directions, for what is recollected has been, is repeated backward,
whereas genuine repetition is recollected forward."[41]

The idea of "recollecting forward" is applicable to the definition of induction that we have examined earlier, and to the reinterpretation of the root *deuk-/*duk- as 'draw continuously
toward a definite goal', with the implication that continuity takes
place through the mental process of connecting like with like. As
we will now see, such a reinterpretation suits the ancient Greek
concept of mimesis as well, which is fundamental to poetry as
performance. In fact, the semantics of mimesis will help us reach
a sharper definition of the mental process of connecting like with
like. From the earliest attested meanings of mimesis, we will see
there must be a definitive model as well as a definite goal.

It is easier to approach the topic of a definitive model if we first
review the idea of a definite goal. In the case of the root *deuk-/
*duk-, we have already seen the example of the Latin compound
verb *ēducāre*, which conveys the idea of raising a child, or a plant,
toward the definite goal of maturity, and this idea is still current
in the English usages of *educate*.[42] We may note, with reference to

[39] Cf. Foley 1991, who shows how the Homeric epithet transcends its immediate
context, that is, its "instance." The referentiality of the epithet is "extrasituational," in
that "epithet and instance harmonize not because the phrase can be reduced – its
complexity conveniently denatured – but rather because it entails a larger reality than
can be presented in any one narrative event" (p. 141). In the "pars pro toto" logic of
oral composition-in-performance, "the ever-incomplete performance or text is the
only medium through which we can completely experience the oral traditional work of
art" (p. 10; cf. p. 58). Meaning is thus "inherent" in the context, not "conferred" exclusively by the context (p. 8).
[40] Kierkegaard 1983 (=1843) 131.
[41] Kierkegaard p. 131.
[42] See p. 47n23 above.

the definite goal of maturity, that the Greek word *télos* can designate either such a goal *or a ritual of initiation.*[43] Further, we have already seen derivatives of the root *deuk-/*duk- such as *indūcere* and the English borrowing *induct* in the sense of 'initiate'. This much said, let us proceed to explore in more depth the meaning of mimesis. As with the root *deuk-/*duk-, where the goal that is implied helps us comprehend the model as well, so also with mimesis. The definitive models of mimesis take shape by way of a process that leads towards definite goals such as initiation and education – which are the very concepts reflected in the Latin words *indūcere* and *ēducāre*.

With the ultimate purpose of arriving at a working definition of mimesis, let us first consider its function in the context of the *khorós* 'chorus, song-and-dance ensemble', a traditional Greek performance medium that serves as an instrument of initiation as well as education in archaic Greek society.[44] A premier example, as we will see, is Alcman fragment 1 (as numbered in the PMG edition of Denys Page), the so-called *Partheneion*, the text of a choral composition destined for performance in archaic Sparta.[45]

As John Herington argues in his *Poetry into Drama*, the performance of a chorus is ordinarily a matter of a seasonally recurring *reperformance.*[46] There are particularly striking examples from Sparta, such as the description in Sosibius FGH 595 F 5, by way of Athenaeus 678bc, of choral performances at the Spartan Feast of the Gymnopaidiai, featuring reperformances of compositions attributed to Alcman and other archaic figures. We may note too the description in Polycrates FGH 588 F 1, by way of Athenaeus 139e, of choral performances at the Spartan festival of the Hyakinthia, where the compositions of Alcman were most likely a part of the repertory (witness the papyrus commentary to Alcman, PMG 10[a].5). Here is the text of Polycrates' vivid description:

> But the middle day of the three days there is a colorful
> spectacle [*théā*] and a great and notable gathering of all

[43] Cf. N 1990a.245–246.
[44] For more on the *khorós* as a medium of initiation and education, see Calame 1977, especially 1 437–439.
[45] Detailed discussion in N 1990a.345–349 (cf. N 1989.50–51) and Clay 1991.
[46] Herington 1985.

[*panéguris*]. Boys wearing girt-up tunics play the lyre, sweeping all the strings with the plectrum as they sing the god in the anapaestic rhythm and at a high pitch. Others pass through the viewing area [*théatron*] on finely caparisoned horses. Massed choruses of youths now enter and sing some of the epichoric songs, while dancers mixed in with them perform the ancient dance-movements to the pipe [*aulós*] and the singing. Next maidens enter, some riding in richly adorned wicker cars, while others make their procession in chariots yoked with mules. And the entire city is astir, rejoicing at the spectacle [*theōríā*]. On this day they sacrifice an abundance of victims, and the citizens feast all their acquaintances and their own slaves. And no one is left out of the sacrifice, but it comes to pass that the city is emptied for the spectacle [*théa*].[47]

Herington concludes, on the basis of this and similar testimony, that "some at least of Alcman's compositions were still being *re-performed* well into the Hellenistic era [emphasis mine]."[48]

In an earlier work, I linked the meaning of mimesis with this medium of the *khorós*,[49] arguing that the primary meaning of mimesis was 're-enactment, impersonation' *in a dramatic sense*, as in a *khorós*, and that the secondary meaning of 'imitation' – which is a built-in aspect of re-enactment – became the new primary meaning of this word only after the dramatic sense of mimesis was destabilized.[50] For present purposes, let us use the word "dramatic" strictly with reference to traditional societies like those of archaic Greece, where drama entails *an interaction of myth and ritual*.[51] As for *myth*, we may define it tentatively as a given

---

[47] This translation of Polycrates FGH 588 F 1 is based on that of Herington 1985.7, who goes on to say about Polycrates: "Even if he lived relatively late in the Hellenistic period, ... Sparta's ritual and musical conservatism was such that he could well have witnessed a celebration of the Hyakinthia in much the same form that it would have had in classical times" (p. 224n8; cf. N 1990a.351, 371n168 and Clay 1991.64). As Victor Bers points out to me, the emphasis on the idea that "no one is left out of the sacrifice" echoes the semantics of a "gathering of all" inherent in *panéguris*.

[48] Herington 1985.25–26. I disagree, however, with his general assumption that the composition of archaic Greek lyric performances required the technology of writing (pp. 41–42): see N 1990a.19n7.

[49] N 1990a.339–413. A pioneering study of mimesis, to which I am much indebted, is Koller 1954.

[50] N 1990a.42–45, 346, 349, 373–375, 381, 387, 411.

[51] N 1990a ch.13.

traditional society's coding of truth-values through narrative.[52] And we may adopt, at least for the moment, Stanley Tambiah's definition of *ritual* as "a culturally constructed system of symbolic communication."[53] Keeping in mind this broad working definition of ritual, I propose that myth – or at least the *performance* of myth as song, poetry, or prose – can even be seen as an aspect of ritual, though of course myth is also potentially distinguishable from ritual.[54]

This working definition of mimesis as 're-enactment, impersonation' is supported by the celebrated description of mimesis in the *Poetics* of Aristotle as the mental process of identifying the representing "this," as in the ritual of acting the drama, with the represented "that," as in the myth that is being acted out by the drama: in Greek this mental process can be expressed by way of the equation *hoûtos ekeînos* 'so this is that!' (1448b17).[55] The restatement of this equation in Aristotle *Rhetoric* 1.1371a21 makes it clear that the media of representation that Aristotle has in mind are not just the visual arts but also the verbal arts, primarily the art of songmaking and poetry as performed in the dramas of Athenian State Theater.

As the discussion proceeds, it will become clear that I think of all song and poetry as mimetic, although in varying degrees – not just the song and poetry of theatrical drama in particular and of performance by a *khorós* in general. My usage of *performance* is analogous, in that I extend the theatrical connotations of this English word to all kinds of song and poetry. For the moment, though, let us consider Aristotle's formulation of mimesis primarily from the viewpoint of song and poetry in drama or, at least, in the framework of a *khorós*. So long as the represented "that" remains absolute – that is, absolutized by the myth – the representing "this" remains a re-enacting "this."[56] So long as "this" imitates an absolute "that," it re-enacts as it imitates; the re-enactment remains primary, and the imitation remains secon-

[52] Elaborations in N 1990b.8; cf. N 1990a.313–317.
[53] Tambiah 1985.128.
[54] Cf. the formulation "myth implies ritual in the very performance of myth" at p. xi of my foreword to Martin 1989 and at N 1990b.317.
[55] N 1990a.44.
[56] N 1990a.42–44.

dary.[57] Once you start imitating something that is no longer absolute, however, you can no longer re-enact the absolute: then you can only make a copy, and your model may be also just a copy. I have just described here the general mentality induced by the destabilization of the conceptual world of mimesis.[58]

It bears repeating that both re-enactment and imitation are genuine aspects of the older conceptual world of mimesis. If you *re-enact* an archetypal action in ritual, it only stands to reason that you have to *imitate* those who re-enacted before you and who served as your *immediate* models. But the *ultimate* model is still the archetypal action or figure that you are re-enacting in ritual, which is coextensive with the whole line of imitators who re-enact the way in which their ultimate model acted, each imitating each one's predecessor.

Pursuing the idea that mimesis was a traditional function of the *khorós*, let us turn to the *Homeric Hymn to Apollo*, which describes a *khorós* of Delian Maidens performing at a festival on the island of Delos.[59] In earlier work, I argued that the Delian Maidens represent an idealization of choral lyric.[60] We may compare Plato's picture of the ultimate divine *khorós*, comprised of the Olympian gods themselves, serving as model for all human choruses (*Phaedrus* 247a, θείου χοροῦ). I also argued that the Delian Maidens are presented in the *Hymn* as archetypes meant to be re-enacted in the local ritual context of real choral performances at Delos − in which context any real chorus-members would be equated, for the ritual moment, with the archetypal Maidens.[61] Such a *re-enactment of a model* would be mimesis in the primary sense just outlined.

The Delian Maidens show the way for others to re-enact them by demonstrating their own power to re-enact all other peoples, in all their varieties. These Maidens are models of mimesis by way of practicing mimesis: they can repeat everyone's voice, *mimeîsthai* (*Hymn to Apollo* 163), and everyone who hears the repetition will

---

[57] Ibid.
[58] Cf. Nehamas 1982.
[59] Burkert 1987.54 interprets lines 162−165 of the *Homeric Hymn to Apollo* as a reference to the "performance of choral lyrics."
[60] N 1990a.43, 375−377.
[61] Ibid.

think that it is his or her own voice (163–164).[62] We may compare this usage of mimesis with the semantics of Latin *inductiō*, meaning not only 'induction' in the sense of initiation but also induction as a mental process *of connecting like with like, thus achieving a continuum through variety*. We may also compare the traditional image of the sacrificing god, as recently studied by Kimberley Patton in a wide variety of different cultures: when gods take the seemingly paradoxical stance of sacrificing, they are simply acting as *models*, authoritatively showing the way for others to sacrifice by being the first to do so themselves.[63]

Similarly in Alcman's *Partheneion*, I propose that archetypal figures, including the primary archetypal figures named Hagesikhora and Agido, are *models* being acted out by real chorus-members in performances held on a seasonally-recurring basis.[64] Even their names designate models – either divine, like Hagesikhora, or royal, like Agido.[65]

We may reconstruct a similar principle at work in the earliest stages of Athenian State Theater: the real chorus-members of a tragedy would be re-enacting an archetypal ensemble that is interacting with archetypal figures of the heroic world, figures acted by actors playing roles differentiated out of the ranks of the chorus.[66]

But the paradox of mimesis is that the archetype to be re-enacted must re-enact, not just enact, in its own right. So also in Song I of Jaufré Rudel, we had seen that the song of the nightingale, which serves as model for the song of the poet, is itself a model of recomposition, not just composition, in that even the songbird is in fact recomposing his own song by virtue of performing it. The nightingale of Provençal songmaking *moves* his song, which is inherently recurrent and recomposed, much as every new season of spring is a joyous event of inherent recurrence and recomposition, even re-creation.

So also in the case of *poludeukḗs*, variant epithet for the nightingale of Homeric songmaking: if the interpretation, 'patterning

---

[62] Detailed discussion in N 1990a.43–44, 375–377.

[63] Patton 1992.

[64] N 1989.50–51, N 1990a.345–370; cf. Clay 1991.

[65] N 1990a.345–348.

[66] On the complex patterns of differentiation that led to the emergence of the first, second, and third actors as distinct from the chorus, see N 1990a.378–379.

in many different ways', is cogent, we see here a model of song-making that is ultimately patterned on its own goal, achieved by maintaining continuity through variety.[67] To maintain this continuity is to keep on re-creating, which is the process of mimesis.[68] In mimesis, every performance is a re-creation. To rephrase the words of Aristotle in the *Poetics*, the representing "this" re-creates the represented "that" (1448b17).

[67] The idea of continuity through variety may be expressed by the metaphor of "breaking." Successive interruptions or "breakings" in a continuum may actually contribute to an overall sense of continuity or non-interruption, as in the pulsation of sound or the *refraction* of light. Here we may note the expression περὶ δέ σφισιν ἄγνυτο ἠχώ 'and the sound [*ēkhō*] was refracted all around them' in the Hesiodic *Shield*, verses 279 and 348 (see n68 on the hiatus – perhaps onomatopoetic – which is etymologically motivated by the loss of initial ϝ- in *ϝαχώ). At verse 348, the expression applies to the neighing of war-horses; at 279, it applies to the sound of choral voices accompanied by herdsmen's pipes. With reference to verse 279, we may compare the metaphors of *refraction* as discussed in ch.1.

[68] The metaphor of "breaking" can express – even mime – discontinuity as well as continuity, as in the expression γλῶσσα ἔαγε 'my tongue has broken down' in Sappho 31.9; the translation 'break down' here connotes the English metaphor of *breakdown* with reference to the operation of a mechanism or faculty – in this case, the faculty of speech. In N 1974.45, I argue that the metaphor of "breakdown" here is reinforced by a "gagging" effect, produced by the hiatus of word-final and word-initial vowels in the actual sequence γλῶσσα ἔαγε 'my tongue has broken down'. Thus the discontinuity in speech is symbolized by the discontinuity in sound. The sound of gagging – that is, the sound of an interrupted voice – is conveyed by hiatus and thus matches an expression that designates the sensation of gagging. And the voice that is being interrupted in Sappho 31 is of course ultimately the *poetic* voice. Such an onomatopoetic effect, as it is pointed out in N 1974.45, could not have evolved if there had not been a pre-existing pattern of hiatus associated with the inherited phraseology of the root ἀγ-, thanks to the loss of initial ϝ- (ϝαγ-). There may also be an onomatopoetic effect in the positive instance of the "breaking" metaphor that we examined earlier, περὶ δέ σφισιν ἄγνυτο ἠχώ 'and the sound [*ēkhō*] was refracted all around them' in the Hesiodic *Shield*, verses 279 and 348; to repeat, the hiatus is etymologically motivated by the loss of initial ϝ- in *ϝαχώ. Cf. Bonanno 1993, especially pp. 62 and 68. While I agree with her that the ancient imitations of Sapphic γλῶσσα ἔαγε, in Lucretius 3.155 and Theocritus 2.108–109 convey the idea of stammering, I maintain that the more basic idea is that of an *interruption* of speech – or, to return to the English idiom, *breakdown* of speech.

3

Mimesis of Homer and beyond

The variant epithet of the Homeric nightingale's voice in *Odyssey* 19.521, *poludeukés* 'patterning in many different ways', applies to Homer himself and – just as important – to those who perform Homer. In making this claim, I am arguing that Homer's nightingale is in effect a model for Homer – and even for performers who model their identities on Homer – in her capacity to maintain continuity through variety. In other words, the song of the nightingale is a metaphor for the mimesis of Homer.

As a point of comparison, we may look back for a moment at the Provençal nightingale, who as we have seen is a model for the *troubadour* – in his capacity to "move" the song. Looking at the actual Greek evidence, we may compare the epithet of the Hesiodic nightingale in *Works and Days* 203, *poikilódeiros* 'having a varied[-sounding] throat',[1] who is in effect a model for Hesiod – in her capacity to raise her voice against the brutality of the hawk, as narrated in the *aînos* 'fable' about the hawk and the nightingale (*Works and Days* 202–212; *aînos* at verse 202); within the framework of this Hesiodic fable, the hawk and the nightingale become

---

[1] In translating *poikilódeiros* as 'having a varied[-sounding] throat' (ἀηδόνα ποικιλόδειρον *Works and Days* 203), I follow the reasoning of Irwin 1974.72–73 on *khlōraúkhēn*, conventionally translated as 'green-throated', which serves as epithet of the nightingale in Simonides PMG 586.2 (ἀηδόνες ... χλωραύχενες): "there is nothing noteworthy about the plumage on the neck of the nightingale to cause Simonides to mention the colour of their necks. The neck or throat is only noteworthy as the source of the music the nightingale sings. If one observes a song-bird, one can see the throbbing of the throat as he pours forth his song." See p. 7n1. The element *poikilo-* 'varied' is parallel to *aiolo-* 'varied', as in the epithet for the nightingale in Oppian *Halieutica* 1.728, *aiolóphōnos* (ἀηδόνος αἰολοφώνου). For more on *aiolo-* 'varied', see also the next note. On the paradox of a monochrome exterior in form and a colorful interior in content, see later on in this chapter.

negative and positive models respectively for king and poet, and the idea of "poet" becomes explicit in the description of the nightingale as an *aoidós* 'singer' (verse 208).[2] The driving idea of maintaining continuity through variety, as reconstructed for the epithet *poludeukés* 'patterning in many ways', is inherent also in the early meaning of *rhapsōidós* 'rhapsode'. The etymology of this word, like that of *poludeukés*, reveals a central metaphor for the mimesis of Homer.

Before we turn to matters of etymology, however, let us review briefly some questions about the actual function of the rhapsode as a professional performer of Homer throughout the historical period of ancient Greek civilization. I have attempted elsewhere an overall diachronic sketch of rhapsodes,[3] concluding that "it is simplistic and even misleading to contrast, as many have done, the 'creative' *aoidós* ['singer'] with the 'reduplicating' *rhapsōidós*."[4] Here the argument is more specific: that the rhapsode cannot be viewed as merely "reduplicating" what Homer had said. The conventional view of the rhapsode as a mere replica of Homer is mainly inspired by Plato's *Ion*, where the rhapsode Ion is metaphorically pictured as the last and weakest link in a long magnetic chain leading all the way back to the real thing, the original magnet, the genius of Homer (533d–536d).[5] This idea of a *reperformed composer*, as we will see, is contradicted by the more archaic mentality of mimesis, which shapes (over a lengthy stretch of time) the alternative idea of a *recomposed performer*, that is, the idea that performers may persist in appropriating to themselves the persona of the composer.

The singer of Homeric poetry begins the song by praying to

[2] N 1979.238–241; also N 1990a.256 and 312. On the poet or *aoidós* 'singer' as an *aēdōn* 'nightingale', see also Theocritus 16.44, where the lyric master Simonides is described as the *aoidós* 'singer' of Keos (ἀοιδὸς ὁ Κήιος), who makes his *aióla* 'varied' songs (αἰόλα φωνέων) to the tune of his many-stringed lyre (on *poikílos* 'varied' as a attribute of the lyre, cf. Pindar *Olympian* 4.2); in Bacchylides 3.98, the poet actually calls himself the nightingale of Keos (Κηΐας ἀηδόνος). While the image of a nightingale serves as an ultimate model for Bacchylides as poet, the image of his maternal uncle Simonides as a nightingale is surely an immediate model. According to Democritus B 154 DK, all human singers are disciples of the nightingale.
[3] N 1990a.21–28; also N 1990b [1982] 40–47.
[4] N 1990b [1982] 42. This conclusion is corroborated by the article of Ford 1988.
[5] Cf. N 1990a.21–22.

his Muse: "sing!" (*Iliad* 1.1) or "tell me!" (*Odyssey* 1.1).[6] What he then tells his audience is supposed to be exactly what he hears from the Muse or Muses, goddesses of memory, who are conceived as the infallible custodians of the *ipsissima verba* emanating from the Heroic Age.[7] The words of Homer are supposed to be the recordings of the Muses, who saw and heard exactly what had happened in that remote age; therefore, what Homer *narrates* is exactly what the Muses *saw*, and what Homer *quotes* within his narrations is exactly what the Muses *heard*.[8]

In line with this pattern of thinking, a Homeric narration or a Homeric quotation of a god or hero speaking within a narration are not at all representations: they are the real thing. When a Homeric hero is quoted speaking dactylic hexameters, it is to be understood that heroes "spoke" in dactylic hexameters, not that they are being *represented* as speaking that way.[9] Further, and this is crucial for the argument at hand, when the rhapsode says "tell me, Muses!" (*Iliad* 2.484) or "tell me, Muse!" (*Odyssey* 1.1), this "I" is not a *representation* of Homer: it *is* Homer. My argument is that the rhapsode is re-enacting Homer by performing Homer, that he *is* Homer so long as the mimesis stays in effect, so long as the performance lasts. In the words of T. S. Eliot (*The Dry Salvages*, 1941), "you are the music/While the music lasts."[10] From the standpoint of mimesis, the rhapsode is a *recomposed performer*: he becomes recomposed into Homer every time he performs Homer.

We will soon be looking at some other sources of information concerning the archaic concept of *rhapsōidós* 'rhapsode', going beyond the premier testimony of Plato's *Ion*. But first it is crucial to examine the etymology of this compound noun *rhapsōidós*, 'he who sews together [*rháptō*] the song(s) [*aoidḗ*]'.[11]

---

[6] Instances of "tell me, Muses!" in the *Iliad*: 2.484, 11.218, 14.508, 16.112. An instance of "tell me, Muse!": *Iliad* 2.761, on which see Martin 1989.238.
[7] N 1990b.26–27; cf. N 1979.15–18.
[8] N 1990b.26–27.
[9] Ibid.
[10] Eliot 1963 (=1941) 199.
[11] Schmitt 1967.300–301 (with a definitive discussion of the morphology of *rhapsōidós*), Durante 1976.177–179, N 1979.298 par. 10n5 and 1990a.28. On the accent of *rhapsōidós*, Durante 1976.177.

The metaphor implicit in the etymology of this word is actually made explicit in the syntax of a song composed by Pindar. More important, this metaphor is placed at the very beginning of that given song, *Nemean* 2.1–3. Most important of all, this metaphor at the beginning of Pindar's song refers to the very beginning of a Homeric performance by the *Homērídai* 'Sons of Homer': ὅθεν περ καὶ Ὁμηρίδαι ῥαπτῶν ἐπέων τὰ πόλλ' ἀοιδοὶ ἄρχονται, Διὸς ἐκ προοιμίου ... 'starting from the very point where [*bóthen*] the *Homērídai*, singers [*aoidoí*] of sewn-together [*rhaptá*] utterances [*épē*], most often take their start [=verb *árkhomai*], from the prelude [*prooímion*] of Zeus ...' (Pindar *Nemean* 2.1–3).

The ultimate starting-point, in the logic of this song, is the ultimate god, Zeus.[12] As such, Zeus is associated with the *prooímion* 'prelude' that introduces the ultimate songs, the songs of Homer. The association of Zeus with the songmaking form of the *prooímion* 'prelude' (plural *prooímia*) in referring to an ultimate starting-point in Homeric songmaking is crucial, since it is precisely within the framework of this form, the *prooímion*, that the author of a given song conventionally identifies himself.[13] The most salient example is the Homeric *Hymn to Apollo*, to which Thucydides explicitly refers as a *prooímion* (3.104.4–5), where the first-person speaker identifies himself as the blind singer of Chios, whose songs will win universal approval in the future (*Hymn to Apollo* 172–173); in effect, the singer of this hymn *claims* to be none other than Homer, "author" of the universally approved Homeric poems.[14] From the standpoint of this *prooímion*, the performer who speaks these words in the first person is not just *representing* Homer: he *is* Homer.[15]

The *prooímia* or 'preludes' are represented in Pindar's song as performances of the *Homērídai* 'Sons of Homer'; this name applies to a lineage of rhapsodes in Chios who traced themselves back to an ancestor called *Hómēros*, or Homer (scholia to Pindar *Nemean* 2.1, Plato *Phaedrus* 252b, Strabo 14.1.33–35, *Contest of*

---

[12] Such a theme is particularly appropriate to a Nemean song celebrating a victory at the Nemean Games, over which Zeus presides: see the scholia to Pindar *Nemean* 2.1a.

[13] N 1990b.53–54.

[14] N 1990a.22 (especially n23), 376.

[15] N 1979.5–6, 8–9; 1990a.375–377.

Homer and Hesiod [p. 226.13–15 Allen]).[16] In terms of this representation in Pindar *Nemean* 1.2, it is the *Homērídai* who *start* the songs of Homer, and yet, paradoxically, they are not Homer himself but a continuum of descendants of Homer who keep on re-starting his song. The idea of continuum is further emphasized in the placement of the adverb *hóthen* 'starting from the very point where' as the very first word of Pindar's song. Here we see another paradox: in the conventions of real *prooímia*, a performative marker like *hóthen* is *transitional*, expected to occur only *after* a given divinity has been invoked.[17] Having observed how Pindar's song begins, let us look ahead to see how it ends: the chorus is called upon to *start* the celebration (*Nemean* 2.25), and the idea of *start* is expressed at this point with the verb *árkhomai*. Here we see yet another paradox: in the conventions of a real *prooímion* this word *árkhomai* 'start' would be expected to occur at the beginning, not the end, of the song. To make such an ending that proceeds into its own beginning produces what has aptly been described by one critic as a looping effect.[18]

Pindar's representation of the Homeric *prooímion* is pertinent to the etymology of this word, which has up to now been translated conventionally as the 'prelude' of a song. It stems from *oímē* 'song', so that the *pro-oímion* is literally the *front* or, better, the *starting end* of the song.[19] Further, *pro-oímion* is the starting end of the *thread* of the song, if indeed the noun *oímē* stems from a verb-root meaning 'sew'.[20] The metaphor implicit in this etymology of

---

[16] A fuller collection of references in N 1990a.23. On an alternative tradition, which attributes the final form of the Homeric *Hymn to Apollo* not to Homer but to Kynaithos of Chios, a rhapsode who supposedly could not trace himself back to Homer (scholia to Pindar *Nemean* 2.1), see N 1990a.22–23, with further bibliography.

[17] Cf. N 1990a.356–357.

[18] Kurke 1991.43; cf. Mullen 1982.234n36 and N 1990a.357.

[19] N 1990a.353. The genitive of *oímē* at *Odyssey* 8.74, marking the point of departure for the performance of the first song of Demodokos, is functionally a genitive of origin, parallel to the origin-marking adverb *hóthen* 'starting from the very point where' in Pindar's representation of the *prooímion* at *Nemean* 2.1.

[20] Durante 1976.176–177, *pace* Chantraine *DELG* 463 and 783. Durante points out (p. 177) that there is an analogous metaphor inherited by Latin *ex-ordium*, the semantic equivalent of Greek *prooímion*. He also argues persuasively (pp. 176–177) that *oímē* is cognate with *oímos*; though the discussion of Chantraine (p. 783) is inconclusive on this matter, at least it is made clear that *oímos* (from **hoímos*, as evident in Attic *phroímion*) cannot be derived from *eími* 'go'. If indeed *oímē* is to be interpreted etymologically as 'song-thread', we may compare the semantics of Latin *filum dēdúcere* 'draw out a thread', as discussed at p. 49.

oímē, where making songs is equated with a process of *sewing together* or *threading* songs, is explicit in Pindar's reference to the Homeric rhapsodes at the beginning of *Nemean* 2, where *rhaptá* 'sewn together' is applied to *épē* in the sense of poetic 'utterances'. The same metaphor is implicit, as we have seen, in the etymology of the actual word for rhapsode, *rhapsōidós*, 'he who sews together [*rháptō*] the song(s) [*aoidḗ*]'.[21]

This metaphor of *sewing together the song(s)* must be contrasted with a related metaphor in archaic Greek traditions, that of *weaving the song(s)*, which is in fact so old as to be of Indo-European linguistic provenience.[22] An example is this phrase of Pindar, F 179: ὑφαίνω δ᾿ Ἀμυθαονίδαισιν ποικίλον ἄνδημα 'I weave [*huphaínō*] a varied [*poikílos*] headband [that is, of song] for the Amythaonidai'.[23] As we see from such passages, song is being

---

[21] Schmitt 1967.300–301, Durante 1976.177–179, N 1979.298 par. 10n5 and 1990a.28.

[22] Schmitt 1967.298–300. I disagree with Scheid and Svenbro 1994.119–138 when they argue that there was no such metaphor in archaic Greek poetics – until a *terminus post quem* which they set in the era of choral lyric, as pioneered by the likes of Simonides and Pindar. I agree with Koller 1956.177 that the expression ἀοιδῆς ὕμνον '*húmnos* of the song' at *Odyssey* 8.429 conveys the idea of the *totality* of performance (cf. N 1990a.354n77 and 1990b.54n56); further, despite the reservations of Chantraine *DELG* 1156, I maintain that *húmnos* derives from *huphaínō* in the metaphorical sense of a 'web' or 'fabric' of song. See also below on the usage of *húmnos* in Hesiod F 357.

[23] Schmitt 1967.300. Scheid and Svenbro 1994.119–138 argue that this kind of explicit reference to weaving as a metaphor for songmaking is absent in Homeric diction. It can be counter-argued that the Homeric usage of *húmnos* and *oímē*, as discussed above, points to a *survival* of metaphors for songmaking as weaving and sewing respectively. It is preferable to say "survival" because Scheid and Svenbro p. 121 seem to me justified in emphasizing that Homeric expressions like the verb *huphaínō* + *mētis* as object, meaning 'I weave a ruse' (e.g. *Iliad* 7.324, *Odyssey* 4.739), or like *rháptō* + *kaká* as object, meaning 'I sew together evil things' (e.g. *Iliad* 18.367, *Odyssey* 3.118), are preoccupied with the idea of constructing evil words or plans to the detriment of others. But we must keep in mind that Homeric poetry portrays many negative or negativized kinds of songmaking and poetry, as in the case of the Sirens in *Odyssey* 12.189–191 (cf. N 1979.271, Pucci 1979). Such a pattern of negativization seems to have extended, at least in part, to the metaphors of weaving or sewing as singing, as we see from the example of *Iliad* 3.125–128, where Helen is represented not as singing while weaving, which is the conventional Homeric image, but as weaving the epic theme of the evils suffered, on her account, by both Achaeans and Trojans in the Trojan War: instead of a positive reference to a woman's *performance* of a song while the woman weaves, the narrative here gives a negative reference to the *composition* of the song, which is not literally sung by Helen but instead woven by her into the fabric (N 1979.294–295 par. 5n7, with further bibliography). Such a substitution of *content* for *form* is parallel to what seems to be a tendency of phasing out, in Homeric diction, the application of metaphors of weaving and sewing to the *form* of singing. If the metaphor tends to become restricted to the *content* of singing, then its explicitness may indeed

visualized as a web, a fabric, a textile (Latin *textilis*, from *texō* 'weave'), or – to use only for the moment an English word that no longer retains its metaphorical heritage – even a text (Latin *textus*, again from *texō*).[24] An apt epithet for the beautiful handiwork of weaving is *poikílos* 'varied, patterned', as we see it applied to that ultimate fabric, the *péplos* that the goddess Athena herself once made with her own hands (πέπλον ... ποικίλον *Iliad* 5.734–735). It follows that the fabric of song is likewise *poikílos*, as we have just seen in the Pindaric quotation and as we saw earlier in the epithet of the Hesiodic nightingale, *poikilódeiros* 'having a varied[-sounding] throat' (*Works and Days* 203).[25]

As we juxtapose these two metaphors for songmaking in ar-

become blurred. When a Homeric character weaves words or sews words together, these words are tantamount to "singing" in that they could be performed or "sung" by the Homeric medium, but they are not explicitly represented as singing. It is important to reconsider in this light the collocation of the verb *huphaínō* 'weave' with *múthos* as object in *Iliad* 3.212, as incisively analyzed by Martin 1989.95–96. In brief, the Homeric tradition may have preserved only vestiges of these metaphors in a positive or at least neutral sense.

[24] Schmitt 1967.14–15, Dubuisson 1989.223; on Latin *textus*, see Scheid and Svenbro 1994.139–162, especially p. 160 with reference to Quintilian *Institutio oratoria* 9.4.13.

[25] This Hesiodic epithet of the nightingale seems to stem from an early version of what we know from later versions as the story of Procne, who was turned into a nightingale. Let us review here the best-known later version of the story, Ovid *Metamorphoses* 6.412–674. After Tereus rapes Procne's sister Philomela, he cuts out her tongue, but Philomela weaves a fabric that tells her sad tale (lines 576–578), and her sister Procne then "reads the pitiful song" (*carmen miserabile legit* 582) from the fabric. Segal 1994.267 remarks: "Procne, the tale's first 'reader,' unrolls (*evolvit* [verse 581]) the woven narrative as a contemporary of Ovid would unroll the poem; and she is the model for the later reader's immediate reaction. What she finds is a tale whose pain lies beyond the power of words [reference to verse 583, quoted above at p. 36n100]." In Ovid's version (verses 667–669), it is not specified which one of the two tragic women is turned into a nightingale and which one into a swallow. In any case, the image of a varied fabric of song is inherent, as already proposed, in *poikilódeiros* 'having a varied[-sounding] throat' (Hesiod *Works and Days* 203; pace West 1978.206). If this proposal is justified, then we have here another counterexample to the argument that the metaphor of weaving as songmaking is not attested before Simonides and Pindar. With reference to the myth of Procne and Philomela, as reflected in Sophocles' tragedy *Tereus* (F 595 Radt), Aristotle *Poetics* 1454b37 takes note of the expression κερκίδος φωνή 'voice of the shuttle [*kerkís*]'. In Aristophanes *Frogs* 1316, the shuttle (*kerkís*) is described as a "singer" (*aoidós*). In *Greek Anthology* 6.174.5, the shuttle (*kerkís*) is metaphorically equated with the nightingale. It may be pertinent to the mythical detail about the cutting-out of Philomela's tongue that the nightingale is described in ["Aristotle"] *Historia animalium* 616b8 as bereft of a tongue-tip (ἴδιον ... τὸ μὴ ἔχειν τῆς γλώσσης τὸ ὀξύ). On the general topic of metaphorical connections between the nightingale and the process of weaving, see Papadopoulou-Belmehdi 1994.155–156; cf. Seaford 1994.56.

65

chaic Greek traditions, *weaving* and *sewing*, we discover that the second of the two is more complex than the first. The idea inherent in *rhapsōidós*, 'he who sews together [*rháptō*] the song(s) [*aoidḗ*]', is that *many and various fabrics of song, each one already made, that is, each one already woven, become re-made into a unity, a single new continuous fabric, by being sewn together.* The paradox of the metaphor is that the many and the various become the single and the uniform – and yet there is supposedly no loss in the multiplicity and variety of the constituent parts.[26] In effect, this metaphor conveyed by the concept of *rhapsōidós* amounts to an overarching esthetic principle, one that may even ultimately settle the everongoing controversy between advocates of unitarian and analytic approaches to Homer.

There is a similar paradox at work in later European traditions about the song of the nightingale. For example, in Poem 23.29–32 (ed. Hartel) of Paulinus of Nola (died 431), we read: *quae uiridi sub fronde latens solet auia rura | multimodis mulcere modis linguamque per unam | fundere non unas mutato carmine uoces, | unicolor plumis ales, sed picta loquellis* '[the nightingale] which, hiding beneath the green foliage, | soothes the pathless countryside with multi-mode modulations and with one tongue | pours forth many voices, changing its tune, | a winged creature that is monochrome of feather, but colorful of speech'.[27] In the preface to the *Philomena* (ed. Stone) of John of Howden (died 1278), we read: *et a non ceste pensee: "Rossignos," pur ce ke si come li rossignos feit de diverses notes une melodie, auci feit ceste livres de diverses matires une acordaunce* 'and this poem is called "Rossignol" ["Nightingale"] because just as the nightingale makes one melody out of diverse notes, this book makes an accord out of diverse materials'.[28]

Eustathius, in his *Commentary on the Iliad* (vol. 1 p. 10), quotes the Pindaric description (*Nemean* 2.1–3) of the *Homērídai* 'Sons of Homer' as ῥαπτῶν ἐπέων ... ἀοιδοί 'singers [*aoidoí*] of sewn-together [*rhaptá*] utterances [*épē*]', interpreting these words as a periphrasis of the concept inherent in the word *rhapsōidoí* 'rhapsodes'. He goes on to offer what he considers a second interpretation

[26] Such a paradox may be viewed as a working convention within the tradition. See N 1992a.45–49.
[27] Cf. Pfeffer 1985.26.
[28] Cf. Pfeffer 1985.38.

(again, 1.10), claiming that this concept of *sewing together* can be taken either in the sense that we have seen made explicit in Pindar's wording or in a more complex sense – a sense that is actually implicit in the same Pindaric wording – which emphasizes the characteristic unity of the *Iliad* and the *Odyssey:* ῥάπτειν δὲ ἢ ἁπλῶς, ὡς εἴρηται, τὸ συντιθέναι ἢ τὸ κατὰ εἱρμόν τινα ῥαφῇ ὁμοίως εἰς ἓν ἄγειν τὰ διεστῶτα. σποράδην γάρ, φασί, κειμένης καὶ κατὰ μέρος διῃρημένης τῆς Ὁμηρικῆς ποιήσεως, οἱ ᾄδοντες αὐτὴν συνέρραπτον οἷον τὰ εἰς ἓν ὕφος ᾀδόμενα 'sewing together [*rháptō*] either in the simple sense, as just mentioned, of putting together or, alternatively, in the sense of bringing different things, in accordance with some kind of sequencing [*heirmós*] in sewing, uniformly into one thing; for they say that Homeric poetry, after it had been scattered about and divided into separate parts, was sewn together by those who sang it, like songs sung into a single fabric [*húphos*]'.

An analogous interpretation is given by the scholia to Pindar *Nemean* 2.1d: οἱ δέ φασι τῆς Ὁμήρου ποιήσεως μὴ ὑφ᾽ ἓν συνηγμένης, σποράδην δὲ ἄλλως καὶ κατὰ μέρη διῃρημένης, ὁπότε ῥαψῳδοῖεν αὐτήν, εἱρμῷ τινι καὶ ῥαφῇ παραπλήσιον ποιεῖν, εἰς ἓν αὐτὴν ἄγοντες 'but some say that – since the poetry of Homer had not been brought together under one thing, but rather had been scattered about and divided into parts – when they performed it rhapsodically [*rhapsōidéō*], they would be doing something that is similar to sequencing or sewing, as they produced it into one thing'.

The scholia to Pindar *Nemean* 2.1d proceed to offer yet another version, which supposedly explains the naming of Homeric performers as rhapsodes: there was a time when each performer of the once-disintegrated Homeric poems sang whatever "part" he wanted, and they were all competitors (τῶν ἀγωνιστῶν) for a prize of a lamb or *arḗn*, so that the performers were then called *arnōidoí*; but later, once the competitors (τοὺς ἀγωνιστάς) started to adjust each "part" so as to achieve a totality (τὴν σύμπασαν ποίησιν ἐπιόντας), these performers were called *rhapsōidoí:* οἱ δέ, ὅτι κατὰ μέρος πρότερον τῆς ποιήσεως διαδεδομένης τῶν ἀγωνιστῶν ἕκαστος ὅ τι βούλοιτο μέρος ᾖδε, τοῦ δὲ ἄθλου τοῖς νικῶσιν ἀρνὸς ἀποδεδειγμένου προσαγορευθῆναι τότε μὲν ἀρνῳδούς, αὖθις δὲ ἑκατέρας τῆς ποιήσεως

εἰσενεχθείσης τοὺς ἀγωνιστὰς οἷον ἀκουμένους πρὸς ἄλληλα
τὰ μέρη καὶ τὴν σύμπασαν ποίησιν ἐπιόντας, ῥαψῳδοὺς
προσαγορευθῆναι, ταῦτά φησι Διονύσιος ὁ Ἀργεῖος 'others
say that previously – since the poetry had been divided part by
part, with each of the competitors singing whichever part he
wanted, and since the designated prize for the winners had been a
lamb – [those competitors] were in those days called *arnōidoí*
[=lamb-singers], but then, later on – since the competitors,
whenever each of the two poems[29] was introduced, were mend-
ing the parts to each other, as it were, and moving toward the
whole poem – they were called *rhapsōidoí*. These things are said by
Dionysius of Argos [between 4th and 3rd centuries BC; FGH 308
F 2]'. We will return to some of the details of these versions at a
later point, especially to the image of a disintegrated totality that
suddenly becomes reintegrated.

Following up on what he considers two different interpretations of Pindar *Nemean* 2.1–3, Eustathius (vol. 1 p. 10) offers a third
one as well: that the concept of sewing together songs is parallel
to the concept of *rhapsōidía*, a word that he uses to designate any
one of the twenty-four books of the *Iliad* or *Odyssey*. At a later
point, we will re-examine from a historical point of view the
eventual division of the *Iliad* and the *Odyssey* into twenty-four
books each.[30] For now it will suffice to remark that, even in
considering this interpretation, Eustathius goes back to connecting the meaning of *rhapsōidoí* 'rhapsodes' with the esthetic principle of sewing songs together into a unified whole. Only, in this
case, the songs are visualized *textually*, as separate *rhapsōidíai* or
'books' of Homer.

In the esthetics of sewing, as conveyed by the verb *rháptō*,
one's attention centers on the totality of the *Gestalt* that has been
sewn together, not on the constituent parts. For an attention-
getting example, we may consider the following description of a
type of fashionably tailored *khitón* worn by the young women of
Sparta to show off their beauty: τῷ γὰρ ὄντι τοῦ παρθενικοῦ
χιτῶνος αἱ πτέρυγες οὐκ ἦσαν συνερραμμέναι κάτωθεν, ἀλλ'

---

[29] The expression ἑκατέρας τῆς ποιήσεως 'each of the two poems' specifies, it
seems, that the *Iliad* and the *Odyssey* are meant.
[30] See ch.6.

ἀνεπτύσσοντο καὶ συνανεγύμνουν ὅλον ἐν τῷ βαδίζειν τὸν μηρόν 'for in fact the flaps of the *khitón* worn by their young women were not <u>sewn together</u> [*rháptō*] at the lower ends, and so they would fly back and bare the whole thigh as they walked' (Plutarch *Comparison of Lycurgus and Numa* 3.4). Just exactly where you sew together – and where you leave off sewing together – becomes an exquisite art of *tailoring* to *suit* the senses and the sensibilities of the viewer.

The esthetic principle of combining many different patterns into one new unified pattern seems to be the basis of a foundation myth that explains the genesis of Homeric poetry, specifically in Athens. According to this myth, the key figures who transmitted this poetry are none other than the *rhapsōidoí*, performers who arguably derive their very identity from the metaphor of sewing together many separate patterns of song into one new unified pattern. The foundation myth in question, like others examined in more detail elsewhere, accounts for an entire institution – in this case, the seasonally-recurring performances of the Homeric *Iliad* and *Odyssey* at the Feast of the Panathenaia in Athens – as if this institution had been created overnight, so to speak.[31] Moreover, the myth centers on historical figures who were in all likelihood genuinely involved in shaping or, better, reshaping not only this institution of the Panathenaia in general but also, in particular, the institution of Homeric performances that became a featured event of this festival. The figures in question are the Peisistratidai – that is, Peisistratos and his sons – who traced themselves back to the heroic-age Peisistratos, son of Nestor (as portrayed in *Odyssey* Book 3) and who ruled Athens as tyrants during the second half of the sixth century BC.[32]

[31] There is a more detailed discussion in N 1992a.45–49.
[32] Summary in N 1990a.52–81 and 1992a.42–53. For bibliography on the claim of the Peisistratidai to be descended from the Homeric Peisistratos, son of Nestor, see N 1990a.155. On the effects of the régime of the Peisistratidai on the contents of Homeric poetry, especially the *Odyssey*, see also Catenacci 1993 (at pp. 7–8n2, he offers a useful summary of Aloni 1984 and 1986). All this is not to deny that there may well have been earlier associations of Nestor and his lineage with the lineages of other historical dynasties, such as those at Colophon and Miletus. See Janko 1992.134, with bibliography. I agree with Janko that the earlier Ionic phase of Homeric transmission is decisive, but I note that he too, like me, posits a later Attic phase as well (p. 37): "the superficial Attic traits in the epic diction do prove that Athens played a major role in the transmission, and this must be related to the Pisistratids' patronage of

The making of identity in performance

A key premise of this foundation myth, preserved in "Plato" *Hipparchus* 228b–c, is the very concept of *rhapsōidoí* as performers of Homer. It is claimed, first of all, that Hipparkhos, son of Peisistratos, introduced the Homeric poems to Athens, and, second, that he "forced" the *rhapsōidoí* to perform them *in a fixed sequence:*

Ἱππάρχῳ, ... ὃς ἄλλα τε πολλὰ καὶ καλὰ ἔργα σοφίας ἀπεδείξατο, καὶ τὰ Ὁμήρου ἔπη πρῶτος ἐκόμισεν εἰς τὴν γῆν ταυτηνί, καὶ ἠνάγκασε τοὺς ῥαψῳδοὺς Παναθηναίοις ἐξ ὑπολήψεως ἐφεξῆς αὐτὰ διιέναι, ὥσπερ νῦν ἔτι οἶδε ποιοῦσιν

Hipparkhos, ... who publicly enacted many and beautiful things to manifest his expertise [*sophía*],[33] especially by being the first to bring over [*komízō*] to this land [=Athens] the poetic utterances [*épē*] of Homer,[34] and he forced the rhapsodes [*rhapsōidoí*] at the Panathenaia to go through [*diiénai*] these utterances in sequence [*ephexês*], by relay [*ex hupolépseōs*], just as they [=the rhapsodes] do even nowadays.

"Plato" *Hipparchus* 228b–c

Homeric poetry." However, I disagree when he goes on to say (ibid.) that the Peisistratidai "probably procured the first complete set of rolls to cross the Aegean." It may be enough to claim that the Peisistratidai introduced the Homeric *performance* tradition from Ionia, probably from Chios.

[33] The archaizing phraseology of the entire passage about Hipparkhos in "Plato" *Hipparchus* 228b–229d, only a small portion of which is quoted above, is strikingly consistent in leaving unspecified the question of authorship and in emphasizing instead the fact of authority, which is expressed as *sophía* 'expertise' in the understanding of poetry; this *sophía* is in turn implicitly equated with *sophía* in *performing* this poetry, without specification of the process of actually *composing* the poetry. For further details, see N 1990a.161.

[34] When Hipparkhos 'brings over', by ship, the poet Anacreon to Athens ("Plato" *Hipparchus* 228c), the word used, *komízō*, is the same verb used earlier to designate his 'bringing over' the *épē* 'poetic utterances' of Homer in the passage quoted here (228b). By providing the people of Athens with the poetry and songmaking of Homer, Anacreon, and Simonides (the latter is coupled with Anacreon, 228c), Hipparkhos ostensibly demonstrates to them that he is not "stinting with his *sophía*" (σοφίας φθονεῖν: cf. N 1990a.161), as if it was his *sophía* that had somehow generated the performances of these poets. We may infer that the application of *komízō* to the songs of Anacreon and, by extension, to those of Simonides is made parallel to the application of this same word to the poetry of Homer because Hipparkhos did not simply invite these poets for a single occasion of performance but rather institutionalized such performances in contests of *kitharōidía* 'lyre-singing' at the festival of the Panathenaia (on which subject cf. N 1990a.98, 104), parallel to contests of *rhapsōidía* at the same festival.

From this source and also from another one, Lycurgus *Against Leokrates* 102, we may infer that the *épē* 'poetic utterances' of Homer performed at the Panathenaia were exclusively the *Iliad* and *Odyssey*.[35] In another attested report about this same subject, Diogenes Laertius 1.57, we find the same emphasis on the rhapsodes' being forced to perform Homer *in a fixed sequence:* τά τε ῾Ομήρου ἐξ ὑποβολῆς γέγραφε ῥαψῳδεῖσθαι, οἷον ὅπου ὁ πρῶτος ἔληξεν, ἐκεῖθεν ἄρχεσθαι τὸν ἐχόμενον 'he [Solon the Lawgiver] wrote a law that the works of Homer were to be performed rhapsodically [*rhapsōidéō*], by relay [*ex hupobolês*], so that wherever the first person left off, from that point the next person would start'. We have here clear traces of different versions of the foundation myth: this time, the culture hero who is given credit for the institutional reality of rhapsodic performances is Solon the Lawgiver, not Hipparkhos, son of the tyrant Peisistratos. Further below, we will examine still other different versions, which attribute the institution to Peisistratos himself. For now, however, let us concentrate not on the transformations of this foundation myth, which serve to suit different political climates in different historical periods, but rather on one single aspect of the myth, the detail about rhapsodic sequencing.

The esthetics of rhapsodic sequencing, where each performer takes up the song precisely where the last one left off, are in fact built into the contents of Homeric poetry: much as rhapsodes sing in sequence, each one taking his turn after another ("Plato," *Hipparchus* 228b and Diogenes Laertius 1.57), so also the *Iliad* represents the heroes Patroklos and Achilles as potentially rhapsodic performers of epic. While Achilles, becoming the ultimate paradigm for singers, is represented as actually performing the epic songs of heroes, *kléa andrôn* 'glories of men' at *Iliad* 9.189, Patroklos is waiting for his own turn, in order to take up the song precisely where Achilles will have left off:

[35] Further discussion in N 1990a.21–24. Lycurgus *Against Leokrates* 102 says that a customary law at Athens required that *only* the *épē* 'poetic utterances' of Homer could be performed at the Panathenaia; he is speaking at a time when "Homer" is generally held to be the "author" of *only* the *Iliad* and *Odyssey*. Cf. N 1992a.37. In the passage from "Plato" *Hipparchus* 228b–c, moreover, it is presupposed that there were already epic performances by the rhapsodes at the Panathenaia before Hipparkhos brought

The making of identity in performance

τὸν δ' εὗρον φρένα τερπόμενον φόρμιγγι λιγείῃ
καλῇ δαιδαλέῃ, ἐπὶ δ' ἀργύρεον ζυγὸν ἦεν,
τὴν ἄρετ' ἐξ ἐνάρων πόλιν Ἠετίωνος ὀλέσσας·
τῇ ὅ γε θυμὸν ἔτερπεν, ἄειδε δ' ἄρα κλέα ἀνδρῶν.
Πάτροκλος δέ οἱ οἶος ἐναντίος ἧστο σιωπῇ,
δέγμενος Αἰακίδην ὁπότε λήξειεν ἀείδων.

And they [the members of the embassy] found him
    [Achilles] delighting his spirit with a clear-sounding lyre,
beautiful and well-wrought, and there was a silver bridge on
    it.
He won it out of the spoils after he destroyed the city of
    Eetion.
Now he was delighting his spirit with it, and he sang the
    glories of men [*kléa andrôn*].
But *Pátroklos*, all alone, was sitting, facing him, in silence,
waiting for whatever moment the Aeacid would leave off
    singing.

Iliad 9.186–191

Both the plural usage here of *kléa andrôn* 'glories of men' (as opposed to singular *kléos* 'glory') and the meaning of the name *Patrokléēs* are pertinent to the rhapsodic implications of this passage: "it is only through *Patrokléēs* 'he who has the *kléa* [glories] of the ancestors' that the plurality of performance, that is, the activation of tradition, can happen."[36] So long as Achilles alone sings the *kléa andrôn* 'glories of men', these heroic glories cannot be heard by anyone but Patroklos alone. Once Achilles leaves off and Patroklos starts singing, however, the continuum that is the *kléa andrôn* – the Homeric tradition itself – can at long last become activated. This is the moment awaited by *Patrokléēs* 'he who has the *kléa* [glories] of the ancestors'.[37] In this Homeric image of

the *épē* of Homer to Athens. It seems, by implication, that these newer *épē* were exclusively the *Iliad* and *Odyssey*.

[36] N 1990a.202.
[37] It could be argued that Patroklos as the solo audience of Achilles becomes interchangeable with the general audience of the *Iliad*. On the Homeric device of creating an effect of interchangeability between characters of epic and members of an audience, see Frontisi-Ducroux 1986; cf. Russo and Simon 1968. For a compelling interpretation of the self-referentiality conveyed by the image of Achilles singing the *kléa andrôn* 'glories of men', see Martin 1989.234–236, who also discusses in this context the special effects of apostrophe in the Homeric passages where the narrator addresses Patroklos in the second person.

72

Patroklos waiting for his turn to sing, then, we have in capsule form the esthetics of rhapsodic sequencing.[38] It is not only these main heroes of Homeric poetry who can perform like rhapsodes. In the myths about the prototypical poets, those figures too become practicing rhapsodes. Thus Homer and Hesiod themselves are conventionally represented in such a way. For example, the scholia to Pindar *Nemean* 2.1 (the source is Philochorus FGH 328 F 212) quote the following verses attributed to Hesiod, who speaks of performing, in competition with Homer, hymns to Apollo:

ἐν Δήλωι τότε πρῶτον ἐγὼ καὶ Ὅμηρος ἀοιδοὶ
μέλπομεν, ἐν νεαροῖς ὕμνοις ῥάψαντες ἀοιδήν,
Φοῖβον Ἀπόλλωνα ...

Then it was, in Delos, that Homer and I, singers [*aoidoí*],
for the first time
sang, in new hymns, sewing together [*rháptō*] the song [*aoidé*],
[sang] of Phoebus Apollo

Hesiod F 357

In the previous chapter, we have seen the Delian Maidens in the Homeric *Hymn to Apollo* show the way for others to re-enact them by demonstrating their own power to re-enact all other peoples, in all their varieties. These Maidens are models of mimesis by way of practicing mimesis (*Hymn to Apollo* 163).[39] So also Homer and Hesiod are models of rhapsodes by way of performing like rhapsodes.[40] Even for Plato (*Republic* 600d), Homer and Hesiod can be visualized as performing like rhapsodes (*rhapsōidéō*). For

---

[38] In Cicero *Laws* 1.3.9 and *Pro Caelio* 18, *con-texō* is used in the sense of taking up the activity of weaving, *texō*, where it had been interrupted and thus left off; this idea is applied metaphorically to the process of literary composition, including poetic composition. Cf. Scheid and Svenbro 1994.150–151. In this sense, con-text is a matter of continuity.

[39] See p. 56.

[40] Scheid and Svenbro 1994.120 concede that the concept of *rhapsōidós* is driven by the metaphor of songmaking as *sewing together*. Still, they argue that this metaphor cannot be taken further back and applied to Homer. In their view, as we have seen, the metaphors of *weaving* and *sewing together* did not exist before the era of Simonides and Pindar. I disagree, having just argued that these metaphors are at least residually attested in even the earliest evidence and that the concept of Homer as rhapsode is basic to Homer.

Plato, a figure like Phemios, represented as a prototypical poet in the *Odyssey*, is likewise a *rhapsōidós* (*Ion* 533c).

The poet as rhapsode is the ultimate performer, but he is also the ultimate composer – at least from the standpoint of myth. The esthetics of sewing as a metaphor for singing highlight, as we will now see, both the technique and the product of poetic craftsmanship.

Let us begin with the name of Homer, *Hómēros*. The meaning of this name can be correlated with the traditional status of Homer as author.[41] The further we go back in time, the greater the repertoire attributed to this author, including in the earlier times all the so-called Cycle, all the Theban epics, and so on.[42] In fact, the very notion of "Cycle" had once served as a metaphor for all of Homer's poetry.[43] I propose that the metaphor of *kúklos* as the sum total of Homeric poetry goes back to the meaning of *kúklos* as 'chariot-wheel' (*Iliad* 23.340, plural *kúkla* at 5.722). The metaphor of comparing a well-composed song to a well-crafted chariot-wheel is explicitly articulated in the poetic traditions of Indo-European languages (as in *Rig-Veda* 1.130.6); more generally in the Greek poetic traditions, there is a metaphor comparing the craft of the master carpenter or "joiner" – the *téktōn* – to the art of the poet (as in Pindar *Pythian* 3.112–114).[44] Further, the root *ar-* of *ararískō* 'join, fit together' (the verb refers to the activity of the carpenter in the expression ἥραρε τέκτων 'the joiner [*téktōn*] joined together [*ar-*]' at *Iliad* 4.110, 23.712) is shared by the word that means 'chariot-wheel' in the Linear B texts, *harmo* (Knossos tablets Sg 1811, So 0437, etc.). Most important of all for my argument, the same root *ar-* is evidently shared by the name of Homer, *Hómēros*, the etymology of which can be explained as 'he who joins together' (*homo-* plus *ar-*).[45] Thus the making of the

---

[41] N 1990a.52–81.
[42] N 1990a.70–79.
[43] Pfeiffer 1968.73; N 1992a.37.
[44] N 1979.297–300, interpreting the evidence assembled by Schmitt 1967.296–298.
[45] N 1979.300. Bader 1989.269n114 attempts to connect the root *seH- 'sew' with the *Hóm-* of *Hómēros*, though she makes clear that her proposed etymology poses some phonological difficulties. While I agree with her that *hómēros* in the sense of 'hostage' may possibly be compatible with the metaphorical world of the root *seH-, *homo-* 'together' plus the root of *ararískō* 'fit, join' is an even more plausible etymology for a noun meaning 'hostage', given the social metaphors inherent in the derivatives of *ararískō* (cf. Chantraine *DELG* 101–102, especially with reference to *arthmós* 'bond,

kúklos by the master poet Homer appears to be a global metaphor that pictures the crafting of the ultimate chariot-wheel by the ultimate carpenter or, better, 'joiner'. This traditional pattern of thinking matches the classification of both the *aoidós* 'singer' and the *tékton* 'carpenter, joiner' under the category of *dēmiourgós* or 'itinerant artisan' at *Odyssey* 17.381–385.[46]

The root of the Greek verb *ar-* 'join' is cognate with the root of the Latin noun *ars/artis* 'craft, art' (also *artus* 'joint'), while the root of the Greek nouns *tékton* 'carpenter, joiner' and *tékhnē* 'craft, art' is cognate with that of the Latin verb *texō*, which means not only 'weave' but also 'join, carpenter' (as in Virgil *Aeneid* 11.326, where the objects that are being carpentered are *ships*).[47] These and other such facts lead to the general conclusion that the metaphor of carpentry as songmaking in Indo-European languages is parallel to the metaphor of weaving.[48] I propose, further, that there is a corresponding parallelism between the concepts of *Hómēros* and *rhapsōidós*.

Implicit in this parallelism is the following complex proportionality of metaphors: the *carpenter* of song is to the *joiner* of song as the one who *weaves* the song is to the one who *sews together* or *stitches* the song, that is, to the *rhapsōidós*. In other words, just as a joiner is a master craftsman, capable of special feats of craftsmanship like the making of a chariot-wheel out of pieces of woodwork already made by himself or by other carpenters, so also the stitcher, one who sews together pieces of fabric already woven, is a master craftsman in his own right, fashioning something altogether "new" that is tailor-made to suit a given form.

league, friendship' and related forms). There is a striking semantic parallel to *phōnēi homēreûsai* 'fitting [the song] together with their voice', describing the Muses at *Theogony* 39: it is *artiépeiai* 'having words fitted together', describing the Muses at *Theogony* 29 (N 1979.297).

[46] N 1979.233–234, 310–311 par. 2n3. As we ponder the archaism of this metaphor of *kúklos*, we may note a curious detail in the chariot inventories of the Linear B texts: there is a dichotomy of red and purple in descriptions of colors painted on these chariots. In Homeric diction, as we will see later, there is a parallel dichotomy of red and purple in descriptions of colors painted on ships. See ch.6, where I connect this dichotomy with an observation made by Eustathius in the Prolegomena to his commentary on the *Iliad* (vol. 1 p. 9): that performers of the *Iliad* wore costumes dyed red and those of the *Odyssey*, purple. The precise colors may be different, but the dichotomy itself seems analogous.

[47] Schmitt 1967.14–15, N 1979.297–300.

[48] Schmitt 1967.298–301.

Thus the metaphor of a joiner or a stitcher, as distinct from a carpenter or a weaver, conveys the idea of a master singer. I hasten to add that the English word *stitcher* may be inappropriate for expressing the esthetics of a master's handiwork, in that *stitch* implies something makeshift, as if stitchwork were simply patchwork. More appropriate than *stitcher* – at least esthetically, perhaps – is *tailor*. Related images that come to mind are *connector* and *conductor*. In any case, just as *Hómēros* is the ultimate 'joiner', so also the poetry of Homer becomes the handiwork of the ultimate *rhapsōidós*, the one who sews the songs together.

Whichever way myth figures the creation of Homeric poetry, whether it be a joiner's chariot wheel or a "tailor's" perfect fit, the actual creation is viewed as happening at a remote point in time, not over time. From the standpoint of the myth, it is as if there had been a "big bang" that produced a fixed pattern of composition, which led to a fixed pattern of performance or both.

Moreover, Homer is not just the creator of heroic song: he is also the culture hero of this song.[49] Ancient Greek institutions tend to be traditionally retrojected, by the Greeks themselves, each to a proto-creator, a culture hero who gets credited with the sum total of a given cultural institution.[50] It was a common practice to attribute any major achievement of society, even if this achievement may have been realized only through a lengthy period of social evolution, to the episodic and personal accomplishment of a culture hero who is pictured as having made his monumental contribution in an earlier era of the given society.[51] Greek myths about lawgivers, for example, whether they are historical figures or not, tend to reconstruct these figures as the originators of the sum total of customary law as it evolved through time.[52] So also with Homer: he is retrojected as the original genius of heroic song, the protopoet whose poetry is reproduced by an continuous succession of performers. We have

---

[49] N 1990a.78–81.
[50] Cf. Kleingünther 1933.
[51] For an illuminating discussion of culture heroes in Chinese traditions, cf. Raphals 1992.53: Yi invents the bow; Zhu, armor, Xi Zhong, the carriage, Qiao Chui, the boat.
[52] N 1985.33.

already noted Plato's *Ion* (533d–536d), where Socrates envisages the rhapsode Ion as the last in a chain of magnetized metal rings connected by the force of the original poet Homer. In this mythical image of Homer and his successors, the magnetic force of the poetic composition weakens with each successive performer. Pictured as the last or at least the latest replicant of Homer, Ion becomes the weakest of all replicants.[53]

From the standpoint of an evolutionary model for the fixation of Homeric poetry, by contrast, the reality is altogether different from the myth: "even if the size of either the *Iliad* or the *Odyssey* ultimately defied performance by any one person at any one sitting, the monumental proportions of these compositions could evolve in a social context where the sequence of performance, and thereby the sequence of narrative, could be regulated, as in the case of the Panathenaia."[54] In quoting this formulation, I have highlighted the idea that an evolving fixity in patterns of performance leads to a correspondingly evolving fixity in patterns of composition, given that performance and composition – or, better, recomposition – are aspects of the same process in this medium.

In myth, the nature of events is radically different, and their order is reversed: a moment of fixation in composition leads to a moment of fixation in performance. As we look back at the foundation myths we have already considered, we see that the establishment of a fixed sequence in Homeric performance is viewed by the myths as a moment in time, coming after the fact of composition, which must go back to an earlier moment in time. The fixity of this composition is visualized as a totality created once upon a time by Homer, the "original" culture hero. In the version of the myth that we are now considering, this totality is then disintegrated, only to become reintegrated at the initiative of a subsequent culture hero, whose role is claimed by a succession of historical figures ranging from Solon to Peisistratos to the son of Peisistratos. The process of reintegration is a matter of making sure that the totality of the "original" composition will be performed in the right sequence. Let us review the wording of

[53] N 1990a.55.
[54] N 1990a.23.

77

The making of identity in performance

Eustathius: ῥάπτειν δὲ ἢ ἁπλῶς, ὡς εἴρηται, τὸ συντιθέναι ἢ τὸ κατὰ εἱρμόν τινα ῥαφῇ ὁμοίως εἰς ἓν ἄγειν τὰ διεστῶτα. σποράδην γάρ, φασί, κειμένης καὶ κατὰ μέρος διῃρημένης τῆς Ὁμηρικῆς ποιήσεως, οἱ ἄδοντες αὐτὴν συνέρραπτον οἷον τὰ εἰς ἓν ὕφος ᾀδόμενα 'sewing together [*rháptō*] either in the simple sense, as just mentioned, of putting together or, alternatively, in the sense of bringing different things, in accordance with some kind of sequencing [*heirmós*] in sewing, uniformly into one thing; for they say that Homeric poetry, after it had been scattered about and divided into separate parts, was sewn together by those who sang it, like songs sung into a single fabric [*húphos*]'. This time, let us concentrate on the idea that the totality had been *scattered about and divided into separate parts*, only to be later reassembled, or *sewn together*, by those who sing it.

In another version of the myth, the idea of a whole fabric that once became divided into separate parts and scattered about but was later successfully sewn back together again extends into the idea of an actual written *text* that was disassembled and then reassembled. I have examined this version at length in my earlier work, citing parallels from other cultures where an oral tradition applies to itself the metaphor of a written text.[55] In that work, the following conclusions were reached: "the intrinsic applicability of *text* as metaphor for *recomposition-in-performance* helps explain a type of myth, attested in a wide variety of cultural contexts, where the evolution of a poetic tradition, moving slowly ahead in time until it reaches a relatively static phase, is reinterpreted by the myth as if it resulted from a single incident, pictured as the instantaneous recovery or even regeneration of a lost text, an archetype."[56] Here I limit myself to offering a brief summary of this alternative version of the foundation myth, where the Homeric poetry produced by the "big bang" is visualized as a written text.

According to this version, four men were commissioned by Peisistratos, tyrant of Athens in the second half of the sixth century BC, to supervise the 'arranging' of the Homeric poems, which were before then 'scattered about' (διέθηκαν οὑτωσὶ σποράδην οὔσας τὸ πρίν: Tzetzes in *Anecdota Graeca* 1.6 ed.

[55] N 1992a.44–49.
[56] N 1992a.45.

78

Cramer).[57] There is a parallel narrative reported in Aelian *Varia Historia* 13.14, where the introduction of Homeric poetry to Sparta by Lycurgus the Lawgiver is explicitly compared to a subsequent introduction of the *Iliad* and *Odyssey* to Athens by Peisistratos. A further detail of interest can be found in Cicero *De oratore* 3.137: Peisistratos, supposedly one of the Seven Sages (*septem fuisse dicuntur uno tempore, qui sapientes et haberentur et vocarentur*),[58] was so learned and eloquent that "he is said to be the first person ever to have arranged the books of Homer, previously scattered about, in the order that we have today" (*qui primus Homeri libros confusos antea sic disposuisse dicitur, ut nunc habemus*).[59] The detail concerning the division of Homeric poems into separate books *which then become separated from each other* reflects the outlook of a later era, when the *Iliad* and *Odyssey* were in fact each divided into twenty-four papyrus rolls. We have already seen the same detail reflected in the third of the three alternative explanations offered by Eustathius concerning the ultimate *sewing together* of the Homeric poems: according to this third version, the separate parts are conceived as books, which are equated with *rhapsōidíai*.[60] We will consider in more detail at a later point the historical division of the *Iliad* and *Odyssey* each into twenty-four books. Suffice it to conclude, for now, that all the various accounts of a supposedly original Athenian reception of Homeric poetry have inspired a modern construct that has come to be known among Classicists as the "Peisistratean recension."[61]

---

[57] Ibid. Allen 1924.233 thinks that the source of Tzetzes here was Athenodorus, head of the Library at Pergamum. Note the parallel wording in the *Greek Anthology*, 11.442, representing Peisistratos as speaker: ὅς τὸν Ὅμηρον ἤθροισα, σποράδην τὸ πρὶν ἀειδόμενον 'I who gathered together Homer, who was previously being sung here and there, <u>scattered</u> all over the place'.

[58] There is emphasis on the idea that each of the Seven Sages except Thales had been head of state (Cicero *De oratore* 3.137: *hi omnes praeter Milesium Thalen civitatibus suis praefuerunt*).

[59] On this passage from Cicero, see Boyd 1996.

[60] See p. 68 above, on Eustathius (vol. 1 p. 10): the *rhapsōidíai* correspond to the twenty-four books of the *Iliad* and *Odyssey*, which are scattered and then reassembled into the totality of the Homeric poems. This particular notion of *rhapsōidíai* corresponds to Cicero's notion of *libri confusi* 'scattered books'.

[61] For a brief restatement and for a survey of primary information pertinent to the concept of a "Peisistratean recension," see Allen 1924.225–238. See also N 1990a.21–22n20. In the scholia to Dionysius Thrax, Codex Venetus 489 (as printed in Allen p. 230), it is reported that the Homeric poems were "sewn together" (συνερράφησαν) by Peisistratos himself.

Despite the metaphor of a written text, this version of the foundation myth, just like the others, centers not on proving the hypothetical existence of some unattested textual transmission of Homer but rather on explaining the institutional reality of ongoing performances of Homeric song at the Feast of the Panathenaia in Athens. That is, the myth is concerned with the performance of Homer, the mimesis of Homer – in the archaic sense of that word. Throughout this chapter, it has been argued that the rhapsode, the performer of Homer, is engaged in a mimesis that re-creates not only the characters of heroic song but also the composer and prototypical performer of that song, Homer himself.

From a modern point of view that sees Homer as the author of a text, the re-creating of a real Homer in the performance of a rhapsode may not even seem to be a matter of mimesis. Even for Plato and Aristotle, a straightforward third-person narration in heroic song is technically a matter of diegesis or 'narration' as opposed to mimesis. In contemplating the "I" of "tell me, Muses" or "tell me, Muse," we find ourselves at a loss in finding the element of the mimetic – or, to say it in a more modern way, the *dramatic*. And yet, my claim is that this "I" is perhaps the most dramatic of all the characters in heroic song – once we see this song on the level of performance as well as composition. This "I" is Homer speaking. For us, however, his role is no longer overt as it had been for audiences of Homeric song, and Homer has lost his power as a dramatic persona.

There is in fact a staggering variety of roles to be played out in all the various performance traditions of ancient Greek songmaking, whether they are overtly dramatic or otherwise. Even in diegesis or 'narration', there is an outer frame of mimesis within which we find an "I" who narrates, whose identity is either highlighted or shaded over in performance.[62] Still, it is justifiable to consider drama, with all its ritual background, as a primary form of mimesis. Moreover, it may well be the ultimate status of drama as State Theater in Athens – and as the near-equivalent of

---

[62] It is essential to make a distinction here between an "I" within mimesis and an "I" outside of mimesis. On the hermeneutics of the latter kind of "I" or "je," see Calame 1986.

Mimesis of Homer and beyond

that concept in other city-states as well – that conferred upon the word mimesis (*mímēsis*) its ultimate importance and seriousness. The word's prehistory, to be sure, suggests that mimesis (*mímēsis*) once had a less important and less serious tone, since it is after all derived from *mîmos*, the meaning of which never really went far beyond the relatively lowly meaning that corresponds to our own notion of 'mime' (Aristotle *Poetics* 1447b10).[63] The eventual importance, however, of the derivative of *mîmos*, that is, mimesis (*mímēsis*), is quite clear even in its earliest attested usage, in the *Homeric Hymn to Apollo*, where we have seen the stately Delian Maidens themselves being described as engaging in the activity of making mimesis, that is, *mimeîsthai* (*Hymn to Apollo* 163).

It could even be said that the attestation of mimesis (*mímēsis*) in the Homeric *Hymn to Apollo* gives us an essential *terminus ante quem* for a functioning institutional complementarity, in Athens, between the performance of drama by actors and chorus at the City Dionysia on the one hand and, on the other, the performance of Homeric epos – and of Homeric hymns that serve as preludes to the epos – by rhapsodes at the Panathenaia.[64] As two premier media of performance that are highlighted at two premier festivals organized by the State, epos and tragedy – the primary form of drama – become complementary forms, evolving together and thereby undergoing a process of mutual assimilation in the course of their institutional coexistence.[65]

We can see clearly the complementarity of epos and tragedy from the wording of Aristotle, at the beginning of the *Poetics*, who puts at the head of his list of poetic forms the pair that he calls *epopoiía* 'making of epos' and *tragōidías poíēsis* 'making of tragedy':

[63] A useful semantic overview in Chantraine *DELG* 703–704.

[64] Cf. N 1990a.391: "The close association of the Peisistratidai of Athens with the City Dionysia, context for performance of drama, and with the Panathenaia, context for performance of epic, is analogous to the association of the tyrant Kleisthenes of Sikyon with innovations in the performance of both epic (Herodotus 5.67.1) and drama (5.67.5)." On the mutual assimilation of Homeric epos and Homeric hymns, see N pp. 353–354. The fact that Thucydides (3.104.4–5) uses the word *prooímion* 'prelude' in referring to the version of the Homeric *Hymn to Apollo* that he knew suggests to me that he heard the *Hymn* performed at the Panathenaia as a prelude.

[65] Cf. N 1990a.388, 390–391; cf. also Herington 1985.138–144 on the "Homeric" repertoire of Aeschylus. On the process of mutual assimilation in the evolution of tragedy and comedy, which follows an earlier era of differentiation between these forms, cf. N pp. 384–388; on the mutual assimilation of tragedy and dithyramb, cf. N 1990a.388–389.

ἐποποιία δὴ καὶ ἡ τῆς τραγῳδίας ποίησις, ἔτι δὲ κωμῳδία, καὶ ἡ διθυραμβοποιητική, καὶ τῆς αὐλητικῆς καὶ κιθαρ-ιστικῆς, πᾶσαι τυγχάνουσιν οὖσαι μιμήσεις τὸ σύνολον · 'the making of *épos* [*epopoiía*] and the making [*poíēsis*] of tragedy, also comedy, and the making [*-poiētiké*] of dithyrambs, and the [making] of reed-songs and lyre-songs – all these are in point of fact forms of *mímēsis*, by and large' (Aristotle *Poetics* 1447a14–15).

In effect, Aristotle is here pairing off the forms of epos and trag-edy as genres, but the status of these forms as genres derives from their complementarity not only as media of composition but also, explicitly, as media of performance. The prerequisite of performance is made explicit by Aristotle's assertion here that all these forms of songmaking are a matter of mimesis. Thus when-ever Aristotle's *Poetics* draws our attention to the tragic features of Homeric epos and to the epic features of evolving tragedy (especially chapters 23–24), we have reason to think that such marks of mutual assimilation between two genres result from complementarity of traditions in performance, not just composi-tion. Such complementarity is reflected in the usage of the verb of mimesis in the Homeric *Hymn to Apollo*.

Elsewhere, I have argued that the Delian Maidens of the *Homeric Hymn to Apollo* offer to make a mimesis of Homer, and Homer responds by making a mimesis of them.[66] In the mythical world of the Homeric *Hymn to Apollo*, epic performance is being notionally assimilated to the mimetic performance of an idealized chorus. This relationship, it can now be argued, reflects what is actually happening in the real world of Athenian state festivals, where epic performance is being historically conditioned by the mimetic performance of drama in State Theater.

All this is not to lose sight of changes in the later history of the word *mímēsis*. Eventually, its authority became destabilized, and in fact we start seeing traces of such destabilization as early as the second half of the fifth century, as for example in some passages of Herodotus.[67] For the moment, however, I stress the surviving authority of the word, suggesting that any eventual diminution in its authority may be simply a symptom of an eventual diminu-

---

[66] N 1990a.376.
[67] See Nehamas 1982.75n49 on e.g. Herodotus 5.67.1; cf. N 1990a.349n58.

tion in the authority of Athenian State Theater itself. Ironically, Plato's negative treatment of mimesis as a concept may be interpreted as a sign of the surviving power and prestige that marked the poetics of State Theater, even in the fourth century.[68]

Ancient Greek dramatic re-enactment, that is, mimesis, could take place in the song and poetry of not only theater, not only choral performance, but even monody. Let us review briefly the conventions of both choral and monodic performance, including epic under the category of "monody," with the aim of finding the broad outlines of the performer's patterns of identification with the contents of the performance. Here I return to a long-range inference reached in my earlier work, which is, that patterns of performance in ensemble help explain patterns of solo performance more effectively than the other way around.[69]

From the standpoint of mimesis, it is essential to make further distinctions concerning performance. Besides the opposition of *solo* and *ensemble*, we may subdivide "ensemble" by distinguishing between *audience* and *group* – corresponding to various distinctions of specialization and non-specialization in songmaking traditions.[70] *Whereas a performer performs for an audience, a group can perform together for each other.* Group performance is possible even if some members take on far more important roles than others, to the extent that an outsider may not even be able to distinguish a group from an audience. So long as the mentality of group performance is there, everyone who is present at a mimesis becomes part of it.

The distinction between *audience* and *group* can be applied to scenes of person-to-person or person-to-group interaction in Homeric narrative. Let us consider as an example any given Homeric narration that pictures a woman singing a lament for the death of someone she loves, as when Andromache mourns the

[68] Cf. N 1990a.42, 44, 349, with extensive further references. Another sign is the attitude of another fourth-century figure like Isocrates, who throughout his own extensive corpus of written work uses the word mimesis (*mimēsis*) in a positive light, without implications of disapproval: in his eyes, mimesis seems to be a matter of utmost importance and seriousness (e.g. *Euagoras* 75, *Antidosis* 3).

[69] N 1990a ch.12. For zoömusicological analogies, see Mâche 1991.158–163, especially p. 158 concerning the synchronized singing of cicadas.

[70] For illuminating examples in the songmaking traditions of India, see Kothari 1989.103.

killing of her husband Hektor in *Iliad* 24.725–745.[71] For those who are the characters inside the narrative, the woman is the performer of a song of lament, which is addressed directly or indirectly to the characters that hear her. For those who are the audience outside the narrative, a performer is re-enacting for his or her audience the woman who is singing the lament. Such re-enactment is a matter of mimesis. The point is, the person-to-person or person-to-group interaction in Homeric narrative mirrors the actual conventions of performer-audience interaction in the "real world" that frames the performance of the narrative.[72] It is as if the lamenting woman were addressing not only her group but also the audience that is listening to the performer as he re-enacts the woman.[73]

Such mirroring is pertinent to the issues raised by Wolfgang Rösler's pioneering book, *Dichter und Gruppe*, which investigates the reception of archaic Greek lyric monody in the specific social context of archaic Lesbos.[74] It can be argued that the interactions of Alcaeus and Sappho with their respective *groups* on one level simply mirrors the performances of the Alcaeus-persona and the Sappho-persona to their respective *audiences* on another level.[75] With this adjustment, we can follow Rösler's argument that there is no "fiction" *per se* on the occasion of, say, an epithalamium or bridal song attributed to Sappho. We may add, though, that there *is* indeed re-enactment. On an occasion like a wedding, there are archetypal situations to be acted out. With specific reference to the songmaking form of a bridal song, for example, we may simply note in passing that the ancient Greek word *númphē* means both 'bride' (e.g. *Iliad* 18.492) and 'goddess', that is, 'nymph' (e.g. *Iliad* 24.616). By implication, the ritual occasion of a wedding, as formalized in a bridal song, collapses the distinction between 'bride' and 'goddess'. In the next chapter, we will explore the poetic implications of such mergers in identity.

When we speak of a "group" in such contexts, it is important to keep in mind not only such dramatic settings as a *hetaireía*

---

[71] On which see Martin 1989.87.
[72] For a far-reaching investigation of such mirroring, see Martin 1989.87–88.
[73] Ibid. Cf. N 1979.95–96, 114.
[74] Rösler 1980.
[75] On the monodic form of Sappho, cf. N 1990a.371.

'assembly of comrades' addressed by Alcaeus himself at one time and one place but also such historical settings as symposia, with all their variations in time and place, where the spirit of *hetaireía* provides a context for re-enactments of, say, Alcaeus' words in song.[76] Thus the dramatic setting of Alcaeus' words addressed to his *hetaireía*, which was primarily the symposium according to Rösler, can be perpetuated in a historical setting that is primarily this same medium, the symposium.[77]

In previous work, I argued extensively that the performance traditions of lyric compositions that were attributed to the likes of Alcaeus and Sappho – as also of non-lyric compositions attributed to the likes of Archilochus and Theognis – were perpetuated by the medium of the symposium, in all its varieties.[78] I also highlighted the other central medium that perpetuated and to some degree transformed these performance traditions, that is, the institution of State Theater in Athens.[79] Thirdly, I linked these two media with the institution of private schools, elitist training grounds that enhanced the artistic competitiveness and bravura inherent in the performance traditions perpetuated by the symposium and the theater.[80] Here it suffices simply to note the fundamental role of mimesis in all these traditions. And mimesis is predicated on the mentality of what we may call the *group*, as distinct from the *audience*.

Once we distance ourselves from the idea of a "fictional" dimension in the performance of archaic Greek song and poetry, we acquire a ready counterargument to Plato's reasoning in the

---

[76] On the poetics of Alcaeus in the context of the symposium, see N, forthcoming, in a chapter of a book on problems of genre, edited by Mary Depew and Dirk Obbink.

[77] Page 1955.185 entertains the possibility of interpreting Alcaeus F 6, a song that describes a storm at sea, as follows: "Alcaeus recreates it as if it were yet to be suffered." He then proceeds to reject this interpretation: "To define a procedure so futile, and so discordant with the practice of ancient poets at any period, is alone enough to condemn it beyond belief." Bowie 1986.17 criticizes Page's condemnation: "what he ignores is the dramatic element in non-dramatic poetry." I agree in part, though I disagree with the description of Alcaic poetry as "non-dramatic." Any song is dramatic to the extent that it is mimetic.

[78] N 1990a.15, 107, 109–110, 112, 113, 115, 340–342, 368, 371, 375, 409, 435, 436 (general statement), 437. Cf. Murray 1990.8, who acknowledges the pioneering work of Reitzenstein 1893 on the symposium as context for performance (for more on the perspectives of Reitzenstein, see also N 1990a.109–110).

[79] N 1990a ch.13 in general.

[80] Ibid.

Laws, which promotes the idea that Athenian State Theater appropriates real genres from real occasions and makes them make-believe. A case in point is the *thrênos*, a kind of lamentation. As Nicole Loraux points out, the condemnation of mimesis as a representative of theater in general and of tragedy in particular is specifically correlated in Plato's *Republic* Book III (395d–e) with the condemnation of imitating women's behavior, especially when it comes to lamentation.[81] For Plato, a lament must be implicitly a lament in "real life," where real living persons mourn for a real dead person in a song that marks a real occasion, while a *thrênos* in tragedy is supposedly an imitation, a fiction, where make-believe persons mourn for a make-believe dead person in a song that merely imitates a real occasion. As we now see, however, from a deeper reading of mimesis as re-enactment, the songs of lamentation in State Theater are really archetypal. They are prototypes, as it were, of the "real-life" laments of "real-life" people. Far from being an intended *imitation* of a "real-life" genre, the dramatized *thrênos* of Athenian State Theater can be seen as an intended *model*. There is an authority inherent in mimesis, and this authority confers an absolute status upon the person or thing to be re-enacted.

So also with laments that are quoted, as it were, in Homeric performance. When the rhapsode performs Andromache's lament, he *is* Andromache, singing her lament, just as he *is* Homer when we hear in the Homeric poems: "tell me, Muses," or "tell me, Muse." So also, finally, with the lament of the nightingale in *Odyssey* 19.518–523: the songbird's beautiful sad song is being chosen by an epic character as a *model* for her own epic self-expression. Moreover, in narrating the lyric lament of the nightingale, epic imitates it as a *model*. This way, epic is not only imitating but actually re-enacting lyric, drawing on its own resources of mimesis.

[81] Loraux 1990.22 and 125n15.

4

Mimesis in lyric: Sappho's Aphrodite and the Changing Woman of the Apache

We turn to a striking example of the equation between a ritual "this" and a mythical "that," as postulated in Aristotle's formulation of mimesis. This example of dramatic re-enactment, taken from a culture that is definitely unrelated to the Greek, is explicitly a case of initiation – a concept that we have seen only implicitly in the semantics of the epithet for the Homeric nightingale, *poludeukḗs* 'patterning in many different ways'.

To make sure that the comparison about to be made serves its intended purpose of allowing us to see the ancient Greek evidence in a new light, it is important to stress that ancient Greek dramatic re-enactment could in fact take place not only in theater, not only in choral performance, but even in monody, the conventions of which are replete with stylized choral roles.[1] Such monody could be performed not only at public "recitals" but also at symposia.[2] An outstanding case in point is the ostensibly monodic poetry of Sappho, whose songs "presuppose or represent an interaction, offstage, as it were, with a choral aggregate."[3]

Our example is a Navajo ritual of girls' initiation into puberty called the *kinaaldá*, customarily performed by and in honor of a young female member of the community on the occasions of her first and second menstruation. Much has been written about the Navajo *kinaaldá* ritual, and it is difficult to do justice to its rich complexities. For my present purposes, the most telling summary of the Navajo evidence is to be found in a book of cross-cultural

---

[1] N 1990a.370–371.
[2] N 1990a.107, 340–342, 368, 371, 375, 409, 435–437.
[3] N 1990a.371.

87

studies concerning the general topic of female initiation.[4] There are related rituals in other societies of the same Athapascan language family to which the Navajo belong, notably in Apache societies, where the term for girls' puberty ritual is *nah-ih-es*.[5]

The focal point of the Navajo myth and ritual is the goddess Changing Woman, also known as White Shell Woman, who is to become the mother of the Divine Twins. More literally, her name means "the woman who is transformed time and again" (p. 25). The Apache analogue is likewise known as Changing Woman, or White Painted Woman (p. 135). In the case of the Navajo *kinaaldá* ritual, most of the proceedings take place in the family *hogan* (the Navajo word for a type of earth-covered edifice) of the girl to be initiated. On the final night of the *kinaaldá*, the ritual program features the performance of what are called the hogan songs, claimed to be originally composed for the *kinaaldá* of Changing Woman herself (pp. 18–19). There are two kinds of hogan songs, corresponding to the girl's first and second menstruations: the Chief Hogan Songs and the Talking God Hogan Songs (p. 22). According to Navajo myth, the power of these same hogan songs enabled the prototypical figures First Man and First Woman to sing the prototypical hogan into existence (p. 18). In the here and now of the ritual, these hogan songs are thought to have the power of re-enacting the prototypical event. The words of the singer's songs, by identifying the family hogan with the first hogan, claim to rebuild and thus renew the identified edifice, as the words themselves say explicitly (p. 18).

Thus the localization of the Navajo family hogan becomes sacred space, where the distinctions between the details of myth and the details of ritual can merge in the minds of those who participate in the ritual (p. 19). In one particular recording of these hogan songs, we can observe the continual repetition of a phrase that can be translated: "I fully understand it" (p. 19).[6] This

---

[4] Lincoln 1981 ch.3: "Kinaaldá: Becoming the Goddess," pp. 17–33. Unless otherwise indicated, page-numbers in the text proper concerning Navajo rituals refer to Lincoln's work.

[5] For an introduction to the Apache *nah-ih-es*, see Haley 1981. Unless otherwise indicated, page-numbers in the text proper concerning Apache rituals refer to Haley's work.

[6] We may compare the element of *assensio* 'assent' in the mental process of induction as analyzed at ch.2.

phrase frames such declarations as "Now with my doorway, now
with my door curtain, the house has come into being, it is said"
and "Now long life, now everlasting beauty, were brought into
the interior, it is said" (p. 19). Within the sacred space of this
interior, the young girl to be initiated becomes *identified* with
the goddess Changing Woman (p. 119n35). In the corresponding
Apache ritual, the family of the girl initiand, before the actual
puberty ritual takes place, conventionally refers to the daughter as
"she who is going to become White Painted Woman" (p. 135).
Since the feasting is open to all, the initiand can be conventionally
designated by the people at large as "she through whom we will
have a big time" (p. 135).

In the course of the Navajo ritual, the young girl initiand has
the *authority* to confer the blessings of prosperity and fertility
upon the participants in the ritual, "thus imparting some of the
powers of growth with which she abounds at this moment of her
life" (p. 20); in the Apache ritual as well, "during those four days
the celebrant was considered to have power" (p. 135).[7] After the
blessings in the Navajo ritual, the initiand leaves the hogan and
runs a race with other young people who are participants in her
initiation, and it is ritually prescribed that she must take the lead
in the race (p. 50). We may compare the authoritative status of
the chorus-leader or *khorēgós* in Alcman's *Partheneion* (which apparently refers to some sort of ritualized race).[8]

In the Navajo ritual, the prescribed course of the race to be
run by the girl initiand is clockwise, heading eastward from the
hogan toward the sun, returning westward to the hogan (p. 20). It
has been observed that "the race is, in effect, her pursuit of the

---

[7] The etymology of *authority* is pertinent to my choice of this word in denoting the
initiand's power: Latin *auctor*, the founding form of *auctoritas*, is attested in the sense of
'he who makes things grow/flourish' (cf. Virgil *Georgics* 1.27; from *augeō*, conveying the
idea of vegetal fertility) and 'he who is first to speak with authority' (cf. Cicero *in
Pisonem* 35 and the comments of Ernout/Meillet *DELL* 57).

[8] On the correlation of female athletic events, especially footraces, with female
choral participation, see Calame 1977 I 335–350 and II 125–131 (with reference to
what seems to be a prescribed footrace between Hagesikhora and Agido in Alcman's
Partheneion); also N 1990a.367 and Clay 1991.60–62. In the previous note, we noted the
semantics of authority as applied to the power of a girl initiand within the sacred space
of a ritual. We may also note the semantics of authorship implied by the usage of the
word *khorēgós* 'chorus-leader'; cf. N 1990a.339–381, where it is argued that the chorus
is the ultimate mimesis of authority in early Greek society, and that the very concept
of authorship is ultimately defined by choral authority.

sun" (p. 20). In the myth of Changing Woman, which is correlated with the race of the girl initiand, the goddess actually mates with the Sun (p. 29).[9] At the moment of intercourse, the Sun takes on the form of a handsome youth (p. 120n55). We may compare a theme that is prevalent in the poetics of Sappho, where the female speaker declares her *érōs āelíō* 'lust for the sun' (Sappho F 58.25–26 V), which parallels a story in Lesbian mythology about the pursuit of a handsome youth Phaon by all the women of Lesbos, headed by Aphrodite herself; the mythical pursuit by Aphrodite corresponds to a poeticized pursuit of Phaon by the principal female speaker featured in Sappho's poetics – let us call her Sappho.[10] Phaon's name (*Pháōn*) means 'shining', parallel to the name Phaethon (*Phaéthōn*), derived from the participle *phaéthōn* 'shining', attested as the ornamental epithet of Helios the sun-god.[11]

The positioning of the participants in the Navajo ritual is regulated so that the *kinaaldá* girl and the chief singer, who leads the ritual events of the evening, are situated next to each other, in the West of the hogan; in the middle of the hogan is a mound of earth and a vessel of water; in the North and South are the women and men respectively (pp. 21–23). In the East is the doorway, where the first rays of the sun will enter at dawn, "just as Sun came to Changing Woman through her hogan's eastern door at the beginning of time" (p. 22). In this setting, the singing of the hogan songs begins. In this context, we may compare the variety of possibilities in choral positioning as implied in the wording of Alcman's *Partheneion*; in that particular song, of course, the main divine referent is a Dawn Goddess (Orthria at line 61, Aōtis at line 87).[12] Such a conceptualization cannot exactly apply to Changing Woman, but there are nevertheless clear parallels, as we may infer from the following description: "Changing Woman's chief concern is fertility of all kinds – the

---

[9] The Divine Twins whom Changing Woman mothers are both connected with this event, though the sun fathers only one of the Twins, the Monster Slayer, while the other, Born for Water, is in different versions fathered by different elements: see Lincoln 1981.29–30. The concept of Born for Water is comparable to the Indo-Iranian concept of *Apām Napāt*, on which god see N 1990b.99–102.

[10] For an extensive discussion of this theme in Sappho's poetics, see N 1990b.261.

[11] N 1990b. 235, 255.

[12] Cf. Clay 1991.54–58, who argues that Orthria and Aōtis are epithets of Artemis.

ebb and flow of birth, death, and rebirth – and in this respect she is similar to the sun, who is also much concerned with the bestowing of new life and with the rhythms of plants and seasons" (p. 30). In the corresponding Apache ritual, the symbols painted on the Puberty Dress of White Painted Woman include the crescent moon, morning star, rainbows, and sunbeams (p. 136).[13]

In the Talking God type of hogan songs in Navajo ritual, the goddess is conventionally described as moving towards the ritually decorated family hogan and then signaling her arrival. As she arrives, the references to the goddess shift from the third to the first person, so that the goddess herself, represented in the words of the singer, now speaks as an "I." A phrase continually repeated in *Talking God Hogan Song* 25 goes like this: "With my sacred power, I am travelling" (p. 23). Towards the end of this song, this repeated phrase frames, on either side, the following declaration: "Now with long life, now with everlasting beauty, I live" (p. 23). This image of a traveling goddess whose climactic epiphany in the here and now signals a shift from third to first person is comparable to the celebrated inaugural song of the Alexandrian edition of songs attributed to Sappho (F 1 V), where Aphrodite shifts from second-person addressee to first person speaker (in a stretch starting at line 18 and lasting through line 24).[14]

In the whole Navajo ritual, the chief purpose "is the identification of the girl initiand with Changing Woman" (p. 24). This identification is explicit in the following Twelve Word Song (p. 24):

> I am here; I am White Shell Woman, I am here.
> Now on the top of Gobernador Knob [a local mountain], I
>   am here.
> In the center of my white shell hogan I am here.
> Right on the white shell spread I am here.
> Right on the fabric spread I am here.
> Right at the end of the rainbow I am here.

[13] Cf. Sydele E. Golston (forthcoming) on the puberty ritual of the Apache.
[14] The full text of *Song* 1 of Sappho is provided later on in this chapter, with further discussion.

We may note the immediacy of this epiphany, comparable with the epiphany of Aphrodite in *Song* 1 of Sappho (F 1 V). Even more important, it seems that the "I" here stands for a composite of the girl initiand and Changing Woman herself, though the actual performer is the chief singer.

In the corresponding Apache girls' initiation ritual, there are similar distributions in roles, though we can expect many variations in the hierarchy of participants in the ritual. In our survey of the Navajo ritual, we noted in particular the role of the chief singer. In the corresponding Apache ritual, there is likewise a chief singer, but in this instance let us shift our attention to a ritual figure who functions as a correlate of the chief singer. She is an attendant, an older and more experienced woman whose task it is to take charge of the girl initiand during the period of the ritual. It has been observed that "some attendants could claim supernatural experience with [White Painted Woman] herself," so that the girl's attendant is placed "more in the role of priestess than true shaman" (p. 136). We may compare Pausanias' description of the Leukippides, historical analogues to the main choral figures of Alcman's *Partheneion*, as *hiéreiai* 'priestesses' (3.16.1).[15] In the Apache girls' initiation ritual, once the attendant is matched with the initiand, the woman and the girl are expected, from that point on, to address each other as mother and daughter respectively for the rest of their lives (p. 136). This relationship seems comparable to the dramatized interactions of heroines and nurses in Greek tragedy, especially the case of Phaedra and her nurse in Euripides' *Hippolytus;* just as the attendant in the Apache ritual is well versed in women's lore, so also is the nurse in Greek tragedy.[16] Despite the importance of the attendant, the overall ritual itself is directed by the chief singer. We are told that "the most sought after singers were old men who, by community observation, had presided over ceremonies that produced a high percentage of healthy, strong, good-natured, industrious women" (p. 136).

Besides the attendant and the chief singer, there is a third key participant in the Apache girls' puberty ritual. This is the shaman

[15] N 1990a.346.
[16] See Karydas 1992 on the influence of the tradition of women's choral poetics on the figure of the nurse in Greek tragedy.

or *di-yin*, whom the girl's family has to select and who has the power, through supernatural beings called the *ganh*-s, to select and prepare dancers for the ritual (p. 136). The *di-yin* is asked to miss the puberty ritual himself, since "the one who dressed and painted the *ganh*-s had to stay in a little camp well removed from the festivity" (p. 136). This phase of the ritual complex is pervaded by a deeply felt sense of *danger*, in that the dancers are to re-enact the powerful *ganh*-s (p. 136), and the *di-yin* is well paid for his troubles in recruiting and training them (p. 136).

On the day that the Apache girls' puberty ritual begins, before dawn, the girl initiand is entrusted to the attendant, who washes her hair; as the sun rises, the initiand faces the East as the attendant prays while adorning her and dressing her in her ritual costume. "From this instant she was a woman, and for the next four days she was [White Painted Woman] and had to be addressed so" (p. 137). As for the ritual edifice to be built for the occasion, there is a great deal of variation from tribe to tribe. A key feature is an alignment with the four directions and a runway to the East. The chief singer is in charge of the Dwelling Songs, which accompany the building of the ritual edifice (p. 138). In response to the mention of the key supernatural figures in the singing, the attendant utters the same ululation with which White Painted Woman had once upon a time greeted the deaths of the monsters that threatened the universal order (p. 138). In fact the attendant is known as She Who Makes the Cry (p. 138). Later, as the crowd gathers, the attendant pushes White Painted Woman out of the East entrance to run clockwise around a basket of offerings placed outside, with other women and men who want good fortune trotting after the girl initiand (p. 139). Meanwhile, the *di-yin* is getting the dancers ready. Morris Opler has collected the *ganh*-making songs that are performed at this part of the ritual, including the following:[17]

> In the middle of the Holy Mountain,
> In the middle of its body, stands a hut,
> Brush-built, for the Black Mountain Spirit.
> White lightning flashes in these moccasins;[18]

[17] Opler 1941.108.

[18] For comparative perspectives on the semantics connecting flashes of fire or light with dancing, see N 1979.331–332.

White lightning streaks in angular path;
I am the lightning flashing and streaking!
This headdress lives; the noise of its pendants
Sounds and is heard!
My song shall encircle these dancers.

I have underscored the last line in order to draw attention to its remarkable metaphor concerning the relationship of song and dance. To ponder the image of song as encircling and thereby *containing* dance is a fitting way to bring to a close our consideration of this extended example of re-enactment as initiation.

It is in this light that we may re-examine an ancient Greek example of re-enactment as genuine initiation. The passage in question is the prophecy spoken by the goddess Artemis as a consolation to the dying virgin hero Hippolytus in lines 1423–1430 of Euripides' *Hippolytus*.[19] These verses describe, briefly but explicitly, a ritual of female initiation, pictured as seasonally recurring in the past, in the present, and for all time to come in the city of Trozen, where the local girls customarily cut their hair and sing songs of lament for the death of Hippolytus as a formal sign of their coming of age. The myth of the hero's death and of Phaedra's unrequited love for him (1430) is described as a sad love-song, 'a troubled thought that happens with songmaking' (*mousopoiós ... mérimna*, 1428–1429).[20]

We may note in passing, for purposes of further comparison, the observation of Vladimir Propp about love-songs in Russian folk traditions: "the songs are about unhappy love more often than about happy love."[21] He goes on to note that traditional Russian women's songs at weddings, including the bride's songs, include instances of formal lamentation;[22] in fact, "the wailing of the bride is one of the richest and artistically complete forms of ancient peasant poetry."[23] Given that weddings are elaborate rites

[19] The following discussion of Euripides' *Hippolytus* recapitulates N 1994/95.51–52.

[20] In Bacchylides 19.11, the same noun *mérimna*, which I translate here as 'a troubled thought', refers to the thought-processes of the poet himself as he is pictured composing his song.

[21] See Propp 1975.13.

[22] Propp 1975.17–23.

[23] Propp 1975.19–20. We may also note in general the important performative distinction, which affects the process of composition/recomposition in Russian folk lyric, between singing that is combined and singing that is not combined with dance

of passage in Russian folk traditions and that "many wedding songs were never performed outside the wedding ritual,"[24] we stand to gain a wealth of comparative insights from detailed descriptions of women's songmaking in the context of weddings, especially in view of Propp's conclusion that traditional Russian wedding songs "are so closely related to love and family lyrics that they cannot be studied outside the framework of women's folk lyrics in general."[25] Of special interest for the study of archaic Greek choral traditions is the Russian tradition of the ritual unplaiting of the maiden's braid as a preparation for the wedding, where the unplaiting is accompanied by songmaking, and where the bride's girl-friends sing *in the name of the bride*.[26]

With specific reference to the ancient Greek girls' initiation ritual described in lines 1423–1430 of Euripides' *Hippolytus*, one commentator has noted that "the Athenian audience felt strongly the continuity of legendary past and present," and that "there is an evident *emotional* satisfaction in the feeling that the events and persons one has been witnessing live on in effect or name into the life of the present day."[27] We may note with special interest the commentator's use of the word "emotional" here because it captures the *subjective* level of *páthos* in Aristotle's reading of tragedy: on this level, *páthos* can be translated as "emotion."[28]

Still, it remains to ask how the choral lyric of real-life girls who are experiencing initiation by lamenting for Hippolytus and the unrequited love of Phaedra in the real-life community of Trozen translates into the "emotional satisfaction" of the Athenian audience of State Theater. I propose that the song of initiation performed on a seasonally recurring basis by the girls' chorus in Trozen is dramatically replayed, or, better, preplayed, as the songs performed by the chorus of young men in Athenian State Theater

(Propp p. 14); also important, for purposes of comparison with archaic Greek choral traditions, is the traditional presupposition in certain forms of song-and-dance that one girl in a given performance will be selected, through the performance, as better in beauty or skill than the other girls, so that the song becomes in effect *her* praise-song by virtue of formally making an admission or acknowledgment of her poeticized superiority (p. 15).

[24] Propp 1975.18.

[25] Ibid.

[26] Propp 1975.23.

[27] Barrett 1964.412.

[28] Further discussion in N 1994/5.50–52.

who are re-enacting a chorus of young women in Trozen as they
sing and dance the choral lyrics of Euripides' *Hippolytus*. With
reference to the second choral lyric, where the chorus emotion-
ally identifies with Phaedra's most intimate thoughts in an ex-
quisitely poeticized escapist reverie *while she is killing herself offstage*
(732–775), one critic has noted the "intersubjectivity" of the
chorus and the hero.[29] This perceptive line of thought can be
extended: in the sacred space of Athenian State Theater, the
páthos or primal ordeal of a hero like Hippolytus or Phaedra
becomes identified with the *páthos* or emotion of the audience
as well, all through the *intersubjectivity* of choral performance.

It has been remarked that, when the maidens of Trozen mourn
for Hippolytus, they mourn for themselves.[30] So too the audience
of the *drâma* that is Athenian State Theater experiences the *páthos*
of the hero through the *páthos* of re-enactment in choral song and
dance.[31]

The mentality of re-enactment requires the idea of an archetype, not just the latest model in a series of previous models. In
diegesis or 'narration' this principle may be latent, though it can
be argued that even diegesis is subsumed by mimesis: if the role
or even the identity of the narrator, the one who performs diegesis, is left unspecified in a narration, then its frame of mimesis
is merely hidden from view.[32] As for mimesis pure and simple, on
the other hand, the principle is overt: mimesis is predicated on
such archetypes as gods or heroes, as we have already noted in
the case of Alcman's *Partheneion*.

We may try to sidestep the central idea of mimesis by telling
ourselves that the pronoun "I" used by the one who re-enacts a
given god or hero is at that moment merely an "actor," no matter
who the speaker may be – a member of a chorus, or a chorus-
leader, or even the one whom we identify as the composer. But
I must insist that this kind of "acting" in the context of ar-

---

[29] Zeitlin 1985.195n41 and 199n72.
[30] Zeitlin 1985.96.
[31] N 1990a.387–388.
[32] Cf. N 1992b.320: "Homeric poetry makes no overt reference to its own social
context, the occasions of its own potential performability." Following Martin 1989,
the argument continues (N 1992b.320): "still, if Homeric narrative itself gives us
'texts' within its own 'text', with appropriate contexts to which these 'texts' refer, then
the outer context, out there in the 'real world', is at least indirectly recoverable."

chaic Greek poetry is not a matter of pretending: it is rather a merger of the performer's identity with an identity patterned on an archetype – a merger repeated every time the ritual occasion recurs.

According to this argument, then, mimesis in the older sense of the word requires that the speaker's identity merge with that of his *role* as speaker, just as the identities of those who are spoken to and spoken about must merge with their respective roles. If the merger is successful, then the model has not been merely copied, that is, imitated. It has been remodeled, that is, re-enacted. What is remodeled can continue to be a model. What is merely copied cannot. The paradox here is that a model implies no change, whereas whatever is remodeled does indeed imply change. That is to say, an explicit idea of unchangeability through time subsumes an implicit idea of change in the here-and-now of the occasion of performance.

The premier metaphor for this paradox of re-enactment is *repetition*, as ideally expressed by adverbs or preverbs meaning 'again', such as Greek *deúte* in *Song* 1 of Sappho:[33]

ποικιλόθρον' ἀθανάτ'Αφρόδιτα,
παῖ Δίος δολόπλοκε, λίσσομαί σε,
μή μ' ἄσαισι μηδ' ὀνίαισι δάμνα,
πότνια, θῦμον,

ἀλλὰ τυίδ' ἔλθ', αἴ ποτα κἀτέρωτα   5
τὰς ἔμας αὔδας ἀίοισα πήλοι
ἔκλυες, πάτρος δὲ δόμον λίποισα
χρύσιον ἦλθες

ἄρμ' ὑπασδεύξαισα· κάλοι δέ σ' ἆγον   10
ὤκεες στροῦθοι περὶ γᾶς μελαίνας
πύκνα δίννεντες πτέρ' ἀπ' ὠράνωἴθε-
ρος διὰ μέσσω.

αἶψα δ' ἐξίκοντο· σὺ δ', ὦ μάκαιρα,
μειδιαίσαισ' ἀθανάτωι προσώπωι
ἦρε' ὄττι δηὖτε πέπονθα κὤττι   15
δηὖτε κάλημμι

---

[33] The discussion that follows is expanded in N 1994a, with reference to Horace *Odes* 4.1 and 4.2.

κῶττι μοι μάλιστα θέλω γένεσθαι
μαινόλαι θύμωι· τίνα δηῦτε πείθω
βαῖσ᾽³⁴ ἄγην ἐς σὰν φιλότατα; τίς σ᾽, ὦ
Ψάπφ᾽, ἀδικήει;   20

καὶ γὰρ αἰ φεύγει, ταχέως διώξει,
αἰ δὲ δῶρα μὴ δέκετ᾽, ἀλλὰ δώσει,
αἰ δὲ μὴ φίλει, ταχέως φιλήσει
κωὔκ ἐθέλοισα.

ἔλθε μοι καὶ νῦν, χαλέπαν δὲ λῦσον   25
ἐκ μερίμναν, ὄσσα δέ μοι τέλεσσαι
θῦμος ἰμέρρει, τέλεσον· σὺ δ᾽ αὔτα
σύμμαχος ἔσσο

You with varied embroidered flowers,³⁵ immortal Aphrodite,
child of Zeus, weaver of wiles, I implore you,
do not devastate with aches and sorrows,
Mistress, my spirit!

But come here, if ever at any other time   5
hearing my voice from afar,
you heeded me, and leaving the palace of your father,
golden, you came,

having harnessed the chariot; and you were carried along by
beautiful
swift sparrows over the dark earth
swirling with their dense plumage from the sky through
the   10
midst of the aether,

and straightaway they arrived. But you, O holy one,
smiling with your immortal looks,
kept asking what is it once again this time that has happened
to me and for what reason   15
once again this time do I invoke you,

---

³⁴ See Petropoulos 1993.51, who adduces evidence from the diction of magical
formulae to support the restoration first proposed by Parca 1982.47–48; I agree with
Petropoulos that the wording in Sappho 1.18–19 is based on the language of love
spells, not on "Homeric allusion," as Parca pp. 49–50 claims. Translation: 'whom am
I, this time once again, to persuade, setting out to bring her to your love?'
³⁵ This translation of *poikilóthronos* will be explained in the discussion that follows.

and <u>what</u> is it that I want more than anything to happen
to my frenzied spirit? "Whom am I <u>once again *this*</u> time to
    persuade,
setting out to bring her to your love? Who is doing you,
Sappho, wrong?   20

For if she is fleeing now, soon she will give chase.
If she is not taking gifts, soon she will be giving them.
If she does not love, soon she will love,
    even against her will."

Come to me <u>even now</u>, and free me from harsh   25
anxieties, and however many things
my spirit yearns to get done, *you* do for me. *You*
become my ally in war.

As the song begins, its female speaker invokes Aphrodite, the
archetype of love, in the form of a prayer.[36] The goddess is then
described as flying down from Olympus, but the action takes
place not in a third-person diegesis but still in the second person,
so that the potential diegesis is subsumed by the syntax of prayer.
Then, as the goddess arrives all the way from her distant celestial
realm, she is quoted by the speaker as speaking directly in the
first person to this speaker, who is now suddenly shifted into the
second person (lines 18–24). Aphrodite's first question is: what
is wrong with you *this* time (line 15)? And she is addressing a
woman whom she calls Sappho (line 20). So we see that the
speaker who had started speaking at the beginning of the song
was Sappho. But now, from the standpoint of performance, the
speaker Sappho is speaking in the first person of Aphrodite (lines
18–24): she is in effect re-enacting the goddess. We have earlier
noted a comparable shift to the first person in the songs of
the Changing Woman rituals. Moreover, at the end of Sappho's
prayer, she asks to be the goddess's equal partner, a *súmmakhos*
'fellow warrior' in the warfare of love. The active *teléssai* in place
of the expected passive *telésthēn* at line 26 suggests that the con-
trolling plan is meant to be the mind of Sappho, as if she were
equivalent to Aphrodite herself.[37]

---

[36] Travis 1990 has written a perceptive study of the poetics of prayer in *Song* 1 of
Sappho.
[37] On the poetic contrast between active *teléssai* and passive *telésthēn* in Sappho's
poetics, see N 1990b.259–260.

The re-enactment of Aphrodite as the archetype of love is made manifest by the adverb *dēute* (δηὖτε) 'again, once again *this* time', which refers to the onset of love in the speaker's heart. It is reinforced by the repetition of this adverb denoting repetition – three times at that. And there is further reinforcement in the triple repetition of *ótti/k'ótti* 'what?'. Yet, in this paradox of repetition, the more you hear "again" or "one more time," the more changes you see. It is all an archetypal re-enactment for the archetypal goddess of love, but for the humans who re-enact love it becomes a vast variety of different experiences by different people in different situations. This paradox of repetition brings to mind the words of Kierkegaard: "The dialectic of repetition is easy, for that which is repeated has been – otherwise it could not be repeated – but the very fact that it has been makes the repetition into something new."[38]

The variety of erotic situations suggested by *dēute* (δηὖτε), and highlighted by the instances of *amor versus* at lines 21 to 24, can also be illustrated by the strikingly plentiful set of examples that we find in the relatively few surviving fragments of Anacreon: at PMG 358 golden-haired Eros throws at me *dēute* (δηὖτε) a purple ball; at 376, ἀρθεὶς δηὖτε ἀπὸ Λευκάδος πέτρης ἐς πολιὸν κῦμα κολυμβῶ μεθύων ἔρωτι 'lifting off *dēute* from the white rock I dive down into the gray eddies below, intoxicated with eros'; at 394b, Alexis is wooing *dēute* (δηὖτε); at 400, one is fleeing Eros *dēute* (δηὖτε); at 413, eros smites me *dēute* (δηὖτε) with a great *pelékus* 'double-axe' like a *khalkeús* 'coppersmith', and it washes me in a wintry torrent; at 428, I love *dēute* (δηὖτε) and I do not love/And I am mad and I am not mad. Surveying these and other instances of *dēute* (δηὖτε) in Greek love lyric, Anne Carson remarks about the constituents δή 'now' and αὖτε 'again': "The particle *dē* marks a lively perception in the present moment: 'Look at that now!' The adverb *aûte* peers past the present moment to a pattern of repeated actions stretching behind it: 'Not for the first time!' *Dē* places you in time and emphasizes that placement: *now*. *Aûte* intercepts 'now' and binds it into a history of '*thens*'."[39]

---

[38] Kierkegaard 1983 (=1843) 149.
[39] Carson 1986.118–119.

We could go on with other illustrations, but the point has already been made. Every time I say to myself, "here I go again," I am repeating the pattern of Aphrodite, but each time it is a different experience for me. No wonder Aphrodite is invoked as *poikilóthronos* in the first word of *Song* 1 of Sappho. This epithet, if indeed it is derived from *thróna* 'embroidered flowers' rather than from *thrónos* 'throne', can be translated 'with varied embroidered flowers'.[40] For those who re-enact her, the goddess of love is as limitlessly varied as the limitless varieties of flowers embroidered on her exterior.

Let us compare the experiences of those initiated in the Changing Woman ritual. Keith Basso, one of the most conscientious collectors of Apache traditions, has recorded the conventional Apache understanding that "Changing Woman's power grants longevity."[41] The reason, as he explains, is that "Changing Woman, unlike other mythological figures, has 'never died.'"[42] It is understood that, "although she grows old, she is always able to recapture her youth."[43] Two different accounts were related to Basso by Apache informants, and here is one of them:

> When Changing Woman gets to be a certain old age, she goes walking toward the east. After a while she sees herself in the distance looking like a young girl walking toward her. They both walk until they come together and after that there is only one. She is like a young girl again.[44]

The old identity is here pictured as finding the young identity. Also, the other way around, the young finds the old. They find each other, young and old, old and young, through an everlasting repetition of the Changing Woman ritual. Each repetition of the Changing Woman ritual, old as it is, brings newness, youth, change. I repeat in this context the words of Kierkegaard: "The dialectic of repetition is easy, for that which is repeated has been

---

[40] Putnam 1960–61, with further bibliography. A decisive passage is *Iliad* 22.441, where *thróna poikíla* (θρόνα ποικίλ') refers to 'varied flower patterns' embroidered into the fabric. On the magical properties of the *thróna*, see Petropoulos 1993.53.

[41] Basso 1966.151.

[42] Ibid.

[43] Ibid.

[44] Ibid.

– otherwise it could not be repeated – but the very fact that it has been makes the repetition into something new."[45]

The idea of a meeting between old and new as the core of the Apache Changing Woman ritual may be compared to the story in Lesbian mythology, already noted, about the pursuit of a handsome youth Phaon by all the women of Lesbos, headed by Aphrodite herself, where the mythical pursuit by Aphrodite corresponds to a poeticized pursuit of Phaon by the principal female speaker in Sappho's songs. Phaon's name (*Pháōn*), as we have seen, means 'shining', that is, 'shining like the sun'. Here we may turn to another story taken from the Lesbian myths about this Phaon (the testimonia are collected in Sappho F 211 V).[46] He is an old man who generously ferries an old woman across a strait, only to discover that the old woman is none other than the goddess Aphrodite in disguise. After Aphrodite crosses over the strait, the old woman changes back into a beautiful young goddess, who then confers beauty and youth on Phaon as well (again, Sappho F 211 V).

I once argued "that the figure of Sappho identifies herself with this figure of an old woman."[47] That is, Sappho identifies herself with the goddess Aphrodite not only explicitly in compositions like *Song* 1 but also implicitly by virtue of her poeticized declaration that she loves Phaon: after all, Aphrodite too loved Phaon. In the Lesbian myths about Phaon, I saw an opportunity for Sappho the author to find a precedent, in that she could love Phaon just as Aphrodite had once loved him. Today I would stress not so much Sappho's own authorial identification as the role of the main female speaker in Sappho's songmaking tradition, the performing *prima donna* who is re-enacting not only Sappho but also Aphrodite herself by declaring her own love for Phaon. In the performance of Sappho's songs, the *prima donna* who sings can become for the moment the archetypal Aphrodite through the intermediacy of Sappho, much as the initiand in the Changing Woman ritual *is* Changing Woman through the intermediacy of the chief singer, so long as the ritual lasts. And we

[45] Kierkegaard 1983 (=1843) 149.
[46] N 1990b.262.
[47] Ibid.

may add: much as a Greek bride is called a *númphē*, which can also mean a goddess, but which means 'bride' while the wedding lasts.[48]

To repeat the words of T. S. Eliot (*The Dry Salvages*, 1941), "you are the music/While the music lasts."[49] While the music of Sappho lasts, Aphrodite is present, and whoever performs the music *is* Sappho, *is* the music of Aphrodite. The performers may keep changing from one person to the next as each new time of performance comes round, but it is the old model of Aphrodite that gets repeated, over and over. Each new performer is recomposed in performance, according to the old model. But the old model is in turn renewed by each new performer. Each performance is a meeting of old and new.

This theme of the old finding the new, the new finding the old, as we see it played out in the exotic Lesbian myths about the old ferryman Phaon and his discovery of the eternally young Aphrodite, can lead us back finally to the semantics of an everyday word like French *trouver*, 'to find', derived from "Vulgar Latin" **tropāre*, derived in turn from the school usage of Greek *trópos* 'modulation' in the ultimate sense of 'continuity through variation'. It is this sense that we have found in the earliest attested Greek traditions, in the word *trōpósa* (τρωπῶσα) at *Odyssey* 19.521, describing the nightingale at springtime as she keeps *changing around* or literally *turning* the sound of her beautiful song.[50] An everyday notion of *find* has led back to an ancient songmaking metaphor that paradoxically told of reaching a goal of novelty by maintaining, in a vast variety of ways, a genuine sense of continuity.

---

[48] See ch.3.

[49] Eliot 1963 (=1941) 199.

[50] Antisthenes F 187 connects the epithet of the nightingale, *trōpósa* at *Odyssey* 19.521, with the epithet of Odysseus, *polútropos* 'of many turns' at *Odyssey* 1.1, reasoning that the hero deserves this epithet in part because he is skillful with words. Cf. also the poetic implications of *atropíē* in Theognis 218, as analyzed in N 1990a.425.

PART II

Fixed text in theory, shifting words in performance

5

Multiform epic and Aristarchus' quest for the real Homer

Multiformity, as conveyed by *poludeukés* 'patterning in many different ways', the variant epithet describing the sound of the nightingale in *Odyssey* 19.521, is a key concept in understanding poetry as performance in ancient Greece. This has been the general argument so far, which will now be applied specifically, in the second part of this work, to the heritage of Homeric poetry as performance. The task at hand is to work out a historical perspective of Homeric poetry as it changes over time.[1]

In confronting the dynamics of change in any songmaking tradition, it is useful to apply criteria of fluidity and rigidity. We will find, it must be emphasized at the outset, that some traditions of songmaking are at any given stage relatively more fluid, while others are more rigid; we may even allow for varying degrees of fluidity and rigidity within any one given tradition.[2] In Athenian tragedy, for example, we may expect more phraseological fluidity in some of its aspects, such as the iambic trimeters declaimed by actors, than in others, such as the songs sung and danced by the chorus.[3]

---

[1] Cf. N 1990b.29: "the language of a body of oral poetry like the *Iliad* and *Odyssey* does not and cannot belong to any one time, any one place: in a word, it *defies synchronic analysis*." Cf. di Luzio 1969.11, where he refers to the "diachronic" nature of oral epic composition; cf. D'Ippolito 1984. In my own work, the terms *synchronic/diachronic* refer not to the internal standpoint of any given structure but only to the external standpoint of one who analyzes that structure (cf. N 1990a.4). Thus it is preferable to say that the analysis of oral composition requires the simultaneous application of synchronic and diachronic perspectives, and that the absence of either of these perspectives can lead to a warped analysis. Di Luzio seems to agree, in a formulation that appears toward the end of his work, p. 138.

[2] Cf. Lord 1995 ch.2.

[3] Cf. N 1990a.45–46.

For this important distinction of fluidity and rigidity, there are striking illustrations to be found in other cultures, as in the case of Hungarian dance traditions: it has been observed that "at a certain threshold, when the collective knowledge of the tradition within the community has reached the point where it will no longer support improvisation, the dance form may become solidified into a set sequence of figures and thus preserved – in a rigid, 'canonical' version – for a considerable time after the disappearance of improvisatory dancing."[4] This formulation is ideal for my purposes, provided we understand "improvisatory" in a strictly ethnographic sense as *reworked on the spot, in performance.*[5] In another description of other dance traditions, one anthropologist observes that various structures of performance, as they become progressively more rigid, can suffer "abrupt confrontation and loss."[6]

With reference to this observation, I had described in my earlier work even the pan-Hellenic period of Homeric transmission as relatively rigid in comparison to still earlier periods.[7] And I substituted a more esthetic metaphor for what I have just described as rigidity, resorting to the image of crystallization.[8] This image served to convey the essential idea of an overall "evolutionary model" of Homeric text-fixation, which I envisage not as a single event but as a long-term process, a general progression from more fluid to more rigid phases.[9]

The term "crystallization," used as a metaphor to describe the evolution of a Homeric text without the aid of writing, can be applied also to the evolution of an individual singer's repertoire. In ballad studies, for example, it has been observed that a given song tends to be more fluid when it is being learned by one singer

---

[4] Kraft 1989.278n18, who continues: "I have the impression that this has been the fate of many Hungarian dance traditions in the villages of Hungary proper." For more on the rigid/fluid distinction, see N 1990a.60–61.

[5] Miller 1982b.15 and pp. 5–15 in general, with a catalogue of instances in contemporary scholarship where the term "improvise" has been oversimplified with reference to oral tradition.

[6] Royce 1977.104.

[7] N 1990a.60–61.

[8] N 1990a.53.

[9] Summary in N 1992a.37–53. See also Seaford 1994.144–154. Cook 1995.5 extends my evolutionary model: "the crystallization of the Odyssean tradition into a written text, the growth of Athenian civic ritual, and the process of state formation in Attica were simultaneous and mutually reinforcing developments."

from another and progressively more rigid when it becomes part of the repertoire of the individual singer.[10]

The term has been applied in other fields as well. To mention a particularly striking example: Peter Marler, a biologist who pioneered in a 1981 article the systematic description of stages in the process of a bird's learning its distinctive birdsong, was the first to use the term "crystallization" to designate the definitive stage of birdsong.[11] Also in the forefront of research in this area is Heather Williams, whose work centers on the zebra finch, a type of semidomesticated cagebird.[12] "Most important for Williams' research, the male bird learns its song in a sixty-day period from the thirtieth to ninetieth day after hatching, and thereafter, absent some intervention from the experimenter, it sticks with the same song for life."[13] To quote Williams' own words on the matter: "They stop learning and fix their song when they come into sexual maturity."[14] We may note especially her use of the expression *fix their song.*

With these considerations of fluidity and rigidity serving as a backdrop, let us proceed to analyze the multiformity of Homeric transmission, with the immediate goal of refining the "evolutionary model" of Homeric text fixation by answering various questions of periodization that are raised by this model. The ultimate goal is to lay down the groundwork for a multitext edition of Homer.[15]

Let us begin with an outline, to be defended in the extensive discussion that follows it, of what I see as five distinct consecutive periods of Homeric transmission, "Five Ages of Homer," as it were, with each period showing progressively less fluidity and more rigidity:[16]

---

[10] Andersen 1991, especially p. 26 (where he uses the term "crystallization"), with further bibliography. At p. 37 he says about one of his informants: "Stanley Robertson is capable of imitating the singing styles of his aunt Jeannie and his cousin Lizzie to perfection, but he will never sing like them in public."

[11] Marler 1981. I owe this information to Professor Heather Williams (*per litteras* 23 September 1993).

[12] The results of Williams' work are cited from the lucid account of M. R. Montgomery, *Boston Globe* 26 August 1993 pp. 61 and 64.

[13] Montgomery, ibid.

[14] Montgomery, ibid., quoting Williams.

[15] Cf. the doctoral thesis of Graeme Bird at Harvard University, who is working toward a new multitext edition of Book 1 of the *Iliad*.

[16] The category of "period," used here in setting up tentative boundaries of periodiza-

(1) a relatively most fluid period, with no written texts, extending from the early second millennium into the middle of the eighth century in the first millennium;

(2) a more formative or "pan-Hellenic" period, still with no written texts, from the middle of the eighth century to the middle of the sixth;

(3) a definitive period, centralized in Athens, with potential texts in the sense of *transcripts*,[17] at any or several points from the middle of the sixth century to the later part of the fourth; this period starts with the reform of Homeric performance traditions in Athens during the régime of the Peisistratidai;

(4) a standardizing period, with texts in the sense of transcripts or even *scripts*,[18] from the later part of the fourth century to the middle of the second; this period starts with the reform of Homeric performance traditions in Athens during the régime of Demetrius of Phalerum, which lasted from 317 to 307 BC;

(5) a relatively most rigid period, with texts as *scripture*,[19] from the middle of the second century onward; this period starts with the completion of Aristarchus' editorial work on the Homeric texts, not long after 150 BC or so, which is a date that also marks the general disappearance of the so-called "eccentric" papyri, to be defined later on in the discussion.

There is progressively less variation in each of the five successive periods, though the third, fourth, and fifth yield us progressively more information about variation in all five periods. In previous work, I treated extensively the periods here described as the first and the second, considering in detail both the phenomenon of pan-Hellenism and the reforms that seem to have taken place later on in Athens during the sixth century BC, the era of tyranny when the Peisistratidai ruled Athens.[20] Here I will limit myself to the third, fourth, and fifth periods of Homeric trans-

tion, is meant to be more precise than the category of "phase" and the subcategory of "stage" as I use those words in N 1992a.52.

[17] The word is used in a narrow sense, to be defined below.
[18] The word is used in a narrow sense, to be defined below.
[19] The word is used in a narrow sense, to be defined below.
[20] Summary in N 1995; cf. Sherratt 1990.

mission, working backward in time and devoting less attention than in my previous work to the pivotal role of Athens in the third period.[21] Suffice it to record in passing, at precisely this point, the importance I attach to (1) the reforms of Homeric performance associated with the Peisistratidai in the sixth century BC, centering on the performance traditions at the Feast of the Panathenaia,[22] and (2) the reforms associated with Pericles in the fifth century.[23] Both sets of reforms fall within what we may call the third period of Homeric transmission.[24] In the present

---

[21] For more about the Athenian impact on the Homeric tradition in what I call here the third period, see N 1992a.39–52. For a discussion of the evidence of vase paintings as a criterion for determining the gradual fixation of Homeric traditions around the middle of the sixth century, especially in Athens, see Lowenstam 1993, especially p. 216.

[22] See pp. 69–71 above.

[23] For a reference to reforms, instituted by Pericles, of performance traditions at the Panathenaia, see Plutarch *Pericles* 13.11: φιλοτιμούμενος δ' ὁ Περικλῆς τότε πρῶτον ἐψηφίσατο μουσικῆς ἀγῶνα τοῖς Παναθηναίοις ἄγεσθαι, καὶ διέταξεν αὐτὸς ἀθλοθέτης αἱρεθείς, καθότι χρὴ τοὺς ἀγωνιζομένους αὐλεῖν ἢ ᾄδειν ἢ κιθαρίζειν. ἐθεῶντο δὲ καὶ τότε καὶ τὸν ἄλλον χρόνον ἐν Ὠιδείῳ τοὺς μουσικοὺς ἀγῶνας 'in the course of his ambitious programme, Pericles at that point for the first time had a decree enacted that called for a seasonal contest [*agōn*] of songmaking [*mousikē*] to be held at the Panathenaia, and he himself was the organizer, having been chosen as *athlothétēs*, of the rules that had to be observed, by those competing, in playing the pipe, in singing, or in playing the lyre; both at that point and during later periods, theater-goers would attend the songmaking [*mousikós*] contests [*agōn* plural] in the Odeum'.

[24] Davison 1968.63 argues that Plutarch's reference to Pericles' reform should not be taken to mean that the institutions he mentions actually began with the reform. Herington 1985.86 infers that the contests of *kitharōidoí* 'lyre-singers', *aulōidoí* 'pipe-singers', *kitharistaí* 'lyre-players', *aulētaí* 'pipe-players' – as indicated by αὐλεῖν ἢ ᾄδειν ἢ κιθαρίζειν, may be understood here as being *in addition to* contests of *rhapsōidoí*. I agree, on the comparative basis of parallel wording in other passages such as Isocrates *Panegyricus* 159, where Homeric performances are described as taking place ἐν τοῖς μουσικοῖς ἄθλοις. We may compare also IG XII ix [Euboea, ca. 340 BC] 189 line 5, τιθεῖν τὴμ πόλιν ἀγῶνα μουσικῆς, and lines 10–15 τὴν δὲ μουσικὴν τιθεῖν ῥαψωιδοῖς, | αὐλωιδοῖς, κιθαρισταῖς, κιθαρωιδοῖς, παρωιδοῖς, | τοὺς δὲ τὴν μουσικὴν ἀγωνιζομένους πάντα[ς] | ἀγωνίζεσθαι προσόδιον τεῖ θυσίει ἐν τεῖ αὐλεῖ ἔ[χο]ντας τὴν σκευὴν ἥμπερ ἐν τοῖ ἀγῶνι ἔχουρ[ι]. For more on *rhapsōidoí* in agonistic contexts where they are mentioned as parallel to *kitharōidoí* and *aulōidoí*, see N 1990a.29, 54, 104 (with reference to the Euboean inscription, IG XII ix 189). In light of the fact that Plutarch describes Pericles as taking on the role of *athlothétēs* (καὶ διέταξεν αὐτὸς ἀθλοθέτης αἱρεθείς), we may compare Aristotle *Constitution of the Athenians* 60.1, where the *athlothétai* are described as arranging the Panathenaic procession and the *agōn* of *mousikē*: διοικοῦσι τήν τε πομπὴν τῶν Παναθηναίων καὶ τὸν ἀγῶνα τῆς μουσικῆς. In a future project, I will argue the following point: when Pericles is represented as saying in Thucydides 2.41.4 that "we" Athenians do not need Homer as an *epainétēs*, an official giver of praise, it is implicit that "we" Athenians already *own* Homer and

chapter, however, and also in two more that follow, we will concentrate on periods 4 and 5. Following a reverse chronological order, we will examine in depth the relevance of Aristarchus to the fifth period and of Demetrius of Phalerum to the fourth. It is important to keep in mind from the start that the point of reference in setting up a scheme of five periods of Homeric transmission is the dimension of *performance*, not of *text*. Accordingly, we need special working definitions for the otherwise purely textual terms *transcript*, *script*, and *scripture*, as assigned to the third, fourth, and fifth periods respectively. By *transcript* I mean the broadest possible category of written text: a transcript can be a record of performance, even an aid for performance, but not the equivalent of performance.[25] We must distinguish a transcript from an inscription, which can traditionally refer to itself in the archaic period as just that, an equivalent of performance.[26] As for *script*, I mean a narrower category, where the written text is a prerequisite for performance.[27] By *scripture* I mean the narrowest category of them all, where the written text need not even presuppose performance. In order to alert the reader that this term will be used metaphorically rather than literally – for reasons that become clear in Chapter 7 – "scripture" will regularly be placed within quotation marks.[28]

It is also important to keep in mind the traditional wording that was used to express the idea of performance during the five periods. The word *rhapsōidoí* 'rhapsodes' designates performers of Homer in the reports about reforms of epic performance under the Peisistratidai ("Plato" *Hipparchus* 228b, Diogenes Laertius

---

therefore do not need to hear "our" ownership made explicit by way of excessive references to Athens in the narrative of Homer. Lardinois 1995.161 argues that *Odyssey* 16.161, οὐ γάρ πως πάντεσσι θεοὶ φαίνονται ἐναργεῖς 'for it is not to everyone that the gods appear as manifest' may be interpreted as an oblique Homeric reference, *in the context of Homeric performance at the Panathenaia*, to the "presence" of Athena at the Panathenaia. According to this interpretation, the Homeric verse implies that those attending the Panathenaia are a privileged audience.
[25] N 1992a.41–43.
[26] N 1992a.41–43, with bibliography.
[27] N 1992a.42.
[28] In any case, my literal understanding of "scripture" is not casual: I take seriously the efforts of Smith 1993 to achieve greater semantic precision in using this word. At p. 209, he notes: "even when scripture is seen as, is understood to be, explicitly written, it is an error to suppose that this means written *rather than* oral." Cf. Graham 1987.7.

1.57),[29] and the same word is regularly used in the same sense throughout the stretch of time that has been divided here into periods 3, 4, and 5, with the most prominent examples to be found in Plato's *Ion*.[30] From an overall diachronic perspective of the concept of *rhapsōidoí*,[31] to repeat, "it is simplistic and even misleading to contrast, as many have done, the 'creative' *aoidós* ['singer'] with the 'reduplicating' *rhapsōidós*."[32] Suffice it to add here that the currency of the term *rhapsōidós* can be reconstructed to extend to an era even before that of periods 3, 4, and 5 all taken together, that is, to an era corresponding to what I call here period 2.[33] Moreover, there is a parallel to be drawn between the rhapsodic transmission of Homer and that of Hesiod.[34]

In brief, then, this scheme of five periods in Homeric transmission brings into play primarily the dimension of performance, in particular the traditions of the *rhapsōidoí*, and, secondarily, the dimension of text as a derivative of performance, where each successive period reflects a progressively narrower concept of textuality, from transcript to script to "scripture." It should be stressed again that the ultimate purpose in drawing up this scheme is to lay the groundwork for an eventual multitext edition of Homer, one that would be expected not only to report variant readings but also to relate them wherever possible to different periods in the history of textual transmission, such as the five

---

[29] See ch.3.

[30] N 1990a.22.

[31] Cf. N 1990a.21–28; also N 1990b [1982] 40–47.

[32] N 1990b [1982] 42. This conclusion is corroborated by the article of Ford 1988.

[33] Again, N 1990b [1982] 42. Citti 1966.8 uses the criteria of *stadio di trasmissione libera* and *stadio di trasmissione rigida* to distinguish what he describes as the era of the *aoidós* from that of the *rhapsōidós*. I agree with the wording of his criteria but not with its application to the concepts of *aoidós* and *rhapsōidós*, in that I am arguing for a broader range of applications in the case of the latter word. Also, in the extensive report on rhapsodes in the scholia to Pindar *Nemean* 2.1e, we may note the usage of *apangéllō* in referring to the performance of rhapsodes in the circle of Kynaithos (οἱ περὶ Κύναιθον ... τὴν Ὁμήρου ποίησιν ... ἐμνημόνευον καὶ ἀπήγγελλον) in light of the usage of this same word in Herodotus 7.142.1, as discussed in N 1990a.168. On the relationship of master and disciple in the traditions of the rhapsodes (as indicated by the expression οἱ περὶ Κύναιθον), see Ritoók 1970.23–24.

[34] N 1990a.29n66 on the *sunthútai Mousôn Hēsiodeíōn* 'fellow-sacrificers to the Hesiodic Muses' at Thespiae, *IG* VII 1785. Cf. the reference to *paideutaí* 'students' belonging to a gymnasium called the *Mimnermeîon* (after the poet Mimnermus) at Smyrna, *Ionia/Smyrna doc.* 661.9; there was a gymnasium called the *Homēreîon* (after Homer) at Chios, *Ionia/Chios doc.* 268b4; cf. also the *Homēreîon* at Smyrna, *Ionia/Smyrna doc.* 703.1, and at Delos, *Inscriptions de Délos* 2.443.faceB.fr b.147.

categories proposed here. An example of this kind of approach is my earlier work on variants in the textual transmission of Theognis, especially on the phenomenon of what may be called "Solonian" and "non-Solonian" doublets, which seem linked with different periods in not only the textual history but also the *political* history of Megara and its daughter cities.[35]

It is essential to stress from the start, moreover, that a multi-text edition of Homer is clearly *not* what Aristarchus, who became ultimately the most influential textual critic of Homer in the ancient world, had in mind. The era of Aristarchus corresponds to what has just been described as period 5 in the history of Homeric transmission, when the text of Homer was becoming equivalent to "scripture." By the time we reach the end of the last chapter, I hope that I will have justified my use of this term, as also the overall scheme of the third, fourth, and fifth periods in the history of Homeric transmission. Let us turn, then, to Aristarchus, as we proceed to review the historical circumstances, working backward in time.

Aristarchus of Samothrace became head of the Library of Alexandria sometime after 180 BC, the estimated date of the death of a distinguished predecessor, Aristophanes of Byzantium; we do not know how soon it was after 180 that the accession of Aristarchus took place, but in any case he held on to the position of head of the Library through the reign of Ptolemy VI Philometor, whose death in 145 set off a chain reaction of events climaxing in the violent removal of Philometor's son Ptolemy VII by Philometor's brother Ptolemy VIII; that same year (145/4) Aristarchus departed from Alexandria and from Egypt altogether, along with many of his pupils and other scholars.[36] "From this *secessio doctorum*," it has been said, "the first crisis ensued in the history of scholarship."[37] Looking further backward, let us focus on another key figure, Aristophanes of Byzantium, who had been head of the Library probably starting with the death of Eratosthenes, perhaps sometime between 196 and 193 BC, until his death, around 180 BC.[38] These two figures,

[35] N 1985.46–51.
[36] Pfeiffer 1968.210–212.
[37] Pfeiffer 1968.212.
[38] Pfeiffer 1968.172.

Aristophanes and especially Aristarchus, are essential for my formulation of period 5.

There is a mass of references to Aristarchus in the Homeric scholia, especially in those of the tenth-century Venetus A manuscript of the *Iliad*.[39] From these references, derived in large part from the reports of Didymus (second half of the first century BC and beginning of the first AD), we may infer that Aristarchus was the author of a *hupómnēma* 'commentary' on Aristophanes' *ékdosis* 'edition' of Homer, also known as *diórthōsis*, and that he later went on to produce his own edition, also writing a commentary to accompany it, which in turn was followed by a revised edition made by members of his school.[40] These *ekdóseis* or *diorthóseis* 'editions' and *hupomnḗmata* 'commentaries', it has been argued, were all still available to Didymus.[41] We know many details about Aristarchus' editorial methodology from the Homeric scholia, especially from the scholia of Venetus A, and we even know from the reports of Didymus (also of Aristonicus, Nicanor, and Herodian), as recorded or paraphrased primarily in the A scholia, about the texts used by Aristarchus and about his editorial judgments concerning their relative worth.[42]

We must immediately confront the problems raised by the concept of *edition* here. The terms *ékdosis* and *diórthōsis*, commonly used in the scholia and elsewhere, may be interpreted to mean 'edition' only within limits, even in the case of critics like Aristarchus.[43] To the extent that he produced his own texts of

---

[39] Edited by Erbse 1969–1988. On the D-scholia, not covered in Erbse's edition, see Montanari 1979.3–25 (cf. Henrichs 1971, especially pp. 100–105).

[40] The historical sequence formulated here, with an Aristophanes edition followed by an Aristarchus commentary followed by an Aristarchus edition followed by a second Aristarchus commentary followed by a second edition by the school of Aristarchus, is essentially the construct of Pfeiffer 1968.217; followed by Janko 1992.26. On the second edition, supposedly produced by Aristarchus' students, see Apthorp 1980.132. On the notion of a *hupómnēma* 'commentary', see Lührs 1992.10, who visualizes it as a combination of what we would call an *apparatus criticus* and a *commentarius criticus*. On the early sources of the D-scholia, especially as mediated in the format of the *hupómnēma*, see Montanari 1979.14–15.

[41] Pfeiffer 1968.217–218.

[42] Janko 1992.26. Also Ritoók 1987.15, who summarizes the Alexandrian editorial criteria of preferring some readings over others as follows: relative age of manuscript, majority of manuscripts showing a given reading, quality of given manuscript, internal evidence.

[43] Allen 1924.307 says that the editions of the Alexandrians "were not editions in the modern sense, that is so many hundred copies (ἴσα) produced by scribes from a

Homer, which were to be used as a point of reference in the Library of Alexandria, the interpretation of *ékdosis* or *diórthōsis* as 'edition' seems to fit.[44] Still, the usage of these same terms in the context of references to the work of other critics may fall short of what we would mean by an edition.[45]

With these qualifications in mind, let us consider the editorial criteria of Aristarchus, as transmitted mainly through the writings of Didymus. It appears that Aristarchus deemed as *khariésterai* 'more elegant' and *khariéstatai* 'most elegant' the texts of Homer that were "edited" by previous scholars, as also the undated texts known as the *politikaí* or 'city editions' stemming from Chios, Argos, Cyprus, Sinope, Massalia, and so on.[46] Conversely, he deemed as *eikaîa* or *eikaiótera* 'random' and *phaûla* or *phaulótera*

---

single original. The words *ékdosis* and *diórthōsis* were often verbals and meant 'proposal for edition', and 'revision'." From the usage of the Homeric scholia, I infer that *ékdosis* means the production of a new copy containing readings based on the procedure of *diórthōsis*. This procedure entails, if we follow Pfeiffer p. 94, the collating of manuscripts and the emending of texts – which would amount to a "recension." We should expect, of course, the quality of the procedure to vary from editor to editor (cf. Cameron 1990.117 on the editorial criteria of Eutocius, early sixth century AD). I prefer the formulation of Blum 1991.65n10, who says that *ékdosis* and *diórthōsis* are practically the same: "there was no *ékdosis* without *diórthōsis*, there were only different degrees of *diórthōsis*."

[44] The work of Apthorp 1980, reinforcing the arguments of Pfeiffer 1968.215–217 against Erbse 1959, argues persuasively that Aristarchus did indeed produce his own texts of Homer. Cf. Lührs 1992.6–13. For reasons about to be discussed, however, I am not persuaded by Apthorp's arguments that the texts of Aristarchus recovered practically all that was genuine in the Homeric tradition, any more than I am persuaded by the arguments of others, also about to be discussed, seeking to prove that Aristarchus' editorial work was riddled with spurious conjectures. Further, we will see that there are important insights to be gained from the position taken by Erbse and defended by Nickau 1977.18–19 against Pfeiffer, especially with reference to the fluidity, however reduced, of textual transmission even after the editions of Aristarchus.

[45] On the vagueness of the term *ékdosis* as used in texts other than the scholia and with reference to the work of other scholars, for example Apollonius Dyscolus, see also Nickau 1977.18–19n39, citing a concession on this point by Pfeiffer 1968.216.

[46] Allen 1924.283–296, 297–299; cf. Janko 1992.22 and Apthorp 1980.47–48. As Apthorp (1980.102n2) points out, feminine adjectives like *khariésterai* presuppose nouns like *ekdóseis* 'editions' (in however limited a sense). I find one clear instance, scholia A to *Iliad* 3.10, where the Chios and the Massalia texts are referred to as *ekdóseis* 'editions'. For reasons that will become clear later, it is important to note the usage of the superlative *khariéstatai* 'most elegant', as in the scholia to *Iliad* 2.53a (A), 2.164a (A), 2.192b (A), 2.196c (T), 3.18a (A), 3.51 (A). Moreover, in the scholia to *Odyssey* 10.70 (hypothesis format), a reading adopted by Zenodotus is followed by the following comment: καὶ ἔστι χαριεστάτη ἡ γραφή 'and it is this way of writing it that is most elegant [*khariestátē*]'.

'inferior' the texts of Homer that were not so "edited."[47] Included under this heading of "worse" were the text or texts called *koiné* in the singular and *koinaí* in the plural, which Richard Janko and others interpret as the 'common' or 'popular' texts, as if they were merely a default category; the same goes for the term *dēmódeis* 'popular'.[48] This version of Homer is the so-called "Vulgate."

In what follows, the argument is that the *koiné*, which I prefer to call not the "Vulgate" but simply the Koine, can be traced back to a distinct category, even if it did indeed in the course of time become merged into a default category along with any other "unedited" and therefore "inferior" manuscripts.[49] In positing an earlier distinct status for the Koine, I will be in partial disagreement with Janko, but for now it is more important to stress my agreement with his argument that Aristarchus was unjustified if he deemed inferior those variants that happen to be recorded in the *koinaí*.[50] I also agree with Janko's argument that the readings of the *koinaí* often "preserve oddities" that the other manuscript traditions level out – oddities "which are now explained from comparative philology or oral composition."[51] But again I disagree, at least in part, with his inference that these "oddities" prove that "the 'common' texts are usually superior."[52] The empirical methods of comparative philology and the study of oral

---

[47] Allen 1924.277–278; cf. Janko 1992.26 and Apthorp 1980.47–48. As Apthorp (1980.102n2) points out, neuter adjectives like *eikaîa* presuppose nouns like *antígrapha* 'copies'.

[48] Janko 1992.22, 26. I find one case, scholia A to *Il.* 17.214, where *koinaí* explicitly describes *ekdóseis*, that is, the word for 'edition' (in however limited a sense) in the plural. Janko 1992.26n29 argues that the references by Didymus epitomators to "all" or "most" manuscripts should be understood to mean all or most of the *named* editions (including that of Aristarchus himself), not the manuscripts in general. There may be, however, an analogous pattern of reference to *unnamed* editions, if Allen 1924.278 is justified in printing the emended reading of scholia A at *Iliad* 8.349, αἱ πλείους τῶν δημωδῶν 'the majority of the *dēmódeis* 'popular (texts)' (emended by Villoison from αἱ πλείους τὴν δημώδη), which would be the equivalent of αἱ πλείους 'the majority' in scholia T.

[49] Cf. the question formulated by Allen 1924.278: "is there ground to believe that the *koiné* originally meant 'usual', 'universal', and that the disparaging sense was secondary?" The discussion that follows will treat in detail Allen's own answer to this question.

[50] Janko 1992.26.

[51] Ibid.

[52] Ibid.

tradition can be used to defend a variant reading as traditional, not as superior. On the basis of comparative studies of textual variation in manuscript traditions that are based on oral traditions, these same empirical methods can be used to defend variant readings that happen to be attested only in manuscripts judged inferior by editors ancient or modern.[53]

The problem is that any given variant reading attested in texts that Aristarchus or his followers deemed "superior" and editors like Janko now deem "inferior" may be suspected of being an ancient editor's conjecture rather than a genuine variant derived from oral traditions. The word *conjecture* is used here in an extreme sense, to indicate a hypothetical situation where an editor rejects all variant readings that he finds in the manuscripts and substitutes a reading of his own invention – his own rewriting – into the master copy.

If indeed it were simply a matter of conjectures, Janko would be justified in treating the Homer texts "edited" by ancient scholars as less valuable for his purposes than the "unedited" manuscripts, which I prefer to describe as the *less edited* manuscripts – less edited, that is, from the standpoint of the Alexandrian critics. But I will now argue that even the more "corrected" texts of Homer, including whatever traces there may be of the editions of Alexandrian Homer critics earlier than Aristarchus, can provide genuine variants stemming from oral traditions. The argument will extend to a still earlier Homer critic, Aristotle.[54]

The problem can be restated this way: if we read a report about an ancient critic who makes a *diórthōsis* or 'correction' in a manuscript of Homer, especially in contexts where the report itself questions the judgment of the given critic, are we to assume that this *diórthōsis* can only be a conjecture?[55] For an example of such a report, let us consider an anecdote in Plutarch *Alcibiades* 7, the

---

[53] Cf. e.g. Davidson 1994.54–72.

[54] On references to a *diórthōsis* of the *Iliad* by Aristotle, see Blum 1991.21–22 and 69–70n45, who nevertheless sides with the view that "the Alexandrian philologists of Homer ... did not pay any attention to the Aristotelian *diórthōsis* of the *Iliad*" (p. 70). On a possible explanation for any gaps in references by Alexandrian critics to the editorial judgments of the Peripatetic School, see below.

[55] The phrasing here reflects the attested usage of *diórthōsis* in the sense of an ad hoc editorial judgment, as distinct from that of an overall editorial procedure. Both senses are well represented in the Homer scholia.

setting of which is to be dated 435 BC, that tells of an Athenian teacher who claims to own a copy of Homer that he himself had corrected; the verb here is *diorthóō* 'correct' (ἑτέρου δὲ φήσαντος ἔχειν Ὅμηρον ὑφ' ἑαυτοῦ διωρθωμένον).[56] Alcibiades follows up with a play on words: he remarks mockingly that the teacher is "correcting" Homer instead of students (Plutarch *ibid.*). We may note in this context another anecdote, this one reported by Diogenes Laertius (9.113) about Timon of Phleious (ca. 320–230 BC), who advised Aratus to read *tà arkhaîa antígrapha* 'the ancient copies' of Homer, not those that were 'already corrected', *édē diō-rthōména* (ἤδη διωρθωμένα); again the verb is *diorthóō* 'correct'. Rudolf Pfeiffer has suggested that Timon was here "alluding no doubt to the editorial work of Zenodotus."[57] Rudolf Blum goes further, associating such an example of *diórthōsis* with the school of Aristotle himself.[58]

Let us start with Zenodotus and then work our way back to Aristotle. The attitude of Timon as it is reported here is indeed clearly antithetical to that of Zenodotus – and even more so to that of Aristarchus. For Aristarchus, copies that were "already corrected" would have been "superior," as we have seen from the testimony of the Homer scholia. We may note again that Pfeiffer immediately associates the very word *diorthóō* 'correct' with the "editorial work" of Zenodotus.[59] He has good reasons, as we will now see from a brief review of relevant facts suggesting that Zenodotus was a methodological forerunner of Aristarchus.

Though there are controversies surrounding the precise date, Zenodotus of Ephesus was put in charge of the Library of Alexandria about a hundred years before Aristarchus became head of the Library.[60] Zenodotus is described in the *Suda* as the first

---

[56] Blum 1991.70n46.

[57] Pfeiffer 1968.98; cf. also the perceptive remarks of Rengakos 1993.15.

[58] Blum 1991.22. We would expect questions of *diórthōsis* to be raised in the six books of Aristotle's *Homeric Questions*, now lost, to which Diogenes Laertius 5.81 makes reference.

[59] Pfeiffer 1968.98.

[60] Blum 1991.101 considers 291 BC as a possible date for Zenodotus' appointment, but he judiciously weighs the alternative possibilities of later datings. On this topic, I await the forthcoming book of J. D. Morgan, who has revived the long-neglected argument that it was Ptolemy II, not Ptolemy I, who appointed Zenodotus head of the Library of Alexandria and tutor to his children, and that Ptolemy III, not Ptolemy II,

diorthōtḗs 'corrector' – let us at least for the moment continue to render this word as 'editor' – of the Homeric poems.[61] In the *Prolegomena* to Tzetzes' excerpts from Scholia on Aristophanes and Dionysius Thrax, there is a catalogue of the earliest Alexandrian critics who *diōrthṓsanto* 'edited' various ancient books, and it is said that "Zenodotus at first and later Aristarchus" should be given credit for "editing" what are vaguely called the "poetic" books (τὰς δὲ ποιητικὰς Ζηνόδοτος πρῶτον καὶ ὕστερον Ἀρίσταρχος διωρθώσαντο).[62] The editorial work of Zenodotus included, besides Homer, Hesiod and Pindar.[63] Pfeiffer summarizes his own interpretation of the data: Zenodotus "was indeed the first *diorthōtḗs* of the Homeric and other poems, revising and emending the text, and [the word *diorthóō*] was the proper technical term."[64] The reference to Aristarchus, he goes on to say, "proves conclusively that this is what the *Prolegomena* mean."[65]

Such a parallel assessment of Zenodotus and Aristarchus brings us back to the problem of determining to what extent we may interpret a *diórthōsis* of Homer by any critic as an 'edition'. Even in the case of Aristarchus, it should be stressed again, there is only a limited conceptual equivalence of *diorthóō* 'correct' with contemporary notions of *edit a text*.[66] There are also other related problems. Is the critic who is responsible for a given *diórthōsis* reliable? Or at least are his methods of *diórthōsis* to be trusted? Further, are the theoretical underpinnings of his methods sound?

---

made Apollonius of Rhodes head of the library and tutor to his son Ptolemy IV, not Ptolemy III. This reassessed chronology makes it possible to date Zenodotus' editorial activity to the reign of Ptolemy II (283–246), after the death of Demetrius of Phalerum in the late 280s (on which subject there is more in ch.7).

[61] For an objective assessment of the *Suda* reference on Zenodotus, see Blum 1991.101. The idea that Zenodotus, in the process of editing Homer, did indeed produce his own *text* is argued – to my mind persuasively – by Rengakos 1993.12–14 (his discussion also provides an admirable bibliographical survey of opposing views). He also argues that Aristarchus had direct access to the Homer edition of Zenodotus, even if Didymus and Aristonicus may not have (p. 14). So too Apollonius of Rhodes and Callimachus, both contemporaries of Zenodotus, had access to such a text (ibid.). More on this point later, p. 138.

[62] Pfeiffer 1968.105–106.
[63] Pfeiffer 1968.117–118.
[64] Pfeiffer 1968.106.
[65] Ibid.
[66] Cf. Allen's argument on *diórthōsis*, as quoted at pp. 115–116n43.

Even if the answers are positive in the case of, say, Aristarchus, can we extend such a positive assessment further back to Zenodotus? The last question can be taken even further back, to Aristotle. It has been shown that Aristotle was very much engaged in research on problems of Homeric textual transmission.[67] Moreover, there is considerable evidence linking him with the very concept of *diórthōsis*. Aristotle consistently uses the verb *diorthóō* 'correct' and its abstract derivative *diórthōsis* in the sense of *provide the right interpretation of a difficult text*, or *provide the right solution to a question (erótēma)*; as in *Sophistici Elenchi* (chapters 18 and 19).[68] In the same work, we even find the expression τὸν Ὅμηρον ἔνιοι διορθοῦνται 'some people correct [*diorthóō*] Homer' (*Sophistici Elenchi* 166b3), with reference to an exegetical problem at *Iliad* 23.328: some critics interpret the OY in the received text as οὖ instead of οὐ (cf. also Aristotle *Poetics* 1461a21).[69] It seems that such "corrections" were envisioned as markings in the margins or diacritics in the text itself.[70] For the sophistic tradition in general and for Aristotle in particular, the format of *diórthōsis* was a matter of marginalia.[71] A case in point is Aristotle's mention of the *parásēmon* 'marginal mark' in *Sophistici Elenchi* 177b, in a context of discussing a variant accentuation (and breathing).[72] We may note as well the wording used to describe a copy of Homer owned by Alexander the Great: φέρεται γοῦν τις διόρθωσις τῆς Ὁμήρου ποιήσεως, ἡ ἐκ τοῦ νάρθηκος λεγομένη, τοῦ Ἀλεξάνδρου μετὰ τῶν περὶ Καλλισθένη καὶ Ἀνάξαρχον ἐπελθόντος καὶ σημειωσαμένου τινά 'it is reported that there was a *diórthōsis* of the poetry of Homer, called "the one from the *nárthēx*," when Alexander with Callisthenes and Anaxarchus went over it and

---

[67] Blum 1991.22.

[68] Laum 1928.105.

[69] Laum 1928.104–105. Aristotle *Poetics* 1461a21 identifies Hippias of Thasos as the initiator of the interpretation οὖ instead of οὐ. What matters here is not the philological validity of the interpretation itself, which is negligible, but the usage of the word *diorthóō* with reference to diacritics. Cf. Hintenlang 1961.76n1, who also gives another example of such issues of interpretation: Aristotle *Poetics* 1461a22–23 (cf. Plato *Republic* 383a) on δίδομεν for δίδομεν at *Iliad* 2.15.

[70] Laum ibid.

[71] Laum 1928.108.

[72] Laum 1928.106. As Andrew Dyck points out to me, it may well be that the mark was "marginal" to the word, not to the text.

made some marks [*sēmeîa*] on it' (Strabo 13.1.27).[73] Elsewhere, we hear that this *nárthēx* edition of Homer resulted from a *diórthōsis* of Aristotle himself, Ἀριστοτέλους διορθώσαντος (Plutarch *Life of Alexander* 8.2).[74] The editorial format or *diórthōsis* of Zenodotus and of those like Aristarchus who came after him was likewise a matter of marginalia. There is in fact a noticeable continuity from Aristotle to Aristarchus not only in the format of *diórthōsis* but also in the discourse associated with it, as evidenced most clearly in the case of Aristarchus himself, whose criteria at times bear a striking resemblance to those represented by the school of Aristotle. Let us take for example Aristarchus' criterion of *khariésterai* 'more elegant' or *khariéstatai* 'most elegant', which as we have seen was applied with reference to the "edited" texts of Homer. I have found the same critical term in an earlier fourth-century context. The speaker is Isocrates, and the work in question is the last oration that he composed, the *Panathenaicus* or "Panathenaic" speech, issued in 339 BC, when the author was ninety-seven years old.[75] As the author makes clear, an illness had prevented him from finishing the work earlier (*Panathenaicus* 267–270), and it seems that he had originally intended to issue the work on the occasion of the Great Panathenaia of 342 BC (*Panathenaicus* 7).[76] We are about to see Isocrates referring negatively to some so-called "sophists in the Lyceum."[77] These sophists are said to practice the art of the rhapsodes (1) as they perform the poems of Homer, Hesiod, or others and (2) as they are *mnēmoneúontes*

---

[73] See Callisthenes FGH 124 T 10; cf. Pfeiffer 1968.71.

[74] The *Vita Marciana* speaks of Aristotle's *ékdosis* of the *Iliad*, which he gave to Alexander (τὰ γεγραμμένα αὐτῷ Ὁμηρικὰ ζητήματα, καὶ ἡ τῆς Ἰλιάδος ἔκδοσις ἣν ἔδωκε τῷ Ἀλεξάνδρῳ Aristotle *Fragments* p. 427.5 Rose). In the *Vita Latina*, this edition is called a *dictamen* (*homerica commenta scripta ab eo et Yliadis dictamen quod dedit Alexandro* Aristotle *Fragments* p. 443.5-6 Rose). For more on the *nárthēx* edition of Homer – and on the reliability of the reports about it – see ch.7.

[75] It goes without saying that, for Isocrates, the writing of a speech, expressed by way of *gráphō* 'write' (cf. *Panathenaicus* 1), is tantamount to the composing and even the notional "delivering" of a speech. On *gráphō* 'write' as a notional speech-act, see N 1990a.233n86.

[76] Cf. Jebb 1893 II 113.

[77] Although the Lyceum cannot be identified specifically with the school of Aristotle until a later period (after the philosopher's death, when his successor Theophrastus institutionalized the school in the Lyceum), the place was known as a sort of forum for philosophers even before the era of Isocrates (cf. e.g. Plato *Lysis* 203a).

'mentioning', in a supposedly derivative way, the *khariéstata* or 'most elegant things' about these poems:

περὶ μὲν οὖν τῶν πεπαιδευμένων τυγχάνω ταῦτα γιγνώσκων. περὶ δὲ τῆς Ὁμήρου καὶ τῆς Ἡσιόδου καὶ τῆς τῶν ἄλλων ποιήσεως ἐπιθυμῶ μὲν εἰπεῖν, οἶμαι γὰρ ἂν παῦσαι τοὺς ἐν τῷ Λυκείῳ ῥαψῳδοῦντας τἀκείνων καὶ ληροῦντας περὶ αὐτῶν, αἰσθάνομαι δ' ἐμαυτὸν ἔξω φερόμενον τῆς συμμετρίας τῆς συντεταγμένης τοῖς προοιμίοις.

Such, then, are my opinions about educated men. As for the poetry of Homer and Hesiod and the others, I [=Isocrates] do have the desire to speak about it, since I think I could silence those who rhapsodically perform [*rhapsōidéō*] their poems in the Lyceum and speak idly about them, but I sense that I am being carried along beyond the proportion set for the introductory remarks.

Isocrates *Panathenaicus* (*Oration* 12) 33

μικρὸν δὲ πρὸ τῶν Παναθηναίων τῶν μεγάλων ἠχθέσθην δι' αὐτούς. ἀπαντήσαντες γάρ τινές μοι τῶν ἐπιτηδείων ἔλεγον ὡς ἐν τῷ Λυκείῳ συγκαθεζόμενοι τρεῖς ἢ τέτταρες τῶν ἀγελαίων σοφιστῶν καὶ πάντα φασκόντων εἰδέναι καὶ ταχέως πανταχοῦ γιγνομένων διαλέγοιντο περί τε τῶν ἄλλων ποιητῶν καὶ τῆς Ἡσιόδου καὶ τῆς Ὁμήρου ποιήσεως, οὐδὲν μὲν παρ' αὐτῶν λέγοντες, τὰ δ' ἐκείνων ῥαψῳδοῦντες καὶ τῶν πρότερον ἄλλοις τισίν εἰρημένων τὰ χαριέστατα μνημονεύοντες· ἀποδεξαμένων δὲ τῶν περιεστώτων τὴν διατριβὴν αὐτῶν ἕνα τὸν τολμηρότατον ἐπιχειρῆσαί με διαβάλλειν, λέγονθ' ὡς ...

But, a short time before the Great Panathenaia, I [=Isocrates] got very annoyed at them [=Isocrates' detractors]. For, according to what was reported to me by some friends that I happened to meet, there were these run-of-the-mill sophists, sitting together in the Lyceum, three or four of them, the kind who tell you that they know everything, the kind who quickly turn up at every occasion, and here they were discussing various poets, and especially the poetry of Hesiod and Homer, saying on their own part nothing about them but rather performing rhapsodically [*rhapsōidéō*] their poems [that is, the poems of Homer, Hesiod, and other poets] and mentioning [*mnēmoneúō*] the most elegant things [*khariéstata*] taken from what has previously been said [about the poems] by others. Then, when the bystanders showed their approval of their [=the sophists'] performance [*diatribḗ*], the most audacious of the lot started trying to slander me, saying that ...

Isocrates Panathenaicus (Oration 12) 18–19

We may note with interest the criterion of *khariéstata* 'the most elegant things' that these men are "mentioning" about poets like Homer, Hesiod, or others. This criterion, attributed to these "sophists in the Lyceum" who perform just like rhapsodes and who allegedly offer no critical judgment of their own about such poets, resorting instead to "what has previously been said by others," seems to me a precursor of the Aristarchean criteria which privilege those Homer editions that are supposedly *khariésterai* 'more elegant' or *khariéstatai* 'most elegant' – and which prefer the variant reading that is supposedly *khariestátē* 'most elegant'.[78]

We may note also the idea that these "sophists in the Lyceum" are *mnēmoneúontes* 'mentioning' received knowledge about these poems, which they are able to perform just like rhapsodes. The question arises: are they not only performing but also 'commenting' or 'making commentaries' on these poems by virtue of 'mentioning' received knowledge about them?[79] We may compare the claim of Socrates, in Plato's *Ion*, that a rhapsode is expected to be a *hermēneús* 'interpreter' of a poet like Homer, and that therefore he must surely know the poet's intention, or *diánoia* (531c). In other words, the rhapsode is expected to make a commentary on the poet he performs.[80] To which Ion replies that he

---

[78] For these usages in the Homeric scholia, see p. 116n46.

[79] On the possibility that the "commentaries" of Zenodotus, accompanying his edition of Homer, had the format of *oral disquisitions* rather than *written texts*, see Rengakos 1993.14. In the case of Aristarchus, on the other hand, we can be more certain that his *hupomnḗmata* 'commentaries' were indeed written texts: see p. 115n40 above.

[80] The verb used in Plato *Ion* 530a for the rhapsode's performance is *diatríbō*, which matches the noun *diatribḗ* that we have seen used in the passage from Isocrates with reference to the performance of the "sophists in the Lyceum." We note again the idea that these "sophists" are *mnēmoneúontes* 'mentioning' received knowledge about the poet they perform; so also in the *Ion*, the rhapsode notes that his attention is always awakened when someone "mentions" Homer, and the verb used is *mimnḗiskomai*

can indeed "speak" most beautifully <u>about Homer</u>, more so than any of his predecessors (καὶ οἶμαι κάλλιστα ἀνθρώπων λέγειν περὶ Ὁμήρου 530c; cf. 533c–d), and that the *diánoiai* that he "speaks" <u>about Homer</u> are more <u>beautiful</u> than those spoken by any of his predecessors (ὡς οὔτε Μητρόδωρος ὁ Λαμψακηνὸς οὔτε Στησίμβροτος ὁ Θάσιος οὔτε Γλαύκων οὔτε ἄλλος οὐδεὶς τῶν πώποτε γενομένων ἔσχεν εἰπεῖν οὕτω πολλὰς καὶ καλὰς διανοίας περὶ Ὁμήρου ὅσας ἐγώ 530c–d).[81]

Although the format of *diórthōsis* was a matter of marginalia for both Aristotle and Aristarchus, we can expect to find important changes or improvements in the system of the Alexandrian critics. One such change is the way in which Aristotle and Aristarchus deal with accentual idiosyncrasies in Homer. For Aristotle, as we have seen, questions of Homeric accent were a matter of *diórthōsis*. For Aristarchus, by contrast, such questions were to be taken up not in the *diórthōsis* – which is by now to be interpreted in a more strict sense, closer to our own notions of 'edition' – but in the *hupomnḗmata* or 'commentaries'. Accents were not part of the text, as Aristarchus understood the concept of text. The assumption of Karl Lehrs and others[82] that the Homer edition of Aristarchus entailed the systematic placement of accent-signs over the words of Homeric verses has been challenged – successfully, I think – by Bernhard Laum.[83] Rather, it appears that Aristarchus' information on accentual variations in Homer was primarily recorded in his *hupomnḗmata* 'commentaries', and that only in a later era did some of this information make its

(ἐπειδὰν δέ τις περὶ Ὁμήρου μνησθῇ 532c); this verb is here made parallel to *dialégesthai* 'engage in discourse' (ὅταν μέν τις περὶ ἀλλοῦ του ποιητοῦ διαλέγηται 532b). Later on in the *Ion*, the same theme of the rhapsode's awakened attention is transferred from the act of making comments on the poet (περὶ μὲν Ὁμήρου ὅταν τις μνησθῇ 536c) to the act of actually performing the poet (ἐπειδὰν μέν τις ἄλλου τοῦ ποιητοῦ ᾄδῃ 536b).

[81] At Plato *Ion* 531a–b, the rhapsode's "speaking about Homer" is now expressed by way of *exēgéomai* – a term even more appropriate to the idea of "commentary."

[82] Lehrs 1882.248–249.

[83] Laum 1928.60. Laum's work remains indispensable, despite the need for some corrections (cf. the bibliography in Turner 1987.159). On the invention, by the Alexandrian critic Aristophanes of Byzantium, of the actual notation-system for ancient Greek accents, see Laum p. 62. At pp. 100–102, Laum prints the testimony from the manuscript Parisinus 2102 reporting Aristophanes' invention, and he traces this testimony, however flawed, to Theodosius of Alexandria, who flourished around 400 AD. Pfeiffer 1968.179n1 questions the reliability of the text as printed by Laum.

way from there into the marginalia of later Homer texts.[84] In sum, it would seem that Aristarchus' information on Homeric accentuation, however valuable it must have been, did not get systematically transferred into the texts of the Alexandrian Homer editions.[85]

The situation was not radically different in the case of texts from outside the Library, as evidenced by the papyri from Hellenized Egypt: even these texts, some of which we may expect to have served as "scripts" – for learning situations or even for performances before audiences – are very seldom marked *systematically* for accent.[86] Still, we can draw some additional inferences from the papyri, given that the accentual notations that we find in these texts, however sporadic the attestations, served a practical purpose. For the Alexandrian critics, questions of accent were primarily though not exclusively a matter of exegesis: since accent may be the only element distinguishing one word from another, it can be crucial to know the accent in order to distinguish one meaning from another.[87] For readers of papyri, by contrast, questions of accent were primarily a matter of getting the pronunciation

---

[84] Laum 1928.62. Of the over 150 mentions of Aristarchean *diórthōsis* that Laum counted in the Homer scholia, he found *in those contexts* only a single reference to an accentual variation noted by Aristarchus (scholia A to *Iliad* 13.191, χρόος instead of χροός).

[85] Laum 1928.327.

[86] Ibid. It can be said in general for Greek literature that only in the Byzantine editions of the ninth and tenth centuries did it become a regular practice to mark the accent on each word in a given text (ibid.). Laum 1928.63n2 finds a dramatic illustration of neglected accent-markings in the case of a papyrus containing Menander's *Perikeiromene*, dated between the first and second centuries AD, with punctuations meticulously supplied (three different categories), with miswritings corrected, with variants added, with elided letters restored, with role-assignments straightened out – *and with no accent-marks.*

[87] Laum 1928.329. It is not the accents of individual words that turn out to be different in the earlier sources: rather, it is the accentuation of word-combinations. For example, though modern editors print a polysyllabic oxytone word consistently with a grave accent when that word is followed by another word without an obvious intervening syntactical break, the evidence of the papyri and of the Homeric scholia indicates that the accent in this context could in fact be acute, not grave: see Laum 1928. 152, 159, 161. (Cf. the formulation of West 1992.199 concerning a general tendency in ancient Greek melodic traditions: "when the accent [is] on the final syllable of a word, and is not circumflex, and not succeeded by a grammatical pause, then the melody does not fall again until after the next accent.") I say "could," not "should," because Moore-Blunt 1978 has found several instances of papyri dated earlier than 400 AD where we do see the spelling of grave as well as acute in this same context (cf. Mazzucchi 1979). Laum treats the earlier pattern of acute spellings as a *constant,*

right.[88] In the papyri, especially in those texts that served as
scripts or quasi-scripts for performance[89] or just for teaching,[90]
we see that accent tends to be marked mostly where it differed
from everyday pronunciation: the maximum accentual difference
– and therefore the maximum accentual marking – is to be found
in the poetic texts and the minimum, in the prosaic.[91]

Despite these difficulties that we encounter in trying to recover
the information that Aristarchus and his predecessors had collected about Homeric accentual idiosyncrasies, this information is
vital for purposes of arguing (1) that there was a continuum from
Aristotle to Aristarchus in the procedures of editing and commenting on the Homeric text and (2) that there was a continuum
in Homeric performance traditions that are indirectly reflected by
these procedures.

The Homeric accentual idiosyncrasies reported by the Alexandrian critics are an ideal test-case, in that even Aristarchus, as we
have seen, treated accents as if they were not integral to the Homeric textual transmission, thus giving us reason to think that
accents were instead part of the Homeric performance tradition
inherited by rhapsodes. Moreover, we have noted a scholarly interest, as early as the fourth century, in the idiosyncrasies of Homeric
accentuation and even in the actual performances of rhapsodes. In
the first case, we have seen that Aristotle himself spoke of Homeric
accentual questions in terms of *diórthōsis*. In the second case, we
have seen Isocrates' disparaging picture of "sophists" acting like
rhapsodes by performing Homeric, Hesiodic, or other such poems
and by delivering learned commentaries about them.[92]

whereas in fact it seems to be a gradually disappearing *tendency*. The point remains – and
Laum says this just as effectively as Moore-Blunt – that earlier patterns of ancient Greek
accentuation are conditioned by the melodic contour, as it were, of the overall syntax.

[88] Laum 1928.63. There is a particularly striking illustration given by Moore-Blunt
1978.161–162: "papyri also demonstrate how, in questions, the final syllable of the last
word (i.e. the final syllable of the sentence) could bear the high pitch, regardless of the
normal [I would prefer to say "lexical"] accentuation of the word." As Moore-Blunt
points out (p. 162), such a spelling of an acute is especially useful where the syntax has
no interrogative particle, as in the case of ἀκηκουκάς at Herodas 5.49.

[89] Laum 1928.63.

[90] Laum 1928.63, 163, 327.

[91] Laum 1928.63 offers the dictum that accentuated texts were meant for students,
not scholars. I hasten to add that the category of "student" needs to include students
of performance traditions.

[92] Isocrates *Panathenaicus* (*Oration* 12) 18–19 and 33, as quoted above.

For an example of the accentual idiosyncrasies in Homer, let us begin with the accentuation of ἀγυιῇ at *Odyssey* 15.441. The pattern that we might expect on the basis of Classical Greek is ἀγυίη, which in this case is also attested as a textual variant in the same verse. In a 1914 article, Jacob Wackernagel proposed that such sporadically attested prosodic anomalies as ἀγυιῇ reveal authentic traditional patterns.[93] *Here the evidence of linguistics, as adduced by Wackernagel, is decisive.* On the basis of comparative Indo-European linguistics, we can be sure that the anomalous final-syllable accentuation of ἀγυιῇ is an archaism and that the recessive accentuation of ἀγυίη is an innovation.[94] Wackernagel proposed further that the authenticity of prosodic anomalies like ἀγυιῇ is supported by the very fact that they caused problems for the ancient critics of Homer and even led to false analogies in the diction of later poets.[95]

The thesis, then, as formulated by Wackernagel and as more recently reformulated by myself and others, is that such transmitted accentual patterns were reported by Alexandrian critics not on the basis of grammatical conjecture but on the basis of the actual pronunciation perpetuated by rhapsodes in their performances of the Homeric poems.[96]

To this thesis I now add two further proposals:

(1) that the reports of the Alexandrian critics about such authentic prosodic anomalies came from the Homeric *hupomnēmata* 'commentaries' of Aristarchus;

(2) that these reports about the accents were based not on the direct experiences of the Alexandrian critics with rhapsodes but on the writings of earlier critics associated with the school of Aristotle.

For the first proposal, let us consider the accentuation of δηιοτῆτι at *Iliad* 3.20. In this case, the scholia attribute this

---

[93] Wackernagel 1953 [1914] 1175.
[94] N 1970.121.
[95] Wackernagel 1953.1176.
[96] Wackernagel 1953 [1893] 1103: "Aber die Zitate basieren doch selbst wieder auf der mündlichen Rezitation der homerischen Gedichte [reference also to Schulze 1892.213n3]; da die Rhapsodik bis an die Anfänge der Philologie hinanreicht, haben wir hier eine ununterbrochene Traditionskette. Daß beim mündlichen Vortrag neben den Versikten auch der musikalische Wortton zum Ausdruck kam, ist unzweifelhaft." Cf. also Lehrs 1882.258, quoted by N 1970.121, where the discussion is taken further.

anomalous accentuation explicitly to the authority of Aristarchus. As Wackernagel points out, the accent of δηιοτής is anomalous when we compare the everyday Greek words κακότης, νεότης, φιλότης.[97] And yet, the accent of δηιοτής can be verified as an archaism in terms of Indo-European linguistics, on the basis of cognate formations, especially in Vedic Sanskrit.[98] What is striking about this example, as well as many others, is that the witness for this anomalous form is specifically named in the scholiastic tradition as Aristarchus. There is an irony here, in that Aristarchus had the reputation, even in his own era and thereafter, of being the supreme Analogist, that is, of seeking to replace, in texts that he edited, anomalous forms with analogous forms.[99]

The second proposal can be found in my earlier work, which accepted Wackernagel's thesis of a rhapsodic performance tradition as the ultimate witness for the archaizing prosodic anomalies preserved in the transmitted Homeric text, and which adduced the work of Karl Lehrs, who, even before Wackernagel, had mentioned the rhapsodes as a possible source for the preservation of prosodic anomalies in the Homeric text.[100] As Lehrs argues, the very fact that a later commentator like Herodian, who flourished in the second half of the second century AD, was quite knowledgeable about the prosodic patterns reported by the earlier

[97] Wackernagel 1953 [1893] 1103.

[98] Wackernagel 1953 [1909] 1119–1120.

[99] The observation of Didymus in the scholia A to *Iliad* 16.467c, that Aristarchus would not leave something *aparamútheton*, in other words, that he would not miss the opportunity of making contextual comparisons with all available internal evidence, does not mean that his priorities ranked internal logic ahead of manuscript evidence: in this regard, I find persuasive the discussion of Ludwich 1885.92, 97, 109 (yes, Aristarchus is an analogist, but not at the expense of the manuscript evidence), 114 (striking examples where Aristarchus reads an anomalous form instead of substituting an analogous form). There is an interesting critique by Janko 1990.332-334 of the analogizing tendencies in the Monro–Allen 1920 Oxford Classical Texts edition of the *Iliad*. With reference to the manuscript reading δ' ἐκάθεν at *Iliad* 13.107, which the OCT edition replaces with δὲ ἑκάς on the analogy of the manuscript reading at *Iliad* 5.791, Janko argues that the manuscript reading δ' ἐκάθεν at *Iliad* 13.107 "is superior *precisely because it is different*, even though it happens to include a more recent linguistic form (which the poet uses elsewhere)." I agree with the wording except for an important detail: I would substitute <u>authentic</u> for <u>superior</u>. Given that Zenodotus and Aristophanes both read δὲ ἑκάς at *Iliad* 13.107, I suggest that this reading too is authentic (I will have more to say presently on Zenodotus and Aristophanes). What is *lectio difficilior* for one period may be *lectio facilior* for another (here again I disagree with Janko, pp. 332–333n21). Cf. Pasquali 1952.122 and di Luzio 1969.144–145.

[100] N 1970.121, following Lehrs 1882.258.

commentator Aristarchus but seemed to have no idea about how
or where Aristarchus got his information suggests that the earlier
critic relied on evidence that goes beyond the level of pure
text.[101] That evidence, Lehrs inferred, may be the testimony of
rhapsodes. A similar inference was made by Martin West in his
1970 Oxford Classical Dictionary article on rhapsodes, where he
cites the arguments of Wackernagel.[102] I now propose instead
that the evidence from rhapsodes is not direct but instead mediated by earlier writings stemming from the school of Aristotle: as
we have seen from the references by Isocrates, it is possible that
this school had intellectual contacts with rhapsodes.

If later Alexandrian critics like Aristarchus did not have direct
access to such intellectual contacts, whether by choice or otherwise, then we have a reason to account for the almost complete
absence of references in the Homer scholia to rhapsodes.[103] The
one exception of which I know is a reference in the scholia bT to
Iliad 21.26 mentioning one "Hermodoros the rhapsode" (Ἑρ-
μόδωρος ὁ ῥαψῳδὸς χεῖρας ἐναίρων ἤκουε "χειροκοπῶν", κα-
τεχρήσατο δέ).[104] Erbse remarks about Hermodoros: "vir aliunde
ignotus."[105] Hermodoros may have been a contemporary of Aristarchus, but it may be more likely that he is from an earlier
era.[106] In any case, to judge from the bit of exegesis attributed to
Hermodoros in the scholia, Aristarchus would surely have held
him in low regard.[107]

A question remains: how exactly did the performance tradi-

[101] Lehrs ibid.
[102] West 1970; see also West 1981.114.
[103] Ludwich 1898.163 remarks on the absence, in the Homer scholia, of any reference to variant readings that are explicitly connected with rhapsodes. The scholia
mention nothing along the lines of "ἀντίγραφα τῶν ῥαψῳδῶν" or the like. Also, I
find no mention of Homeridai in the Homer scholia edited by Erbse.
[104] The uniqueness of this attestation is verified by the Thesaurus Linguae Graecae.
[105] Erbse 1969–88.v.130.
[106] Cf. also the extract quoted in *Suda*, omicron 760: δειξάτω, οὗ κεῖται Ὁμήρου
ῥαψῳδιῶν στίχος. ἀλλ᾽ οὐδ᾽ ἂν ˉΙωνα δοκῶ τὸν ῥαψωιδὸν ἐξευρεῖν 'let him show
where a line of Homer's *rhapsōidíai* is attested; but I don't think that even Ion the
rhapsode could find it'.
[107] We may note in this context an anecdote reported by Vitruvius about Aristophanes of Byzantium, T 17 in the Aristophanes edition of Slater 1986. The text is
given in the Appendix. In this narrative, the idea of reading aloud is equated with
the idea of oral performance, and the details about the competition at the *ludi* suggest that
earlier versions of this narrative concerned rhapsodic traditions of performance. Particularly noteworthy is the detail about the fixed sequence of competing poets.

tions of rhapsodes preserve the archaic and ultimately anomalous accent patterns? The answer, I suggest, has to do with the inherited melodic contours of the Homeric hexameter, however reduced the component of melody may have become in hexameter as opposed to the lyric meters, with their overt melodies.[108] These reduced melodic contours, as perpetuated in the performance traditions of rhapsodes, would have aided in preserving archaisms in the pitch accentuation – archaisms that were otherwise leveled out in everyday Greek.[109] My reformulation here is built not only on the work of Wackernagel, which goes back to 1893,[110] but also on a 1951 work by Meinrad Scheller, whose own reformulation had originally led me to appreciate Wackernagel's insights.[111] Scheller adduces a rule in traditional Greek music, to the effect that unaccented syllables did not have higher pitch than

[108] In N 1990a.20–28, there is an extended discussion of the phenomenon that I call *reduced melody* or *recitative* in hexameter traditions as performed by rhapsodes. For more on the melodic contours of the hexameter, see West 1986.45, who argues that the epic singer of the eighth century "followed the contours given by the word accents"; also, that "this tradition was perpetuated by the rhapsodes, but in a gradually decaying form," and that "the rhapsodes preserved many archaic accentual features of Homeric Greek into the Hellenistic age"; cf. also West 1981.114 and 1992.208–209. I agree with most of these formulations, though I resist the idea of a "decaying form." On the concept of *recitative*, see van der Werf 1967. In the traditions of the Old French *chansons*, as he argues, there are cases of distinctly recitative melodies and distinctly arioso ones but there are other compositions where "we can no longer discern whether the original of a given line was a recitative on *d* or an arioso melody with *d* as a tonal center." (van der Werf 1967.234) In other words, there are instances where "we cannot conclude from the preserved music whether a manuscript gives us a simplified variant of an arioso original or an ornamented variant of a strict recitative." (ibid.) It is clear that "a trouvère recitative could easily be transformed into a trouvère arioso, or an arioso transformed into a recitative." (ibid.) Though it is impossible at times to determine in which direction the shift is headed, whether it is from arioso to recitative or vice versa, it is clear that these two styles were not "two rigorously separated styles for the jongleurs, notators, and scribes at the end of the thirteenth century." (ibid.) We may compare the ancient Greek traditions associated with the "lyric" Stesichorus and the "epic" Homer, as discussed in N 1990a.49–51.
[109] On the distinction between sung hexameter and rhapsodic hexameter, see West 1986.44. At pp. 43–45, West collects valuable comparative evidence on distinctions between repeated and varied melodic contours in line-by-line epic performance (especially with reference to the French chansons de geste, p. 43n12, and Kirghiz epic, p. 44n15).
[110] Wackernagel 1953 [1893] 1103, quoted at p. 128n96 above.
[111] Scheller 1951. At p. 10 Scheller resists the negative judgment of Wilamowitz 1916.8–9 about the value of the Alexandrian tradition on accents. According to Wilamowitz, this tradition represents an arbitrary application of analogy principles, revealing an unawareness of etymology and of the fundamental principles of word-formation; he thinks that linguists should be the last people on earth to pay so much

the acute-accented syllable: with such preexisting rules, argues
Scheller, embedded patterns of archaic accentuation could be
preserved within a traditional melodic frame.[112] Such a frame is
what I have just called the melodic contour.[113]

By now we have a variety of reasons to justify the idea that the
Homer scholarship of the Alexandrian critics, especially when it
comes to information about performance, was a continuation of
traditions set by the school of Aristotle. A basic question, remains, however: where do we find a historical point of contact
between the Homeric research of Aristotle and that of the Alexandrian critics? I will argue in the course of the next two chapters
that the missing link, as it were, was Demetrius of Phalerum.

Before we consider this link, however, we must follow through
in confronting the more basic question, which is, how reliable
is the editorial judgment of Alexandrian critics? Their reliability,
as we have seen, must be tested with special reference to cases

attention to these patterns. It is thanks to the research of Wackernagel, as Scheller
points out, that the negative judgment of Wilamowitz can be "modified." Besides accent, there are also variations in breathings that must have survived by way of performance traditions: see Householder and Nagy 1972.66 on such Homeric contrasts as
ἀμός vs. ἄμμι, ὑμός vs. ὔμμι (see Laum 1928.365 on the spelling ἄμμι in a papyrus for
Bacchylides 17.25).

[112] Scheller 1951.9n3. See further Comotti 1989.91 on the Delphic Hymns, where
syllables having acute or even grave accent in any given word consistently avoid any
pitch that is lower than the other pitches assigned to the other syllables in the same
word. For more on the relationship of pitch accent and melody in ancient Greece,
especially on the more archaic pattern where the melodic patterns are conditioned by
the accentual patterns, see N 1990a.39 and n113. Cf. West 1981.115, 1986.45,
1992.199. See also Comotti p. 91 on the concept of *logôdes mélos* 'speech-like melody' in
Aristoxenus *Harmonics* 1.18 p.23.14 Da Rios. Comotti p. 92 juxtaposes this concept
with the arguments of Dionysius of Halicarnassus *De compositione verborum* 11.58ff, p.
40.17 Usener-Radermacher, who insists that melody controls the words, not the words
the melody, and who cites Euripides *Orestes* 140–142 (making mistakes with the accents of some words: see Comotti p. 92n6). According to Comotti, Dionysius is
slanting his argument by citing Euripides, who is musically the most innovative of the
tragedians. He argues that the Delphic Hymns are musically far more conservative than
the lyric compositions of Euripides. I agree. West 1992.199 attempts to explain the
melodies of Euripides' *Orestes* in terms of constraints imposed by the principle of
responsion between strophe and antistrophe.

[113] Cf. Laum 1928.164 on a convention found in the papyri: there is a tendency to
signal an acute accent belonging to only one word within a given string of words, instead of signalling all the acutes belonging to all the words (for example, P.Oxy. III
448, from *Odyssey* 22.184: τηι δ'ετερηι σακος ευρύ γερον, which is spelled by modern
editors as τῆι δ' ἑτέρηι σάκος εὐρὺ γέρον). To mark the one acute is perhaps a reflex
of marking the highest point of the melodic contour. (On the practice of marking
polysyllabic oxytones with acute rather than grave in some clause-medial situations,

where they report variant readings. On the matter of variant readings in accentuation, I have already concluded that the testimony of Aristarchus is indeed reliable. But we have yet to examine variants in actual wording. To test the authenticity of such variants as reported by the Alexandrian critics, we may use the criteria of comparative philology and formulaic analysis, just as Janko has done in testing the authenticity of readings taken from the Homer texts called *koinaí* by Aristarchus. The difference is that I will use these criteria to test only authenticity, not correctness. To repeat my previous point, the empirical methods of comparative philology and the study of oral tradition can be used only to defend a variant reading as traditional, not to establish it as the superior reading – let alone the correct reading.[114]

Let us start with the earliest of the three major Alexandrian Homer critics, Zenodotus. For purposes of the present argument, a telling example of a variant that is backed up by the authority of Zenodotus and that turns out to be justified through the application of comparative philology and through the study of the attested formulaic system of Homeric diction is the phrase ἔλπομαι εὐχόμενος 'I hope, praying ...' at *Iliad* 8.526, as opposed to εὔχομαι ἐλπόμενος 'I pray, hoping ...', the reading that is found in the majority of manuscripts and that is supported by the authority of Aristarchus himself.[115] In his 1976 monograph on the formulaic behavior of the Homeric verb εὔχομαι, Leonard Muellner shows convincingly that in fact both manuscript variants, ἔλπομαι εὐχόμενος as well as εὔχομαι ἐλπόμενος, can be generated syntactically from parallel formulaic patterns attested elsewhere in the Homeric text even as we have it.[116] In this case, we happen to find more internal evidence as precedent for the reading given by Zenodotus, but there are clear indications that

see p. 126n87 above.) It may be possible to compare this kind of pattern with what we find in the Homeric scholia, which frequently refer not to individual words but to strings of words (e.g. Laum 1928.379), reflecting a practical mode of commenting on texts that had once been spelled without word-divisions. In the scholia, there is a tendency to comment on only one accent belonging to only one word within a given string of words instead of commenting on all the accents belonging to all the words (e.g. Laum 1928.143).

[114] See p. 117 above. Cf. di Luzio 1969.141 and D'Ippolito 1984.224–225.

[115] Van der Valk 1964.76 reviews the facts; as the discussion that follows will show, I do not share his interpretation of the facts.

[116] Muellner 1976.58–62; also p. 24 with n18.

the "Vulgate" reading – or, as I prefer to call it, the Koine reading – is "genuine epic diction" as well.[117]

To take the argumentation further, I insist that neither variant in this example has a claim to be the original reading or, to put it positively, that both variants are traditional multiforms. In a multitext format of editing Homer, we would have to take both forms into account, and then we could still pursue the question whether one variant was more suitable than another at a given time and place. An ideal example is Zenodotus' reading οἰωνοῖσί τε δαῖτα at *Iliad* 1.5 (reported in Athenaeus *Epitome* 12f), as opposed to the reading attested in all the manuscripts, οἰωνοῖσί τε πᾶσι.[118] There is evidence that Zenodotus' reading follows a version that was current in the Athenian performance traditions of the fifth century, the era of the three canonical tragedians: witness the expression in Aeschylus *Suppliants* 800–801: κυσὶν δ' ἔπειθ' ἕλωρα κἀπιχωρίοις | ὄρνισι δεῖπνον.[119] Yet there is evidence that the manuscript reading οἰωνοῖσί τε πᾶσι, apparently defended by Aristarchus against Zenodotus, was also authentic: we have not only the external testimony of the manuscripts but

---

[117] Muellner, ibid.

[118] Zenodotus athetized *Iliad* 1.4–5 according to Athenaeus 12f, which means that he considered what he had read in these lines to be un-Homeric. But the point is, at least as I understand it, that οἰωνοῖσί τε δαῖτα is indeed what he had read at *Iliad* 1.5. On athetesis as an editorial judgment rather than an act of omission – a judgment that may or may not affect manuscript transmission – see p. 138n134. Kirk 1985.53 remarks on Zenodotus' reading οἰωνοῖσί τε δαῖτα: "Aristarchus (who is evidently Athenaeus's source, through Aristonicus, at [Ath.] 12e–13a, cf. Erbse I, 9) tried to refute [it] on the erroneous ground that Homer never uses δαίς of animal food – as he does in fact at [24.]43." Ludwich 1885.87 points out that we cannot be sure what exactly Aristarchus said. So I would reply to Kirk: whatever the merits, or even the substance (which, to repeat, we do not know for sure), of Aristarchus' arguing on internal grounds for οἰωνοῖσί τε πᾶσι at *Iliad* 1.5, his primary reason for preferring this reading over οἰωνοῖσί τε δαῖτα was surely not internal evidence but the external evidence of what he considered the "superior" manuscript versions (cf. Ludwich 1885.89). More on this point presently.

[119] For the view that Aeschylus was aware of the version οἰωνοῖσί τε δαῖτα at *Iliad* 1.5, see e.g. Pfeiffer 1968.111, with further examples from tragedy (we may note that Pfeiffer would have assumed that such an awareness was based on the existence of such a version in the manuscript tradition, not in the performance tradition of Homer); see also Pasquali 1952.236–237. See also Janko 1992.23, who accepts the idea that Zenodotus' reading may go back to the fifth century BC but who still prefers to think of it as "an early emendation" – meant "to remove the 'problem' that not all birds eat flesh" (cf. the reasoning in the scholia b to *Iliad* 1.5; Eustathius 19.45, 256.8). Kirk 1985.53 describes Zenodotus' reading as "a fussy change of the vulgate." Rengakos 1993.30n1 draws attention to Kirk's assumption of "change" here.

also the internal testimony of formulaic expressions, found throughout the Homeric poems, with the same idea of "hyperbolic allness" that we find in the idea that the corpses of heroes were prey to "all" birds.[120]

Let us pursue further the central question, whether any given variant reported on the authority of, say, Zenodotus, or even of Aristarchus, can be treated as just that, a variant, or whether it is merely a conjecture. The credibility of all Alexandrian editors, Aristarchus included, as witnesses to authentic variants was already seriously questioned in the eighteenth century by Friedrich August Wolf.[121] In recent times, the work of Marchinus van der Valk is most prominently cited for its sustained polemics against the credibility of all major Alexandrian scholars.[122]

There have been many variations in the history of such polemics. Earlier scholars could be selective in their approaches, concentrating their attacks on the reliability of some Alexandrian scholars while defending that of others. Thus for example Ulrich von Wilamowitz-Moellendorff and Giorgio Pasquali tended to favor Zenodotus at the expense of Aristarchus, while Karl Lehrs and Arthur Ludwich championed Aristarchus, often at the expense of Zenodotus.[123] T. W. Allen relied heavily on Aristar-

[120] The Homeric examples adduced by Ludwich 1885.89n55, where the notion of "all" is logically a matter of hyperbole, are for me persuasive (especially *Iliad* 5.52, *Odyssey* 18.85). As for Zenodotus' reading οἰωνοῖσί τε δαῖτα, we have in its defense some internal testimony as well, most notably the picture of a ravenous lion who lunges for his meal in *Iliad* 24.43 (ἵνα δαῖτα λάβῃσιν). We have already seen this passage cited by Kirk 1985.53 – though he was of course not defending Zenodotus but attacking Aristarchus.

[121] Wolf 1795. An indispensable summary of Wolf's position is Pfeiffer 1968.215–218. Apthorp 1980.xiii, in line with the arguments of Bolling 1925, uses the term "Wolfian vulgate" in a negative sense to characterize post-Wolf Homer editions that tend to discount the judgments of Alexandrian critics, especially with reference to criteria of excluding lines in the Homeric corpus. Such an edition is the Monro–Allen 1920 Oxford Classical Texts version of the *Iliad*. Pfeiffer 1968.214–215 outlines the efforts of Lehrs 1882 and Ludwich 1884/1885 to rehabilitate the authoritativeness of Aristarchus as editor of Homer, as also the arguments of Erbse 1959 challenging this rehabilitation. In offering his own counterarguments to Erbse's position, Pfeiffer begins by saying (1968.215): "it looks to me as if by a sort of unconscious counter-revolution Wolf has now been put back on the throne from which Lehrs had driven him."

[122] Van der Valk 1949, 1963/1964.

[123] For Zenodotus: Wilamowitz 1916 (e.g. pp. 120–121, 261n2, 262n2; cf. van der Valk 1964.10) and Pasquali 1952 (e.g. pp. 207, 235–236; cf. van der Valk 1964.15). For Aristarchus: Lehrs 1882, Ludwich 1884/1885. Given that there is unanimous manuscript

chus,[124] and the trustworthiness of Aristarchus was also a cornerstone in the overall account of Rudolf Pfeiffer's *History of Classical Scholarship*.[125]

More recently it has been the negative assessment of van der Valk that seems to dominate a number of influential works on Homer. With reference to the Alexandrian critics and to the so-called *politikaí* or 'city books' of Homer, valued as independent textual sources by both Zenodotus and Aristarchus, Geoffrey Kirk in the introduction to his *Iliad* commentary has this to say about the polemics of van der Valk:

> Moreover the city and individual texts, when their readings are taken as a whole, seem to be very erratic and to possess no special ancient authority; indeed the 'common' or 'worse' ones often appear, by modern criteria, more reliable than the 'ancient' or 'more refined' ones! Obviously this is a large and difficult topic; most scholars from Nauck and Wilamowitz on have held that Aristarchus sometimes made conjectures and on other occasions relied on earlier texts. That seems like a reasonable view on *a priori* grounds, but on the whole I side with van der Valk, who in *Researches [on the text and Scholia of the Iliad]* II, 86 records his opinion reached after astute if sometimes arcane studies, that 'Aristarchus' readings are nearly always subjective and personal conjectures', and that the cited texts, whatever their description, are comparatively recent products of Hellenistic and especially Alexandrian criticism. That applies *a fortiori* to Zenodotus also, whose distinctly shorter text, in particular, is clearly the result of his applying stringent and sometimes

---

authority for the reading οἰωνοῖσί τε πᾶσι at *Iliad* 1.5 as opposed to Zenodotus' reading οἰωνοῖσί τε δαῖτα (as reported in Athenaeus 12f), Ludwich 1885.89 defends the first reading and rejects the notion that it was a conjecture of Aristarchus. As indicated earlier (n120), I agree with Ludwich that it was not a conjecture. But I do not agree with him that the alternative reading, οἰωνοῖσί τε δαῖτα, is therefore a conjecture. We have already seen evidence that Zenodotus' reading follows a version that was current in the Athenian performance traditions of the fifth century, the era of the three canonical tragedians (see p. 134). In order to maintain the idea that this reading was a conjecture or interpolation, Ludwich is forced to say that it must have been an "old" one indeed (see also the position of Janko as cited at n119). For a critique of the position taken by Ludwich and others, that the Aristarchean text comes closest to a Homeric "original," see di Luzio 1969.6–9.

[124] Allen 1924.302–327.
[125] Pfeiffer 1968.210–219.

foolish standards of τὸ πρέπον, 'what is appropriate' in Homer, rather than being due to any authoritative special sources which modern criticism can discern.[126]

A similar though far more moderate position is taken by Richard Janko in the introduction to his commentary on Books 13–16 of the *Iliad*, part of the overall *Iliad* commentary that has been put together under the general editorship of Kirk.[127] Although I have benefited a great deal from Janko's discussion, and although I agree with much of what he has to say, I object when he writes: "I agree with van der Valk and Kirk (vol. 1, 43) that most readings where the Alexandrians lack support in the papyri and other codices are conjectures."[128] Janko speaks of van der Valk's "radical re-evaluation" of Alexandrian scholarship, "which Allen had prized too highly."[129]

I disagree, arguing that van der Valk's efforts to discredit in general the reliability of the Alexandrian scholars and in particular the value of the variant readings that they report must be systematically juxtaposed with the efforts of earlier scholars like Arthur Ludwich, and even earlier ones like Karl Lehrs, whose work persuades me that variant readings attributed by later ancient sources to editors like Aristarchus were just that, variants attested in the extant manuscripts or manuscript traditions available to these editors, and that these variants did not as a rule stem from conjectures supposedly made by these editors or by their predecessors.[130] As for Zenodotus, a recent study by Klaus Nickau concludes after a thorough analysis that, even if this critic *may* have made conjectures, it is impossible in any given instance to

---

[126] Kirk 1985.43. Editions of the *Iliad/Odyssey* by Nauck, 1877/1875. On the position of Wilamowitz, see p. 135 above. Kirk's position is disputed by Rengakos 1993.22n3.

[127] Janko 1992.22–29.

[128] Janko 1992.2–25. His reference is to Kirk's commentary, 1985.43. Cf. also van Thiel 1991 and the comment of Janko 1994.291: "T.'s attitude to the Alexandrians (p. ix–xiii) derives, like mine, from the great work of van der Valk."

[129] Janko 1992.21n6.

[130] Lehrs 1882; Ludwich 1884/1885, 1898. The principle is most forcefully stated, as "Lehrs' Law," by Ludwich 1884.86. I agree with the criticism of van der Valk's methods by Nickau 1977.31n1. I resist in general the idea that the Alexandrian editors would have contemplated any kind of theory-driven policy for making conjectures. Their theories may well have led them to argue for some variants over others, but that is a far cry from the idea that they rewrote the text as they saw fit.

prove it.[131] Moreover, using the textual evidence of the actual
surviving poems of Apollonius of Rhodes, Callimachus, and
other Hellenistic authors, Antonios Rengakos has argued convincingly that these poets "cited" Homer – other Classicists
would rather say "alluded" to Homer – on the basis of various
privately-owned Homeric texts that either stem from the Homer
text of Zenodotus, a contemporary of Apollonius and Callimachus, or are at least closely related to it; he argues, further, that
the variants contained in these pre-Aristarchean texts are exactly
that, variants, not conjectures.[132]

Further support for the thesis that the Alexandrian editors of
Homer preserved authentic variants comes from the work of
M. J. Apthorp, who argues that the edition of Aristarchus, taken
as a whole, contained practically the sum total of genuine Homeric verses.[133] According to Apthorp, and here he follows the
position of George M. Bolling, the *numerus versuum* of Aristarchus'
Homer edition is a functional norm, reflecting the conventions of
an earlier era in Homer transmission.[134] Janko in fact implicitly

---

[131] Nickau 1977.48; cf. Slater 1989.42n17. Slater goes on to say at a later point:
"ultimately, as Nickau [1972 column 34] says, no amount of generalizing theory re-
lieves the modern critic from assuming that every reading of an early grammarian
could be a variant until some alternative is demonstrated."

[132] Rengakos 1993 (especially pp. 11, 23, 31). He insists on the concept of *citation* –
as distinct from *allusion* – as a way of underlining the fact that, for the Alexandrian
poets, Homer was the absolute *source*, not only the unsurpassable *model* (p. 9). Beyond
the poetry of Apollonius and Callimachus, Rengakos draws special attention to the
text of another Hellenistic poet, Rhianos, as witness to a set of variants derived from a
Homer text that is markedly different from the Homer texts of Zenodotus, Aristophanes, and Aristarchus (p. 10). The value of the Homeric textual sources used by
other poets, including "Euripides," Antimachus, Philitas, and Aratus, is also discussed
(Rengakos 1993.11).

[133] Apthorp 1980. We may note in this context Apthorp's severe criticism (p. xiv)
of van der Valk's methods.

[134] Apthorp's valuable work (1980) builds on the findings of Bolling 1925, which he
summarizes as follows (p. xiv): "where a line is weakly attested by the medieval
manuscripts and papyrus evidence was available, then that line was almost invariably
absent from the papyrus or papyri." Apthorp adds (ibid.): "papyri published since
1925 have served only to confirm Bolling's position, sometimes dramatically." (It is
important to note that Apthorp is referring here to papyri dated after, not before, 150
BC or so.) In terms of Bolling's position, the evidence of the papyri indicates (to follow Apthorp's wording, ibid.) that "the *numerus versuum* of our medieval vulgate, when
purged of these weakly-attested lines, is identical with the *numerus versuum* of Aristarchus." Apthorp notes the important distinction (p. xv) between athetesis, where
Aristarchus marks with an obelus a verse that he deems non-authentic *though he leaves
it in the text*, and outright omission; as he points out (ibid.), "the evidence shows

agrees with Apthorp's inference that the plus-verses, that is, those verses that were evidently not included in Aristarchus' edition, are "interpolations," to be excised from modern editions of Homer.[135]

Despite my disagreement, for reasons to be elaborated presently, with Apthorp's argument that *only* the verses contained in Aristarchus' edition are "genuine," I accept his judgment that Aristarchus' *numerus versuum* is indeed genuine *to the extent that it cannot be simply the cumulative result of conjectural selections.*[136] I even accept his idea that the plus-verses are "interpolations" in the medieval manuscript tradition – *though they would be so only retrospectively*, from the hindsight of an Aristarchean editorial tradition.[137] But I find it difficult if not impossible to reconcile Janko's

conclusively that [Aristarchus] omitted only lines which were absent from the vast majority of his manuscripts." For further insights on Aristarchus' methodology – on the levels of (1) manuscript evidence and (2) content – in deciding whether or not a Homeric line was authentic, see Lührs 1992. I find especially important the observations of Lührs p. 11 concerning instances where Aristarchus excluded verses in his Homeric text and then apparently signaled in his commentaries (that is, in his *hupomnémata*) that these plus-verses had been included in the Homer text of Zenodotus: as Lührs argues, Aristarchus did not think of such verses as conjectures made by Zenodotus but rather, more simply, as verses deemed authentic by Zenodotus and non-authentic by himself. Presumably, such verses must have been attested in some manuscripts and absent in others for them to be included and excluded in the Homer texts of Zenodotus and Aristarchus respectively (Lührs ibid.)

[135] Janko 1992.21n6: "interpolations" (see also Janko 1990.334). Despite this position taken by Janko, we see that a few pages later in his commentary (1992.27–29) he defends, I think successfully, the authenticity of what he calls "the most notorious case" of such plus-verses, *Iliad* 9.458–461. This passage, missing in the medieval manuscript tradition and omitted from a papyrus that covers this stretch of the *Iliad*, happens to be known only from a citation by Plutarch (*Quomodo adolescens poetas audire debeat* 26f), who claims that Aristarchus omitted these lines "out of fear" (the lines concern Phoenix as he contemplates killing his father).

[136] In other words, I infer that the omission or non-omission of a verse is really a question of variation, not conjecture, in that Aristarchus will omit a verse – whatever contextual reasons he may adduce for such an omission – only when the documentary evidence allows him to do so. This extreme conservatism of Aristarchus, Apthorp notes (1980.xv), was appreciated by Ludwich and Bolling – but definitely not by van der Valk.

[137] Apthorp (1980.xvi) goes on to argue that "the numerous lines absent from *all* our manuscripts which we know to have been pre-Aristarchean but *absent* from Aristarchus' edition – some cited by the scholia, some present in extant Ptolemaic papyri, some included in ancient quotations or discussions of Homer – stand condemned as interpolations alongside the weakly-attested lines of the mediaeval manuscripts." I object to this condemnation, as also to Apthorp's followup remark (p. xxvn2): "Thus the attempt by A. di Luzio [1969] to defend numerous plus-verses of the Ptolemaic papyri on so-called linguistic and stylistic grounds must be pronounced unsuccessful." I remain unconvinced that a verse must be an interpolation if it is both non-Aristarchean and pre-Aristarchean.

acceptance of Apthorp's privileging of Aristarchus' edition when it comes to variations in the number of verses – Bolling's *numerus versuum* – with his simultaneous acceptance of van der Valk's discrediting of this same edition when it comes to variations in the actual wording of verses.[138]

I propose that variations, both in wording and in *numerus versuum*, be treated as parallel phenomena as we reconsider the editorial task that confronted the Alexandrian Homer critics. With the establishment of any final text of Homer by Aristarchus, however faithfully this critic may have collected all the facts that he knew from all the available manuscript evidence, we would have to expect that he was left with a mass of variants, on the level of wording within lines, that would have to be omitted in the text established by him. If such a text becomes a definitive edition, from then on the re-entry of any of these variants may indeed be considered an interpolation *retrospectively*, from the standpoint of the hypothetical edition. Let us apply the same reasoning to the problem of *numerus versuum*. In this connection, we cannot lose sight of the mechanism of fluctuating expansion and compression in oral poetics, a phenomenon discussed at length elsewhere.[139] This phenomenon produces fluctuation between more and fewer lines, and the very fact of this fluctuation must be, at least in some cases, a matter of *variants*. Granted, if a shorter version is accepted into a canonical edition established by Aristarchus, then a longer version could re-enter the tradition represented by that edition only as an interpolation – even if this longer version is diachronically a variant of the given shorter version.

As for Kirk's acceptance of the position taken by van der Valk, it is far more extreme than Janko's: for Kirk to go even further than August Nauck – not to mention Wilamowitz – in insisting, as we have seen in the passage quoted above, that the Alexandrian editors invented and imposed their own readings is to ignore the arguments that Arthur Ludwich had worked out specifically to counter the arguments of Nauck and Wilamowitz concerning the alleged "conjectures" of the Alexandrian critics.

---

[138] Janko 1992.21n6. Apthorp 1980.110n64 speaks of "the limited influence of Aristarchus on the text of the subsequent tradition *within* his *numerus versuum*," with further discussion at pp. 37–38.

[139] N 1992a.39–40.

On the other hand, I disagree with some aspects of the further inferences drawn by Ludwich and others from the evidence that they collected – evidence meant to show that the Homer edition of Aristarchus was a reliable collection of genuine readings. Even if it is justified to infer that Aristarchus' edition accurately reflected an official Athenian version of Homer, and we will presently review some reasons for arguing such a possibility, we cannot infer further that Aristarchus' edition therefore reflects the "original" Homer. We have already seen one decisive argument against this further inference, which is, that there are variant readings stemming from the editions known as *koinaí* – and rejected by Aristarchus – that are authentic as well.

There are also at least two other arguments against the inference that the Aristarchus edition of Homer represents the only genuine Homer. The first comes from the evidence of the so-called "eccentric" papyri.[140] As Stephanie West describes them, these papyri are "characterized by a high proportion of variants and additions," and they can be dated mostly before around 150 BC; they generally "die out" after this terminus, while "later papyri offer a text which differs little from that of the medieval manuscripts."[141] West allows for the possibility – and this is as far as she is willing to concede – that these "eccentric" papyri from the Ptolemaic period contain variants derived from the performance traditions of rhapsodes.[142] The case could be made more forcefully.[143]

West and others explain the disappearance of "eccentric" versions as due directly or indirectly to the influence of Aristarchus' new edition of Homer, which apparently was finished also around 150 BC.[144] Earlier versions of this theory were resisted by Allen, who argued that such a strategy of explanation, which requires

---

[140] The term "eccentric papyri" is claimed by Allen: see 1924.302.

[141] [S.] West 1988.45; cf. also 1967.15.

[142] [S.] West 1967.13; cf. Apthorp 1980.60.

[143] Cf. D'Ippolito 1984.224–225, especially p. 224n12. In what follows, it will be clear that I generally accept the arguments of di Luzio 1969 (see n137 above) that these "eccentric" Ptolemaic papyri of Homer, dated mostly before around 150 BC, contain a significant number of authentic variants, reflecting an ongoing rhapsodic tradition. In his article, di Luzio offers case-by-case counterarguments about Homeric variants discounted by West and by other critics (cf. Del Corno 1960 and 1961) who have examined the "eccentric" Homer papyri.

[144] [S.] West 1988.45; Apthorp 1980.1–3.

that an Alexandrian critic's edition *caused* the obsolescence of the "eccentric" versions, "is an excellent example of the argument *post hoc ergo propter hoc*."[145] West herself raises a problem with this theory: that even the papyri dated after 150 BC. "offer too wide a range of variants to allow the hypothesis that they might all be copies of a single edition."[146] Allen's own explanation, which will be criticized in the discussion that follows, is that these "eccentric" versions "had depended on the rhapsode," but now they "withered of themselves" as the rhapsodic art withered.[147] In this connection, we may note with interest the argument, advanced by Aldo di Luzio, that the linguistic peculiarities of the "eccentric" Homer papyri reflect a phase of rhapsodic transmission emanating from Athens.[148]

The subject of rhapsodes leads us to yet another argument against the inference that the Aristarchus edition represents the only genuine Homer. This time, the evidence comes from the works of Plato, whose citations of verses from Homer have been systematically studied by Jules Labarbe.[149] In the era of Plato, as we can deduce from these citations, there seems to have been no single Athenian Homer *text* of the sort posited by Ludwich and others in their arguing for some kind of archetype as a source for Aristarchus' Homer edition. Labarbe finds demonstrably authentic variants that are distinct from those adopted by Aristarchus,[150] and some variants are in fact attested only in Plato and nowhere in the medieval manuscript tradition of Homer.[151] There is even an instance, *Iliad* 23.335, where Plato and Xenophon each report variant readings, each differing from the other, which do not survive into the medieval manuscript tradition.[152]

---

[145] Allen 1924.303.

[146] [S.] West 1988.47.

[147] Allen 1924.326; cf. also 320.

[148] Di Luzio 1969.7–8.

[149] Labarbe 1949. The attempt of Lohse 1964 to refute the findings of Labarbe is in my opinion unconvincing: the criteria that Lohse sets up (especially pp. 5–7) for determining what is or is not oral poetry seem to me too rigid to be applicable to Homeric performance traditions in the fourth century BC. For the purposes of my own argumentation, it is essential simply to stress Lohse's concession that any Homer text used by Plato was *at least to some degree* different from what we have (e.g. p. 7). I concede that there may well be instances of Homeric quotations where Plato has selectively introduced his own rewordings (cf. Lohse 1967).

[150] Labarbe 1949.419.

[151] Labarbe 1949.415–416.

[152] Labarbe 1949.424; also pp. 90–94, 98–99.

Labarbe allows for the possibility that Plato used *an* Athenian text of Homer for his citations.[153] Still, there is no way to equate such a text with some kind of Athenian "archetype" as reconstructed by Ludwich and others.[154] More important, some of the Homeric variations attested in Plato, whether or not they were mediated by way of *a* text, must derive ultimately from the oral tradition: the criteria that Labarbe applies to test whether or not any Homeric variant cited in Plato is "genuine" are soundly based on Milman Parry's methodology of formulaic analysis, and to this extent Labarbe is justified in claiming that at least some of the Homeric variations attested from the citations of Plato must stem from the performance traditions of rhapsodes.[155]

And yet, even though I resist the idea that a Homer text owned by Plato can be derived from an archetypal Athenian text of Homer, there is one aspect of Plato's "text" that does indeed suggest the existence of at least a conceptual Athenian archetype. Unlike the "eccentric" papyri that are dated from around 300 to 150 BC, Plato's Homer is not characterized by plus-verses.[156] Labarbe attributes this aspect of stability in Plato's Homer text to the hypothetical existence of a "control text," which he equates tentatively with the so-called "Peisistratean Recension," the popular influence of which would have regulated the *numerus versuum* even of commercial copies, such as the one that Plato presumably possessed.[157] In previous work, I have already given reasons to doubt the construct of such an early "control text," arguing instead that a crystallizing Athenian performance tradition of Homer at the Panathenaia could be sufficient in and of itself to account for the quasi-textualization of Homeric poetry in the era of the Peisistratidai.[158] Patterns of stabilization in length of performance need not presuppose the agency of a written text.[159]

---

[153] Labarbe 1949.423. To this extent, I can accept the formulation of Erbse 1959.301 concerning an "Athenian Recension" of Homer; cf. Lohse 1967.230n14.

[154] Labarbe 1949.423.

[155] Labarbe 1949.423–425. I am not convinced by the specific discussions offered by Lohse (e.g. 1965.259n21, 262n27) concerning criteria for determining what is or is not genuine formulaic variation.

[156] Labarbe 1949.423. Cf. Lohse 1967.229. On the concept of plus-verses, see p. 139 above.

[157] Ibid.

[158] N 1992a.38–41.

[159] N 1992a.40.

More important for now, the stabilization of the *numerus vers-uum* in papyri after 150 BC can hardly be due to the influence of a new Aristarchean edition – if indeed it is true that the Homer citations of Plato already reveal a similar pattern of stabilization, one that we find in place as early as the fourth century.[160] In the discussion that follows, extending into the next two chapters, I prefer to argue that any stabilization of the Homeric *numerus vers-uum* in the fourth century is due to the regulation, by the Athenian State, of rhapsodic performance traditions, and that the "eccentric" papyri dating from around 300 to 150 BC, with their plus-verses, reveal a later and relatively more fluid phase of rhapsodic tradition when such regulation by the State was no longer in effect.[161]

That the "eccentric" papyri become obsolete in a still later phase, after around 150 BC, raises the possibility that we are witnessing the beginnings of some new kind of interference by the State, in this case the state of Ptolemaic Egypt.[162] Such a possibility, however, is not necessarily incompatible with Allen's theory that the performance tradition of the rhapsodes had by this point "withered." Granted, Allen's metaphor surely overstates the case in that we cannot say that the performance traditions of Homer simply died out around 150 BC. As we will see,

[160] Apthorp 1980.3 points out that the *numerus versuum* of Aristarchus does not match that of his predecessor Aristophanes in six known cases, and in each case the readings in papyri dated after 150 BC back up Aristarchus, not Aristophanes. On these grounds, he argues against supposing "that our manuscripts are descended from some other recension which just happened to largely coincide with that of Aristarchus." I would argue rather that Aristarchus may have simply surpassed Aristophanes in his editorial efforts to recover an Athenian version, on which more later. Apthorp concedes (ibid.) that Aristophanes' *numerus versuum* was indeed very similar to that of Aristarchus.

[161] We may note with interest the observation of Laum 1928.33 that papyri from the fourth and third centuries BC tend to be less prone to archaizing tendencies – from a palaeographical point of view – as opposed to papyri from the second century BC to the second AD.

[162] As J. D. Morgan points out to me (*per litteras* 30 November 1993), this dating for the obsolescence of the "eccentric" papyri is delineated by 145/4 BC, the date for the departure of Aristarchus and the other grammarians when Ptolemy VIII came to power (see p. 114 above). Morgan suggests further: "it was the grammarians who were interested in collecting and copying such papyri, and when they left, almost nobody was left to take an interest in them." From another point of view, however, the phenomenon of "eccentric papyri" needs to be linked with the book trade, not so much with the activity of grammarians. I am grateful to Andrew Dyck for broadening my general perspective on this problem.

they persisted for several centuries beyond that point, even in areas like Hellenized Egypt. But at least the higher levels of flexibility in the rhapsodic tradition as reflected in the "eccentric" papyri do indeed seem to have ceased after 150 BC or so, and this cessation coincides with the emergence of the Aristarchean text of Homer as the only version of Homer.

The ultimate outcome, with the atrophy of the "eccentric" papyri after 150 BC or so, is that both the later performance traditions and the later commercial books of Homer revert to reflecting more closely an earlier and more canonical Athenian rhapsodic tradition that pre-dates the era of the "eccentric" papyri. There will be more to say about such a rhapsodic tradition in the next two chapters. Further, these patterns of reversion in the popular Homer do indeed correspond to the canonical new edition that had just been prepared by Aristarchus – an edition that reflects most closely a canonical Athenian tradition. Thus it may be more apt to find a metaphor other than *withering away*, such as *sclerosis*, in describing the fate of the performance tradition of Homer after 150 BC. We may prefer, however, a metaphor that leaves room for the esthetic possibilities of the envisaged process, and thus I revert to the image with which we started this chapter, that of crystallization.

Let us return to the important implications of what Labarbe had discovered in his study of Plato's Homer. We have seen that at least some of the variations that are attested in this instance of Homeric transmission reveal clearly the performance traditions of rhapsodes. "If Labarbe and other modern critics are right," as van der Valk comments, then "the Homeric text was originally transmitted orally."[163] "It is obvious," he continues, "that the acceptance of this theory has far-reaching consequences."[164] In fact, "the whole basis of our Homeric text becomes uncertain."[165] To put it another way: if Labarbe is right, *we can no longer determine the archetype.*

Van der Valk's reaction is to posit a purely textual rather than oral transmission, going back all the way to a time when "Homer

[163] Van der Valk 1964.266–267.
[164] Van der Valk 1964.267.
[165] Ibid.

put down his poems in writing."[166] Whereas I prefer Labarbe's findings about a rhapsodic phase of transmission and resist van der Valk's radical alternative, Labarbe makes further inferences about his findings that I cannot share. According to Labarbe, we simply do not know exactly what the real Homer said, but we do know that the rhapsodes could change it in the context of a continuing oral tradition.[167] So this critic too, like those who believe in a purely textual transmission, posits an archetype, albeit an unwritten one, setting up yet again the choice between right variants that supposedly come from this archetype and wrong ones that come from elsewhere. According to Labarbe's model, there are inferior variants stemming from the rhapsodes and superior ones, from Homer, so that only the second category is allowed to be "authentic."[168] And yet, the criteria for establishing what is superior or inferior, right or wrong, seem to me subjective.

What is needed is a set of objective editorial criteria that take into account the phenomenon of variation in reperformance. This phenomenon is reflected not only in the textual variants that we find in Plato's Homer but also in those reported by Alexandrian critics like Aristarchus. Again I find that most arguments about whether a given variant is spurious or genuine, inferior or superior, are unfounded. We are entitled to like or dislike any given variants that the various Alexandrian critics had chosen from time to time, and we may even classify these critics according to their methods or prejudices in choosing one kind of variation over another, but what we cannot do is simply assume that they have made a conjecture just because their choice of a reading does not suit our own sense of editorial verisimilitude.[169]

---

[166] Van der Valk 1964.269. See also Bolling 1925.33–34, who claims that all Homeric variants result from a written rather than oral tradition, and that this tradition has a single "fountain-head," which is "an Athenian text not earlier than the sixth century."

[167] Labarbe 1949.423–425.

[168] Labarbe 1949.425.

[169] This point applies even to situations that we could consider minimal conjecture, such as athetesis. When an Alexandrian editor athetizes, he does not propose to change any reading in the text proper but simply questions the genuineness of a line with an obelus in the margins. There is evidence that, at least in the case of Aristarchus, the editor formed his judgment about the alleged spuriousness of a line quite methodically, on the basis of not only the internal evidence *but also the external evidence*

A rigorous case-by-case review of instances where van der Valk has argued that ancient critics substituted conjectures for genuine readings can lead to conclusions quite different from his. The case-by-case review of Ludwich 1884/1885 remains in my opinion a most valuable aid.

There has been one such review by Vittorio Citti, in which many of the variant readings stemming from the *politikaí* or 'city editions' of Homer have been defended, in my opinion successfully, from van der Valk's arguments against their authenticity.[170] Though I disagree wherever Citti concludes that a given reading of the *politikaí* is "superior" to that of the surviving manuscript traditions,[171] or for that matter wherever he says that a reading is "inferior,"[172] we may note with interest that he treats some variants, like the reported reading χέει ἄσπετον of the Massaliotike at *Iliad* 12.281(scholia AT) and the reading χέει ἔμπεδον of the surviving manuscripts (and of Aristarchus: scholia AT), as "both ancient" (*ambedue antiche*).[173] The central question is not even whether both such readings are *ancient* but more simply whether both are *authentic*.

---

of the manuscript traditions. In the case of Aristarchus' editorial work, Apthorp 1980 has demonstrated the consistency of his method. With reference to the tag *perissós* 'extraneous' in the transmitted judgments of Alexandrian critics of the Homer text, Reeve 1972.250 observes: "but if in one single case an Alexandrian athetesis can be shown to have rested on documentary evidence, the possibility must always be reckoned with that *perissós* has documentary authority behind it." He then gives three examples of Alexandrian *perissós* verdicts that are indeed backed up by documentary evidence: at *Iliad* 23.92, 4.88, 21.290 – in that order. In the second case, there is an outright omission of the given line, an omission attributed to Zenodotus (actually, it is line 89 that he left out of his edition, while he leaves in 88 with wording that differs from what survives in the medieval manuscript tradition), and his judgment is backed up by the evidence of Papyrus 41 (the numbering follows the Monro–Allen 1920 OCT edition of the *Iliad*), on which see Apthorp 1980.1–2, 81.

[170] Citti 1966 (cf. Rengakos 1993.74n5). See also Apthorp 1980.116n112, who finds "unconvincing" van der Valk's efforts to dismiss as conjectures the variant readings of the *politikaí*. In the case of the Chios edition, Apthorp (p. 76) dates it earlier than Zenodotus. Citti (p. 32) dates the *politikaí* back to the fourth century BC. He also points out (p. 30) an important fact about the Homer citation in Aeschines *Against Timarchus* 149, where the verse from *Iliad* 23.77 contains a variant οὐ γὰρ ἔτι that is shared by some of the *politikaí* (scholia A: ἔν τισι τῶν πολιτικῶν) as opposed to the variant οὐ μὲν γάρ of the surviving manuscript traditions: the verses that Aeschines here is asking the *grammateús* 'clerk' to read out loud come from a Homer edition that clearly had plus-verses.

[171] E.g. Citti 1966.10, 43; at p. 17, there is even talk about an "original" reading.

[172] E.g. Citti 1966.14, 18, 23, 43.

[173] Citti 1966.15.

In general, a most convincing proof of a variant's authenticity is its relative archaism. A particularly striking example is the reported reading δούρασιν ἄμφω of the Massaliotike at *Iliad* 21.162 (scholia AT), with an archaic indeclinable ἄμφω (also attested in *Homeric Hymn to Demeter* 15), as opposed to the reading δούρασιν ἀμφίς of the surviving manuscripts. Still, δούρασιν ἀμφίς may be just as archaic in terms of a formulaic system that could generate both forms.[174] What turns out to be an even more striking example of proven archaism appears in a variant: at *Iliad* 21.351, where the surviving manuscripts read ἠδὲ κύπειρον, the *politikaí* read ἠδὲ κύπαιρον (scholia AT: αἱ ἐκ τῶν πόλεων ἠδὲ κύπαιρον εἶχον). Citti thinks that *kúpairos* is a "Dorism" as distinct from Ionic *kúpeiros*,[175] while van der Valk says that *kúpairos* "is, in my opinion, a corruption or an instance of local orthography."[176] I propose instead that *kúpairos* is an archaism, which could have entered the oral poetic tradition at a relatively early period, perhaps even as early as the second millennium BC: in the Linear B documents, for example, we find the form *ku-pa-ro₂* = *kuparyos*, ancestor of *kúpairos*.[177] It is precisely this same form *kúpairos* that we find attested in the "city editions." Even in this case, however, I would argue that *kúpeiros* too is an authentic variant.

It is instructive in the context of this discussion to assess van der Valk's opinion about a pair of variant readings that we have already considered, the case of the phrasing ἔλπομαι εὐχόμενος 'I hope, praying ...' at *Iliad* 8.526, which is the reported reading of Zenodotus and is found in a minority of manuscripts, as opposed to εὔχομαι ἐλπόμενος 'I pray, hoping ...', which is the reported reading of Aristarchus and is found in a majority of manuscripts. In this case, van der Valk concludes from the sense of the Homeric passage in question that "Zenodotus' reading seems to be the better one."[178] So Zenodotus is here exceptionally being rescued from the charge of conjecture. But now the blame is shifted to Aristarchus instead: according to van der Valk, if Zenodotus

---

[174] *Iliad* 5.723 and 14.123 are comparable instances of verse-final ἀμφίς.
[175] Citti 1966.27.
[176] Van der Valk 1964.7n33.
[177] Ventris and Chadwick 1973.557–558, with special reference to Pylos tablets Un 249 and Un 267.
[178] Van der Valk 1964.76.

did not make a conjecture in this case, then surely Aristarchus must have.[179] Whoever has the "better" reading, if we follow this line of thought, must be using the real text. Whoever has the "worse" reading, to continue in this line, must be making a conjecture. The problem with such an approach, as Muellner's findings reveal, is that the question of a "better" or "worse" reading is moot here, once we re-examine the question from the standpoint of formula analysis: both readings can in fact be shown to be authentic.

Thus I reaffirm my position that we need to take all authenticated variants into account in establishing a multitext format for the editing of Homer. Only within such a multitext editorial framework can we turn to questions of whether one variant was more suitable than another at a given time and place. But it is important also to reaffirm that Aristarchus and his predecessors, even though they collected a wide range of variants, had in mind an editorial goal very different from the one I am advocating. They treated the textual traditions of Homer as primary evidence and the performance traditions, which as we will see were still alive in their time, as mostly irrelevant to their primary goal, which was the recovery of an original Homer.[180]

In this respect, Aristotle may have had a different outlook, if I am not mistaken in detecting in his work traces of a sustained interest in the performative aspects of Homer. A clear example is his critique, in *Poetics* 1462a, of the techniques of a rhapsode called Sosistratos, otherwise unknown to us, *as an actor.*[181] It may also be pertinent to cite the anecdote that has Plato giving Aristotle the sobriquet *anagnóstēs* 'the one who reads out loud' (*Vita Marciana*, Aristotle *Fragments* 428.2 Rose).[182] Rudolf Blum remarks about this sobriquet: "in order to understand the joke one must remember that in Antiquity people read aloud, but that well-to-do gentlemen had slaves read aloud to them."[183] We may note that *anagnóstēs* can designate, more specifically, a slave who is trained

---

[179] Ibid.

[180] An illuminating discussion: Ritoók 1987.17.

[181] Just as the art of the dramatic actor, *hupokritikḗ*, is associated here in Aristotle *Poetics* 1462a with the art of the rhapsode, so also in Plato *Ion* 536a, Ion is both *rhapsōidós* 'rhapsode' and *hupokritḗs* 'actor'.

[182] Pfeiffer 1968.71n2 gives further information, which is of great interest.

[183] Blum 1991.70n47.

to read out loud *to copyists* in the process of book-production.[184] As we will see in the next chapter, however, to say this much about the meaning of *anagnóstēs* may not be enough, especially in view of a custom current in an earlier historical period, conveyed by the verb *paranagignóskō*, of reading out loud to *performers*.[185] For now, however, it is enough to ask whether the sobriquet *anagnóstēs* shows that Aristotle was interested in how the text of Homer should sound, as it were.

By contrast, as we move forward in time to the era of Aristarchus and his followers, we find that they were interested almost exclusively in the textual rather than the performative dimensions of Homeric transmission.[186] To that extent they were not all that different from many contemporary investigators of the Homeric text, who assume that their task is a quest to recover the original composition despite the historical reality of multiformity in the text – a reality that reflects multiformity in performance.

The intellectual framework, then, of this quest for the real Homer was pioneered by the likes of Aristarchus. It seems clear that they believed in a real Homer, an original Homer. And to believe this much is of course nothing new. It was not only the editors of Homeric texts who posited an original: so too did myth, and myth posits an original author as well, called Homer.[187] The further back we go in time, the greater the repertoire of this Homer, including in the earlier times all the so-called Cycle, all the Theban epics, and so on; as we have seen, the very notion of "Cycle" had once served as a metaphor for all of Homer's poetry.[188]

The further we go forward in time, by contrast, the less there is that Homer did himself. Not only is his repertoire becoming restricted to the *Iliad* and *Odyssey*: there are many parts even of

[184] Sealey 1990.129 and 183n17, with reference to a successful publisher in the Roman era, T. Pomponius Atticus, who is said to have employed men described as *anagnostae optimi et plurimi librarii* 'the best readers [*anagnôstai*] and the greatest number of scribes' (Nepos *Life of Atticus* 13.3). Sealey 1990.129 adds that "one could achieve multiple production on a small scale by setting one slave to read a text aloud while many slaves sat around him and wrote down what they heard."
[185] See ch.6.
[186] See the discussion of Hermodoros the rhapsode at p. 130 above.
[187] See ch.3 above.
[188] Ibid.

these epics that now become suspect: for example, Homer surely could not have composed the Shield of Achilles in *Iliad* 18.483–608, in the opinion of Zenodotus (scholia A to *Iliad* 18.483a).[189] And the original Homer of this more critical and suspicious age becomes all the more specific and even brittle in identity, reflecting ever more the critics' understanding of his archetypal creation, his text. For Aristarchus, it appears that Homer was an Athenian who lived around 1000 BC, in the time of Athenian migrations (Proclus F a 58–62 Severyns; cf. *Life of Homer* p. 244.13, p. 247.8 Allen; cf. scholia A to *Iliad* 13.197);[190] moreover, the scholiastic tradition stemming ultimately from Aristarchus implies that Homer *wrote* his poems (scholia A to *Iliad* 17.719) and that Hesiod actually had a chance to *read* them (scholia A to *Iliad* 12.22a).[191]

Even though Aristarchus, following the thought-patterns of myth, posited a Homeric original, he nevertheless accepted and in fact respected the reality of textual variants. He respected variants because, in terms of his own working theory, it seems that any one of them could have been the very one that Homer wrote (and Hesiod read). That is why he makes the effort of knowing the many different readings of so many manuscripts. He is in fact far more cautious in methodology than some contemporary investigators of Homer who may be more quick to say which is the right reading and which are the wrong ones. Aristarchus may strike us as naïve in reconstructing an Athenian Homer who "wrote" around 1000 BC, but that kind of construct enables him to be more rigorous in making choices among variants.[192]

What, then, would Aristarchus have lost, and what would we stand to lose, if it really is true that the variants of Homeric textual tradition reflect for the most part the multiforms of a

---

[189] On the factor of changing esthetics in the process of Homeric transmission, see also di Luzio 1969.142.

[190] Cf. Davison 1955.21, Pfeiffer 1968.228, Janko 1992.32 (n53), 71.

[191] Porter 1992.83.

[192] This is not to say, of course, that his choices are necessarily "right." We may recall the remark of Reeve 1972.258 about the dilemma faced by modern editors who restrict their choices to the evidence of the manuscript transmission as they have reconstructed it: "an editor who prints a reading when he regards another as more probable is not doing his job, and an editor who fancies he can avoid arbitrary procedure by sticking to the transmitted text is making a judgement of probability just as arbitrary as if he were to change it."

performance tradition? If you accept the reality of multiforms, you forfeit the elusive certainty of finding the original composition of Homer but you gain, and I think this is an important gain, another certainty, an unexpected one but one that may turn out to be much more valuable: you recover a significant portion of the Homeric repertoire. In addition, you recover a sense of the diachrony. From the sketch of Homeric periodization that I have just offered, one can develop a sense of different Homers for different times, such as a relatively "proper Homer" for the late fourth century and thereafter, periods 4 and 5, as opposed to a "primitive Homer" in, say, periods 1 and 2, the era before the reforms of the Peisistratidai. As for period 3, we will see in the next chapter that the most appropriate description may be the "common" Homer – or let us say the Homer of the Koine.

Let us return to the fact that some Homer experts who accept Lord's formulation of "oral" poetry seem ready at times to discount the value of Aristarchus' editorial repertoire of variants, which go far beyond the Koine or "Vulgate" texts of Homer. There is an irony here. It would be more understandable for proponents of a "writing Homer" to reject variant X or Y, accepting Aristarchus' implicit premise that only one variant can be right and that Homer could not have written X or Y for such-and-such reasons. It is unnecessary, however, for proponents of an "oral Homer" to insist on one and only one right version, unless they are also willing to believe that the oral tradition ground to a dead halt sometime around the second half of the eighth century BC, after the text was supposedly dictated.[193] In earlier work, presenting arguments that challenge the idea of an early dictation, I substituted an "evolutionary model" to account for the process of Homeric text-fixation.[194] Here I have refined that model with a scheme of five consecutive periods of Homeric tradition culminating with the text of Aristarchus. Still, we are left with the clear impression that multiformity, however reduced, remains a persistent feature even in the terminal phases of this tradition.

[193] For the theory that the *Iliad* and *Odyssey* were indeed dictated in the eighth century, see Janko 1992.22, 26.
[194] Summary, with bibliography, in N 1992a.37–53.

6

Homer as script

The Athenian Koine or "Vulgate" version of Homer, even if it were to have no claim to be the original Homer any more than the text established by Aristarchus, represents a crucial era in the history of Homeric performance traditions. This is the next argument to be made, added as a qualification to my earlier argument that we cannot simplistically apply the criteria of right or wrong, better or worse, original or altered, in the editorial process of sorting out the Homeric variants transmitted by Aristarchus or by earlier sources. It is indeed justifiable, however, to ask whether a variant is *authentic* or not – provided we understand "authentic" to mean *in conformity with traditional oral epic diction.*[1]

Further, it is justifiable to ask whether a given variant can be assigned to a particular period. In the scheme of five periods in the history of Homeric transmission, formulated at the beginning of the previous chapter, I propose that the variants attributed by Didymus and, ultimately, by Aristarchus to the Koine version of Homer tend to converge toward period 3, while the variants often preferred by Aristarchus himself or by other Alexandrian critics are typical of periods 4 and 5. This is not going so far as to say that some variants go all the way back to period 3 while others go only as far back as periods 4 and 5. It is only to say that certain kinds of variants seem to predominate at certain periods within the continuum of Homeric transmission. And it still remains to ask what if any distinguishing features we may find in an Athenian Koine version of period 3 – an era defined in the previous chapter

[1] The criteria of any "traditional oral epic diction," it is important to repeat, are hardly universal: they have to be studied within the different historical contexts of different cultures.

as extending from the middle of the sixth century BC to the later part of the fourth.

Let us briefly review the terminology. T. W. Allen's summary concerning the terms *koiné* (singular) and *koinaí* (plural) is instructive:

> We conclude that the *koiné* or vulgate adduced by Didymus in his commentary – if not by the Alexandrians themselves – consisted of the ordinary or uncorrected copies produced by the book trade, whose general characteristic was an increasing modernity in syntax, vocabulary, and phonetics. In most of these points the vulgate was 'careless' and even 'bad'. The principal aim of the professional critic, Alexandrian and other, was to stay the course of the modernizing process by restoring older forms and words.[2]

Allen's notion of "modernism" is also instructive: "In an unfenced text the single tendency that is constant is that to modernism, the effect of the ambient: our printed Bibles, Shakespeares, Miltons have long since been adduced."[3]

There is a problem with this formulation. As we have seen in the previous chapter, the variants in the Koine textual tradition of Homer are in fact frequently more archaic than those found in the edited versions of the Alexandrian scholars. Thus the Koine is by no means the most "modernistic" version of Homer. Some, in fact, would claim just the opposite. For example, Richard Janko and others who agree with the theory of a dictated Homer text interpret the archaisms of the Koine as proof that this particular textual tradition comes closest to a hypothetical archetype, a dictated text stemming from the eighth century BC.[4] According to this theory, the Koine is a sort of default category, a core text that reflects the Homeric "archetype" more closely and accurately than do the texts of Aristarchus and the other Alexandrian scholars who came before him.[5]

But there is a problem with this formulation as well. As we have also seen in the previous chapter, many Homeric variants

---

[2] Allen 1924.282.
[3] Allen 1924.281.
[4] Janko 1992.22, 26.
[5] Ibid.

reported by the Alexandrian scholars as alternatives to the variants in the Koine can be shown to be just as authentic in their own right. So if indeed the Koine textual tradition of Homer is no more "original" than other traditions, then the question is: what if anything makes the Koine distinct?

In terms of my evolutionary model of Homeric text fixation, what stands out about the Koine is precisely the fact that it is not at all some kind of systematically "modernized" version, and to this extent I resist Allen's quoted description. On the other hand, we can in principle accept Allen's notion of an *unfenced* text – provided we restrict the description "unfenced" to Homeric Koine texts as *transcripts* of performances. The point is, however, that the actual performance traditions as reflected by the posited transcripts seem to be anything but unfenced. A salient example is the principle of a fixed *numerus versuum*: as suggested in the previous chapter, this principle of Homeric transmission can be explained as a *performative* as well as *textual* norm.[6] Patterns of stabilization in length of performance need not presuppose the agency of a written text.[7] Following up on this line of thinking, I raised the possibility that these and other patterns of performance stabilization are connected with patterns of performance regulation by the Athenian State.[8] That possibility will now be explored in depth.

Let us adopt for the moment the standpoint of Homer experts who do not reckon with the dimension of performance in the history of Homeric transmission. For them, the evidence of a fixed *numerus versuum* argues for the concept of an Athenian Homer *text* as a historical reality.[9] From this standpoint, the Athenian Homer is in effect a "fenced" text, not an "unfenced" one as it is for Allen.[10] From the standpoint of my argument, however, it is an oversimplification to posit a "fenced" Athenian

---

[6] See p. 143.

[7] Cf. p. 144. See again N 1992a.40.

[8] Ibid.

[9] Bolling 1925, followed by Apthorp 1980.

[10] Those who envisage an Athenian version of Homer purely in textual terms can disagree radically about the reliability of the Alexandrian critics in transmitting such a version: see Rengakos 1993.15–16, who lists various experts representing what he sees as the two opposing sides (it may be noted here that many other radical disagreements separate those who are supposedly members of each side). See further below at p. 185n118.

text. The Koine or "Vulgate" version of Homer may be traced back to a "fenced" *tradition of performance*, located primarily in Athens during "period 3," which extends from the middle of the sixth century BC to the later part of the fourth. Granted, we may expect that the concept of such a "fenced" Athenian tradition was indeed moving toward the status of a text, especially toward the end of "period 3," but it is useful for now to maintain a distinction between this kind of "text" and the ultimate form of Homer. An apt term for the "fenced" Homer tradition at the end of "period 3" is *script*.

I will introduce several different pieces of evidence to justify the application of this term to the late Koine version of Homer, as also to later versions. The centerpiece will be a passage taken from Athenaeus 620b–c, which suggests that Homeric performance traditions were reformed in Athens at the initiative of Demetrius of Phalerum. This is the Demetrius who, as we learn from other sources, came to power at Athens in 317 and ruled until 307 BC, when he was overthrown.[11] Since our basic attested source concerning Demetrius and his reform of Homeric performance traditions is going to be this single passage from a relatively late author, Athenaeus of Naucratis (who flourished around 200 AD), and since the wording of this passage, as we are about to see, is opaque and difficult to interpret, it is essential for the sake of an overall perspective to begin with a brief outline of some historical facts, as known from other sources, concerning Demetrius as a reformer of Athenian traditions.[12] It is only from the perspective of this historical background that we may then more fully appreciate the implications of the relevant passage in Athenaeus 620b–c, to be quoted and analyzed later on.

For purposes of the present argument, the most important historical fact to keep in mind about Demetrius of Phalerum is that he was the reformer of many Athenian institutions. He is best known for having initiated a major reform of Athenian State

[11] Basic works on Demetrius of Phalerum: Bayer 1942, Dow and Travis 1943, Wehrli 1968.
[12] On the cultural reforms of Demetrius in Athens, and on his connections with the school of Aristotle, see in general Williams 1987 (who also surveys the bibliography, which is vast).

Theater in the fourth quarter of the fourth century,[13] following the patterns of an earlier reformer, the statesman Lycurgus, in the third quarter.[14] Demetrius took the decisive step of abolishing the *khorēgía*, that is, the duty imposed on wealthy citizens to finance the choruses of State Theater.[15] From around 309 BC onward, the Athenian State went beyond the earlier pattern of paying salaries to the actors, hereafter paying salaries also to the chorus and even financing its costumes.[16]

Demetrius is also credited with other reforms, each of which was seemingly intended to insure the prevalence of canonical forms. For example, he was responsible for a collection of a corpus of popular tradition that has come down to us as the Fables of Aesop (Diogenes Laertius 5.80: ἀλλὰ μὴν καὶ λόγων Αἰσωπείων συναγωγαί; at 5.81, in the bibliographical listing of his works: Αἰσωπείων α′).[17] He also had a role in establishing a canonical form for the ongoing lore about the Seven Sages (Stobaeus 3.79 and 43.131).[18] Demetrius of Phalerum is the same man, it should be emphasized, who was author of two volumes entitled "On the *Iliad*" (Περὶ 'Ιλιάδος α′ β′) and four volumes entitled "On the *Odyssey*" (Περὶ 'Οδυσσείας α′ β′ γ′ δ′), according to Diogenes Laertius 5.81.

With this historical background, let us now turn to the key passage suggesting that Demetrius had reformed the institution of Homeric performances in Athens:

[13] Blum 1991.24.

[14] On Lycurgus as a cultural forerunner of Demetrius, see Mossé 1989. In the discussion that follows, I propose to compare briefly the reforms of Athenian State Theater undertaken by Lycurgus and Demetrius.

[15] Blum 1991.24.

[16] Ibid.

[17] Cf. FGH no. 228 p. 957. Cf. Adrados 1983. Jacoby FGH no. 228 Notes p. 644 points out that the bibliography of Demetrius' works as listed in Diogenes Laertius 5.80–81 tends to prove Demetrius' connection with the Library of Alexandria (T 6b, e), in that ordinarily there are no such lists for "modern" authors. The total list, as given in Diogenes Laertius 5.80–81, is staggering. This cumulative bibliography of Demetrius, which is supplemented in Wehrli 1968.518–522, is reproduced in the Appendix.

[18] Χρειῶν α′ in the bibliography of Demetrius as given in Diogenes Laertius 5.81 has been identified with this lore about the Seven Sages: Jacoby FGH no. 228 Notes p. 644 (see DK 11 214). In Diogenes Laertius 1.22, we read about Thales of Miletus: καὶ πρῶτος σοφὸς ὠνομάσθη ἄρχοντος 'Αθήνησι Δαμασίου, καθ' ὃν καὶ οἱ ἑπτὰ σοφοὶ ἐκλήθησαν, ὥς φησι Δημήτριος ὁ Φαληρεὺς ἐν τῇ τῶν 'Αρχόντων ἀναγραφῇ (Demetrius of Phalerum FGH 228 F 1).

οὐκ ἀπελείποντο δὲ ἡμῶν τῶν συμποσίων οὐδὲ ῥαψῳδοί.

ἔχαιρε γὰρ τοῖς Ὁμήρου ὁ Λαρήνσιος ὡς ἄλλος οὐδὲ εἷς, ὡς λῆρον ἀποφαίνειν Κάσανδρον τὸν Μακεδονίας βασιλεύσαντα, περὶ οὗ φησι Καρύστιος ἐν Ἱστορικοῖς ὑπομνήμασιν ὅτι οὕτως ἦν φιλόμηρος ὡς διὰ στόματος ἔχειν τῶν ἐπῶν τὰ πολλά· καὶ Ἰλιὰς ἦν αὐτῷ καὶ Ὀδυσσεία ἰδίως γεγραμμέναι. ὅτι δ᾽ ἐκαλοῦντο οἱ ῥαψῳδοὶ καὶ Ὁμηρισταὶ Ἀριστοκλῆς εἴρηκεν ἐν τῷ περὶ Χορῶν. τοὺς δὲ νῦν Ὁμηριστὰς ὀνομαζομένους πρῶτος εἰς τὰ θέατρα παρήγαγε Δημήτριος ὁ Φαληρεύς. Χαμαιλέων δὲ ἐν τῷ περὶ Στησιχόρου καὶ μελῳδηθῆναί φησιν οὐ μόνον τὰ Ὁμήρου, ἀλλὰ καὶ τὰ Ἡσιόδου καὶ Ἀρχιλόχου, ἔτι δὲ Μιμνέρμου καὶ Φωκυλίδου. Κλέαρχος δὲ ἐν τῷ προτέρῳ περὶ Γρίφων "τὰ Ἀρχιλόχου, φησίν, [ὁ] Σιμωνίδης ὁ Ζακύνθιος ἐν τοῖς θεάτροις ἐπὶ δίφρου καθήμενος ἐραψῴδει." Λυσανίας δ᾽ ἐν τῷ πρώτῳ περὶ Ἰαμβοποιῶν Μνασίωνα τὸν ῥαψῳδὸν λέγει ἐν ταῖς δείξεσι τῶν Σιμωνίδου τινὰς ἰάμβων ὑποκρίνεσθαι. τοὺς δ᾽ Ἐμπεδοκλέους Καθαρμοὺς ἐραψῴδησεν Ὀλυμπίασι Κλεομένης ὁ ῥαψῳδός, ὥς φησιν Δικαίαρχος ἐν τῷ Ὀλυμπικῷ. Ἰάσων δ᾽ ἐν τρίτῳ περὶ τῶν Ἀλεξάνδρου Ἱερῶν ἐν Ἀλεξανδρείᾳ φησὶν ἐν τῷ μεγάλῳ θεάτρῳ ὑποκρίνασθαι Ἡγησίαν τὸν κωμῳδὸν τὰ Ἡσιόδου,[19] Ἑρμόφαντον δὲ τὰ Ὁμήρου.

Nor were rhapsodes [*rhapsōidoí*] missing from our symposia. For Larensis took delight in the works of Homer as no one else could, so much so that he made even Cassander, the one who was King of Macedonia, look superficial. About whom [Cassander] it is said by the Carystian in his *Historikà hupomnémata* that he was such a Homer enthusiast [*philómēros*] that he could orally quote much of the epic poetry. And he [Cassander] made his own private transcript of the *Iliad* and *Odyssey*.[20] That the rhapsodes [*rhapsōidoí*] were also called *Homēristaí* is reported by Aristocles

---

[19] Valckenaer emends, maybe unnecessarily, from Ἡροδότου.

[20] J. D. Morgan comments (*per litteras* 6 June 1994): "This is certainly evidence for Cassander's high level of interest in Homer and possibly even for his concern for the proper constitution of the text of Homer." For Cassander to commission transcripts of the *Iliad* and *Odyssey* is effectively to produce his own private edition. I suspect that Aristotle himself did so, and that he may in fact be the model for what Cassander is reported to have done. Cassander, son of Alexander's regent Antipater, was the ruler of Macedon from 317 to 297. He was on close terms with Aristotle's successor, Theophrastus, who composed a book entitled Πρὸς Κάσανδρον περὶ βασιλείας Ἡo

in his work *On choruses*. Demetrius of Phalerum was the first to introduce those who are nowadays called *Homēristaí* into the theaters. Chamaeleon, in his work *On Stesichorus*, says that not only the poetry of Homer was melodically sung but also that of Hesiod and Archilochus, even that of Mimnermus and Phocylides. Clearchus, in the first of the two books of his work entitled *On riddles*, says: "Simonides of Zacynthus, seated on a stool, used to perform rhapsodically [verb *rhapsōidéō*] the poetry of Archilochus in the theaters."[21] Lysanias, in the first book of his work *On the iambic poets*, says that Mnasion the rhapsode [*rhapsōidós*] used to act [*hupokrínomai*] in his performances [*deíxis* plural] some of the iambs of Simonides.[22] As for the *Katharmoi* of Empedocles, Kleomenes the rhapsode [*rhapsōidós*] performed them rhapsodically [verb *rhapsōidéō*] at Olympia, as Dicaearchus says in his work, *The Olympic*. Jason says, in the third book of his work *The sacred institutions of Alexander*, that Hegesias the performer of comedies acted [*hupokrínomai*] in the Great Theater in Alexandria the poetry of Hesiod, and Hermophantos, the poetry of Homer.

Athenaeus 620b–c

According to this passage, the contents of which are repeated by Eustathius 4.937.19–24, Demetrius of Phalerum transferred the performances of Homer "into the theaters," as we see from the underscored wording, and the performers of this reformed performance tradition are "nowadays" called *Homēristaí*. The wording here allows a variety of interpretations. My own is this: that the *Homēristaí* eventually replaced the earlier category of *rhapsōidoí* or rhapsodes. Since Athenaeus is linking performances *in theaters* by *Homēristaí* with historically attested performances *in theaters* by *rhapsōidoí*, we may infer that he thinks of the *Homēristaí* as continuing in the traditions of the rhapsodes – this despite the

Cassander, on Kingship' (Diogenes Laertius 5.47, Athenaeus 144e). In the discussion that follows, I will take note of Cassander's relationship with Demetrius of Phalerum.

[21] On the dating of Clearchus, who flourished between 300 and 250 BC, see Bartol 1992.67, with further references.

[22] Lysanias was reportedly the teacher of Eratosthenes (*Suda* s.v. Eratosthenes); the latter flourished in the third century BC, so that Lysanias is roughly contemporaneous with Clearchus. I draw attention to the dates of Clearchus (previous note) and Lysanias because both these relatively early sources seem to associate the art of the rhapsodes with theatrics. Such an association is important for later stages of my argumentation.

likelihood that the performance traditions of the *Homēristaí*, as we will see below, evolved into something quite different from the traditions of the earlier rhapsodes. As we begin to recognize the differences, however, we should at the same time keep in mind that the performance traditions of fifth- and fourth-century rhapsodes, who apparently declaimed in recitative style, without musical accompaniment, were in turn quite different from those of the even earlier *aoidoí* 'singers' as they are actually portrayed by the Homeric narrative.[23]

I argue, then, for a historical connection between *rhapsōidoí* and *Homēristaí* on the basis of the passage just quoted from Athenaeus 620b–c. These arguments are in general agreement with conclusions reached by the papyrologist Geneviève Husson, and we will examine presently some of the supporting evidence that she adduces.[24] In earlier work on this Athenaeus passage, I had already posited a continuity between the *rhapsōidoí* and the *Homēristaí*, though at the same time I stressed the differences between the two designations of performers, recognizing that the testimony of Athenaeus may well have conflated various different stages in the evolution of performance traditions.[25]

Granting that there are differences, I propose to defend the connection between *rhapsōidoí* and *Homēristaí* made by our source here, Athenaeus of Naucratis (around 200 AD), who cites the

---

[23] For an extensive discussion of the recitative format of rhapsodic performance traditions: N 1990a.19–28.

[24] Husson 1993, who stresses the pertinence of Athenaeus 620b–c to the history of Homeric performance traditions. She argues also that the comments by Robert 1936 = 1969.673n4 and 1983.182–184 on *Homēristaí* need to be modified, if ever so slightly, on the basis of this passage. Further discussion below.

[25] N 1990a.26–27 (cf. West 1970.919), where I offer a detailed diachronic explanation of such concepts as represented by the word *melōidēthēnai* 'to be sung melodically' (in the passage quoted from Athenaeus 620c), arguing that it is anachronistic to translate this word as 'to be set to music'. Although the fifth and especially the fourth centuries mark an innovative phase in songmaking traditions where even poetic forms with reduced melody, such as hexameters and iambic trimeters, can indeed be "set to music" (1990a ibid.), there is a more basic principle to be kept in mind: that even recitative poetic forms like the hexameter stem ultimately from traditions of singing (N 1990a.24–26). Thus we may expect the modified survival of traditional patterns of melody even in poetic forms with ultimately reduced melody, like the hexameter. We may also expect the performance traditions of rhapsodes to reflect such patterns, which in turn would promote the preservation of archaic patterns of pitch accent (N 1990a. 29). More below on the subject of accent-patterns preserved in performance.

authority of Aristocles (between first century BC and first century AD).[26] I will also defend the connection that Athenaeus makes between Demetrius of Phalerum and the shifting of performances of Homer "into the theaters," in which context Athenaeus identifies the performers as the *Homēristaí*.[27] Then, on the basis of morphological parallels about to be adduced, we will consider the possibility that the term goes as far back as Demetrius himself. As we proceed, it is important to keep in mind that, even if the word *Homēristaí* goes as far back as the era of Demetrius of Phalerum, it does not follow that Homeric performers known by such a name in the late fourth century BC would have been just like the *Homēristaí* in the era of Athenaeus, at the beginning of the third century AD, about half a millennium later.[28]

Let us begin by considering a premier example of rhapsode-style performance in theaters, as cited by Athenaeus in the same passage quoted above: he is someone called Hermophantos, who is described, towards the end of our passage, as "acting" the poems of Homer at a performance in the Great Theater of Alexandria. The authority cited by Athenaeus for this information, Jason of Nysa (first century BC), takes us back to the Ptolemaic era.[29] We may compare another passage that deals with the performance of a rhapsode in the Ptolemaic era of Alexandria:

καὶ ὁ μὲν ῥαψῳδὸς εὐθὺς ἦν διὰ στόματος πᾶσιν, ἐν τοῖς Πτολεμαίου γάμοις ἀγομένου τὴν ἀδελφὴν καὶ πρᾶγμα δρᾶν ἀλλόκοτον ⟨νομιζ⟩ομένου καὶ ἄθεσμον ἀρξάμενος ἀπὸ τῶν ἐπῶν ἐκείνων·

Ζεὺς δ᾿ Ἥρην ἐκάλεσσε κασιγνήτην ἄλοχόν τε [*Iliad* 18.356][30]

---

[26] Cf. Husson 1993.94–95. On this point, I disagree with Boyd 1994, who argues that the connection between *rhapsōidoí* and *Homēristaí* is unjustifiable.

[27] Cf. Husson 1993.95. She thinks that the usage of the term *Homēristaí* can be linked with the era of Athenaeus.

[28] Timothy Boyd draws my attention to Diomedes *Ars Grammatica* 3.484.12–16 (fourth century AD), where the word *rhapsōidía* is associated with performance, in theatrical contexts, by *Homēristaí*.

[29] Husson 1993.95.

[30] It is crucial to note the use of δέ at the beginning of a rhapsodic performance. The fact that correlative μέν and δέ can be found separated by Homeric book-divisions, as at *Odyssey* 2.434 (μέν) and 3.1 (δέ), has been used along with other facts to argue that the division of the *Iliad* and *Odyssey* into twenty-four books each is "not

The rhapsode [*rhapsōidós*] was the talk of everybody – the one who, at the wedding of Ptolemy who, in marrying his own sister was considered to be committing a deed unnatural and unholy,[31] began with the following words:

'And Zeus summoned Hera his sister, his wife' [*Iliad* 18.356]

Plutarch *Quaestiones convivales* 736e

There is also earlier and to that extent even more valuable evidence connecting the performance of Homer with theatrical traditions. Already in Plato's *Ion*, we see the figure of Socrates making an explicit equation between the *rhapsōidós* 'rhapsode' and the *hupokrités* 'actor' (536a).[32] The rhapsode Ion himself is vividly portrayed as a master of histrionics (535c).[33] Aristotle too in his *Poetics* notes an overlap between the art of the rhapsode and that of the actor in drama, commenting on what he considers to be overacting on the part of one particular rhapsode, Sosistratos by name, specifically with regard to this man's use of physical dramatic gestures (1462a6).[34]

We find further evidence for a relatively early theatricalization of rhapsodic traditions when we look beyond the references to a specifically *Homeric* repertoire on the part of rhapsodes. Let us begin with Plato's *Ion*, where we learn that a rhapsode's repertoire could include not only Homer and Hesiod but also Archilochus (531a, 532a).[35] In the light of this information, we may look back at the extended passage in Athenaeus 620b–c, where we saw sources from the third century BC reporting rhapsodic performances of Archilochean poetry in particular (Clearchus) and

original but most likely a product of the Hellenistic age": see S. Douglas Olson, in a paper presented 28 December 1993 at the annual convention of the American Philological Association (APA 1993 Abstracts p. 41). On the basis of the anecdote that we have just seen, however, I would argue that such separations of correlative μέν and δέ are traditional rhapsodic practice: the δέ of *Iliad* 18.356, beginning a performance at the wedding of Ptolemy II, is syntactically correlated with a μέν in an earlier Iliadic verse, 18.354. More below on the possibility that Homeric book-divisions were based on rhapsodic practices.

[31] The historical occasion is the marriage, in the first quarter of the third century before our era, of Ptolemy II Philadelphus to his sister, Arsinoe, in accordance with the practice of Egyptian pharaohs – and in violation of Hellenic practices.

[32] See also Plato *Ion* 535b; cf. Husson 1993.95.

[33] Cf. Boyd 1994.

[34] See Dupont-Roc and Lallot 1980.407.

[35] N 1990a.25.

"iambic" poetry in general (Lysanias).³⁶ We may note in both sets of testimony the strong emphasis on the theatrical aspects of performance: the rhapsodic performance of Archilochean poetry by Simonides of Zacynthus is said to take place in theaters [*théatra*] (Clearchus), while Mnasion the rhapsode is said to act [*hupokrinomai*] in his performances [*deíxis* plural] of *iamboi* 'iambs' (Athenaeus 620c).

In this connection, it is crucial to compare a statement made by Aristotle in his *Politics* (1336b20–22): τοὺς δὲ νεωτέρους οὔτ' ἰάμβων οὔτε κωμῳδίας θεατὰς θετέον, πρὶν ἢ τὴν ἡλικίαν λάβωσιν ἐν ᾗ καὶ κατακλίσεως ὑπάρξει κοινωνεῖν ἤδη καὶ μέθης, καὶ τῆς ἀπὸ τῶν τοιούτων γιγνομένης βλάβης ἀπαθεῖς ἡ παιδεία ποιήσει πάντως 'it should be ordained that younger men not be theater-goers [*theataí*] of *iamboi* or of comedy until they reach the age where they have the opportunity to participate in lying down together at table and getting intoxicated [that is, to participate in symposia], at which point their education [*paideía*] will make them altogether immune to the harmful effect of these things'.³⁷ I infer that Aristotle is contrasting professional performance by rhapsodes or actors in theaters with amateur performance at symposia, and that he has in mind such poets as Archilochus

³⁶ See p. 159 above.

³⁷ Cf. Bartol 1992.66. My interpretation of this Aristotle passage depends on whether the *paideía* here refers to whatever the boy learns – by way of songs and the erotic sensibilities conveyed in the songs – as preparation for participation in the symposium. See Calame 1989, with reference to a red-figure painting by Douris on a drinking-cup produced between 490 and 480 BC (ARV² 431, 48 and 1653; CVA II pp. 29–30, with plates 77 and 78): the painting illustrates in rich detail two scenes, "A" and "B," where boys are being educated in the learning and the performance of song and musical accompaniment. On the left in both scenes A and B, a seated ephebe (B) or adult (A) is playing the reed (B) or the lyre (A). On the right in both scenes, a seated pedagogue, with a cane, looks on. In the middle is a young boy standing and facing a seated ephebe who holds a tablet, on which he is writing (B) and a young boy standing and facing a seated adult who holds a roll of papyrus, which he is reading (A). Another young boy is standing and facing the seated reed-playing ephebe on the left (B), and a seated lyre-playing ephebe faces the seated lyre-playing adult on the left (A). In scene A, there are musical instruments – both lyres and reeds – represented as levitating above the action, and they are framed on either side by representations of drinking-cups shaped just like the one painted by Douris. As Calame argues (p. 53), the songmaking apprenticeship of the boys, with distinct implications of homoerotic undertones (on both sides, there is an erotic inscription designed to touch the lips of whoever drinks from the cup), is being represented as a prerequisite for the integration of adolescents into the symposia of adult citizens, which is the context for which the drinking-cup of Douris is destined.

when he speaks of the performance of *íamboi,* presumably by rhapsodes, as parallel to the performance of comedy by actors.[38]

Let us pursue further, now moving considerably ahead in time, the connection made by the third-century BC sources of Athenaeus 620b–c between rhapsode-style performance and the setting of theaters. There is an incidental reference to theatrical performances of Homer in Achilles Tatius 3.20.4: τῶν τὰ Ὁμή- ρου τῷ στόματι δεικνύντων ἐν τοῖς θεάτροις 'those who perform [*deíknumi*] the poems of Homer orally in theaters'.[39] Let us now consider a related passage, by the same author, where the art of performing Homeric poems is designated by the verb *Homērízō.* It is this verb, of course, from which *Homēristaí* is derived. As we examine this passage, we will note various allusions to the theatricality of Homeric performance in what seems to be a parody of the very ideology of *paideía* 'education' in the arts. The context is this: in a legal wrangle, a speaker is attacking his opponent by portraying him as a moral degenerate. The man's degeneracy is being expressed metaphorically in a humorous narrative about his counterfeit *paideía* 'education' in the arts, as it were, where the idea of practicing the art par excellence seems to be equated mockingly with a theatrical image of "playing the *Homēristés.*" The central joke is in the word itself, since the form *Homērízō* is being used here as a pun to convey a sexual *double entendre* (*mēr-* in the sense of 'thigh'):

καί τοί γε νέος ὢν συνεγίνετο πολλοῖς αἰδοίοις ἀνδράσι
καὶ τὴν ὥραν ἅπασαν εἰς τοῦτο δεδαπάνηκε. σεμνότητα
δ' ἔδρακε καὶ σωφροσύνην ὑπεκρίνατο, παιδείας προσ-
ποιούμενος ἐρᾶν καὶ τοῖς εἰς ταύτην αὐτῷ χρωμένοις
πάντα ὑποκύπτων καὶ ὑποκατακλινόμενος ἀεί. καταλι-
πὼν γὰρ τὴν πατρῴαν οἰκίαν, ὀλίγον ἑαυτῷ μισθωσά-
μενος στενωπεῖον, εἶχεν ἐνταῦθα τὸ οἴκημα, ὁμηρίζων
μὲν τὰ πολλά, πάντας δὲ τοὺς χρησίμους πρὸς ἅπερ
ἤθελε προσηταιρίζετο δεχόμενος. καὶ οὕτω μὲν ἀσκεῖν
τὴν ψυχὴν ἐνομίζετο, ἦν δ' ἄρα τοῦτο κακουργίας
ὑπόκρισις.

---

[38] Further discussion at p. 218.
[39] On this passage, see Jones 1991.189, especially with reference to the use of weapons as props, as it were, for Homeric performance. See also p. 167 below.

When he was a boy, he would consort with many respect-
able men, and in fact he prodigiously spent the entire
bloom of his youth in this pursuit. He put on the look of
solemnity and played the role [*hupokrínomai*] of moderation,
pretending to be passionately devoted to *paideía* and behav-
ing consistently in a submissive and abjectly self-abasing
way towards those who became involved with him in this
pursuit. Leaving his father's house, he rented a little shack.
So he had his ménage there, being the *Homēristés*[40] for the
most part, while all along playing host and making friends
with anyone who would prove useful for whatever he
wanted. And in this way, the thinking was, he was edifying
his spirit. Of course, all this was acting [*hupókrisis*], a thing
of perversion.

Achilles Tatius 8.9.2–3

Given that the art of the rhapsode was becoming ever more
theatrical and mimetic over time, as we see from the testimony of
Plato and Aristotle already in the fourth century BC, we have
reason to expect Athenaeus, near the beginning of the third century AD, to assume that the theatrical tradition of the *Homēristaí*
was ultimately derived from an earlier rhapsodic heritage. Further, on the basis of Aristotle's remark about stylized physical
gestures in the mimesis of Homer – let us say the *acting* of Homer
– we have reason to expect such specific aspects of mimetic
performance to become ever more pronounced with the passage
of time. Let us consider a case in point, with explicit reference
to *Homēristaí*. In the *Interpretation of Dreams* by Artemidorus (4.2
ed. Pack), dated to the second century AD, there is an anecdote about a surgeon who once dreamed that he was acting
Homer, expressed by the verb *Homērízō* (ὁμηρίζειν νομίσας), and
the reason given for this dream is a mechanical analogy between
the motions made by surgeons as they make their incisions and
the motions made by *Homēristaí* as they make their gestures of
wounding opponents with weapons and drawing blood: καὶ γὰρ
οἱ ὁμηρισταὶ τιτρώσκουσι μὲν καὶ αἱμάσσουσιν, ἀλλ' οὐκ
ἀποκτεῖναί γε βούλονται· οὕτω δὲ καὶ ὁ χειρουργός 'for just

---

[40] In LSJ s.v. *Homēristés*, it is pointed out that the word conveys a sexual *double entendre* in this context. For another such sexual pun involving *mēr-* in the sense of
'thigh', see Crates, *Greek Anthology* 11.218.

as the *Homēristaí* make wounds and draw blood, without any intention of killing, so also does the surgeon'.[41]

There is a comparable reference to *Homēristaí* in Petronius, *Satyricon* 59.2–6, where the histrionics of these performers are being ridiculed as an abstruse exercise in art, on display for pretentious but ludicrously ignorant connoisseurs.[42] In this humorous account, the host Trimalchio starts by saying (59.2–3): ... *simus ergo, quod melius est, a primitiis hilares et* <u>*Homeristas*</u> *spectemus* 'so let us be festive, which is better, right from the start; let us watch the *Homēristaí*'. At that point (59.4–6), *intravit factio statim hastisque scuta concrepuit. ipse Trimalchio in pulvino consedit, et* <u>*cum Homeristae Graecis versibus colloquerentur, ut insolenter solent, ille canora voce Latine legebat librum.*</u> *mox silentio facto "scitis" inquit "quam fabulam agant? Diomedes et Ganymedes duo fratres fuerunt. horum soror erat Helena. Agamemnon illam rapuit ..."* 'there entered right away a troupe [of *Homēristaí*], beating on their shields with their spears. Trimalchio himself sat down on his cushion and, <u>while the *Homēristaí* were having their dialogues in Greek verses</u>, in their usual pompous manner, <u>he</u> [Trimalchio], in a sonorous voice, was <u>reading along, in Latin, from a book</u>.[43] Then after a moment of silence, he said: "Do you know what story they are acting? Well, Diomedes and Ganymedes were two brothers. They had a sister, Helen, and Agamemnon abducted her ..."'[this display of Trimalchio's faulty education continues through section 6]. When Trimalchio finishes (59.6): *haec ut dixit Trimalchio, clamorem Homeristae sustulerunt,...* 'when Trimalchio said these things, the *Homēristaí* raised a clamor ...'.

These passages from Artemidorus and Petronius show clear signs of a newer and ever more theatrical stage in the lengthy history of Homeric performance traditions – a stage where these traditions come closest to our own contemporary notion of a "script." We begin to appreciate from these later sources just

---

[41] Cf. Jones 1991.189. For a related passage, Achilles Tatius 3.20.4, see p. 164 above.

[42] Cf. also Jones, ibid.

[43] The humorous effect that is intended here may be this: one would expect an educated person to read along from a libretto written in the original Greek, as it were, but Trimalchio has to resort to a Latin translation. The implications of this detail, where someone is described as reading along while the Homeric performers recite their lines, may be pertinent to a custom dating back to fourth-century Athens, as discussed below.

how far the theatrical conventions in the performance of Homer have evolved from the conventions envisioned by earlier sources. We have just seen in the passage from Artemidorus that the *Homēristaí* actually act out the wounding of opponents with weapons. Now we see in Petronius that such explicitly mimetic gestures are being reinforced by stage props, as it were, such as spears and shields.[44] Moreover, in the passage from Petronius, it appears that different players take on different roles in enacting a Homeric scene. The players seem to have speaking parts, delivered in Greek verses (to be contrasted with Trimalchio's Latin), apparently representing the speeches of Homeric heroes engaged in combat with each other. I infer that these dialogues were dramatically excerpted – or let us say "scripted" – from actual combat scenes contained by the overall Homeric narrative. Thus I propose to adjust, ever so slightly, a formulation concerning the Artemidorus and the Petronius passages: according to Louis Robert, the *Homēristaí* mimed battles.[45] Surely the activity of miming does not exclude the factor of speaking parts, *delivered in Greek verse*. Still, my use of the expression "speaking parts" shows just how far removed we now are, as we contemplate this particular moment in the history of Homeric performance, from the early traditions of the rhapsodes. The text of Homer has achieved the status of a "script."[46]

The usage of calling the performers of Homer *Homēristaí*, as made explicit in the literary passages surveyed so far, is confirmed by the attested references in documentary papyri to live performances of Homer in Hellenized Egypt:[47]

[44] In some contemporary epic performance traditions of India, various characters of epic are re-enacted by performers who dance wielding specific weapons: for example, Arjuna with a bow and arrow, Draupadī with a scythe, and so forth. These weapons, once used in performance, are venerated as sacred objects. See Sax 1991.

[45] Robert 1936 = 1969.673n4 and 1983.182–184. In the *Corpus Glossariorum Latinorum*, the *Homēristaí* are mentioned s.v. *atellani*; see Husson 1993.94n6, who cites e.g. CGL II p. 22 lines 40–42 and VI p. 108 (we note the verbal association of *atellani* with *skēnikoí* and *biológoi* as well as *Homēristaí*).

[46] I should add: what is already "scripture" for Aristarchus may continue to be a "script" for the *Homēristaí*. More on the notion of "scripture" in ch.7.

[47] I first discussed these papyri in a paper presented 28 December 1992 at the annual convention of the American Philological Association ("Prosodic Anomalies in Homer: Evidence for Rhapsodic Performance Traditions?" APA 1992 Abstracts p. 89). The perceptive analysis of these same papyri by Husson 1993 has added valuable new information about these texts, which I now list in the order that she prefers. C. P.

1. P.Oxy. 3.519 fr. A 3–4 (Oxyrhynchus; ii AD) ὁμηριστῇ (δραχμαί + number 448)
2. P.Oslo 3.189.16 (place?; iii AD) ἀπόδιξις ὁμηρι[στῶν],[48] ἀγὼν ποιητῶν at line 19
3a. SB 4.7336.26 (Oxyrhynchus iii AD) ὁμηριστῇ
3b. same document, line 29 [ἄλλ]ῳ ὁμηριστῇ[49]
4. P.Oxy. 7.1050.26 (Oxyrhynchus ii/iii AD) ὁμηρισ[τῇ]
5. P.Oxy. 7.1025.8 (Oxyrhynchus; iii AD) καὶ Σαραπᾷ ὁμηριστῇ

Let us start with papyrus 5, which is the text of a contract formalized by the magistrates of the metropolis of Oxyrhynchus for the engagement of a *Homēristḗs* and a dramatic mime (*biológos*) who are to travel all the way to the metropolis of Arsinoe in order to perform at a seasonally-recurring festival of Kronos.[50] From the context, Geneviève Husson infers that Oxyrhynchus must have had a special reputation for producing artisans of this kind.[51] Next we look at papyrus 1: here the performance of, again, a *Homēristḗs*, who is to be paid 448 drachmas, is slated to occur after that of a mime, who is to get 496 drachmas, and before that of a dancer, whose wages can be reconstructed at somewhere between 100 and 200 drachmas.[52] In papyrus 4 as well, a *Homēristḗs* and a mime are listed alongside each other.[53] As Husson notes, all these occasions of performance by *Homēristaí* are festivals.[54] Moreover, the dates of all these occasions are not far removed from the era of our main source about *Homēristaí*, Athenaeus of Naucratis (around 200 AD). It is realistic, no doubt, to be reminded again that we are by now over 500 years removed from

Jones points out to me that an inscription published by Marek 1993.144 (no. 28; cf. also p. 109) seems to refer to a *Homēristḗs* (though the actual term is not used in this case).

[48] Of great interest to me is the collocation here of *Homēristaí* with the word *apódeixis* in the sense of 'performance'; I discuss the concept of *apódeixis* at length in N 1990a, especially pp. 222–224, 320, 344, 364, 411. We have already noted at p. 164 above the implications of *Homēristaí* and the verb of *apódeixis* in Achilles Tatius 3.20.4.

[49] In the case of examples 3a and 3b, which come from the same document, *Homēristḗs* is in collocation with *anagnṓstēs*.

[50] For the term *biológos*, cf. n45 above.

[51] Husson 1993.96–97.

[52] Husson 1993.98.

[53] Ibid.

[54] Husson 1993.97.

the glory days of Demetrius of Phalerum, whom Athenaeus credits with the theatricalization of rhapsodes. But it is also realistic to keep in mind the continuity, however transformed, of Hellenic culture even half a millennium later. As Husson points out, for example, the metropolis of Oxyrhynchus had a theater with a seating capacity of over 10,000.[55] Such theaters were to be found throughout the Hellenic cities that dotted the Egyptian hinterland or *khóra*, and Husson reminds us that the cultural vitality of urban life in that era can in no way be imagined as a phenomenon restricted to a small handful of "gymnasium élite."[56] It is clear even from the theatrical events mentioned in our Oxyrhynchus papyri that Hellenic institutions actively coexisted with Egyptian counterparts: in the papyrus mentioning the festival of Kronos, for example, on which occasion there was a *Homēristēs* contracted to perform, it appears that the cult of the god Anubis also figures prominently.[57]

For yet another attestation of *Homēristēs*, we turn to an inscription, published by Charlotte Roueché,[58] that was found by excavators on the side of a doorway leading into Room 6 behind the stage front of the theater at Aphrodisias in Caria: it reads Δημητρίου ὁμηριστοῦ διασκευη 'equipment of Demetrius the *Homēristēs*',[59] and its date cannot be much later than the end of the third century AD.[60] As in the case of the evidence from Oxyrhynchus, the naming of this *Homēristēs* occurs in a context associated with mimes: the inscriptions on the sides of other doorways leading into other rooms behind the stage designate mimes (as in the case of Room 1: Παρδαλᾶ μειμολόγου).[61] In this era, however, it must be kept in mind that such an association does

[55] Husson 1993.99.

[56] Ibid.

[57] Husson 1993.98–99, along with other striking illustrations of Greek-Egyptian cultural coexistence in the context of the festivals noted in these Oxyrhynchus papyri.

[58] Roueché 1993.18; this evidence was kindly brought to my attention by Geneviève Husson, *per litteras* (29 November 1994).

[59] Roueché 1993.22: "In Room 6 it is clear that more than one text had been inscribed and erased. [The Room 6 inscription] seems to have read Δημητρίου ὁμηριστοῦ διασκευη; the description ὁμηριστοῦ, after Demetrius' name, is in a different hand, and was presumably either added to the inscription, or possibly, left over from a previous inscription which Demetrius replaced with his own." On *diaskeuē* in the sense of 'theatrical equipment' (perhaps 'costume'), see Roueché p. 20.

[60] Roueché 1993.24.

[61] Roueché 1993.16.

not reflect negatively on the *Homēristaí*, since the status (and prestige) of mimes was ascending exponentially throughout the Hellenic areas of the Empire at around the time of the third century.[62] The question, then, is not whether the status of *Homēristaí* was declining with the passage of time: what needs to be determined, rather, is to what extent their very identity was becoming assimilated to that of mimes.[63] The mimetic connotations of this particular attestation of a *Homēristḗs* at Aphrodisias in the third century AD bring us to a remarkable additional detail: inscribed above the name of Demetrius the *Homēristḗs* is the following: ἐγενήσθη [*sic*] Ἀλέξανδρος 'he became Alexander'.[64] Here is an interpretation, considered by Rouché: 'he was (acted) Alexander, i.e. Paris'.[65]

The picture that we see emerging in the second and third centuries AD, that of Homer as an obviously excerpted "script" to be performed by *Homēristaí* in a stylized mimetic format, can be seen as a terminal or at least near-terminal stage in the history of Homeric performance.[66] This has been my argument so far.

---

[62] Rouché 1993.24, who also points out that two of the mimes mentioned in the Aphrodisias inscriptions, Philologos (Room 4) and Autolykos (Room 3), were "almost certainly mimes who were competitors at 'sacred' contests at some time in the third century." See also p. 25: "It does seem to be the case ... that the two types of performance which had been increasing in popularity in the Roman period – the pantomime and the mime – dominated the late Roman period." The evidence of ancient testimony surveyed by Rouché pp. 26–27 makes it clear that the performances of pantomimes and mimes involved singing as well as dancing; cf. p. 26: "While the dancer himself did not speak, he was normally accompanied by a choir who would sing the story; ... the songs themselves might be picked up and sung at home by the spectators [with reference to Libanius, iv AD, *On Dancing* 93])." Cf. also Lucian *On Dance* 68.

[63] The passage about the *Homēristaí* in Petronius *Satyricon* 59.4–6, as discussed above, is instructive in this regard: *intravit factio statim hastisque scuta concrepuit. ipse Trimalchio in pulvino consedit, et cum Homeristae Graecis versibus colloquerentur, ut insolenter solent, ille canora voce Latine legebat librum. mox silentio facto "scitis" inquit "quam fabulam agant? Diomedes et Ganymedes duo fratres fuerunt. horum soror erat Helena. Agamemnon illam rapuit ..."* 'there entered right away a troupe [of *Homēristaí*], beating on their shields with their spears. Trimalchio himself sat down on his cushion and, <u>while the *Homēristaí* were having their dialogues in Greek verses, in their usual pompous manner, he</u> [Trimalchio], in a sonorous voice, was <u>reading along, in Latin, from a book</u>. Then after a moment of silence, he said: "<u>Do you know what story they are acting?</u> Well, Diomedes and Ganymedes were two brothers. They had a sister, Helen, and Agamemnon abducted her ..."'.

[64] Rouché 1993.18. The actual reading of the verb, however, is in serious doubt.

[65] Rouché 1993.22. If this particular interpretation is right, then Demetrius the *Homēristḗs* is known for his acting – or, let us say, re-enacting – of Paris in the *Iliad*.

[66] To repeat an ongoing point: what is already "scripture" for Aristarchus may continue to be a script for the Homēristaí.

To be sure, any continuum entails discontinuities as well as continuities – one might say that this is the essence of Hellenism, even of tradition itself – but I maintain that the cumulative evidence of the traces that we have examined up to now does indeed seem to bear out the suggestion made in the passage of Athenaeus that the *Homēristaí* continued the traditions of the *rhapsōidoí*.

There are further traces of *Homēristaí* to be found, in Eustathius. Here we must be even more cautious, given that this scholar of the twelfth century AD often makes spectacular mistakes in his own internalized chronology of the cultural history of Classical and post-Classical Athens, Ptolemaic and post-Ptolemaic Egypt. At the very beginning of his Prolegomena to his Commentary on the *Iliad* (p. 1 ed. van der Valk), for example, he treats Aristarchus as a predecessor of Zenodotus, and he assigns both scholars to the era of Peisistratos. Still, Eustathius had access to information that was often more complete than what we now have, as for example in the case of the Athenaeus text that he used for reference, and thus the actual information that he gives can be valuable even when his own interpretation of that information may not be so.[67] Let us begin with two cases of the noun itself, *Homēristaí*. In one case (Eustathius 4.937), the information replicates what we have just read in Athenaeus 620b–c.[68] In the other case (Eustathius 4.970), the reference is *en passant*, as if *Homēristaí* had once been the standard word for 'performers of Homer': ταῦτα δὲ πάντα καὶ ὅσα τοιαῦτα ὑποκρουσάμενος τοῖς Ὁμηρισταῖς ὁ ποιητὴς αὐτὸς αὖθις ἐπελύσατο διά τε θείων προσώπων καὶ διὰ λόγων δεξιότητος ... 'being faulted for all these things [that is, various narrative inconsistencies] and for however many other such things by the *Homēristaí*, the poet himself provided explanations by way of divine personae and deft wording ...'. I find this second reference significant precisely because it is used so casually – not just by Eustathius but also, possibly, by his ancient source.[69]

---

[67] For example, Eustathius used an epitome of Athenaeus that was in several respects fuller in detail than the C and E versions that have come down to us; see van der Valk 1971.lxxxv.

[68] For a general discussion of the possibilities of recovering, by way of Eustathius, fuller versions of the Athenaeus text tradition, see van der Valk 1971.lxxix–lxxxv.

[69] Besides the two cases of the noun *Homēristaí* in Eustathius, we find also the verb *Homērízō*. In Eustathius 1.553, the expression κατά τε Ὅμηρον καὶ τοὺς ὁμηρίζοντας,

Let us note in this connection a further comment, made at an earlier point by Eustathius in the Prolegomena to his commentary on the *Iliad* (1.9), that performers whom he describes as "those in a later period" had "acted Homeric poetry in a more dramatic fashion," with performers of the *Iliad* wearing costumes dyed red and those of the *Odyssey*, purple (εἰ δὲ καὶ τὴν Ὁμηρικὴν ποίη-σιν οἱ ὕστερον ὑπεκρίνοντο δραματικώτερον, τὴν μὲν Ὀδύσσειαν ἐν ἁλουργοῖς ἐσθήμασι, τὴν δὲ Ἰλιάδα ἐν ἐρυθρο-βαφέσιν).[70] Eustathius makes this comment in the context of conceding that Homeric poetry had indeed been acted like tragedy, even though it was not called drama (οὐ μὴν δράματα, ὡς τὰ παρὰ τοῖς τραγικοῖς). Given the explicit association of the *Homēristaí* with the theatricalization of Homeric performance traditions, as we have seen from the passage in Athenaeus, I infer that Eustathius – or, better, perhaps his source, who may be Athenaeus – is referring to the *Homēristaí* when he speaks here of "those in a later period" who "acted Homeric poetry in a more dramatic fashion" (to repeat, τὴν Ὁμηρικὴν ποίησιν οἱ ὕστερον ὑπεκρίνοντο δραματικώτερον).

Let us return to the evidence of the extant papyri, all dated to the second or third century AD, concerning the performances of *Homēristaí*. It is important to note that these attestations come

may imply that the *Homērízontes* (from *Homērízō*) are the equivalent of *Homēristaí*. In Eustathius 1.1, the author is saying that no poet would miss the opportunity to imitate Homer, πάντα ποιῶν δι' ὧν ὁμηρίζειν δυνήσεται 'doing everything that enables him to be a *Homērízōn*'. It seems as if the idea of a poet's *imitating* Homer is being implicitly equated with the idea of *performing* Homer.

[70] Eustathius (again 1.9, in his Prolegomena to the *Iliad* commentary) may perhaps be guessing when he attributes to "the ancients" this rationale for the distinct color-schemes: that red stands for the blood shed in war, and purple, for the sea, as the setting of Odysseus' wanderings. Still, his report about the actual color dichotomy seems to be grounded in tradition. In Homeric diction, we find a parallel dichotomy of red and purple in descriptions of colors painted on ships: *nêes miltopárēioi* in *Iliad* 2.637 and *Odyssey* 9.125 vs. *néas phoinikopárēious* in *Odyssey* 11.124 and 23.271. Moreover, the inventories of chariots in the Linear B tablets show yet another parallel dichotomy of red and purple in descriptions of colors painted on chariots: the noun i-qi-ja 'chariot' is described as either mi-to-we-sa = *miltówessa* 'red' as in Knossos tablet Sd 4407 (Ventris and Chadwick 1973.562 compare *nêes miltopárēioi* in *Iliad* 2.637) or po-ni-ki-ja = *phoinikíā* 'purple' as in Knossos tablet Sd 4402 (Ventris and Chadwick 1973.573 compare *néas phoinikopárēious* in *Odyssey* 11.124). For the translation 'purple' in the latter case, I note φοινικόβαπτα ἐσθήματα in Aeschylus *Eumenides* 1028. At *Iliad* 23.716–17, the same notion of purple may even fit σμώδιγγες ... αἵματι φοινικόεσσαι, if the reference is to a special kind of discoloration associated with welts.

from a relatively late era – considerably later than that of the "eccentric" Homer papyri of 300 to 150 BC or so. I have already argued that a phase of relatively more fluidity in the Homeric performance tradition, as reflected in the "eccentric" papyri, was coming to a halt by around 150 BC, after which time both the performance tradition and the commercial books of Homer could revert to reflecting more closely an earlier and more canonical Athenian rhapsodic performance tradition.[71] But we have yet to consider fully whether the very term *Homēristaí* is related to such an earlier, more canonical, rhapsodic tradition.

True, the attestations of this term are so relatively late that we cannot be sure, at this point in the argument, whether it is justifiable to date the institution of *Homēristaí* as far back as the fourth century BC. For now, at least, the only direct textual evidence we have for this argument is the passage in Athenaeus 620b–c, already quoted, which suggests that the *Homēristaí* are offshoots of Homeric performance traditions as reformed by Demetrius. What follows, however, is additional textual evidence for taking the actual term *Homēristaí* all the way back to the era of Demetrius. Also, I will present arguments for linking this term with the idea of a fourth-century "State Script."

We have already noted that Demetrius of Phalerum, apparently credited in Athenaeus 620b–c with a reform of Homeric performance traditions at Athens towards the end of the fourth century, is definitely to be credited with a major reform of Athenian State Theater. By abolishing the *khorēgía*, he brought about the ultimate professionalization of the chorus, that former bastion of non-professional and "liberal" education.[72] Thanks to the reforms of Demetrius, as we have seen, the Athenian State was hereafter paying salaries not only to the actors, as it had already before, but also to the chorus, even financing its costumes.[73] In other words, Demetrius legitimated the evolution of a relatively more professionalized corps of actors in State Theater.[74] This

[71] See pp. 141, 144.

[72] Blum 1991.24

[73] Ibid. Perhaps it is pertinent to recall the remark of Eustathius, in the Prolegomena to his commentary on the *Iliad* (1.9), about the red and the purple costumes worn by performers of the *Iliad* and *Odyssey* respectively.

[74] I hasten to add that any increased inclusiveness of membership in an actors' corps, as implied by the professionalization of the chorus in Athenian State Theater,

historical fact suggests that a new detail can be added to the
argument: extrapolating from Athenaeus 620b–c, I now propose
that Demetrius legitimated the evolution of a corps of Homeric
performers who were relatively more *professionalized* than earlier
performers – and who may have been actually called *Homēristaí*.

There are in fact historical precedents, beyond the reform of
Athenian State Theater instituted by Demetrius himself in the
fourth quarter of the fourth century, for this same man's reform
of Homeric performance traditions. A few years earlier, in the
third quarter of the fourth century, we find that Lycurgus of
Athens had instituted something that seems analogous: this
statesman had initiated reforms in the performance traditions of
State Theater in Athens, legislating an official "State Script" for
the tragedies of three poets and three poets only, Aeschylus,
Sophocles, and Euripides.[75] The crucial piece of evidence comes
from a compressed and problematic passage in "Plutarch" *Lives
of the Ten Orators* 841f.[76] According to this passage, Lycurgus introduced a law requiring that the Athenians erect bronze statues
of Aeschylus, Sophocles, and Euripides, *and that the State make
official the texts of the tragedies of these three poets* in the following way:

> ... τὰς τραγῳδίας αὐτῶν ἐν κοινῷ γραψαμένους
> φυλάττειν καὶ τὸν τῆς πόλεως γραμματέα παραναγιν-
> ώσκειν τοῖς ὑποκρινομένοις· οὐκ ἐξεῖναι γὰρ αὐτὰς
> ὑποκρίνεσθαι

> ... that they were to transcribe their tragedies [that is, the
> tragedies of Aeschylus, Sophocles, and Euripides] and keep

seems symptomatic of a decreasing flexibility in the inherited repertoire. By the time
of Demetrius, the ancestral choral traditions in Athens seem to have grown so obsolete as to require revitalization by professionals. The trend of professionalism in the
fourth century BC is made clear by Pickard-Cambridge [1988] 279–280, who traces this
trend forward in time into the norms of professionalism that prevail in the early third
century BC and thereafter, under the general heading of *Dionúsou tekhnîtai* 'Artists of
Dionysus': see his illuminating chapter "The Artists of Dionysus," pp. 279–321. He
also points out that this category of *Dionúsou tekhnîtai* included "professional reciters
of epic" (p. 92n4). Cf. Stephanes 1988, especially pp. 573–574 (index of *rhapsōidoí*).
More on this subject at n89 below.
[75] Cf. Wilamowitz 1895.132 and 148, followed by Blum 1991.42, on Lycurgus'
"theater reform." As the discussion that follows makes clear, I do not agree with the
opinion of Wilamowitz that the texts of the Athenian tragedians came into being as
books intended for a reading public.
[76] See Bollack 1994.

them under control in common possession,[77] and that the recorder [*grammateús*] of the city[78] was to read them as a model [*paranagignóskō*][79] to those acting in the tragedies, for otherwise it was not permitted to act them [that is, the tragedies].[80]

"Plutarch" *Lives of the Ten Orators* 841f

With reference to this passage about Lycurgus, one scholar has suggested the following possible interpretation: "Did the recorder [*grammateús*] perhaps attend rehearsals ... with the official text in front of him, following the rehearsal in his text and pointing out whenever the actors departed from it, so as to ensure that they got it right in the actual performance?"[81] Another possibility is that the *grammateús* read out the text in advance,[82] in which case we may interpret *paranagignóskō* as 'read out loud as a model'.[83] Either way, the implication is clear: the actors of tragedy were bound to an Athenian "State Script."

---

[77] I interpret ἐν κοινῷ γραψαμένους φυλάττειν to mean 'that they were to transcribe them [that is, the tragedies] and keep them under control in common possession', with ἐν κοινῷ linked directly with φυλάττειν and not with γραψαμένους (thus I disagree with the interpretation 'that they were to transcribe them [that is, the tragedies] all together [that is, as an ensemble] and keep them under control' – if I understand Blum 1991.83n155 correctly). On ἐν κοινῷ 'in common possession' as opposed to ἰδίᾳ 'in private possession', cf. Demosthenes *In Leptinem* 24: εἰ ἐν κοινῷ μὲν μηδ' ὁτιοῦν ὑπάρχει τῇ πόλει, ἰδίᾳ δέ τινες πλουτήσουσ' ἀτελείας ἐπειλημμένοι. Cf. Isaeus 7.16.

[78] Cf. *grammateús* as "recorder of memory" (so LSJ) in Plato *Philebus* 39a. Bollack 1994 compares another mention of "the recorder [*grammateús*] of the city" in Thucydides 7.10.

[79] In LSJ s.v., we may note the translation of *paranagignóskō* as 'read beside, compare, collate one document with another.' One of the most interesting attestations of *paranagignóskō* is Aeschines *De falsa legatione* 135 (the orator asks his audience to listen to a reading ἐκ τῶν δημοσίων γραμμάτων).

[80] Editors have usually adopted the reading οὐκ ἐξεῖναι γὰρ ⟨παρ'⟩ αὐτὰς ὑποκρίνεσθαι 'for it was not possible to be acting in contradiction of them' (e.g. the Teubner text of J. Mau, Leipzig 1971). Even without the conjectured ⟨παρ'⟩, however, the text as it is makes sense: 'for otherwise it was not permitted to act them [that is, the tragedies]'. For the usage of γάρ in the sense of 'for otherwise', see Denniston 1954.62–63.

[81] P. G. McC. Brown, *per litteras* (14 July 1993).

[82] Cf. Cameron 1990.124, with an inventory of important parallels.

[83] It seems that the formula ἐκδόσεως παραναγνωσθείσης + dative of agent X, as in the explicit to the commentary of Eutocius of Ascalon (sixth century AD) on Book I of Archimedes, *De sphaera et cylindro* (see Cameron 1990.103–107 for this and other examples of the formula), may be interpreted 'with the edition [*ékdosis*] read out loud, as a model, by X'. The *ékdosis* 'edition' in question is the text of the work about which the commentary is written, not the commentary itself, and this text is "corrected" by

There is further testimony about such an Athenian text: *tragoedias primus in lucem Aeschylus protulit, sublimis et grauis et·grandilocus saepe usque ad uitium, sed rudis in plerisque et incompositus; propter quod correctas eius fabulas in certamen deferre posterioribus poetis Athenienses permisere; suntque eo modo multi coronati* 'the first to bring out tragedies was Aeschylus – sublime, severe, and often grandiloquent to a fault, but unpolished in many ways and disorganized; on account of which the Athenians allowed later poets to introduce into dramatic competitions the <u>corrected</u> versions of his dramas, and in this way many of these later poets won the crown of victory' (Quintilian *Institutio oratoria* 10.1.66). We note with special interest the expression *correctas*, which seems to me analogous to the concept of *diórthōsis*, which in turn may be related to the concept of *paranagignóskō*.

In this context, as we contemplate further the usage of *paranagignóskō* in the sense of 'read out loud as a model', we may perhaps find a deeper level of meaning in the sobriquet reportedly applied by Plato to Aristotle, *anagnóstēs* 'the one who reads out loud' (*Vita Marciana*, Aristotle *Fragments* p. 428.2 Rose).[84] It may even be pertinent that the *Vita Latina* of Aristotle refers to his own edition of Homer as a *dictamen* (Aristotle *Fragments* p. 443.5–6 Rose).[85] Given the theatrical context of *paranagignóskō* in the passage about Lycurgus' reform of performance traditions in Athenian tragedy, we may compare *anagnóstēs* with the French stage-word *souffleur*.[86] Such an interpretation of *anagnóstēs*

---

the one who "reads it out loud as a model" (this editor is sometimes but not always the same person as the commentator), with variant readings placed at the margins of the "edited" text (Cameron pp. 116–117). I suggest that the idea of "reading out loud as a model" – presumably to copyists who are being dictated the "new edition" – may be a way of expressing the establishment of a definitive text as if it were a speech-act.

[84] See p. 149.

[85] See p. 122n74.

[86] My suggestion, in a lecture given on 13 January 1993, entitled "Démétrius et les rhapsodes," in the seminar of Françoise Létoublon at the Centre d'Etudes Anciennes, Ecole Normale Supérieure. It may be pertinent that in Aristophanes *Frogs* 52–53, Dionysus is represented as *anagignóskōn* 'reading' to himself (ἀναγιγνώσκοντί μοι ... πρὸς ἐμαυτόν), on a ship, the *Andromeda* of Euripides. Given the self-referential jokes, throughout the *Frogs*, about Dionysus as god of State Theater, the self-representation of Dionysus as reading to himself may be interpreted not so much as an act of "silent reading" (for bibliography on which see Dover 1993.196) but rather as a comic reference to a script reading, as it were, performed out loud by the god of the script himself.

may help explain this word's occurrence alongside *Homēristḗs* in the papyrus SB 4.7336, dealing with Homeric performance.[87] In other words, the parallelism of *Homēristḗs* and *anagnṓstēs* in this papyrus implies that the recitation of Homer, like the acting of drama, depended on a "script." Moreover, if indeed the actors of drama in Athens were regulated on the basis of a "script" imposed by the State, the same may be said about the *Homēristaí*.

In continuing the argument for a relationship between the *Homēristaí* and an Athenian "State Script" of Homer, I posit the following sequence of events:

(A) A new state-controlled performance tradition *and* "script," associated with the *Homēristaí*, is founded by Demetrius in Athens sometime between 317 and 307 BC.

(B) Then, with the fall of Demetrius in 307 BC, the Athenian State loses or at least relaxes control of Homeric performance traditions, with the result that more variations can proliferate in Athens and elsewhere.[88] Such variations are reflected in the so-called "eccentric" Homer papyri. This period of instability in performance traditions lasts until around 150 BC. During this period from 307 BC to 150 BC, we can expect the generic designation of Homeric performers to default to the older term *rhapsōidoí* 'rhapsodes'.[89]

(C) After this burst of variation peters out, around 150 BC, the performance traditions of the *Homēristaí* reassert themselves, matching closely the more canonical textual traditions as reconstituted by Aristarchus.[90]

---

[87] See p. 168n49 above. I owe this observation to Geneviève Husson, *per litteras* (20 February 1994).

[88] For possible references in New Comedy to the fall of Demetrius of Phalerum and to a subsequent relaxation of governmental control over the conventions of Athenian State Theater, see MacKendrick 1954; cf. Wiles 1984.

[89] To cite an example: at the Amphictyonic festival of the Soteria at Delphi, as reflected in third-century inscriptions, the professionalized guild of performers known as the *Dionúsou tekhnítai* 'Artists of Dionysus' includes, besides such categories as *tragōidoí* 'tragic actors' and *khoreutaí* 'chorus-performers' (both boys' and men's choruses), the category of *rhapsōidoí* 'rhapsodes' (e.g. *SIG*³ 424, where two rhapsodes are mentioned); see Pickard-Cambridge [1988] 283–284. On the *Dionúsou tekhnítai* in Alexandria, there is a reference in Athenaeus 198c, in the context of a report describing a spectacular procession during the reign of Ptolemy II Philadelphus (282–246 BC); see Pickard-Cambridge p. 287, who adduces the corroborating evidence of two decrees dated around 240 BC.

[90] This is not to say that we should still expect to see patterns of "fenced" performance traditions, which I have posited in general for the earlier "period 3," dating

In terms of this hypothetical scenario, the relatively late attestations of the word *Homēristaí* in the papyri can be correlated with the relatively most rigid period in the evolution of Homeric transmission.

In arguing for the emergence of the term *Homēristaí* already in the late fourth century, the era of Demetrius of Phalerum, I find crucial evidence in the parallel formations of other terms used in parallel contexts. One such form that is parallel to *Homēristaí* features the verb-suffix *-izō* from which the derivative noun-suffix *-istēs* / *-istaí* is derived.[91] The word in question is *Thamuríddontes* (Θαμυριδδόντων), the Boeotian dialectal equivalent of *Thamurízontes,* attested in an inscription from Boeotia that is dated to the first half of the fourth century BC (*Supplementum Epigraphicum Graecum* 32.503). The inscription records a ritual event, mentioning twenty-two participants, and among them is a *hiararkhíōn* 'hierarch' and two *Thamuríddontes,* all of whom Paul Roesch connects with a hero-cult of the prototypical poet Thamyris in the Valley of the Muses.[92] Pausanias reports having seen a statue of Thamyris in the Valley of the Muses, where this prototypical poet is represented as already blinded, holding on to his broken lyre (9.30.2): the best-known version of the story of Thamyris and his punishment for insulting the Muses is told in *Iliad* 2.594–600.[93]

There is another early parallel to the formation *Homēristaí*. The form in question is *Puthagoristaí,* a designation for followers of

from the era of the Peisistratidai in the sixth century all the way to the era of Demetrius toward the end of the fourth. From the middle of the second century BC onward, the performance traditions of Homer would have been a far cry from those of earlier periods, as we may infer from the anecdotes about *Homēristaí,* reviewed above. My point is simply that the performance traditions of the *Homēristaí* were bound, by default, to a more canonical *textual* tradition of Homer. Though I cannot rule out the possibility that the *Homēristaí* may have taken liberties with the Homeric text, any such textual excerptings or even adjustments would be a far cry from the dynamics of variation within an oral performance tradition. As for P.Oxy. 3001 (second century AD; see Parsons 1974.8–12), I doubt that these fragments can be viewed as some sort of an adaptation of epic passages taken from the *Iliad* (especially from Book 23), let alone that such a creation could be attributed to the *ad hoc* activities of *Homēristaí* (tentative suggestion of M. L. West, as reported by Parsons 1974.9). It is more likely, I think, that these fragments represent a poetic creation that has its own literary history.

[91] On *Homēristaí* as derivative of *Homērízō,* see pp. 164, 171–172n69.

[92] On which see Roesch 1982.138–142. I am grateful to Albert Schachter, who alerted me to this inscription and to the observations of Roesch.

[93] On the poetic implications of the name *Thámuris* as a parallel to *Hómēros*: N 1979.311 par. 2n6.

Pythagoras, which is attested already in a comedy from the fourth century BC (Aristophon F 9.2, 12.3 Kassel/Austin; the word is attested in a comedy of Aristophon's bearing the actual title *Puthagoristḗs*). These *Puthagoristaí* are to be distinguished from the ostensibly more "legitimate" line of Pythagoreans, called the *Puthagóreioi*: unlike the *Puthagóreioi*, the *Puthagoristaí* are professionalized and therefore ostensibly more lowly, as we are explicitly told by the Iamblichean *Life of Pythagoras* (18.80). The lowly characterization of the *Puthagoristaí* is also indicated by the context of the reference to them in Theocritus 14.5 (in Dorian dialect, *Puthagoriktaí*).[94] We may compare the morphology of the more elevated name *Puthagóreioi* with that of the name *Kreōphúleioi*, designating a lineage of rhapsodes from Samos who had been rivals of the *Homērídai*, the lineage of rhapsodes from Chios.[95] The archaic ethos of the suffix *-eioi* in the forms *Puthagóreioi* and *Kreōphúleioi* is to be contrasted with the innovative ethos of the suffix *-istaí* in *Puthagoristaí* – and *Homēristaí*. It is worth stressing again that Athenaeus seems to link the reforms of Homeric performance at Athens in the fourth century BC with the term *Homēristaí*.

I propose that the term *Homēristaí* replaced the earlier *Homērídai*,[96] and we may see in this replacement of terms a pattern of displacement in authority, in that we know of traditions that report of claims to authority and even legitimacy made by the earlier *Homērídai*.[97] These traditions even report of instances where the *Homērídai* disclaimed as illegitimate a given performer

---

[94] Cf. again Aristophon 9.2, 12.3. See also the scholia (vetera) to Theocritus (Prolegomena anecdote 14, section 5b, lines 4–10: τῶν Πυθαγόρου οἱ μὲν ἦσαν περὶ θεωρίαν καταγινόμενοι, οἵπερ ἐκαλοῦντο σεβαστικοί, οἱ δὲ περὶ τὰ ἀνθρώπινα, οἵπερ ἐκαλοῦντο πολιτικοί· οἱ δὲ περὶ τὰ μαθήματα· τὰ γεωμετρικὰ καὶ ἀστρονομικά, οἵπερ ἐκαλοῦντο μαθηματικοί. τούτων οὖν οἱ μὲν αὐτῷ συγγινόμενοι τῷ Πυθαγόρᾳ ἐκαλοῦντο Πυθαγορικοί, οἱ δὲ τούτων μαθηταὶ Πυθαγόρειοι, οἱ δὲ ἄλλως ἔξωθεν ζηλωταὶ Πυθαγορισταί 'Some of the followers of Pythagoras were concerned with *theōría*, and they were called *sebastikoí*; others were concerned with human affairs, and they were called *politikoí*; others were concerned with mathematics and geometry and astronomy, and they were called *mathēmatikoí*. And of all these followers, those who were companions of Pythagoras himself were called *Puthagorikoí*. And the disciples of these were the *Puthagóreioi*, while those who were outsiders – but otherwise zealous followers – were the *Puthagoristaí*'.

[95] Detailed discussion, with bibliography, in N 1990a.23, 74, relying especially on Burkert 1972. More on the *Kreōphúleioi* in the Appendix.

[96] Further arguments in N 1990a.26.

[97] N 1990a.22–23. I note in this context the report of Eustathius *Iliad* Commentary 1.6 concerning the Contest of Homer and Hesiod: εἰ δὲ καὶ ἤρισεν Ὅμηρος Ἡσιόδῳ

of Homer, as in the case of the sixth-century figure Kynaithos.[98] It seems that the claim of the *Homērídai* had been that they were the only authorized performers of Homer.[99] Given the exclusiveness of the *Homērídai* as distinct from the *Homēristaí*, we may again compare the distinction made between the ostensibly more "legitimate" line of Pythagoreans, called the *Puthagóreioi*, and the less-connected and therefore ostensibly more lowly *Puthagoristaí*. I propose also that an increased inclusiveness in membership, as implied by the displacement of *Homērídai* by *Homēristaí*, may be symptomatic of a decreasing flexibility in the inherited repertoire, to be correlated with an increasing professionalism needed to ensure the survival of performance traditions. There is a similar correlation in the history of Athenian State Theater, where Demetrius' reform of performance traditions goes hand in hand with a trend toward intensified professionalization.[100] Let us return to the comment, made by Eustathius in the Prolegomena to his commentary on the *Iliad* (vol. 1 p. 9), that performers whom he describes as "those in a later period" had "acted Homeric poetry in a more dramatic fashion" (εἰ δὲ καὶ τὴν Ὁμηρικὴν ποίησιν οἱ ὕστερον ὑπεκρίνοντο δραματικώτερον). I have already suggested that Eustathius – or, better, perhaps his source, which may have been a fuller version of Athenaeus than the one we have – is referring to the *Homēristaí*. This reference of Eustathius to "later" conventions in Homeric performance implies also a contrast with what he describes in the same context (p. 10) as earlier conventions of "the ancients," the majority of whom had referred to the totality of Homeric poetry as *rhapsōidía*

τῷ Ἀσκραίῳ καὶ ἡττήθη, ὅπερ ὄκνος τοῖς Ὁμηρίδαις καὶ λέγειν 'if indeed Homer had a contest with Hesiod of Ascra and was defeated – which was tabu for the *Homērídai* even to talk about'. Cf. N 1990b.78–79.

[98] N 1990a.22–23, 73–75.

[99] I infer from Plato *Ion* 530d that the *Homērídai* may have served as official judges in the competition of rhapsodes at the Feast of the Panathenaia at Athens.

[100] See pp. 173–174. Perhaps the very name of Demetrius the *Homēristḗs*, in the inscription on the wall of Room 6 in the Theater at Aphrodisias (Rouché 1993.18), is significant; there is a possibility that the mime Philistion (named in the inscription of Room 1) was a namesake of one of the reputed founders of the art of the mime (Rouché p. 21, citing Bonaria 1955 II *fasti* nos. 516–40; on Philistion as a contemporary of Menander, cf. nos. 536, 537, 540). Could it be that the namesake of Demetrius the *Homēristḗs* is Demetrius of Phalerum, if indeed he was the founder of the *Homēristaí*?

'rhapsody' and to those who sing it, as *rhapsōidoí* 'rhapsodes' (οἱ δὲ πλείους τῶν παλαιῶν τήν τε ὅλην Ὁμηρικὴν ποίησιν ῥαψῳδίαν λέγουσι καὶ ῥαψῳδοὺς τοὺς αὐτὴν ᾄδοντας 'but the majority of the ancients refer to the totality of Homeric poetry as *rhapsōidía* and to those singing it as *rhapsōidoí*').[101] This earlier practice is then contrasted explicitly (Eustathius, top of p. 10) with the later practice of designating as *rhapsōidía* each of the twenty-four units of the *Iliad* and *Odyssey*, with each *rhapsōidía* corresponding to a letter of the alphabet. I now propose to link this reportedly "later" practice with the era of Demetrius of Phalerum and with the traditions of the *Homēristaí*.

In the era of Demetrius, it appears that the equivalent of *rhapsōidía* is still a matter of performance – though the emphasis may have shifted from the *process* of putting together the units of performance to the *status* of each unit's being divided from the other. In this matter I agree with the opinion of Stephanie West, who infers that "the use of the term *rhapsōidía* for what we call each 'book' of Homer indicates that the system was based on rhapsodic practice."[102] I disagree, however, with her further inference that the custom of naming after a letter of the alphabet each one of the twenty-four units of both Homeric poems, each designated as *rhapsōidía*, goes back to the earlier era of the Peisistratidai.[103] The farther back we go in time, the less textual the

---

[101] I repeat the claim of Eustathius (vol. 1 p. 10) that the process of *sewing together*, as implicit in the traditional concept of *rhapsōidós*, is what confers upon the Homeric poems their unity: ῥάπτειν δὲ ἢ ἁπλῶς, ὡς εἴρηται, τὸ συντιθέναι ἢ τὸ κατὰ εἱρμόν τινα ῥαφῇ ὁμοίως εἰς ἓν ἄγειν τὰ διεστῶτα. σποράδην γάρ, φασί, κειμένης καὶ κατὰ μέρος διῃρημένης τῆς Ὁμηρικῆς ποιήσεως, οἱ ᾄδοντες αὐτὴν συνέρραπτον οἶον τὰ εἰς ἓν ὕφος ᾀδόμενα 'sewing together [*rháptō*] either in the simple sense, as just mentioned, of putting together or, alternatively, in the sense of bringing different things, in accordance with some kind of sequence [*heirmós*] in sewing, uniformly into one thing; for they say that Homeric poetry, after it had been scattered about and divided into separate parts, was sewn together by those who sang it, like songs sung into a single fabric [*húphos*]'.

[102] [S.] West 1988.40. When we consider the rareness of the word *rhapsōidós* in the Homer scholia, the frequency of *rhapsōidía* as a designation of a given "book" of the *Iliad* or *Odyssey* stands out all the more.

[103] [S.] West 1988.39–40. I note the story, in the T scholia to *Iliad* 10.1, reporting that the *rhapsōidía* that we know as Book 10 had been composed by Homer separately, not as part of the *Iliad*, and that it was later arranged, *tetákhthai*, by Peisistratos to fit into the *Iliad*. *In terms of this story*, I suppose that such an insertion is imagined to happen at a time when there was as yet no ongoing convention of dividing the *Iliad* into twenty-four units – from either a performative or even a textual point of view. On the

idea of *rhapsōidía* becomes: and we may certainly expect patterns of performance-segmentation – as reflected in the very word *rhapsōidía* – to vary over time.[104] Accordingly, let us pursue the argument that the era of Demetrius of Phalerum, who according to Athenaeus 620b–c introduced *Homēristaí* into the theaters, is a more likely setting for canonical divisions of the *Iliad* and the *Odyssey* into twenty-four units of performance.

Again, I agree with Stephanie West[105] in resisting the idea that the divisions of the Homeric poems into twenty-four books originated with the school of Aristarchus ("Plutarch" *Life of Homer* 2.4) or not much earlier.[106] I propose instead that the school of Aristarchus *re-established* the divisions of the Homeric poems into twenty-four units.[107] Before the era of the Alexandrian critics, according to this proposal, the division into twenty-four units was a convention primarily of performance, supervised by the Athenian State.

apparent appropriateness of the contents of *Iliad* 10 to the ideology of the Peisistratidai, see Catenacci 1993.18n34.

[104] Further discussion in N 1992a.49–50; also at p. 41n24, where I consider the theory of a three-night performance division of the *Iliad*, as formulated by Taplin 1992.

[105] [S.] West 1988.39–40.

[106] That idea is accepted by Janko 1992.31n47. So also Olson, whose arguments are summarized above at pp. 161–162n30. There we noted the rhapsodic practice of beginning a Homeric performance by starting with a δέ that picks up, midstream, a narrative that had contained a preceding μέν. In the same discussion, I compared this phenomenon with the splitting of a μέν / δέ construction by way of a Homeric book-division.

[107] If it had been Aristarchus – or at least the school of Aristarchus – that really pioneered the divisions of the *Iliad* and *Odyssey* into twenty-four books each, it is difficult to explain the claim of the scholia to *Odyssey* 23.296, according to which Aristarchus as well as Aristophanes of Byzantium thought that this line marks the end of the authentic *Odyssey* (Ἀριστοφάνης καὶ Ἀρίσταρχος πέρας τῆς Ὀδυσσείας ποιοῦνται and τοῦτο τέλος τῆς Ὀδυσσείας φησὶν Ἀρίσταρχος καὶ Ἀριστοφάνης). That this claim of the scholia means what it says, the end of the *Odyssey*, is argued by Rossi 1968; cf. Garbrah 1977 and Catenacci 1993.14. It would be typical of Aristarchus' editorial practice to adhere to an earlier convention – in this case, let us say, a division into twenty-four books – even when such a convention was not "original" to Homer according to his own scholarly assessment. Further, even if Aristarchus thought that the "original" *Odyssey* ended at 23.296, such an opinion did not seem to stop him from making further distinctions between what he thought were more or less authentic portions of the *Odyssey* beyond 23.296. For example, the *Odyssey* scholia report that Aristarchus athetized 23.310–343, where Odysseus retells to Penelope the story that he had told Alkinoos about his adventures. The scholia (QV) speak of thirty-three lines. I find it striking that Aristotle *Rhetoric* 1417a13, in referring to the same *Odyssey* passage, speaks of sixty lines, not thirty-three. I infer that Aristotle's version of the *Odyssey* did not stop at 23.296.

In the era of Aristarchus as distinct from the era of Demetrius, the twenty-four units of the *Iliad* and *Odyssey* could have become reconceptualized, shifting their identity from quasi-textual *rhapsōidíai*, numbered according to the twenty-four letters of the Athenian State Alphabet, to veritable "books" of the *Iliad* and *Odyssey*. In general, however, Aristarchus' organization of the Homeric text was perhaps closer to Demetrius' earlier organization than to what we find attested in the so-called "eccentric" Homer papyri. Conventions of book-production in the early Ptolemaic era, as reflected by the "eccentric" Homer papyri, seem to ignore the canonical division of the Homeric poems into the relatively small units marked off by the twenty-four letters of the alphabet. Following the calculations of Jean Irigoin and others, John Van Sickle argues that the pre-Aristarchean Ptolemaic norm for the size of a papyrus roll or "book" of Homer could have been the length of, say, one of the four books of the *Argonautica* by Apollonius of Rhodes (I, 1362 verses; II, 1285; III, 1407; IV 1781) – or for that matter the length of an Athenian tragedy or comedy – in any case, within the range of 1000 to 2000 lines.[108] By contrast, the post-Aristarchean norm for the size of a papyrus roll or "book" of Homer averages around 500 to 650 lines – and these lengths match the book-divisions that have come down to us through the medieval manuscript tradition.[109] Moreover, as Van Sickle shows, the norm of *any* book in the literary world of the post-Aristarchean era actually became reconceptualized to approximate the size of the Homeric book.[110] The two prime examples are Virgil's *Aeneid*, the books of which average 850 verses, and Ovid's *Metamorphoses*, where the average is 800.[111]

To repeat, the so-called "eccentric" Homeric papyri of the pre-Aristarchean period tend to fall within the range of 1000/2000 lines, *without* regard for divisions into twenty-four units: "these early Ptolemaic papyri of Homer ... show no explicit signs of the division into 'books' designated by letters of the alphabet."[112]

---

[108] Van Sickle 1980.8, following Irigoin 1952.41.

[109] Van Sickle 1980.9.

[110] Van Sickle 1980.9 and following.

[111] Van Sickle 1980.12. It seems to me that the average size of the books in Virgil's *Aeneid* comes closer to 825 verses.

[112] Van Sickle 1980.9. Cf. Rengakos 1993.93–94.

This preference for 1000/2000 line-groupings, Van Sickle suggests, "must represent the custom and convenience of an earlier period, stemming not as yet from Alexandria but from more distant centers, including Athens itself."[113] It is possible, however, that already in Athens there were stricter customs coming to the fore toward the end of the fourth century, at which point my hypothesis calls for the development of something that approximates an Athenian "State Script" of Homer, formalized by Demetrius of Phalerum. The post-Aristarchean era, with its Homeric texts divided into twenty-four books, represents in my opinion not an innovation but a reversion to something like a "State Script" – if not to the actual norms of Homeric performance in late fourth-century Athens.

In support of the notion that the Homer text as formalized by Aristarchus was much closer to such an Athenian "State Script," as I have called it, than to the intermediate texts represented by the "eccentric" Homer papyri, there is an analogy in the textual history of the *Rule* of St. Benedict.[114] The *Rule* was written down in the sixth century, and Benedict's manuscript was preserved at Monte Cassino by the Benedictine Order until 896, when it was destroyed in a fire. An "improved" version of the *Rule*, known as the *traditio moderna*, was evolving ever since the inception of the text in the sixth century till the end of the eighth century. At that point, Charlemagne himself visited Monte Cassino and acquired a copy of the original manuscript. This copy of the original *Rule* then became "the basis for the diffusion of the text throughout the reformed monasteries of the Carolingian kingdom."[115] Ironically, however, "the concern for the establishment of an accurate text led copyists to insert into the margins readings from the *traditio moderna*, thus recorrupting the text away from Benedict's original."[116]

To restate the analogy, we could say that the evolution of the *Rule* in the *traditio moderna* matches the evolution of the Homeric tradition in the era of the "eccentric" Homer papyri, and that the return to the earliest layer of the *Rule* at the initiative of

[113] Van Sickle 1980.9.
[114] On Benedict's *Rule*, see Zetzel 1993.103–104, following Traube 1910.
[115] Zetzel 1993.103.
[116] Ibid.

Charlemagne matches the return to an earlier layer of the Koine
tradition, at the initiative of Aristarchus. The "recorruption" of
the Benedictine *Rule* matches the eventual "recorruption" of the
Aristarchean version of Homer in the post-Aristarchean manuscript traditions.[117] A major difference that offsets the analogy,
however, is that the earlier layer of the Koine text, as restored by
Aristarchus, does not match the archetypal quality of the earliest
layer of the Benedictine *Rule*. Moreover, for reasons that we will
examine in the next chapter, the history of the Athenian text as
restored by Aristarchus covers its tracks, as it were.

For now, however, the argument runs as follows: that the
performance traditions of fifth-century tragedy and even those of
Homer were concurrently reaching a relatively rigid stage in the
era of the Athenian reforms starting in the third quarter of the
fourth century. It will be important to keep this era in mind as we
consider the succeeding era of Alexandrian scholarship, with all
its intense editorial activity – which is the central topic of the
next chapter. The present argument is that the medieval text traditions of Homer stem, at least in part, not from the Alexandrian
era but rather from this earlier Athenian era.[118] In terms of the

[117] The term "corruption" is of course valid only from the standpoint of Benedict's
original. Similarly, it is valid only from the standpoint of what we understand to be
Aristarchus' editorial principles.

[118] There are also other theories of a pre-Alexandrian Homer text, founded on arguments different from mine. I note in particular the position taken by Ludwich 1898
(defended by Allen 1924.327), according to whom the Homeric text is pre-Alexandrian, to be traced back to Athenian copies and continuing as the basis of the medieval manuscript tradition. At least on this point, the views of van der Valk 1964.609 are
similar: he argues that a pre-Aristarchean "vulgate" had "preserved the authentic
text," and that this text "was also transmitted by the vulgate of the medieval manuscript." Van der Valk and Ludwich agree also in positing that this textual transmission
bypassed the editions of the Alexandrian critics, especially that of Aristarchus. For van
der Valk, what are thus bypassed are "conjectures," whereas Ludwich affirms that
Aristarchus did not make conjectures. For Ludwich, what are bypassed by the "vulgate" are for the most part better readings. For van der Valk, the "vulgate" version is
superior to the Aristarchean version; for Ludwich, it is the reverse. [S.] West 1988.46
argues that "we should certainly reject the theory that an official Athenian copy, never
mentioned because everywhere taken for granted, provided the basis for Aristarchus'
text." At an earlier point, West (1988.39) posits a sixth-century Athenian "recension"
of Homer, which "must be regarded as the archetype of all our Homeric manuscripts
and of the indirect tradition represented by ancient quotations and allusions." On the
implications of Ludwich's attempt to discredit the authenticity of the "eccentric" early
Ptolemaic papyri, see Nickau 1977.31–32n3. My main problem with all these theories
is that they concentrate almost exclusively on questions of textual traditions, without
sufficient regard for questions of performance traditions.

scheme of periodization as outlined in the previous chapter, the
Homeric textual tradition that we know today by the vague designation of the Koine or "Vulgate" is typical of period 3, while
period 4 begins with the emergence of a "State Script" of Homeric performance traditions as reformed under the régime of
Demetrius of Phalerum.

There may indeed have been a textual prototype, in the loosest
sense of the word, for the kind of "State Script" that reflects the
performance reforms instituted under this régime. Such a prototype could have been influenced by, or even derived from, a copy
of Homer that Aristotle and his school had used for their own
research, which would surely have included his *diórthōsis* as marginalia.[119] Be that as it may, we could expect the "State Script"
that inaugurates period 4 to be based on the Koine *performance*
traditions of the earlier period 3. As a *text*, however, such a script
would have been considered superior, from the standpoint of its
editors, to any earlier commercial transcript of Koine performance traditions. Whether or not such a script stemmed directly
from Aristotle's own *diórthōsis* of the Koine, we will see in the
next chapter that it reflected an ultimate *diórthōsis* that had been
promoted and perhaps even executed by Demetrius of Phalerum,
student of Theophrastus, who in turn was student and direct
successor of Aristotle.[120]

---

[119] See pp. 121–122. Blum 1991.21–22 and 69–70n45 argues, despite the skepticism
of a host of predecessors, for the existence of a *diórthōsis* of Homer by Aristotle. The
key passage is Plutarch *Life of Alexander* 8.2, concerning a copy of the *Iliad* known as ἐκ
τοῦ νάρθηκος 'from the casket [*nárthēx*]', a copy that Alexander kept under his *proskephálaion*, 'headrest' and that had been "corrected by Aristotle," Ἀριστοτέλους διορθώσαντος (8.2). In the next chapter, there are further arguments for the existence of
such a *diórthōsis* of Homer.

[120] On Demetrius, Diogenes Laertius 5.75 says: οὗτος ἤκουσε μὲν Θεοφράστου
'he attended the lectures of Theophrastus'.

7

Homer as "scripture"

Let us turn to the last of the five periods in the history of Homeric transmission, as formulated at the beginning of the fifth chapter. For the later Alexandrian scholars starting with Aristarchus, whom I put into period 5 of Homeric transmission, that is, into the most "rigid" period, the script or scripts stemming from the Athenian State tradition became "scripture." This is the next thesis, which I will now develop by re-examining some key terms – and the ideas behind them.[1] Even before we consider the reasons for my use of the term "scripture," however, we must start with the relevant Greek terms.

When a scholar like Aristarchus referred to the *koiné* or to the *koinaí*, I will argue that he was citing, from his own point of view, copies derived from the Athenian "City Edition" of Homer. Not that this version was *the* text for the Alexandrian scholar: it was *a* text, which had to be considered alongside other texts that the school of Aristarchus seems to have valued more highly for variant readings, like the "city editions" of Chios, Argos, Massalia, and so on. I think that Minna Skafte Jensen says it most incisively when she claims that the Koine too was a "city edition" – I would say the city edition by default – that is, the city edition of Athens.[2] It seems remarkable, she reasons, that a *politiké* or 'city edition' of Athens is never mentioned in the Homer scholia, in light of the numerous references to the *politikaí* of other cities. A ready explanation is that the *politiké* of Athens is indeed the *koiné*.

---

[1] For a historical analysis of the term "scripture," see Smith 1993; cf. also Graham 1987, especially pp. 92–95 on the Arabic word *qur'ān* as a common rather than proper noun meaning 'act of recitation'.

[2] Jensen 1980.109.

In this connection, I agree with T. W. Allen's view that the very word *koinế* had once conveyed in the context of Homeric transmission the fundamental idea of 'common' in the sense of 'universal'.[3] The built-in Athenian ideology, I would further suggest, is that this text was *koinế* or 'common' to all because it *was* standard, authoritative.[4]

I also agree with Allen that the usage of the word *koinế* developed the negative connotation of 'common' in the sense of 'vulgar' only secondarily, in the context of the scholiastic tradition stemming ultimately from the school of Aristarchus, for whose followers *koiná* in the negative sense of 'common' (the neuter plural is cited for the sake of symmetry with the forms still to be cited) and *dēmốdē* in the negative sense of 'vulgar' become synonymous with such descriptions as *eikaîa* 'random' or *eikaiốtera* 'random by comparison' and *phaûla* 'base' or *phaulốtera* 'base by comparison' in scholiastic references to the less "edited" versions of Homer, as opposed to the more "edited" ones described as *khariếstera* 'more elegant' and the like.[5]

Let me anticipate my conclusions. In an earlier era, at a time when an "edited" text of Homer was not yet conceptually distinguishable from any other text, I hold that the expression *koinế* in everyday usage would indeed have meant something like the Athenian "City Edition." Such a usage could have been appropriate even in a later era, as in the time of Demetrius of Phalerum. For Demetrius himself, as reformer and standardizer of

---

[3] Allen 1924.278.

[4] In Plato *Phaedrus* 252b, there is a quotation of a pair of hexameters about Eros, nowhere else attested, that are supposedly taken from *apótheta* reported by "some of the Homeridai" (λέγουσι δὲ οἶμαί τινες Ὁμηριδῶν ἐκ τῶν ἀποθέτων δύο ἔπη εἰς τὸν Ἔρωτα). As Lohse 1964.26 points out, following Lobeck 1829.861–863, *apótheta* conveys the idea of 'removed from common usage and known only to a few' ("communi usu exempta paucisque nota") rather than 'esoteric' or 'reserved'. Without entering the debate over whether these two hexameters are "genuine," I simply draw attention to the idea of *common usage* as a principle ascribed to the repertoire of the Homeridai.

[5] Allen 1924.278. On the implications of *khariếstera* 'more elegant' from the earlier standpoint of the fourth century BC, see p. 122 above. The semantic heritage of *dēmốdēs* 'vulgar' is also of interest. In Plato *Phaedo* 61a, Socrates implies that all *mousikế* except for philosophy is *dēmốdēs*, in the context of explaining why he chose to engage in the *mousikế* of composing 1) a hymn to Apollo and 2) poetic versions of fables of Aesop (60c–d). Both of these poetic forms, he says, are a matter of *múthos*, not *lógos* (ἐννοήσας ὅτι τὸν ποιητὴν δέοι, εἴπερ μέλλοι ποιητὴς εἶναι, ποιεῖν μύθους ἀλλ' οὐ λόγους 61b).

Homeric performance traditions, there would have been a positive sense of 'common' inherent in *koiné* – a sense also connected in Athenian usage with the concept of control by the State.[6] The *koiné* would be considered 'common' to all, the prized possession of all – of all Athenians, at least.[7] Such a positive sense of *koiné* would have signaled the standardization – and, from the Athenian point of view, the universalization – of Homeric performance traditions. Any standardization of performance traditions could have led to relative standardization of written copies as well, including commercially available copies. Moreover, standardization of performance traditions could have provided an added incentive for the commercial production and sale of the Homeric text, to the extent that the very concept of a Standard Version of Homer implies to the buyer a prized and even unique possession.

All this is not to say that the standardization of Homeric performance – or perhaps even the concept of *koiné* – started with Demetrius. The idea of making the poetry of the heroic age a common possession can be traced back all the way to the middle of the sixth century BC, the era when the régime of the Peisistratidai was already reforming the rhapsodic performance traditions at the Panathenaia.[8] And the idea continues in the fifth

---

[6] In the report of "Plutarch" *Lives of the Ten Orators* 841f we have seen the expression *en koinôi* 'in common possession', that is, in the possession of the Athenian State, with reference to the texts of the tragedies of Aeschylus, Sophocles, and Euripides that the State had commissioned to be transcribed and kept under its control: τὰς τραγῳδίας αὐτῶν ἐν κοινῷ γραψαμένους φυλάττειν καὶ τὸν τῆς πόλεως γραμματέα παραναγινώσκειν τοῖς ὑποκρινομένοις· οὐκ ἐξεῖναι γὰρ αὐτὰς ὑποκρίνεσθαι '... that they were to <u>transcribe</u> their tragedies [that is, the tragedies of Aeschylus, Sophocles, and Euripides] and <u>keep them under control in common possession</u>, and that the recorder [*grammateús*] of the city was to read them as a model [*paranagignōskō*] to those acting in the tragedies, for otherwise it was not permitted to act them [that is, the tragedies]'.

[7] For an example of *koinós* in this sense, see Demosthenes 18.170: ἦν γὰρ ὁ κῆρυξ κατὰ τοὺς νόμους φωνὴν ἀφίησι, ταύτην κοινὴν τῆς πατρίδος δίκαιον ἡγεῖσθαι 'for the voice that the herald emits in accordance with the laws, it is just that it be considered the <u>common possession</u> of the fatherland'. As Victor Bers points out to me, Isocrates 15.296 claims that the Attic dialect is the lingua franca of Greece because of its *koinótēs*, that is, because of its quality of being *koiné*, the common possession of all Greeks.

[8] Cf. N 1990a.160–162, with special reference to the promotion, by the Peisistratidai, of an Athenian ideology of shared poetic culture, as articulated in "Plato" *Hipparchus* 228d. Cf. also Aloni 1984 and 1986, along with the assessment of Catenacci 1993.7–8n2.

century, the era of Pericles.[9] Still, the idea of a standard, as arguably realized by Demetrius through his specific reform of what I have been calling a State Script, implies a semantic narrowing that can be schematized as a progression from a "Common Homer" to a "Standard Homer," corresponding respectively to period 3 and period 4. In other words, the concept of *koinē* may apply to both period 3 and period 4, with an intensification or specialization of ideology in period 4, when Homer becomes not only common to all – at least, from an Athenian point of view – but also the enforced standard for all.

In period 5, by contrast, which I equate with the era of Aristarchus and his school, the same word *koinē* could have come to mean, more generally, the Athenian City Text. The alternation of singular *koinē* and plural *koinai* in the scholia reporting the views of Aristarchus suggests that he found some degree of variation within this textual tradition of an earlier era, but the Aristarchean convention of consistently juxtaposing the readings of the *koinē* or *koinai* with the readings of other textual transmissions suggests that Aristarchus treated the *koinē* or *koinai* as a distinct manuscript family. For him, the *koinai* at his disposal may have been mostly commercial copies.

We know that Aristarchus also had access to the private copies of earlier Homer critics dating back to the era of Demetrius and even before, whose editorial work would have survived mostly in marginalia anchored in copies of the Homeric text.[10] Still, it appears that he would not have valued all that highly the work of the earliest critics – though he did value the earliest manuscripts. To put it positively, Aristarchus would have valued more highly the work of later critics like Aristophanes of Byzantium, who came far closer to his own standards of editorial judgment and practice.[11]

Still, it seems remarkable that there are in the Homer scholia practically no references at all to anything resembling the activity of "editing" the text of Homer in the fourth century – let alone fourth-century Athens.[12] We might have expected the most likely

---

[9] See p. 111n23.

[10] See p. 121.

[11] Cf. Ludwich 1884.118–122 and the critique of Janko 1992.26.

[12] Pfeiffer 1968.72 argues: "the only pre-Hellenistic editor of Homer" was Antimachus of Colophon (late fifth century BC). Pfeiffer means "editor" here in a strictly

candidates to be Aristotle and the whole Peripatetic School.[13]
This school surely included Demetrius of Phalerum.[14]

Despite this silence, we have seen instances where Aristotle
clearly speaks in terms of *diórthōsis* as an editorial procedure involving a Homeric reading.[15] So even if we agree that Aristotle

qualified sense: "we have no reason to assume that Antimachus made a 'recension' of
the Homeric poems, collating manuscripts and emending the text; his work is never
called a '*diórthōsis*'" (p. 94).

[13] Pfeiffer 1968.72 interprets the silence of the Homer scholia concerning any "edition" of Homer by Aristotle to be proof that there was no such thing. On the general
failure of the Homer scholia to mention Aristotle in the context of references to Aristarchus' Homer research, see Lührs 1992.14, who goes on to survey instances where
Aristarchus seems nonetheless to show an awareness of Aristotle's views (pp. 13–17).

[14] There are sporadic instances in the Homer scholia where the editorial judgment
of a critic called "Demetrius" is actually still on record. In most of these situations,
however, it is difficult if not impossible to know for sure whether Demetrius of Phalerum is meant. One obstacle is that there were other critics by the name of Demetrius, such as Demetrius Ixion, a contemporary of Aristarchus (in the Homer scholia,
sometimes called Demetrius, sometimes Ixion; seven attestations where both parts of
the name are given), mentioned prominently by Janko 1992.203. An even bigger obstacle, of course, is the nature of scholiastic writing, where the perspective of the
latest scholiast tends to displace the perspectives of earlier ones. What may be obviously Demetrius of Phalerum to an earlier scholiast may easily be reinterpreted as, say,
Demetrius Ixion by a later one. Nor does it help that the earlier Demetrius, as we will
see, eventually became *persona non grata* in Alexandria. Even if certainty is precluded,
we find some examples from the Homer scholia. In the scholia A to *Iliad* 6.414c, Demetrius is cited as an authority for the reading ἀμόν (Δημήτριός φησιν ἀντὶ τοῦ ἐμόν).
In the scholia AT to 13.5b, he is said to interpret ἀγαυῶν as 'splendid-looking'
(Δημήτριος δὲ ἀγαυοὺς τοὺς εὐειδεῖς). The scholia A to *Iliad* 14.221a report that Aristarchus reads γε νέεσθαι where Demetrius reads γενέεσθαι, a form that the scholia
reject as a false analogy (γε νέεσθαι τουτέστι πορεύεσθαι· οὕτως Ἀρίσταρχος.
Δημήτριος δὲ "γενέ(ε)σθαι" ἀντὶ τοῦ γενήσεσθαι, βιαίως πάνυ· οὐδὲ γὰρ τὸ
"πυθέσθαι" πυθέεσθαι γίνεται οὐδὲ τὸ λαβέσθαι λαβέεσθαι, ἵνα καὶ τὸ "γενέσθαι"
"γενέεσθαι" γένηται); Janko 1992.203 seems sure that we are dealing with Demetrius
Ixion. In the scholia A to *Iliad* 15.194, where the attested manuscript tradition reads
βέομαι φρεσίν, we see that Demetrius reads ἀποβήσομαι in the sense of 'I will yield'
(διὸ οὐκ ἂν κατὰ τὴν αὑτοῦ γνώμην βιώσομαι, ἀλλὰ κατὰ τὴν ἐμαυτοῦ.
Δημήτριος δὲ ἀποβήσομαι, εἴξω); Janko 1992.248 again seems sure that we are
dealing with Demetrius Ixion. The only case in the Homer scholia where a reference
to Demetrius of Phalerum is incontrovertible can be found at *Odyssey* 3.267, where the
scholia give πὰρ γὰρ ἔην καὶ ἀοιδός· οὕτω Δημήτριος ὁ Φαληρεύς: that is to say,
Demetrius read what the majority of our attested manuscripts give, πὰρ γὰρ ἔην, as
opposed to πὰρ δ' ἄρ' ἔην, the minority reading (and the reading chosen in the
OCT). In Athenaeus 5.4 Kaibel (177ef), there is a report of Demetrius' negative
judgment of the ethos reflected in *Iliad* 2.409. Bayer 1942.146–147 argues that the
technical language expressing Demetrius' criticism, as in the case of the word *parálēpsis*, is
anachronistic. I propose, however, that we give this report the benefit of the doubt, given
the implications of marginal notation in this term *parálēpsis*. As we have seen, explicit
references to marginal notation are a characteristic of Peripatetic text criticism.

[15] See again ch.5.

had no direct role in the production of a Homer "edition" – and I do not necessarily agree – he still speaks knowledgeably about the editorial activities of others. We have also noted other evidence for the existence of scholarly research on Homer in the fourth century. There was for example Isocrates' negative account of "sophists" who deliver in public learned commentaries, in the style of rhapsodes, about Homer and Hesiod.[16]

And there must have been scholarly research on other poetic traditions as well in the fourth century. Since the later Alexandrian critics seem not to have taken an active interest in performance traditions, whereas the earlier Athenian critics clearly did so, it seems to me most likely that the initial impetus for editing various non-Athenian songmaking traditions, including those of Alcman, Sappho, and Alcaeus, can be traced back to fourth-century Athens. I say this because the textual transmission of these songmaking traditions, mediated by the Alexandrian editors, reveals a wealth of details on the levels of dialect, prosody, and even orthography that could not have been preserved except through performance traditions.[17] And such traditions would be a most likely topic of research for scholars in fourth-century Athens.

I believe I have found an example of such a fourth-century scholar: in Isocrates *Letter* 8, *To the Rulers of Mytilene* (dated around 350), Isocrates is pleading for the restoration from exile of one Agenor of Mytilene in Lesbos, currently living in Athens and serving as the "music teacher" of Isocrates' grandsons (*paideuthéntes . . . tà perì tèn mousikén*, section 1). The father of these boys is Aphareus, a poet of tragedy. Isocrates goes on to say about Agenor of Mytilene (section 4): αἰσχρὸν γὰρ τὴν μὲν πόλιν ὑμῶν ὑπὸ πάντων ὁμολογεῖσθαι μουσικωτάτην εἶναι καὶ τοὺς ὀνομαστοτάτους ἐν αὐτῇ παρ' ὑμῖν τυγχάνειν γεγονότας, τὸν δὲ προέχοντα τῶν νῦν ὄντων περὶ τὴν ἱστορίαν τῆς παιδείας ταύτης φεύγειν ἐκ τῆς τοιαύτης πόλεως 'it is a shame that, while your city [= Mytilene] is acknowledged by all to be the most "musical" and the most famed figures in that field [ἐν αὐτῇ] happen to have been born in your city, yet he who is preeminent

---
[16] Isocrates *Panathenaicus* (*Oration* 12) 18–19 and 33, as quoted in ch.5.
[17] Pathfinding work by Risch 1946 on the early textual history of these poets.

192

among those who are currently engaged in the *historia* of this *pai-deía* [maybe the ἐν αὐτῇ refers proleptically to this *paideía*] is an exile from such a city'.

This passage suggests to me that around the middle of the fourth century there was in Athens an ongoing tradition of research in Lesbian songmaking, and I think that Lesbian songs were at this time still represented primarily by Sappho and Alcaeus. We may note Isocrates' use of the word *historia*, which I interpret as referring to Agenor's research in establishing texts of these songs, as well as the word *paideía*, referring surely to the practical activity of teaching youths how to perform these songs. Isocrates goes on to argue (section 9) that Agenor and his kin, if they were restored from exile, would not be offensive to the older generation of Mytilene, whereas ... τοῖς δὲ νεωτέροις διατριβὴν παρέχειν ἡδεῖαν καὶ χρησίμην καὶ πρέπουσαν τοῖς τηλικού-τοις 'to the younger generation, they provide an activity [*diatribé*] that is pleasant, useful, and appropriate'.[18] Again we may note the ideology of *paideía*.

Let us return, however, to our immediate problem: why is it that we see in the Homer scholia practically no references to the activity of "editing" the text of Homer in the fourth century? There is a solution to be found if we can establish that the *koiné* tradition of Homer was linked to the editorial scholarship of the Peripatetic School in general and of Demetrius in particular. If that is the case, then there are clear and understandable reasons to account for any disinclination on the part of critics in the Library of Alexandria, from Zenodotus onward, to authorize explicitly this stream of scholarship – even if they themselves were the continuators of that scholarship. We will turn to these reasons presently.

The use of *koiné* 'common' in the positive sense of 'standard' – and therefore, by implication, 'universal' – is to be found in reference not only to the text of Homer, as just argued, but also to the sacred text of *scripture*, specifically the Hebrew Bible as translated into the Greek. Here I come to the original reason for my using the word "scripture" – with specific reference to the era of Aristarchus.

---

[18] We may compare the usage of *diatribé* as 'performance' in Isocrates 12.19, as quoted at pp. 123–124.

In Jerome's *Epistle to Sunnia and Fretella* (106.2), the word *koiné*, glossed in Latin as the *vulgata* or 'vulgate', is cited as designating two different Greek versions of the Hebrew Bible, namely, that of Lucianus and that of the Septuagint, as edited by Origen.[19] As we see from the context of Jerome's reference, these two versions were 'common' in different regions of the early Church. The fact that *koiné* is the word used here to refer to the Septuagint is of special interest to Allen, who detects analogies between the status of the Septuagint in Origen's edition of the Hebrew Bible and the status of the Koine in Aristarchus' edition of Homer.[20]

The Septuagint is the fifth *selís* or 'column' in the six-column format of Origen's edition of the Hebrew Bible, known as the Hexapla: the first column is the Hebrew text, the second is a transliteration into the Greek alphabet, and the third through the sixth are Greek translations, of which the fifth column represents the privileged but hardly exclusive authority of the Septuagint (Eusebius *Historia Ecclesiastica* 6.16).[21] Origen avoided the insertion of conjectures or emendations in the Septuagint column of his Hexapla; also, wording that was present in the Septuagint but absent in the corresponding Hebrew texts – that is, wording that Origen would have considered to be "interpolated" – was retained in the Hexapla and simply marked in the margins by the obelus.[22]

Allen envisages an analogous method in Aristarchus' edition of Homer, with the Koine occupying a distinct *status* that is at least conceptually comparable to the distinct *column* occupied by that other Koine, the Septuagint, which Origen had annotated with such editorial marks as the obelus, the lemniscus, the hypolemniscus, and the asterisk (Epiphanius *On Measures and Weights* 2 and 7).[23] In the case of the Hebrew Bible, as Allen concludes, *koiné* could refer to different editions in different parts of the

[19] Allen 1924.278, 317, who also cites Basil *In Esaiam* 2 p. 447d ed. Garnier, where *koiné* refers, again, to a Greek version of the Hebrew Bible.

[20] Allen 1924.315–320.

[21] Allen 1924.315–317, quoting other texts as well besides Eusebius. We may note with interest the use of the word *ktêma* 'possession' in the passage from Eusebius that is cited here.

[22] Neuschäfer 1987 I 99–100; cf. Lührs 1992.8n27.

[23] Allen 1924.316; cf. Neuschäfer 1987 II 388n175.

world, but in any case it meant, wherever it was used, "the general or usual text."[24] Allen goes on to argue that it once had meant "the general text" of Homer as well.

More than that: just as *koiné* designates a text that is *sacred* as well as *common* in the case of the Septuagint, so also the *koiné* text of Homer is sacred, in Allen's judgment.[25] He justifies his specific use of the word "sacred" with reference to the Homeric *koiné* by arguing for its scriptural status in the editorial practice of the Alexandrians: "critics expressed their opinion of the genuineness of parts of it by signs appicted on its margin (as they did to Hippocrates also ...), without removing a jot or tittle from it (as they did not from Hippocrates either)."[26]

Although Aristarchus may have valued other textual traditions more highly, I agree with Allen that this Alexandrian critic treated the *koiné* version of Homer with some measure of respect, as *a* standard. I also agree that Aristarchus would have thought of the hypothetical archetype of the *koiné* version of Homer as a sacred text – sacred as far as the Athenians were concerned.

Here we return to the term *Homēristaí*, which Athenaeus (620b–c) seems to connect with a reform of Homeric performance traditions under the régime of Demetrius of Phalerum – and which I have tried to connect with the idea of an Athenian "State Script" of Homer. In the previous chapter, we have seen that the same term *Homēristaí* was actually used in Hellenized Egypt with reference to Homeric performers. Now I propose to go one step even further: the standard "script" tradition of Homeric performers in Egypt, who were known as *Homēristaí*, may have been derived from a "State Script" instituted for Homeric performers in Athens under the régime of Demetrius of Phalerum, who were also known as *Homēristaí* according to my interpretation of the passage from Athenaeus.

In any case, I must insist that the Koine tradition was for Aristarchus simply *a* "scripture," not *the* "scripture." Similarly, the Septuagint was simply *one* of six columns in the six-column format of Origen's edition of the Hebrew Bible, the Hexapla.

[24] Allen 1924.320.
[25] *Ibid.*
[26] Ibid. Allen's relevant remarks about the editing of the Hippocratic corpus are to be found at his 1924.313.

Mention of the Hebrew Bible brings us to the crucial testimony of the *Letter of Aristeas,* dated around 100 BC.[27] This document dramatizes the genesis of the Septuagint in mythological terms that I think are closely analogous to a wide variety of narrative traditions where the synthesis of oral and textual traditions is pictured as an instantaneous cohesion, a spontaneous generation, a "big bang." I have treated at length this type of narrative about the genesis of Homeric poetry in my 1992 article, "Homeric Questions."[28] Here I need only add two points. First, the narrative of the spontaneously inspired collective translation of the Septuagint by 72 assembled wise men, as reported in the *Letter of Aristeas* and other sources, fits neatly the specific rhetoric of distinct Alexandrian Jewish identity, as a 1991 article by Naomi Janowitz has shown clearly.[29] Second, it fits also the general rhetoric of generating an aetiology for a sacred text. As an aetiology, it reveals some remarkable parallels with the various aetiologies about the genesis of Homeric poetry.

The testimony of the *Letter of Aristeas* is relevant to our discussion not only because of the parallelisms between the status of the Septuagint and the status of Homeric poetry. Even more important, the *Letter of Aristeas* credits none other than Demetrius of Phalerum, the historical figure whom Athenaeus (620b–c) credits with reforming the Athenian traditions of Homeric performance, as the agent responsible for the actual commissioning of the Septuagint. On the basis of Strabo 9.1.20, Diodorus Siculus 20.45, and Diogenes Laertius 5.78, we know that Demetrius fled in 307 from Athens to Thebes, which had been refounded by his patron, Cassander, and then, after the death of Cassander in 297 BC, he found refuge at the court of Ptolemy I in Alexandria, whose first wife, Eurydike, happened to be the sister of Cassander;[30] in Alexandria, Demetrius had a key role in instituting the collection of books that resulted ultimately in the Library of Alexandria.[31] More than that, the *Letter of Aristeas* represents Demetrius as

[27] On which see Murray 1987.

[28] N 1992a.45–51.

[29] Janowitz 1991.

[30] This crucial link between Demetrius and Ptolemy I was brought to my attention by J. D. Morgan (*per litteras* 30 November 1993).

[31] Cf. Blum 1991.100–101, reviewing the discussions of Wilamowitz 1924 I 22 and 165, Pfeiffer 1968.96, 99–104. Both these earlier discussions stress the academic links

advising King Ptolemy to commission the Septuagint for a specific purpose, that is, so that the régime may possess the sacred text of the Alexandrian Jews. Even though the narrative of the *Letter of Aristeas* confuses Ptolemy I with Ptolemy II,[32] the ideology that is being dramatized here is historically verifiable.[33] The Ptolemies developed the policy of possessing official sacred texts representing each of the major cultural constituents of their kingdom, a prominent example being the history of Egypt by Manetho.[34]

The partly mythologized role of Demetrius as the agent responsible for the Ptolemies' acquisition of the Septuagint can be drawn into a parallel with his historical role in the acquisition of Classical Greek books for the Library of Alexandria (*Letter of Aristeas* 9–10).[35] The parallelism itself is of great historical interest.[36] With regard to the role of Demetrius as a collector of the

of Demetrius with the school of Aristotle. Pfeiffer 1968.99 remarks: "Demetrius was always a great favourite with Wilamowitz."

[32] J. D. Morgan comments (*per litteras* 30 November 1993): "I heartily agree with your argument that the *Letter of Aristeas* is evidence that Demetrius played a crucial role in collecting books under Ptolemy I, and that when it refers to Ptolemy II, that is a slip, whereas most previous scholars had thought that the *Letter* had right the name of the Ptolemy but had got wrong Demetrius' role. It needs to be emphasized that confusion of one Ptolemy with another is a common error: e.g. *P.Oxy.* 1241, our primary source for the librarians, confuses Ptolemy I with Ptolemy IV and Ptolemy Philopator with Ptolemy Philometor."

[33] It is clear from the arguments assembled by Bayer 1942 (especially p. 99) that Demetrius was formally associated with Ptolemy I. On this detail, as Blum 1991.100 points out, the *Letter of Aristeas* has it wrong in referring to Ptolemy II. Blum 1991.116–117n27 takes to task Pfeiffer 1968.98 for making too much of the attested references to Ptolemy I instead of II. Blum 1991.101: "one should not diminish the role of [Demetrius of Phalerum] in the foundation of the Alexandrian Library, as Pfeiffer and others have done." Ptolemy II "supported the library during his forty years of government so lavishly that he was thought to have been its founder already in the second century BC." (Blum 1991.102, who as we have seen dates *Letter of Aristeas* at around 100 BC.)

[34] See Blum 1991.103, who points out that the *History of Egypt* by Manetho was dedicated to Ptolemy II Philadelphus. Blum ibid. also adduces a "translated" book on magic by "Zoroaster," again in the reign of Ptolemy II, listed by the Callimachean Hermippus. Blum ibid. puts the Septuagint into a comparable context.

[35] The relevant passage, as well as reinforcing passages from Tzetzes' *Prolegomena* to his commentary on Aristophanes, are conveniently quoted by Pfeiffer 1968.100–101.

[36] Although the *Letter of Aristeas* says that Demetrius of Phalerum was head of the Library under Ptolemy II, other sources indicate Ptolemy I, not II (Eusebius *Historia Ecclesiastica* 5.8.11 = Irenaeus *Adversus Haereses* 3.21.2) while still other sources give both possibilities (Clement of Alexandria *Stromateis* 1.48). J. D. Morgan comments (*per litteras* 30 November 1993): "With such variation in our sources regarding the identity

Greek Classics, it has been argued that it was in fact he who became the first *de facto* head of the Library of Alexandria, and that
Zenodotus took over at the Library only around 291 BC – or
maybe even as late as 283 BC, when Ptolemy II Philadelphus
became sole ruler. In any case, 283 BC marks the point when
Demetrius, who had miscalculated in the politics of succession,
became a *persona non grata* to the new king and was banished.[37]
Demetrius had been a protégé of Eurydike, the first wife of
Ptolemy I and sister of Cassander, Demetrius' deceased patron;
Ptolemy II, on the other hand, was the son of Berenice, the sec-
ond wife of Ptolemy I.[38]

Here I return to my earlier argument that, for earlier Homer
critics like Demetrius himself, the *koiné* could have meant the
Athenian "City Text," as reshaped through the *diórthōsis* of Aristotle and the Peripatetic School, while for later critics like Aristarchus, the same designation would have meant, more generally
and more simply, copies derived from the Athenian "City Text."
Now that we see how Demetrius became *persona non grata* to
Ptolemy II and his descendants, we may ask whether such a de-
bacle may have produced radical changes in any reference by later
Alexandrian critics – starting already with Zenodotus, the protégé
of Ptolemy II – to the Athenian "City Text" of Homer. Any
reference by Alexandrian critics to the Athenian text, from that
point onward, would be likely to underplay or even slight what
may once have been a key role played by the Peripatetic figure
Demetrius in a *diórthōsis* of this text – and even in its transformation into a Ptolemaic possession.[39]

of the Ptolemy and no variation regarding the role of Demetrius of Phalerum, it is
clearly more systematic to give precedence to the latter."
[37] Blum 1991.101, 117n32, 127. Ptolemy II was a former pupil of Philitas of Cos:
Pfeiffer 1968.124.
[38] See p. 196n30. J. D. Morgan comments (*per litteras* 30 November 1993), "The connection is now clear. Upon the death in 297 of his protector Cassander, Demetrius of
Phalerum sought refuge at the court of Cassander's sister, and while there promoted the
interests of his protectress, with ultimately fatal consequences to himself." So finally the
relationship of Cassander and Demetrius, which had seemed as if it were merely a random
association in the passage of Athenaeus (620b–c) that we considered in the last chapter,
becomes evident. Morgan continues: "I think it is easy to suppose that one of the important personal links between the two was a common enthusiasm for studying the
text of Homer, with each inspired by the earlier work of Aristotle on this topic."
[39] The formulation of Pfeiffer 1968.95 is instructive: "the line Philitas-Zenodotus-
Callimachus, of which we have stressed the non-Aristotelian character, met in Alexandria

We see such a pattern of slighting even when it comes to the ultimate service performed by Demetrius for the Ptolemies. There is a celebrated remark by Strabo 13.1.54 about Aristotle's prestige as a renowned collector of books, and in this context it is he rather than Demetrius who gets the credit – despite the historical evidence indicating otherwise – for "teaching" the Ptolemies how to achieve the greatest book-collection of them all, the Library of Alexandria: Ἀριστοτέλης ... πρῶτος ὧν ἴσμεν συναγαγὼν βιβλία, καὶ διδάξας τοὺς ἐν Αἰγύπτῳ βασιλέας βιβλιοθήκης σύνταξιν 'Aristotle ... was the first that we know of to collect books, and <u>he taught the kings in Egypt how to put together a library</u>'.

This is not to say that Zenodotus and the Alexandrian critics that came after him slighted the Peripatetic tradition of Aristotle – all on account of the fallen Demetrius, that most visible of Peripatetics in early Alexandria.[40] I am saying only that a Homeric *diórthōsis* by Aristotle, if it was strongly identified with the subsequent editorial and political activities of Demetrius of Phalerum at the Library of Alexandria, would have faded from official memory along with the man who brought it from Athens. Or, even more likely, such a *diórthōsis* of Aristotle could have changed identities many times over, becoming transformed into the *diórthōsis* of Demetrius and then into the *diórthōsis* of Zenodotus, whose own editorial reshaping could easily have justified in any case such a change of nomenclature.[41]

The point remains that the pieces of evidence concerning the

with a genuine Peripatetic line from Athens." At its earliest stages at Alexandria, the Peripatetic line was represented most visibly by Demetrius of Phalerum (Pfeiffer 1968.96). For a discussion of instances in the Homer scholia where the views attributed to Aristarchus imply an awareness of Aristotle's views on Homer, see Lührs 1992.13–17.

[40] I agree with Slater 1989.42, who argues that the tradition of the Alexandrian school, which "is best represented in our surviving scholia," was "rooted in the methods of the sophists as redefined by Aristotle." Still, there are clear signs of anti-Peripatetic tendencies, especially in the line of thought represented by Callimachus: see Pfeiffer 1968.136–137.

[41] In this connection, we may note that Rengakos 1993.11 cautions against the reductionist mentality, evident already in the ancient world, of crediting Zenodotus, by retrojection, with all or most pre-Aristarchean variant readings of Homer. On Zenodotus' methods in editing Homer, see Rengakos 1993.18–21 (with whom I agree that the variants reported by Zenodotus are genuine textual variants, not glosses or cited parallels, as van Thiel 1992 argues).

activities of Demetrius of Phalerum add up to a premier example
of a historical fact: that the ideology of actually possessing the
text, whether by commissioning or by acquisition, was a key
principle in the genesis of the Library of Alexandria. Witness this
anecdote in Plutarch *Regum et imperatorum apophthegmata* 189d:
Δημήτριος ὁ Φαληρεὺς Πτολεμαίῳ τῷ βασιλεῖ παρῄνει τὰ
περὶ βασιλείας καὶ ἡγεμονίας βιβλία κτᾶσθαι καὶ ἀνα-
γινώσκειν· "ἃ γὰρ οἱ φίλοι τοῖς βασιλεῦσιν οὐ θαρροῦσι
παραινεῖν, ταῦτα ἐν τοῖς βιβλίοις γέγραπται" 'Demetrius of
Phalerum gave King Ptolemy this advice [*paraínesis*]: that he
should possess [*ktásthai*] and read [*anagignṓskein*] books about
kingship and hegemony, giving this as a reason: "those who are
near and dear to kings do not dare to give them advice [*paraínesis*]
about the kind of things that are written in these books."'

In this regard, not enough attention has been paid to a detail
recorded in Plutarch's *Life of Alexander* 8.2, on the authority of
Onesicritus FGH 38 F 134 (who actually accompanied Alexander
on his campaigns), concerning a copy of the *Iliad* known as
ἐκ τοῦ νάρθηκος 'the one from the casket [*nárthēx*]', which
Alexander the Great reputedly used to keep under his *proskephálaion* 'headrest' as he slept. This copy, Plutarch says, had been
"corrected by Aristotle," Ἀριστοτέλους διορθώσαντος (8.2): in
other words, it featured the *diórthōsis* of Aristotle. Rudolf Blum
is helpful in suggesting ways to visualize the *nárthēx* 'casket' as a
container big enough to accommodate the text of the *Iliad*: he
estimates the dimensions at 40 × 30 × 25 centimeters.[42] The discussion that follows offers a way to visualize the idea of a *nárthēx*
under the *proskephálaion*, sometimes mistranslated as a 'pillow'.
But first I should note simply my conviction that the wording
that is used here to describe Aristotle's work on this copy, *diorthóō*
'correct', may yet vindicate the historicity of Plutarch's description, thus removing the doubts expressed by Rudolf Pfeiffer
concerning whether or not Aristotle had produced his own
edition of Homer.[43]

We have already seen some historical evidence linking this
technical word *diorthóō* with the school of Aristotle.[44] Also, in

[42] Blum 1991.69–70n45.
[43] Pfeiffer 1968.71–72.
[44] See p. 121 above.

light of Aristotle's traditional sobriquet *anagnóstēs*, I find it significant that Plutarch's *Life* describes Alexander, precisely in the
context of his possessing Aristotle's edition of Homer, as *philan-
agnóstēs* (8.2).[45] In this same context, Alexander is said to have
taken along on his military campaigns not only this text of Homer
as "edited" by Aristotle but also texts of the tragic poets Aeschylus, Sophocles, and Euripides, as well as texts of the dithy-
rambic poets Telestes and Philoxenus (8.3).[46] These texts of the
three tragedians must be related to the official Athenian State
Script of Aeschylus, Sophocles, and Euripides, commissioned by
the statesman Lycurgus ("Plutarch" *Lives of the Ten Orators* 841f).[47]
In this connection, we may note the opinion of Rudolf Blum and
others that Aristotle himself was the one who had produced, *at
the initiative of Lycurgus*, these official Athenian texts of tragedy.[48]
Like Aristotle, Lycurgus had studied in Plato's Academy.[49]

What is essential for the present argument is not whether this
story of Plutarch about Alexander stems from a historical fact.
What matters is whether the *use* of the story is indeed a historical
fact. I suggest that it is, and that it reflects an ideology promoted
by the dynasty of the Ptolemies when they came to power
in Egypt. The premise of this ideology, I suggest further, is that
the Ptolemies had succeeded in taking possession of the most
canonical text owned by Alexander the Great, his own copy of
the *Iliad*. When the Library of Alexandria was founded in the
reign of Ptolemy I, the core of its acquisitions may indeed have
included texts from Alexander's own library. The expression ἐκ
τοῦ νάρθηκος 'the one from the *nárthēx*' (8.2), designating Alexander's copy of the *Iliad*, seems typical of the terminology used
for cataloguing new acquisitions in the Alexandrian Library.[50]

Let us return to the detail in Plutarch's *Life of Alexander* 8.2

---

[45] On Aristotle as the *anagnóstēs*, see p. 149 above. For a mention, in passing, of a
rhapsōidós 'rhapsode' who performed at a grand feast, the context of many other performances as well, arranged by Alexander the Great, see the whole narrative of the
feast in Athenaeus 538c–539a, reporting the account of Chares in his *History of
Alexander*. Cf. Pickard-Cambridge 1968.280.

[46] Telestes and Philoxenus are dated to the late fifth and early fourth centuries.

[47] On which see pp. 174–175 above.

[48] Blum 1991.42.

[49] Ibid.

[50] Witness the designation of a certain category of acquired texts as ἐκ τῶν πλοίων
'straight off the boats' (Galen 17.1.606.13–14), to be discussed at p. 204 below.

concerning a copy of the *Iliad* kept in a box that was placed under the *proskephálaion* of Alexander the Great as he slept. I prefer to translate *proskephálaion* as 'headrest'. The point is that the text was under the king's head, so that the notion "under the headrest" translates into "under the bed under the headrest under the head." As we will now see, not only did the king possess the text: in the logic of the story, the text possessed the king – specifically the king's head – in his sleep.

The narrative of the *Life of Alexander* tells of a dream that Alexander had after he conquered Egypt (νύκτωρ κοιμώμενος ὄψιν εἶδε θαυμαστήν 26.3), and according to my interpretation this dream was caused, in terms of the story, by the presence of the Homeric text under Alexander's head. For the story of the dream, Plutarch cites as his source Heraclides Ponticus (F 140 Wehrli), and he adds explicitly that this was the story "believed by the people of Alexandria" (26.3) – that is, that this story was accepted as a charter myth, as it were, of Alexandria.[51] Moreover, the story of the dream is explicitly connected by Plutarch with Alexander's choosing to store the Homeric *Iliad* in a container (αὐτὸς ἔφη τὴν 'Ιλιάδα φρουρήσειν ἐνταῦθα καταθέμενος 26.2). This container had been his most precious war-prize by far, a *kibótion* 'box' that had been captured from his defeated enemy, King Darius (26.1). The *kibótion* 'box' as described here by Plutarch is clearly identical with the *nárthēx* that we have already seen at an earlier point in the narrative (8.2).[52]

The dream of Alexander takes place after he has been pondering where he should found the ultimate Hellenic city; in the dream, an old man with gray hair appears to him and declaims the verses that we know as *Odyssey* 4.354–355 (Plutarch *Life of Alexander* 26.5). When Alexander awakens, he realizes that the apparition was Homer and that the mention of Pharos in the Homeric verses meant that he was destined to found the ultimate city at the very site that was to become Alexandria (26.5 and following). I see here a *charter myth* reflecting what I have just described as the ideology of the Ptolemaic dynasty in Egypt – and,

---

[51] On the concept of *charter myth*, cf. Leach 1982.5, following Malinowski 1926.

[52] On the use of the word *kibōtós* 'box' and its derivatives to designate the special storage place of texts containing a powerful political message, see N 1990a.171–172, 431.

more directly, the early ideology of the Library of Alexandria. This charter myth, to repeat, would have been founded on the idea that the Ptolemies now possessed the texts of Alexander the Great, especially Aristotle's text of Homer. According to this charter myth, as Alexander reportedly inferred after his dream, he now had Homer as his military companion (οὔκουν [οὐκ] ἀργὸς οὐδ' ἀσύμβολος αὐτῷ συστρατεύειν ἔοικεν Ὅμηρος 26.3) – and so too, according to this version of the story as believed by "the people of Alexandria," did the Ptolemies (εἰ δ', ὅπερ Ἀλεξαν-δρεῖς λέγουσιν Ἡρακλείδῃ [F 140 Wehrli] πιστεύοντες, ἀληθές ἐστιν *ibid.*).[53] What was "believed" by "the people of Alexandria" was the ideology of the Ptolemies. And this ideology, I propose, goes back to a time when Demetrius of Phalerum was still help-ing Ptolemy I acquire all the available books of Greek civilization, the most treasured of which could have been the text of Homer's *Iliad,* the product of a *diórthōsis* executed by Aristotle himself.

Another prominent example of this driving idea, that the Li-brary of Alexandria was predicated on the ideological principle of possessing the canonical texts, is the report of Athenaeus (3a–b) concerning the patron of Zenodotus, none other than King Ptolemy II himself, who reigned from 283 to 246 BC: the king purchased the whole library of Aristotle from one Neleus, to whom it had been handed down by Theophrastus, who in turn had inherited it from his teacher Aristotle himself. Included in this collection, we might expect, were other valuable copies of Homer. But given the fact that Demetrius of Phalerum was a student of Theophrastus, we might also expect that any "State Script" of Homer, instituted under the régime of Demetrius while he was still in power in Athens, would have already in-corporated the *diórthōsis* of Aristotle. If Demetrius had brought with him from Athens an authorized copy of such a "State Script" at the time when he was welcomed to Alexandria by Ptolemy I, then the later purchase of Aristotle's whole library by Ptolemy II need not have significantly affected the Alexandrian textual transmission of Homer. This line of reasoning may ex-plain in part why we find in the Homeric scholia no mention, attributed to the Alexandrian critics, of a Homeric *diórthōsis* by

[53] On Alexander as a "second Achilles," see Plutarch *Alexander* 5.8, 15.9.

Aristotle; the results of such a *diórthōsis* would have been already
incorporated into the text as reshaped under the régime of
Demetrius of Phalerum – and as further reshaped through the
Homeric *diórthōsis* by Zenodotus and by the later Alexandrian
critics.[54]

Yet another prominent example of such an acquisition of texts
comes from Galen (17.1.607–608, *Commentary* on the Hippocratic
Epidemiai Book 3.2.4). He tells of Ptolemy III Euergetes, who
reigned from 246 to 221 BC. It seems that this king had borrowed
from the Athenians, who accepted a deposit of 15 talents, a state-
owned text described as containing the dramas of Aeschylus,
Sophocles, and Euripides, which was to be copied for the Library of Alexandria – and which was then never returned to the
Athenians.[55] This text is evidently the same State Text of the
tragedians that had been instituted in the era of the Athenian
statesman Lycurgus ("Plutarch" *Lives of the Ten Orators* 841f).[56]

Galen tells the anecdote about Ptolemy III and the State Text
of the three canonical poets of tragedy in the context of having
recounted how a copy of Book III of the Hippocratic *Epidemiai*
found its way to the Library at Alexandria. This copy, he says,
belongs to the τῶν ἐκ πλοίων category (Galen 17.1.606), that is,
one of the old books that had been borrowed "straight off the
boat," in that Ptolemy had the policy of requiring that any tra-
velers to Alexandria should hand over whatever old books they
owned so that these could be copied, whereupon originals would
be kept while new copies would be given back to their owners.
Galen then goes on to say that the extent of just how far Ptolemy
would go in pursuit of his policy is illustrated by the case of the
Athenian State Text of tragedies. The deposit of this large sum of
fifteen talents indicates the exceptional nature of this acquisition.
Moreover, we see in the very fact of the acquisition a transformation in the status of the text from script to "scripture."

So also with the acquisition of Homeric texts: what had been a

---

[54] See p. 199 above. Even before the Ptolemaic acquisition of the library of Aristotle, we may expect that the Library at Alexandria already had selective access to the
works produced by the school of Aristotle, as eventually represented by his successor
Theophrastus: Blum 1991.59.
[55] Pfeiffer 1968.82.
[56] On which see pp. 174–175 above.

script in Athens becomes scripture in Alexandria for the scholars of the Library. And a major figure in this transition is Demetrius of Phalerum himself. More than that, he is an actual agent of transition. In terms of the sequence of five periods of Homeric transmission that I postulated at the beginning of the fifth chapter, the activities of Demetrius not only overlap between period 3 and period 4: they even anticipate period 5. With reference to the transition from period 3 to period 4, we have examined a source claiming that Demetrius was instrumental in the theatricalization of traditions in Homeric performance. If we accept this claim, we can say that Demetrius was primarily responsible for the mentality of what I have been calling the *script*. With reference to the eventual transition from period 4 to period 5, we have also examined a source claiming that Demetrius was a key figure in the founding of the Library of Alexandria during the interim years after he had fled from Greece and before he fell from grace with Ptolemy II in Alexandria. If we accept this claim, we can say that Demetrius had been instrumental in the Library's acquisition of a copy or copies of the Koine, the more heavily edited versions of which I identify with the new Athenian State Script of Homer, instituted under his old régime. A parallel phenomenon is the later acquisition by the Ptolemies of an older Athenian State Script, the corpus of the three tragedians.[57] These scripts of the Athenian State become the "scripture" for a later Alexandrian editor like Aristarchus.

As we contemplate the standardizing or "scriptural" period of Homeric transmission, the era of Alexandrian transmission, it is enough to repeat one last time what I argued in the fifth chapter: that Aristarchus and his predecessors, even though they collected a wide range of variants, had in mind an editorial goal very different from the one I am advocating. They insisted on the idea of an original version of Homer, which must be reconstructed by way of sorting out the variants attested in surviving texts. I insist, by contrast, on the historical fact that the performance tradition of Homer stayed alive well beyond the sixth century BC, and that

---

[57] We may note with interest the comment of Pfeiffer 1968.192: "in contrast to comedy, tragedy seems to have been neglected by the scholars of the third century." See also Blum 1991.83n155.

a primary heritage of this tradition – at least until the era of Aristarchus – was multiformity.

In the end, the textual tradition of Homer, as most strongly represented by Aristarchus, won out. Or, to put it more aptly, the performance tradition, as by now most weakly represented by the Homer performers of Hellenized Egypt, lost out to an ever more uniform text.

Epilogue: dead poets and recomposed performers

There is a late twelfth-century *lai* by Marie de France, entitled *Laüstic*, about a nightingale that was killed by a jealous knight who had been told by his wife, when asked why she would leave the bed so often at night and stand by the window, that "there is no joy in all the world like hearing the nightingale" (*il nen ad joïe en cest mund | ki n'ot le laüstic chanter*, verses 84–85).[1] Till then, there had been a series of nightly contacts, purely by voice, between the wife and her secret lover, whose window was nearby:

> *des chambres u la dame jut,*
> *quant a la fenestre s'estut,*
> *poeit parler a sun ami*
> *de l'autre part, et il a li.*

> From the rooms where the lady lay,
> when she stood by the window
> she could talk to her lover
> and, from the other side, he could talk to her.
> Marie de France, Laüstic verses 39–42

To warn her lover that the secret has been discovered – an inference that follows, without explanation, from the death of the nightingale – the lady sends the body of the dead songbird to him. She starts by saying:

---

[1] There is a related narrative, this one centering on the figures of Tristan and Iseut, in a late twelfth-century poem entitled *Donnei des Amants* (see p. 22 n50): hearing Tristan imitating the song of birds – and the first bird to be mentioned in the text is a nightingale – Iseut leaves the bed where King Mark is sleeping, following Tristan's seductive sound. See Pfeffer 1985.154–156; also in general her ch.7, "Sex and the Single Nightingale."

Epilogue

"le laüstic li trametrai,
l'aventure li manderai."
en une piece de samit
a or brusdé et tut escrit
ad l'oiselet envolupé;
un suen vaslet ad apelé,
sun message li ad chargié,
a sun ami l'ad enveié.

"I will send the nightingale to him,
I will pass on to him the story."
In a piece of silk,
embroidered with gold and with writing all around,
she wrapped up the bird.
She called one of her servants
and charged him with her message
which she sent to her lover.

Marie de France, Laüstic verses 133–140

When the lover receives the body of the dead songbird, he en-
shrines it in a reliquary, which he carries around on his person for
the rest of his life.[2]

This story of the nightingale, according to the interpretation of
one critic, draws a parallel between the song of the bird and the
medium of the *lai*, but the parallelism is enigmatic:

> Nowhere in the *lai* is the presence of a voice anything but a
> substitute for something else. The lovers are never present to
> each other, and the nightingale never sings to the lovers. It is
> itself nothing more than the sign of a ruse or lie told to calm
> the jealous husband's suspicions, an invention synonymous
> with the *lai* itself. Moreover, the dead bird is embroidered and
> written (*a or brusdé et tut escrit*) and sent like a poetic *envoi* to
> the lover once consummation or the presence of bodies is
> no longer even imaginable. Nor was it ever. Presence in the
> *lai* is always deferred.[3]

---

[2] See Pfeffer 1985.157–168, who compares the narrative of Marie de France with
several other versions of the "nightingale's death" theme in medieval literature, including an obscene treatment in Boccaccio's *Decameron*, Day 5 Story 4 ("Caterina and
Ricciardo"). I am grateful to Rupert T. Pickens for showing me a copy of his forthcoming paper, "The Bestiary of Marie de France's *Lais*," in which he gives the background for visualizing the two art objects featured in the *lai* of the nightingale: 1) the
finely-crafted box or reliquary and 2) the luxuriant silk embroidered with gold thread
and wrapped around an object to be treasured – in this case, the body of the nightingale.
The embroidered message on the silk could not be "read" unless it was unwrapped.

[3] Bloch 1988.71.

This formulation is offered in the larger context of a disagreement with Paul Zumthor's hermeneutics of oral poetry, who claims that medieval literature is driven by the primacy of what he calls the living voice.[4] As an alternative to Zumthor's model, it is suggested that "the Old French text is a tomb of the voice which it betrays."[5] I agree, at least to the extent that the voice of the nightingale has indeed been "betrayed" or revealed by the text:

> *la dame prent le cors petit,*
> *durement plure e si maudit*
> *ceus ki le laüstic <u>traïrent</u>*

> The lady took the small body.
> She lamented bitterly and cursed
> those who <u>betrayed</u> the nightingale.
>
> Marie de France, *Laüstic* verses 121–123

And yet, it is not just the text that betrays the voice of the nightingale. Even the voice of poetic performance betrays the songbird's voice. In the logic of the song, the nightingale sings a secret language, to be understood by lovers only, and the songbird is therefore betrayed if his love-song is made public, that is, if his secret language is sung to the public, the poet's public.

To appreciate more fully the poetic implications of this theme of betrayal, it is instructive to begin with the poem *Philomena praevia temporis amoeni* by John Pecham (died 1292). This poet reshapes along religious lines the related theme of the nightingale's love-song, and the legend it implies can be summarized as follows:

---

[4] Bloch 1988.63, especially with reference to Zumthor 1983, 1984. At p. 66, Bloch challenges Zumthor's emphasis on the "biological" aspects of "orality."

[5] Bloch 1988.73, who argues that *traire* 'betray' is treated in this work as a synonym of *traire* 'transmit'. Since, however, we expect the two words to be distinct, that is, pronounced differently (*traïr* 'betray' vs. *traire* 'transmit'), such an argument can work only on the level of the written word (cf. Pickens 1994.68). Bloch (ibid.) goes on to say: "To write or treat ("traire") is to betray ("traire"); or, to carry this idea further, to write immanence, whether figured as the body or the voice, is to betray it, and, as in the case of the nightingale, to ensnare and contain it, kill it and, ultimately, to entomb the living voice in the dead letter of a text, to silence it. This is why, I am convinced, silence is such an obsessive theme in Old French literature: every work silences a voice." Cf. Vance 1986.51–85 ("Roland and Charlemagne: The Remembering Voices and the Crypt"), especially p. 85 on "two modes of experiencing language, one proper to an oral culture, the other to a culture of writing, *though the former cannot be known except as a dialectical myth of the latter.*"

[The] nightingale knows before-hand the time of her death and when she perceives that it is near, flies to the top of a tree and there, at daybreak, pours out her soul in many songs. At the hour of Prime her voice rises higher and in her singing she knows neither respite nor repose. About the time of Tierce, the gladness and the passion increase, until at noon, her heart is ready to break as she cries *oci! oci!* ['kill! kill!'], and her strength begins to fail, until at None she dies."[6]

The songbird's cry of love and death signals the theme of betrayal. In *Song* 18 of the *troubadour* Guillaume le Vinier, for example, the nightingale utters this cry *oci! oci!* 'kill! kill!' (verse 4) precisely because he is denouncing the *trahitour* 'traitors' (verse 7), that is, those who betray true lovers.[7] It is a central convention of the *troubadour* traditions to represent the nightingale as a loyal messenger sent to the beloved by the lover, by the maker of a love-song: thus in Peire d'Alvernha, *Song* 1.1–4, the songbird is both the discreet communicator and the faithful guardian of the lovers' secrets.[8] In the logic of this poetic tradition, the language of the nightingale is like the language of secret lovers: it cannot be understood by the uninitiated. This same language, it follows, is the language of the poet. In an early thirteenth-century poem by Peire Cardenal, Song 56 (verses 33–40), the homology is made explicit:

a mos ops chant e a mos ops flaujol,
car homs mas ieu non enten mon lati;
atretan pauc com fa d'un rossinhol
entent la gent de mon chant que se di.
ez ieu non ai lengua fiza ni breta
ni sai parlear flamenc ni angevi,
mas malvestatz que los escalafeta
lor tol vezer que es fals ni es fi.

---

[6] Raby 1951.445–446. On the vernacular background of the onomatopoeia implicit in the cry *oci! oci!* 'kill! kill!', see Pfeffer 1985.41. On the mythological background for the theme of death by "killing," see Pfeffer pp. 136–137, 140.

[7] Pfeffer 1985.134–137, 140.

[8] Pfeffer 1985.111–113. On the theme of the nightingale as a messenger of lovers in modern French folksongs, see p. 214.

I sing and I play the flute for myself.
For no man except me understands my language.
As little as they understand the nightingale
do the people understand what my song says.
And I do not have a tongue that shakes or stutters,
nor do I know to speak Flemish or Angevin,
but the meanness which contains them
takes away the vision of what is false, what is true.[9]

To betray the nightingale, then, is to betray the lovers' secrets, which they communicate to each other through their love-song.[10] To betray the songbird's secret love-song is to *make it public*. The irony here is that the death of the nightingale becomes essential for the continuity of the bird's song *as art*: to betray and thus make public this love-song, with all its beautiful heartache, is to keep it alive – in the form of the song that the *troubadour* sings to his public.[11] If the poet compares himself directly to the nightingale,'as we have just seen in the stanza from Peire Cardenal, it is more appropriate for him to stage himself at that very moment as being alone, without a public, singing to himself a song misunderstood by the uninitiated.

What, then, is the secret theme of the nightingale's song in the *lai* of Marie de France? In the logic of the *lai* – or of the lady's lament in the *lai* – the songbird's betrayal and death signal both the lovers' feeling of powerlessness to consummate their love and the expression of this feeling in song. It may be that this feeling of unfulfilled love *is* the secret theme of the nightingale's song. This theme can be linked with a medieval belief that the nightingale ceased to sing and lost his singing voice once his songs finally led to the long-awaited moment of success in copulating.[12] There is a related theme in the troubadour tradition, as in Song 35 of Gaucelm Faidit, where the poet himself is pictured as dying from an inability to express his love fully in song.[13]

[9] Translation after Pfeffer 1985.107.

[10] Just as the nightingale is a model of discretion for lovers, other birds, like the starling, become models of indiscretion: on this counter-theme, see Pfeffer 1985.113–114.

[11] For a similar theme, see Schur 1994 on Kafka's *Josefine, die Sängerin oder Das Volk der Mäuse*.

[12] This belief is played out in the Old French *jeux-partis* tradition of the *trouvères*, as in *Princes del Pui, mout bien savés trouver*, analyzed by Pfeffer 1985.141–150, 175.

[13] Analyzed by Pfeffer 1985.101–102.

My aim, however, is not to reflect any further on the feelings conveyed by the nightingale's song but to explore the meaning of the song as a symbol of continuity in spite of death, even because of death. Within the story of Marie de France, to repeat the formulation that we saw earlier, the nightingale is "the sign of a ruse or lie told to calm the jealous husband's suspicions, an invention synonymous with the *lai* itself." Beyond the story, however, the song of the nightingale is the very opposite of an ad hoc invention: it is a sign of continuity, of a sad but compellingly beautiful song that cannot end with the death of the songbird. Marie de France draws attention to her use of a Breton word, *laüstic*, for 'nightingale': *ceo est 'russignol' en franceis / e 'nihtegale' en dreit engleis* 'that is, *russignol* in French and *nihtegale* in proper English' (*Laüstic* verses 5–6). Even in this word of Celtic origin, *laüstic*, we find an indirect historical indication of continuity in an oral and non-Latin tradition.[14] The image of the nightingale as oral poet persists to this day in the poetic traditions of the Celtic world: for example, the cognate of Breton *laüstic* in Welsh, *eos* or *eosig*, means both 'nightingale' and 'bard'.

The letters embroidered on the silk that enshrouds the nightingale, preserved in the reliquary kept by the lover, are the transcript, as it were, of the song he once sang. To that extent, letters are indeed the tomb of performance.[15] In Greek traditions as well, "the poet seems to be saying that [his] poetry is his *sēma* 'tomb'."[16] This formulation has been applied in interpreting some cryptic verses of Theognis, where the poet's words mirror the language of inscriptions actually found on tombs:[17]

> Αἴθων μὲν γένος εἰμί, πόλιν δ' εὐτειχέα Θήβην
> οἰκῶ, πατρῴας γῆς ἀπερυκόμενος
>
> I am Aithon by birth, and I have an abode in well-walled
>   Thebes,
> since I have been exiled from my native land.
>
> Theognis 1209–1210

---

[14] In the forthcoming article mentioned at n2 above, Rupert T. Pickens discusses the reliance on Celtic oral traditions (*matiere de Bretagne*) – alongside Latin written traditions (*matiere de Rom*) – in the *lais* of Marie de France, whose literary activity is historically linked with the court of Henry II of England.

[15] As the discussion still to come makes clear, however, it does not follow that the symbol of the tomb reflects the permanent death of the entombed.

[16] N 1990b.222n62.

[17] N 1990b.273–274. Cf. Svenbro 1993.84.

It appears that the poet here is picturing himself as already dead, speaking from a tomb.[18] The verb *oikéō* in parallel contexts refers to the establishing of a corpse in a sacred precinct for the purposes of hero cult.[19] After the cryptic words of Theognis 1209–1210, and some further cryptic words that go beyond the scope of this inquiry (1211–1213), the poet reiterates that he is an exile (1213–1214), and then he announces that his abode is next to the Plain of Lethe (1215–1216) – clearly, the realm of the dead (cf. Aristophanes *Frogs* 186).[20]

And yet, the image of the tomb in this and other archaic Greek passages conveys a message of life after death, achieved through the dead poet's words.[21] Moreover, *sēma* means not only 'tomb' but also the 'sign, signal, symbol' that *is* the poem.[22] So long as the sign of the dead poet is there, the song may continue to live. A sign *authorizes*, making the poet an *author*.[23] The same may be said of the medieval traditions that we have considered: so long as the sign of the dead nightingale is there, the song of the poet may continue.

Still, it would not be enough to think that the death of the nightingale – the death of the poet – ensures the continuity of the song. The one who continues the song must somehow find a point of engagement with the dead poet, through the dead poet's words. In his 1919 essay "Tradition and the Individual Talent," T. S. Eliot says that, for the modern poet, the "most individual parts of his work may be those in which the dead poets, his ancestors, assert their immortality most vigorously."[24] For a culture like that of the ancient Greeks, where performance is still needed to bring the composition to life, Eliot's words can be reapplied if we take for a moment the performer's point of view: all I need

---

[18] For analogous themes in Irish and Welsh poetry, see Ford 1987: in the Celtic traditions, a given poem can represent its poet as if he were already dead. Ford connects this convention with attested rituals of poetic initiation.

[19] N 1990b.274n20.

[20] Detailed analysis in N 1985.76–81. Cf. N 1993 on Alcaeus F 129 and 130 V, where the persona of the poet seems to be speaking from the dead.

[21] N 1985.76–81.

[22] N 1990b.221–222; cf. Ford 1985.91, 95. On the etymology of *sēma*, see Ivanov 1993b.

[23] On the conceptual link between authorizing and authorship, see N 1990a.79–81, 169–70, 350, and 412–413. It is hazardous, however, to retroject to the ancient world our contemporary notions of the "author" – notably the *individual* author. On the semantic problems of retrojecting our notions of the individual, see Held 1991.

[24] Eliot 1975 (= 1919) 38.

for the moment is to reword *his work* as *his performance*. Let me recompose, then: for a performer, *the most individual parts of his performance may be those in which the dead poets, his ancestors, assert their immortality most vigorously*. In other words, the reperformed composer becomes the recomposed performer.

Here we return to the subject of mimesis in Greek poetic traditions. This book has consistently stressed the fundamental role of mimesis in the performance of song and poetry in the theater, in choral events, in professional citharodic or aulodic events, in rhapsodic events, and even in the symposium.[25] So long as the authority of mimesis continues, we must reckon with its power to reshape the identity of those who take part in the process of performing a song or poem. Just as every performance becomes a potential re-creation in mimesis, that is, a virtual recomposition, so also the very identity of the performer stands to be re-created, recomposed. When the performer re-enacts an identity formerly enacted by previous performers, he or she is re-creating his or her own identity for the moment. That is to say, a performer's identity is recomposed *in performance*.

From the standpoint of the Alexandrian period, an era that inaugurates terminal rigidity in the performance traditions of both tragedy and Homer, it is reasonable to expect the perception of a veritable chasm between the actor of, say, a Sophoclean drama and Sophocles himself, or between the immediate rhapsode and Homer, the ultimate Singer. We have seen a striking example of such a chasm at an even earlier date, already in the fourth century: it is the metaphor of the magnet in Plato's *Ion*, with the rhapsode Ion pictured as the last and weakest link in a long magnetic chain leading all the way back to the genius of Homer (533d–536d). Still, I maintain my earlier objection to this idea that a rhapsode is a mere replica: such a mentality is contradicted by the more archaic mentality of mimesis, which shapes the idea of a recomposed performer, in that performers may still appropriate to themselves the persona of the composer.

In a performance tradition that is markedly more fluid, as in the case of the *troubadour* songs represented by Jaufré Rudel, we have seen that any distinction between the so-called "original" composer and the performer is in fact so blurred as to lead a modern editor to talk about multiple authorship. Let us recall the striking formulation of Rupert Pickens: "The conventions and traditions of the courtly lyric have conspired to efface the author and to create at least as many Jaufré Rudels as there are medieval anthologies."[26]

A comparative perspective, taking into account the differences we have observed so far, leads to the following two axioms:

(1) The greater or smaller the degree of *mouvance*, the smaller or greater respectively is the distinction between composer and performer.[27]
(2) Where the distinction between the composer and performer requires it, the performer's identity becomes re-shaped – recomposed – to fit the ideology of his or her distinctness from the supposedly prototypical composer, the author.

All this is not to renounce the historical reality or even the very concept of authors, of earlier composers of earlier compositions in oral tradition. What I resist is simply the insistence of some scholars on the notion that an original composer of an original composition in oral tradition can be recovered *as a synchronic reality*. The parallel of historical linguistics imposes itself. Within the conceptual framework of this discipline, we can claim to be reconstructing a given earlier phase of a language on the basis of cognate forms, but we cannot ever say that we have recovered an original phase.[28] The different details that we reconstruct cannot be reassembled into one synchronic reality, one glorious instance of real speech as really spoken in one time and one place. All we can do is predict the relationships that the reconstructed details

[26] Pickens 1978.40.

[27] This formulation restricts the term *mouvance* to mean a phenomenon of variation in oral poetics as shown by the evidence of manuscripts, not the manuscript evidence showing that phenomenon. As Laurence de Looze points out to me, the presence or absence of manuscript evidence in any given case may be an accident of history. It often may not be possible, therefore, to work out quantitative or comparative criteria for measuring *mouvance*. My axiom is meant merely as a practical index of *mouvance*.

[28] Cf. Householder and Nagy 1972.49: "it can happen that in a given set of cognates ... the least common denominator of the semantic sphere is no longer extant in any of the Indo-European languages with relevant ... evidence."

maintain with each other within a continuum that is diachrony. Our predictions must take the form of hypothetical cross-sections of synchrony that correspond to genuinely attested cross-sections, that is, to recordings of living speech.

So also in the study of oral tradition, we cannot expect, as Lord warns us, to recover an "original," in this case an original composition. Nevertheless, following the model of historical linguistics, we may indeed hope to reconstruct earlier stages or cross-sections of traditions in composition. In my earlier work, I used the letters L M N and so on as symbols for various reconstructed stages of authorship in oral traditions, avoiding the sequence of letters A B C and so on with the implicit purpose of emphasizing that a model of reconstruction cannot start with *the* beginning, only with *a* beginning.[29] To start with L M N and so on is thus symbolically apt, in line with the archaic Roman custom, derived from earlier conventions in the writing traditions of Semitic languages, of dividing the alphabet into two halves for teaching purposes, with the recto, as it were, starting at A-B-C and the verso, at L-M-N. Thus by learning the essentials of language, one would learn concurrently one's A-B-C-s and L-M-N-s. The idea of L-M-N-s as implicit essentials, alongside the A-B-C-s as explicit ones, helps explain the etymology of Latin *elementum*, alongside *abecedarium*, as Michael Coogan has argued persuasively.[30] To use Coogan's metaphor, the sequence L M N in one particular Qumran student's practice *abecedarium* represents "a fresh start."[31]

This etymology of *elementum* can serve as a fitting symbol for the elements of authorship in oral tradition. As we attempt to trace a progression of originators within an oral poetic tradition, we will predictably fail if we start with an originator standing at a starting line, as it were, but we may indeed succeed in catching up, along the way, with successive relays of continuators, each of whom becomes an originator for the next continuator.

The continuators, of course, need a continuum – a continuous setting, to match any original setting. We may link such "original"

[29] N 1990a.80.
[30] Coogan 1974, 1990; cf. Ivanov 1993a, especially pp. 1–2.
[31] Coogan 1974.61.

settings as the *hetaireía* 'assembly of comrades' addressed by Alcaeus at one time and one place with such historically continuing settings as the symposium, in all its varieties throughout many times and many places, where the spirit of *hetaireía* writ large provides a fitting context for re-enactments of Alcaeus' words in song.[32] To this extent, I accept Wolfgang Rösler's dictum that the identity of Alcaeus as a lyric poet was a function of his social group, his *hetaireía*: "ohne Hetairie kein Lyriker Alkaios."[33] I even accept the notion of Alcaeus as an author. I must insist, however, that the *hetaireía* is diachronic – and so too, for that matter, is the persona of Alcaeus. That is to say, the persona of Alcaeus may be adaptable through time, fitting a wide variety of situations – both positive and negative – affecting the very idea of *hetaireía*. Just as the society reflected by Alcaeus – let us continue to call it his *hetaireía* – changes over time, so also the persona of Alcaeus may change along with it. If indeed Alcaeus was transmitted primarily through the symposium, then Alcaeus the author will change as the symposium changes through time.

The symposium can serve as an ideal example of a setting for performance, since this institution happens to be more conservative than most in maintaining a continuum of traditional values in the history of Hellenism.[34] And the stronger the continuity, the stronger we may expect to be the sense of potential identification between composer and performer. For example, the sympotic persona of Alcaeus, conveyed in the varieties of ethos that are being acted out in the songs attributed to him, makes it all the more natural for any sympotic performer of Alcaeus to develop a relatively strong sense of identification with him in performance. The same can be said of monodic poetry composed in elegiac couplets, as in the case of Theognis: "the figure of Theognis speaks less as a generalized choral personality and more as a specialized sympotic personality" (cf. especially Theognis 239–243).[35] Even the verses of Archilochus, at least

---

[32] See pp. 84–85

[33] Rösler 1980.40.

[34] Cf. Murray 1990.

[35] N 1990a.368n159. See also Bowie 1986. Perhaps it is not necessary to postulate, as does Bowie on p. 14, that the elegiac verses of a figure like Theognis must have been accompanied by an *aulós*. In N 1990a.25–26 it is argued that such accompaniment may have been optional but not obligatory.

those composed in elegiac couplets, were suited for performance at symposia.[36]

We may recall in this connection the opinion of Aristotle, for whom the *paideía* 'education' that a younger man acquires in the symposium, presumably by way of performing as well as hearing the kind of songs that were traditionally performed in that context, provides an immunization against the potentially harmful effects of attending theatrical performances of *íamboi* 'iambs' and comedy, where we would expect the mimesis to concentrate on negative varieties of ethos: τοὺς δὲ νεωτέρους οὔτ᾽ ἰάμβων οὔτε κωμῳδίας θεατὰς θετέον, πρὶν ἢ τὴν ἡλικίαν λάβωσιν ἐν ᾗ καὶ κατακλίσεως ὑπάρξει κοινωνεῖν ἤδη καὶ μέθης, καὶ τῆς ἀπὸ τῶν τοιούτων γιγνομένης βλάβης ἀπαθεῖς ἡ <u>παιδεία</u> ποιήσει πάντως 'it should be ordained that younger men not be theatergoers [*theataí*] of *íamboi* or of comedy until they reach the age where they have the opportunity to participate in lying down together at table and getting intoxicated [that is, to participate in symposia], at which point their education [*paideía*] will make them altogether immune to the harmful effect of these things' (*Politics* 1336b20–22).[37] By implication, the *paideía* of mimesis in the symposium – even the cumulative ethos of the symposium – provides a proper balance for Hellenic youth in their educational experience of learning the variations of ethos. The symposium, it seems, provides a "safe" occasion for morally vulnerable younger men to hear things that might be "unsafe" to hear in the theater. Presumably even the roguish blame poetry of Archilochus becomes a "safe" topic in the symposium.

In this connection, we may note Aristotle's tendency to use specific passages from the poetry of Archilochus when he tries to reconstruct the prototypes of comedy (for example, *Poetics* 1449a9ff, apparently with reference to Archilochus F 120 W);[38] we may note too his theory that *íamboi* are a prototype of comedy and that they stem from blame poetry (*Poetics* 1448b32–1449a6).[39] And yet, it seems that Aristotle does not rule out the symposium as

---

[36] Bowie 1986.16–18, especially with reference to Archilochus F 4 W (also F 2).
[37] See p. 163 above. Cf. again Bartol 1992.66.
[38] N 1990a.394–395.
[39] N 1979.253; cf. Rosen 1988.

a context for performing this kind of poetry, despite its frequent representation of rogues who exemplify a negative morality.

An example of such roguishness is Archilochus F 4.7–8 W, where the speaker says that "we" cannot endure guard-duty without drinking wine. The question imposes itself: is the speaker referring to a real situation? One critic offers this answer: "I think it far more probable that Archilochus is evoking a situation with which his audience was all too familiar but which they could thank the gods was not their actual situation while they sang."[40] I agree, but my point of emphasis is different: *the negative morality that is being represented in this composition is being framed by the positive morality of the symposium as the setting of the representation.* If I understand Aristotle correctly, the same representation in a setting that is different from the symposium, such as the theater, would make it easier for impressionable youth to become vulnerable to the negative morality that is being dramatized. In other words, Aristotle seems to be saying that the symposium provides a proper frame for moral discrimination, whereas the theater is more hazardous.

In the mimesis of a rogue's persona, as in the case of Archilochus, we may expect an intensification of distinctions between composer and performer in the symposium. A similar point can be made about other personae as well, as in the case of Sappho. We know that Sappho's songs, like those of Archilochus, were performed at symposia. In one source, Solon himself is pictured as becoming enraptured by a song of Sappho as sung by his own nephew at a symposium (Aelian via Stobaeus 3.29.58).[41] The point is, for a male singer to act out a woman's persona implies a radical reshaping of personality in performance. One critic

[40] Bowie 1986.16.

[41] Cf. Herington 1985.35. For more on the singing of Sappho's songs at symposia, see Plutarch *Sympotic Questions* 711d: ὅτε καὶ Σαπφοῦς ἂν ᾀδομένης καὶ Ἀνακρέοντος ἐγώ μοι δοκῶ καταθέσθαι τὸ ποτήριον αἰδούμενος 'even when Sappho's songs are sung, or Anacreon's, I feel like putting down my drinking-cup, out of respect'; also 622c: ἐζητεῖτο παρὰ Σοσσίῳ Σαπφικῶν τινων ᾀσθέντων 'there was a debate at the house of Sossios, after some songs of Sappho had been sung ...'; cf. Rösler 1980.101. Also Aulus Gellius *Noctes Atticae* 19.9 (mention of Anacreontic and Sapphic songs sung at a symposium by both boys and girls). I am grateful to Dimitrios Yatromanolakis for the last reference.

remarks, in arguing for a contrast between the ease with which a symposiast may perform the words of Theognis addressing his boy-love Kyrnos and the difficulty with which the same symposiast may perform the dramatized words of Aphrodite addressing Sappho: "Contemporaries will have had little difficulty in singing a song addressed to [Kyrnos]; they might, however, have felt some oddity in singing Sappho [F] 1, with its give-away τίς σ' ὦ Ψάπφ', ἀδικήει; ['who, Sappho, is doing you wrong?']; or reciting such lines as Hipponax [F] 32.4 W δὸς χλαῖναν Ἱππώνακτι ['give a cloak to Hipponax!']."[42] So also with such songs as Alcaeus F 10 V and Anacreon PMG 385: in each case, the dramatized persona who is speaking is clearly female.

We must distinguish, however, between a dramatized "I" who simply plays out a conventional role in a conventional situation and a dramatized "I" who claims to be the author, as when a rhapsode intones "tell *me*, Muses" or "tell *me*, Muse," thereby *becoming* Homer the author, Homer the culture hero of epic. Here we return to the second axiom: where the distinction between the composer and performer requires it, the performer's identity becomes reshaped – recomposed – to fit the ideology of his or her distinctness from the supposedly prototypical composer, the author. When a rhapsode performs the lament of a woman, the lamenting "I" is surely distinct from the narrating "I" of Homer the author.[43] Granted, the equation of the rhapsode's "I" with Homer's "I" is itself an act of mimesis, but the further equation with a lamenting woman's "I" surely intensifies the mimesis. In the same way, a sympotic performer's "I" is surely less mimetic when it renders an "I" overtly equated with Archilochus *as author* or with Sappho *as author* and more mimetic when it renders an "I" that seems distinct from the authors.

Even so, the identity of the author is at risk. Let us reconsider the various songs in which an "author" is speaking through what is understood to be his or her own persona. The variety of situations conjured up even in such appropriated songs may lead to a commensurate variety of speaking personae. In other words, the demands of mimesis may lead toward an intensified multiplicity in ethos even for the author, with the persona of an Archilochus or a Sappho becoming transformed into multiple personalities that fit multiple situations. Just as the performer may be recomposed in multiple ways, so too this multiplicity may be retrojected all the way to the supposedly prototypical composer, the author. A case in point is the persona of Sappho, which becomes refracted into multiple personalities that eventually become distinguished from the "real" poetess in various *Life of Sappho* traditions: one such "fake" Sappho is a lyre-player who reputedly jumped off the cliff of Leukas (Suda σ 108, iv 323 Adler; cf. Strabo 10.2.9), while another is a courtesan (*hetaíra:* Aelian *Varia Historia* 12.19, Athenaeus 596e), even a prostitute (*publica:* Seneca in *Epistles* 88.37). Despite the verifiable reality of recomposition-in-performance, of change in identity within the process of mimesis, the songmaking tradition may continue to insist on its unchangeability. The tradition may even claim that mimesis itself is the visible sign or *seal* of unchangeability for the song and, by extension, for its author. Such a traditional mentality is evident in two passages from Theognis of Megara.

In the first passage, the persona of Theognis claims that he is placing a *sphragís* 'seal' upon his words as he identifies himself by name:

Κύρνε σοφιζομένῳ μὲν ἐμοὶ σφρηγὶς ἐπικείσθω
τοῖσδ' ἔπεσιν, λήσει δ' οὔποτε κλεπτόμενα
οὐδέ τις ἀλλάξει κάκιον τοὐσθλοῦ παρεόντος.
ὦδε δέ πᾶς τις ἐρεῖ· Θεύγνιδός ἐστιν ἔπη
τοῦ Μεγαρέως· πάντας δὲ κατ' ἀνθρώπους ὀνομαστός.
ἀστοῖσιν δ' οὔπω πᾶσιν ἁδεῖν δύναμαι

Kyrnos, let a seal [*sphrāgís*] be placed by me, as I practice my
   skill [*sophía*],
upon these my words. This way, it will never be undetected
   if they are stolen,
and no one can substitute something inferior for the
   genuine thing that is there.
And this is what everyone will say: "These are the words of
   Theognis
of Megara, whose name is known among all mortals."
But I am not yet able to please [= verb *handánō*] all the
   townspeople [*astoí*].

Theognis 19–24

It has been argued about the "seal":

> Like the code of [a] lawgiver, the poetry of Theognis pres-
> ents itself as static, unchangeable. In fact, the *sphragís* 'seal'
> of Theognis is pictured as a guarantee that no one will ever
> tamper with the poet's words. Outside this ideology and in
> reality, however, the poetry of Theognis is dynamic, subject
> [like the law code of Lycurgus] to modifications and accre-
> tions that are occasioned by an evolving social order. And
> the poet is always there, observing it all – despite the fact
> that the events being observed span an era that goes well
> beyond a single lifetime.[44]

With his "seal," then, the figure of Theognis is authorizing himself, making himself the author.[45] There is an explicit self-
description of this author as one who succeeds in *sophía*, the 'skill'
of decoding or encoding poetry.[46] On the basis of this success,
the author lays claim to a timeless authority, *which resists the necessity of changing* just to please the audience of the here and now,
who are described as the *astoí* 'townspeople'.[47] The author must
risk alienation with the audience of the here and now in order to
attain the supposedly universal acceptance of the ultimate audience, which is the cumulative response of Panhellenic fame.[48]

Such fame is achieved, as we see from the second Theognis
passage, through the authority and authenticity of mimesis. Implicitly, only the pleasure of exact reperformance, which is sup-

[44] N 1985.33. Cf. Ford 1985.85: "Theognis is not simply the name of a marvelous performer but the lock and key fixing a body of poetry and guaranteeing its prove-nience."

[45] Cf. Batchelder 1994 on the poetics of the *sphragís* 'seal' in the *Electra* of Sophocles. Here too, as in Theognis, the seal functions as a sign that authorizes the author. In this case, there are two levels of successful authorization and authorship: inside the dramatic frame, Orestes takes control of the state – and of his own drama – as he competes with his rivals for control, while Sophocles himself maintains ultimate control of the frame from the outside, as the definitive dramaturge.

[46] On *sophós* 'skilled' as a programmatic word used by poetry to designate the 'skill' of a poet in encoding the message of the poetry, see N 1990a.148. See also N 1990a.374n190: "A successful encoder, that is, poet, is by necessity a successful de-coder, that is, someone who has understood the inherited message and can therefore pass it on. Not all decoders, however, are necessarily encoders: both poet and audi-ence are decoders, but only the poet has the authority of the encoder."

[47] In this and related contexts, *astoí* 'townspeople' seems to be the programmatic designation of local audiences, associated with the special interests of their own here and now. See N 1990a.273–275.

[48] This theme of the alienated poet is examined at length in N 1985.30 and following.

posedly the ongoing achievement of mimesis, is truly lasting, while the pleasure elicited through changes in response to an immediate audience is ephemeral. In this second passage, the persona of Theognis declares that only the one who is *sophós*, that is, 'skilled' in the decoding and encoding of poetry, can execute a mimesis of Theognis:

οὐ δύναμαι γνῶναι νόον ἀστῶν ὅντιν' ἔχουσιν·
οὔτε γὰρ εὖ ἔρδων <u>ἀνδάνω</u> οὔτε κακῶς·
μωμεῦνται δέ με πολλοί, ὁμῶς κακοὶ ἠδὲ καὶ ἐσθλοί·
<u>μιμεῖσθαι</u> δ' οὐδεὶς τῶν <u>ἀσόφων</u> <u>δύναται</u>.

I am unable to decide what disposition it is that the
    townspeople [*astoí*] have towards me.
For I do not <u>please</u> [= verb *handánō*] them, either when I do
    for them things that are advantageous or when I do
    things that are disadvantageous.[49]
There are many who find blame with me, base and noble
    men alike.
But no one who is not <u>skilled</u> [*sophós*] can <u>re-enact</u> [*mim-
    eîsthai*] me.

Theognis 367–370

Here the notion of mimesis becomes an implicit promise that no change shall ever occur to accommodate the interests of any local audience in the here and now, that is, of the *astoí* 'townspeople'. The authorized reperformance of a composition, if it is to be a true re-enactment or mimesis, can guarantee the authenticity of the "original" composition. The author is saying about himself: "But no one who is not skilled [*sophós*] can re-enact my identity."

Here is an occasion to conjure up, yet again, the reworded words of Eliot: for a performer, *the most individual parts of his performance may be those in which the dead poets, his ancestors, assert their immortality most vigorously*. These words bring us back to the paradox of mimesis, which demands a never-changing identity for the author through an ever-changing identification with whatever the author chooses to represent:

---

[49] The "doing," of course, may amount simply to the performative level of "saying" *by way of poetry*.

The concept of mimesis, in conveying a re-enactment of the realities of myth, is a concept of authority as long as society assents to the genuineness of the values contained by the framework of myth. Correspondingly the speaker who frames the myth, or whose existence is re-enacted as framing the myth, is an author so long as he or she speaks with the authority of myth, which is supposedly timeless and unchanging. The author has to insist on the timelessness and unchangeability of such authority, which resists the pressures of pleasing the interests of the immediate audience by preferring the pleasure of timeless and unchanging values transmitted to an endless succession of audiences by way of mimesis.[50]

To this extent, there is indeed such a thing as an author in oral tradition – or at least, there are different kinds of author in different traditions. In pre-Islamic poetry, for example, as critics contemplate the myriad variants constituting the corpus of a single poet, they claim they can sense the author's presence in the creation – and re-creation – of his poetry:

Thus, although we may not possess the verbatim record of [Imru' al-Qays]' *mu'allaqa* as uttered by the poet himself on a specific occasion, we do possess something perhaps even more valuable: a verse-by-verse delineation of a fine and majestic living poem in all its protean states of oral existence – a carefully developed multiple exposure, as it were, of a fluctuating poetic organism that still kept its own unique identity so as to be recognized by all who knew and heard it.[51]

To recognize the song, then, is to recognize the singer. And yet, the singer cannot be independent of the song, as it continues to be performed and re-performed. We may heed the words of Thomas Hardy,[52] echoing the poems of Wordsworth, Keats, and many others:

The Selfsame Song

A bird sings the selfsame song,
With never a fault in its flow,
That we listened to here those long
　　　Long years ago.

[50] N 1990a.373–374
[51] Zwettler 1978.221.
[52] Hardy 1978 (= 1929) 221. Thanks to Steven Meyer (31 March 1994).

Dead poets and recomposed performers

A pleasing marvel is how
A strain of such rapturous rote
Should have gone on thus till now
    Unchanged in a note!

– But it's not the selfsame bird. –
No: perished to dust is he....
As also are those who heard
That song with me.

Appendix

1. Testimonia on the Kreophuleioi of Samos

In Plutarch *Life of Lycurgus* 4.4 we read how Lycurgus the Lawgiver acquired the Homeric poems from the descendants of Kreophylos in Samos and brought the poems back to the Spartans: ἐκεῖ δὲ καὶ τοῖς Ὁμήρου ποιήμασιν ἐντυχὼν πρῶτον, ὡς ἔοικε, παρὰ τοῖς ἐκγόνοις τοῖς Κρεοφύλου διατηρουμένοις, καὶ ... ἐγράψατο προθύμως καὶ συνήγαγεν ὡς δεῦρο κομιῶν. ἦν γάρ τις ἤδη δόξα τῶν ἐπῶν ἀμαυρὰ παρὰ τοῖς Ἕλλησιν, ἐκέκτηντο δὲ οὐ πολλοὶ μέρη τινά, σποράδην τῆς ποιήσεως, ὡς ἔτυχε, διαφερομένης· γνωρίμην δὲ αὐτὴν καὶ μάλιστα πρῶτος ἐποίησε Λυκοῦργος. (Besides Κρεόφυλος, Κρεώφυλος is also attested in the textual transmission, as in Strabo 14.1.18 C638; also Callimachus *Epigram* 6.4, where the ω is guaranteed by the meter.) In Aristotle F 611 Rose, we read: Λυκοῦργος ἐν Σάμῳ ἐτελεύτησε. καὶ τὴν Ὁμήρου ποίησιν παρὰ τῶν ἀπογόνων Κρεοφύλου λαβὼν πρῶτος διεκόμισεν εἰς Πελοπόννησον. The expression *hoi apógonoi Kreōphúlou* 'the descendants of Kreophylos' is equated with the epithet *Kreōphúleios* in Iamblichus *Life of Pythagoras* 2.11: μετὰ τοῦ Ἑρμοδάμαντος μὲν τὸ ὄνομα, Κρεοφυλείου δὲ ἐπικαλουμένου, ὃς ἐλέγετο Κρεοφύλου ἀπόγονος εἶναι, Ὁμήρου ξένου τοῦ ποιητοῦ. On the contacts of Pythagoras with Hermodamas the *Kreōphúleios*, see Neanthes FGH 84 F 29, Diogenes Laertius 8.2 (cf. Richardson 1975.75). See also Porphyry *Life of Pythagoras* 2: ἐπανελθόντα δ' εἰς τὴν Ἰωνίαν ἐντεῦθεν τὸν Πυθαγόραν πρῶτον μὲν Φερεκύδῃ τῷ Συρίῳ ὁμιλῆσαι, δεύτερον δ' Ἑρμοδάμαντι τῷ Κρεοφυλείῳ ἐν Σάμῳ ἤδη γηράσκοντι. Also *Life of Pythagoras* 15: νοσήσαντα δὲ τὸν Φερεκύδην ἐν Δήλῳ θεραπεύσας ὁ Πυθαγόρας καὶ ἀποθανόντα θάψας εἰς Σάμον ἐπανῆλθε πόθῳ τοῦ συγγενέσθαι Ἑρμοδάμαντι τῷ Κρεοφυλείῳ. Also *Suda* π 3120: ⟨Πυθαγόρας,⟩ Σάμιος, φύσει δὲ Τυρρηνός, Μνησάρχου υἱὸς δακτυλιογλύφου. νέος δὲ ὢν σὺν τῷ πατρὶ ἐκ Τυρρηνίας ᾤκησεν εἰς Σάμον.

Appendix

οὗτος ἤκουσε πρῶτος Φερεκύδου τοῦ Συρίου ἐν Σάμῳ, εἶτα Ἑρμοδάμαντος ἐν τῇ αὐτῇ Σάμῳ, ὃς ἦν ἀπόγονος Κρεοφύλου, εἶτα ....
The story as reported by Aristotle, in the passage already cited, that Lycurgus died in Samos, the same place where he acquired the Homeric
poems for the Spartans, can be compared to the variant story that he
died in Crete, the same place where he acquired the Laws for the Spartans (on the latter variant, see N 1985.78).

2. An ancient bibliography of the writings of Demetrius of Phalerum

The bibliography of Demetrius of Phalerum, as given by Diogenes
Laertius 5.80-81: Πλήθει δὲ βιβλίων καὶ ἀριθμῷ στίχων σχεδὸν
ἅπαντας παρελήλακε τοὺς καθ᾽ αὐτὸν περιπατητικούς, εὐπαίδευτος
ὢν καὶ πολύπειρος παρ᾽ ὁντινοῦν· ὧν ἐστι τὰ μὲν ἱστορικά, τὰ δὲ
πολιτικά, τὰ δὲ περὶ ποιητῶν, τὰ δὲ ῥητορικά, δημηγοριῶν τε καὶ
πρεσβειῶν, ἀλλὰ μὴν καὶ λόγων Αἰσωπείων συναγωγαὶ καὶ ἄλλα
πλείω. ἔστι δὲ τὰ Περὶ τῆς Ἀθήνησι νομοθεσίας α΄ β΄ γ΄ δ΄ ε΄, Περὶ
τῶν Ἀθήνησι πολιτειῶν α΄ β΄, Περὶ δημαγωγίας α΄ β΄, Περὶ πολιτ-
ικῆς α΄, β΄, Περὶ νόμων α΄, Περὶ ῥητορικῆς α΄ β΄, Στρατηγικῶν α΄ β΄,
Περὶ Ἰλιάδος α΄ β΄, Περὶ Ὀδυσσείας α΄ β΄ γ΄ δ΄, Πτολεμαῖος α΄,
Ἐρωτικὸς α΄, Φαιδώνδας α΄, Μαίδων α΄, Κλέων α΄, Σωκράτης α΄,
Ἀρταξέρξης α΄, Ὁμηρικὸς α΄, Ἀριστείδης α΄, Ἀριστόμαχος α΄, Προ-
τρεπτικὸς α΄, Ὑπὲρ τῆς πολιτείας α΄, Περὶ τῆς δεκαετίας α΄, Περὶ τῶν
Ἰώνων α΄, Πρεσβευτικὸς α΄, Περὶ πίστεως α΄, Περὶ χάριτος α΄, Περὶ
τύχης α΄, Περὶ μεγαλοψυχίας α΄, Περὶ γάμου α΄, Περὶ τοῦ δοκοῦ α΄,
Περὶ εἰρήνης α΄, Περὶ νόμων α΄, Περὶ ἐπιτηδευμάτων α΄, Περὶ καιροῦ
α΄, Διονύσιος α΄, Χαλκιδικὸς α΄, Ἀθηναίων καταδρομὴ α΄, Περὶ Ἀν-
τιφάνους α΄, Προοίμιον ἱστορικὸν α΄, Ἐπιστολαὶ α΄, Ἐκκλησία ἔνορ-
κος α΄, Περὶ γήρως α΄, Δίκαια α΄, Αἰσωπείων α΄, Χρειῶν α΄.

*3. An anecdote indirectly reflecting on the custom of consecutive recitation by
rhapsodes and on the negative attitude of Alexandrian scholars concerning the
performance of poetry:*

Vitruvius on Aristophanes of Byzantium, T 17 in the Aristophanes edition of Slater 1986. Vitruvius preface to 7.4–7, ed.
Fensterbusch: *reges Attalici magnis philologiae dulcedinibus inducti cum
egregiam bybliothecam Pergami ad communem delectationem instituissent,
tunc item Ptolemaeus infinito zelo cupiditatisque incitatus studio non mino-
ribus industriis ad eundem modum contenderat Alexandriae comparare.*

Appendix

Cum autem summa diligentia perfecisset, non putavit id satis esse, nisi propagationibus inseminando curaret augendam. itaque Musis et Apollini ludos dedicavit et, quemadmodum athletarum, sic communium scriptorum victoribus praemia et honores constituit. his ita institutis, cum ludi adessent, iudices litterati, qui ea probarent, erant legendi. rex, cum iam sex civitatis lectos habuisset nec tam cito septumum idoneum inveniret, retulit ad eos, qui supra bybliothecam fuerunt, et quaesiit, si quem novissent ad id expeditum. tunc ei dixerunt esse quendam Aristophanen, qui summo studio summaque diligentia cotidie omnes libros ex ordine perlegeret. itaque conventu ludorum, cum secretae sedes iudicibus essent distributae, cum ceteris Aristophanes citatus, quemadmodum fuerat locus ei designatus, sedit. primo poetarum ordine ad certationem inducto cum recitarentur scripta, populus cunctus significando monebat iudices, quod probarent. itaque, cum ab singulis sententiae sunt rogatae, sex una dixerunt, et quem maxime animadverterunt multitudini placuisse, ei primum praemium, insequenti secundum tribuerunt. Aristophanes vero, cum ab eo sententia rogaretur, eum primum renuntiari iussit, qui minime populo placuisset. cum autem rex et universi vehementer indignarentur, surrexit et rogando impetravit, ut paterentur se dicere. itaque silentio facto docuit unum ex his eum esse poetam, ceteros aliena recitavisse; oportere autem iudicantes non furta sed scripta probare. admirante populo et rege dubitante, fretus memoriae certis armariis infinita volumina eduxit et ea cum recitatis conferendo coegit ipsos furatos de se confiteri. itaque rex iussit cum his agi furti condemnatosque cum ignominia dimisit, Aristophanen vero amplissimis muneribus ornavit et supra bybliothecam constituit.

Bibliography

Adrados, F. R. (1983) "Les collections de fables à l'époque hellénistique et romaine," *La fable: Huit exposés suivis de discussions* (ed. F. R. Adrados) 137–195 (Fondation Hardt, Entretiens sur l'antiquité classique 30). Geneva.

Alexiou, M. (1974) *The Ritual Lament in Greek Tradition*. Cambridge.

Allen, T. W. (1924) *Homer: The Origins and the Transmission*. Oxford.

ed. (1931) *Iliad: editio maior*. 3 vols. Oxford.

Allen, W. S. (1973) *Accent and Rhythm. Prosodic Features of Latin and Greek: A Study in Theory and Reconstruction*. Cambridge.

(1987) *Vox Graeca: The Pronunciation of Classical Greek*. 3rd ed. Cambridge.

Aloni, A. (1984) "L'intelligenza di Ipparco. Osservazioni sulla politica dei Pisistratidi," *Quaderni di Storia* 19:109–148.

(1986) *Tradizioni arcaiche della Troade e composizione dell' Iliade*. Milan.

Andersen, F. G. (1991) "Technique, text, and context: formulaic narrative mode and the question of genre," *The Ballad and Oral Literature* (ed. J. Harris) 18–39 (Harvard English Studies 17). Cambridge, Mass.

Angelou, M. (1969) *I Know Why the Caged Bird Sings*. New York.

Apthorp, M. J. (1980) *The Manuscript Evidence for Interpolation in Homer*. Heidelberg.

Austin, J. L. (1962) *How to Do Things with Words*. Oxford.

Austin, N. (1975) *Archery at the Dark of the Moon: Poetic Problems in Homer's Odyssey*. Berkeley and Los Angeles.

Back, F. (1883) *De Graecorum caerimoniis in quibus homines deorum vice fungebantur*. Berlin.

Bader, F. (1986) "De Pollux à Deukalion: la racine *deu-k- 'briller, voir'," *Festschrift für Ernst Risch zum 75. Geburtstag* (ed. A. Etter) 463–488.

(1989) *La langue des dieux, ou l'hermétisme des poètes indo-européens* (Testi Linguistici 14). Pisa.

Bakker, E. (1993a) "Activation and preservation: the interdependence of text and performance in an oral tradition," *Oral Tradition* 8:5–20.

(1993b) "Discourse and performance: involvement, visualization and 'presence' in Homeric poetry," *Classical Antiquity* 12:1–29.

Barker, A., ed. (1984) *Greek Musical Writings* 1. Cambridge.

Barrett, W. S., ed. (1964) *Euripides: Hippolytus.* Oxford.

Bartol, K. (1992) "Where was iambic poetry performed? Some evidence from the fourth century BC," *Classical Quarterly* 42:65–71.

Basso, K. H. (1966) "The gift of Changing Woman," *Smithsonian Institution, Bureau of American Ethnology Bulletin* 196:113–173 (Anthropological Papers No. 76). Washington, D.C.

Batchelder, A. G. (1994) *The Seal of Orestes: Self-Reference and Authority in Sophocles' "Electra."* Lanham, Maryland.

Bäuml, F. H. (1986) "The oral tradition and Middle High German literature," *Oral Tradition* 1:398–445.

Bausinger, H. (1980) *Formen der "Volkspoesie."* 2nd ed. Berlin.

Bayer, E. (1942) *Demetrios Phalereus der Athener* (Tübinger Beiträge zur Altertumswissenschaft 36). Stuttgart.

Bédier, J. (1928) "La tradition manuscrite du Lai de l'ombre," *Romania* 54:161–196, 321–356.

Benveniste, E. (1946) "Structure des relations de personne dans le verbe," *Bulletin de la Société de Linguistique de Paris* 43:1–12. Reprinted in Benveniste 1966.225–236.

(1949) "Le système sublogique des prépositions en latin," *Travaux du Cercle linguistique de Copenhague* 5:177–185. Reprinted in Benveniste 1966.132–139.

(1966) *Problèmes de linguistique générale.* Paris.

(1969) *Le vocabulaire des institutions indo-européennes.* 1. *Economie, parenté, société.* 11. *Pouvoir, droit, religion.* Paris.

(1973) *Indo-European Language and Society.* Translation by E. Palmer of Benveniste 1969. London.

Bertolini, F. (1992) "Il palazzo: L'epica," *Lo spazio letterario della Grecia antica.* 1. *La produzione e la circolazione del testo* (ed. G. Cambiano, L. Canfora, D. Lanza) 109–141.

Bird, G. (1994) "The textual criticism of an oral Homer," *Prudentia* 26:35–52. *Nile, Ilissos and Tiber: Essays in Honour of Walter Kirkpatrick Lacey* (ed. V. J. Gray). Auckland.

Blackburn, S. H., Claus, P. J., Flueckiger, J. B., and Wadley, S. S. eds. (1989) *Oral Epics in India.* Berkeley and Los Angeles. Abbreviated as OEI.

Blackburn, S. H., and Flueckiger, J. B. (1989) "Introduction," OEI 1–11.

Blackburn, S. H. (1989) "Patterns of development for Indian oral epics," OEI 15–32.

Bloch, R. H. (1988) "The voice of the dead nightingale: orality in the tomb of Old French literature," *Culture and History* 3:63–78.

(1990) *See* Nichols 1990.

Blum, R. (1977) *Kallimachos und die Literaturverzeichnung bei den Griechen.* Frankfurt.

(1991) *Kallimachos: The Alexandrian Library and the Origins of Bibliography.* Translation by H. H. Wellisch of Blum 1977. Madison.

Bollack, J. (1994) "Une action de restauration culturelle. La place accordée aux tragiques par le décret de Lycurgue," *Mélanges Pierre Lévêque* (eds M.-M. Mactoux, E. Geny) 13–24. Paris.

Bolling, G. M. (1925) *The External Evidence for Interpolation in Homer.* Oxford.

Bonanno, M. G. (1993) "Saffo 31,9 V.: γλῶσσα ἔαγε," *Quaderni Urbinati di Cultura Classica* 43.61–68.

Bonaria, M. (1955) *Mimorum Romanorum Fragmenta.* I. *Fragmenta.* II. *Fasti Mimici et Pantomimici.* Genoa.

Bornstein, G., and Williams, R. G., eds. (1993) *Palimpsest: Editorial Theory in the Humanities.* Ann Arbor.

Bowie, E. L. (1986) "Early Greek elegy, symposium and public festival," *Journal of Hellenic Studies* 106:13–35.

Boyd, T. W. (1994) 'Where Ion stood, what Ion sang," *Harvard Studies in Classical Philology* 96.

(1996) "Libri confusi," *Classical Journal* 91:1–11.

Bundy, E. L. (1962 [1986]) "Studia Pindarica I: The eleventh Olympian Ode; II: The first Isthmian Ode," *University of California Publications in Classical Philology* 18.1–2:1–92. Both articles reissued 1986 as *Studia Pindarica.* Berkeley and Los Angeles.

Burkert, W. (1972) "Die Leistung eines Kreophylos: Kreophyleer, Homeriden und die archaische Heraklesepik," *Museum Helveticum* 29:74–85.

(1987) "The making of Homer in the sixth century BC: rhapsodes versus Stesichorus," *Papers on the Amasis Painter and His World* (ed. M. True, C. Hudson, A. P. A. Belloli, B. Gilman, and others) 43–62. Malibu.

Burnett, A. P. (1983) *Three Archaic Poets: Archilochus, Alcaeus, Sappho.* Cambridge, Mass.

(1988) "Jocasta in the west: the Lille Stesichorus," *Classical Antiquity* 7:108–154.

Calame, C. (1974) "Réflexions sur les genres littéraires en Grèce archaïque." *Quaderni Urbinati di Cultura Classica* 17:113–123.

(1977) *Les choeurs de jeunes filles en Grèce archaïque* I: *Morphologie, fonction religieuse et sociale.* II: *Alcman.* Rome.

(1986) *Le récit en Grèce ancienne*. Paris.

(1989) "Apprendre à boire, apprendre à chanter: L'inférence énonciative dans une image grecque," *La part de l'oeil* 5:45–53.

Cameron, A. (1990) "Isidore of Miletus and Hypatia: on the editing of mathematical texts," *Greek, Roman and Byzantine Studies* 31:103–127.

Cantarella, R. (1929) *L'edizione polistica di Omero. Studii [sic] sulla tradizione del testo e le origini dei poemi*. Salerno.

Carson, A. (1986) *Eros the Bittersweet: An Essay*. Princeton.

Catenacci, C. (1993) "Il finale dell'*Odissea* e la *recensio* pisistratide dei poemi omerici," *Quaderni Urbinati di Cultura Classica* 44:7–22.

Cerquiglini, B. (1989) *Eloge de la variante: Histoire critique de la philologie*. Paris.

Chantraine, P. (1968, 1970, 1975, 1977, 1980) *Dictionnaire étymologique de la langue grecque* I, II, III, IV-1, IV-2. Paris. Abbreviated as *DELG*.

Chaytor, H. J. (1967) *From Script to Print: An Introduction to Medieval Vernacular Literature*. New York.

Citti, V. (1966) "Le edizioni omeriche 'delle città'," *Vichiana* 3:3–43.

Claus, P. J. (1989) "Behind the text: performance and ideology in a Tulu oral tradition," *OEI* 55–74.

Clay, D. (1991) "Alcman's *Partheneion*," *Quaderni Urbinati di Cultura Classica* 39:47–67.

Comotti, G. (1989) "Melodia e accento di parola nelle testimonianze degli antichi e nei testi con notazione musicale," *Quaderni Urbinati di Cultura Classica* 32:91–108.

Coogan, M. D. (1974) "Alphabets and elements," *Bulletin of the American Schools for Oriental Research* 216:61–63.

(1990) "*'lp- 'To be an abecedarian,'*" *Journal of the American Oriental Society* 110:322–323.

Cook, E. F. (1995) *The "Odyssey" in Athens: Myths of Cultural Origins*. Ithaca.

Curschmann, M. (1967) "Oral poetry in medieval English, French, and German literature: some notes on recent research," *Speculum* 42: 36–52.

Davidson, O. M. (1985) "The crown-bestower in the Iranian Book of Kings," *Acta Iranica, Hommages et Opera Minora 10: Papers in Honour of Professor Mary Boyce*, 61–148. Leiden.

(1988) "A formulaic analysis of samples taken from the *Shāhnāma* of Ferdowsi," *Oral Tradition* 3:88–105.

(1994) *Poet and Hero in the Persian Book of Kings*. Ithaca.

Davison, J. A. (1955) "Peisistratus and Homer," *Transactions of the American Philological Association* 86:1–21.

(1958) "Notes on the Panathenaia," *Journal of Hellenic Studies* 78:23–41 = 1968:28–69.

Bibliography

(1968) *From Archilochus to Pindar: Papers on Greek Literature of the Archaic Period*. London.

Dejeanne, J.-M.-L., ed. (1909) *Poésies complètes du troubadour Marcabru.* Toulouse.

Del Corno, D. (1960) "I papiri dell'Iliade anteriori al 150 a. Cr.," *Rendiconti d. Istit. Lomb., Cl. Lett., Sc. mor. e stor.* 73–116.

(1961) "I papiri dell' Odissea anteriori al 150 a. Cr.," *Rendiconti d. Istit. Lomb., Cl. Lett., Sc. mor. e stor.* 3–54.

Demos, M. (1991) "Lyric quotation in Plato." Ph.D. dissertation, Harvard University.

Denniston, J. D. (1954) *The Greek Particles.* 2nd ed. revised by K. J. Dover. Oxford.

Detienne, M. (1973) *Les Maîtres de vérité dans la Grèce archaïque.* 2nd ed. Paris.

D'Ippolito, G. (1977) *Lettura di Omero: il canto V dell' "Odissea."* Palermo.

(1984) "Papiri ed ecdotica omerica," *Atti del xvii congresso internazionale di papirologia* II 221–228. Naples.

Dover, K. J., ed. with commentary (1993) *Aristophanes: Frogs.* Oxford.

Dow, S., and Travis, A. (1943) "Demetrius of Phalerum and his lawgiving," *Hesperia* 12:144–165.

Dronke, P. (1977) *The Medieval Lyric.* 2nd ed. London.

Dubuisson, D. (1989) "Anthropologie poétique. Prolégomènes à une anthropologie du texte," *L'Homme* 111–112:222–236.

Ducrot, O., and Todorov, Tz. (1972) *Dictionnaire encyclopédique des sciences du langage.* Paris.

(1979) *Encyclopedic Dictionary of the Sciences of Language.* Translation by C. Porter of Ducrot and Todorov 1972. Baltimore.

Duggan, J. J. (1973) *The Song of Roland: Formulaic Style and Poetic Craft.* Berkeley.

Dupont, F. (1994) *L'Invention de la littérature: de l'ivresse grecque au livre latin.* Paris.

Dupont-Roc, R., and Lallot, J., ed. with commentary (1980) *Aristote: La Poétique.* Paris.

Durante, M. (1976) *Sulla preistoria della tradizione poetic greca.* II. *Risultanze della comparazione indoeuropea* (Incunabula Graeca 64) Rome.

Dyck, A. R. (1993) "The Fragments of Heliodorus Homericus," *Harvard Studies in Classical Philology* 95:1–64.

Edmunds, L. (1981) "The cults and the legend of Oedipus," *Harvard Studies in Classical Philology* 85:221–238.

Edmunds, S. T. (1990) *Homeric Nēpios.* New York.

Eliot, T. S. (1963) *Collected Poems* 1909–1962. New York.

(1975) *Selected Prose of T. S. Eliot* (ed. F. Kermode). London.

Erbse, H. (1959) "Über Aristarchs Iliasausgaben," *Hermes* 87:275–303.

ed. (1969–1988) *Scholia Graeca in Homeri Iliadem* I–VII. Berlin and New York.

Ernout, A., and Meillet, A. (1959) *Dictionnaire étymologique de la langue latine: Histoire des mots.* 4th ed. Paris. Abbreviated as *DELL*.

Ferguson, W. S. (1911) *Hellenistic Athens: An Historical Essay.* London.

Figueira, T. J., and Nagy, G., eds. (1985) *Theognis of Megara: Poetry and the Polis.* Baltimore.

Fleischman, S. (1990). *See* Nichols 1990.

Flueckiger, J. B. (1989) "Caste and regional variants in an oral epic tradition," OEI 33–54.

Foley, J. M. (1991) *Immanent Art: From Structure to Meaning in Traditional Oral Epic.* Bloomington and Indianapolis.

Ford, A. L. (1985) "The seal of Theognis: the politics of authorship in archaic Greece," Figueira and Nagy 1985:82–95.

(1988) "The classical definition of PAΨΩIΔIA," *Classical Philology* 83:300–307.

Ford, P. K. (1987) "The death of Aneirin," *The Bulletin of the Board of Celtic Studies* 34:41–50.

Foucault, M. (1969) "Qu'est-ce qu'un auteur?" *Bulletin de la Société française de la philosophie* 64:73–104. = "What is an author?," *Textual Strategies: Perspectives in Post-Structuralist Criticism* (ed. J. V. Harari) 141–160. Ithaca.

Foulet, A., and Speer, M. B. (1979) *On Editing Old French Texts.* Lawrence.

Frisk, H. (1970–1980) *Griechisches etymologisches Wörterbuch.* Heidelberg. Abbreviated as *GEW*.

Frontisi-Ducroux, F. (1986) *La cithare d'Achille. Essai sur la poétique de l'Iliade.* Rome.

Gabler, H. W. (1984) with Steppe, W., and Melchior, C. *James Joyce, Ulysses: A Critical and Synoptic Edition.* 3 vols. New York.

(1993) "On textual criticism and editing: the case of Joyce's *Ulysses*," Bornstein and Williams 1993:195–224.

Gadamer, H.-G. (1975) *Truth and Method.* New York.

Garbrah, K. A. (1977) "The scholia on the ending of the *Odyssey*," *Würzburger Jahrbücher für die Altertumswissenschaft* 3:7–16.

Gentili, B. (1985) *Poesia e pubblico nella Grecia antica: da Omero al V secolo.* Rome / Bari.

(1988) *Poetry and Its Public in Ancient Greece: From Homer to the Fifth Century.* Translation, with introduction, by A. T. Cole of Gentili 1985. Baltimore.

Glare, P. G. W., ed. (1982) *Oxford Latin Dictionary.* Oxford.

Goff, B. (1990) *The Noose of Words: Readings of Desire, Violence and Language in Euripides' Hippolytus.* Cambridge.

Goldhill, S. (1991) *The Poet's Voice: Essays on Poetics and Greek Literature.* Cambridge.

Gow, A. S. F., and Scholfield, A. F., eds. (1953) *Nicander: The Poems and Poetical Fragments.* Cambridge.

Graham, W. A. (1987) *Beyond the Written Word: Oral Aspects of Scripture in the History of Religion.* Cambridge.

Grant, J. N., ed. (1989) *Editing Greek and Latin Texts* (Papers given at the Twenty-Third Annual Conference on Editorial Problems, University of Toronto, 6–7 November 1987). New York.

Greetham, D. C. (1993) "Editorial and critical theory: from modernism to postmodernism," Bornstein and Williams 1993:9–28.

Haley, J. L. (1981) *Apaches: A History and Culture Portrait.* New York.

Halleran, M. R. (1991) "*Gamos* and destruction in Euripides' *Hippolytus*," *Transactions of the American Philological Association* 121:109–121.

Halliwell, S. (1986) *Aristotle's Poetics.* Chapel Hill.

Hardy, T. (1978 [1929]). *Chosen Poems* (ed. F. S. Puk). New York.

Hartel, W. von, ed. (1894) *Paulinus of Nola. Corpus Scriptorum Ecclesiasticorum Latinorum* 30.194–206.

Harvey, A. E. (1955) "The classification of Greek lyric poetry," *Classical Quarterly* 5:157–175.

Havelock, E. A. (1986) *The Muse Learns to Write: Reflections on Orality and Literacy from Antiquity to the Present.* New Haven.

Held, D. t. D. (1991) "Why 'individuals' didn't exist in classical antiquity," *New England Classical Newsletter and Journal* 18:26–29.

Henrichs, A. (1971 / 1973) "Scholia Minora zu Homer I, II, III / IV," *Zeitschrift für Papyrologie und Epigraphik* 7:97–149, 229–260, 8:1–12 / 12:17–43.

Herington, J. (1985) *Poetry into Drama: Early Tragedy and the Greek Poetic Tradition.* Berkeley and Los Angeles.

Herzfeld, M. (1993) "In defiance of destiny: The management of time and gender at a Cretan funeral," *American Ethnologist* 20:241–255.

Higbie, C. (1995) *Heroes' Names, Homeric Identities.* New York.

Hintenlang, H. (1961) *Untersuchungen zu den Homer-Aporien des Aristoteles.* Dissertation Heidelberg.

Householder, F. W., and Nagy, G. (1972) *Greek: A Survey of Recent Work.* The Hague.

Husson, G. (1993) "Les Homéristes," *The Journal of Juristic Papyrology* 23:93–99.

Irigoin, J. (1952) *Histoire du texte de Pindare.* Paris.

Irwin, E. (1974) *Colour Terms in Greek Poetry.* Toronto.

Ivanov, V. V. (1993a) "On the etymology of Latin *elementa*," *Elementa: Journal of Slavic Studies and Comparative Cultural Semiotics* 1:1–5.

(1993b) "Origin, history and meaning of the term 'semiotics'," *Elementa: Journal of Slavic Studies and Comparative Cultural Semiotics* 1:115–143.

Jaeschke, H., ed. (1921) *Der Trobador Elias Cairel* (Romanische Studien 20). Berlin.

Janko, R. (1982) *Homer, Hesiod and the Hymns: Diachronic Development in Epic Diction.* Cambridge.

(1990) "The *Iliad* and its editors: dictation and redaction," *Classical Antiquity* 9.326–334.

(1992) *The Iliad: A Commentary. Volume IV: Books 13–16.* Cambridge.

(1994) Review of van Thiel 1991. *Gnomon* 66:289–295.

Janowitz, N. (1991) "The rhetoric of translation: three early perspectives on translating Torah," *Harvard Theological Review* 84:129–140.

Jeanroy, A. (1916) *Bibliographie sommaire des chansonniers provençaux.* Paris.

ed. (1924) *Les Chansons de Jaufré Rudel.* 2nd ed. Paris.

ed. (1934) *La Poésie lyrique des Troubadours.* 2 vols. Toulouse and Paris.

Jebb, R. C. (1893) *The Attic Orators.* 2nd ed. 2 vols. London.

Jensen, M. Skafte (1980) *The Homeric Question and the Oral-Formulaic Theory.* Copenhagen.

Jones, C. P. (1991) "Dinner theater," *Dining in a Classical Context* (ed. W. J. Slater) 185–198. Ann Arbor.

(1993) "Greek drama in the Roman Empire," *Theater and Society in the Classical World* (ed. R. Scodel) 39–52.

Karydas, H. Pournara. (1992) "The *trophos* from Homer to Euripides as a figure of authority." Ph.D. dissertation, University of Washington.

Kaster, R. (1988) *Guardians of Language: The Grammarian and Society in Late Antiquity.* Berkeley and Los Angeles.

Kierkegaard, S. [1983]. *Fear and Trembling. Repetition.* Translation, with introduction and notes, by H. V. Hong and E. H. Hong. Princeton.

Kirk, G. S. (1962) *The Songs of Homer.* Cambridge.

ed. (1985) *The Iliad: A Commentary. Volume I: Books 1–4.* Cambridge.

Kleingünther, A. (1933) *ΠΡΩΤΟΣ ΕΥΡΕΤΗΣ: Untersuchungen zur Geschichte einer Fragestellung.* Leipzig. (Philologus Supplementband 26).

Koller, H. (1954) *Die Mimesis in der Antike.* Bern.

(1956) "Das kitharodische Prooimion: Eine formengeschichtliche Untersuchung," *Philologus* 100:159–206.

Kolsen, A., ed. (1910) *Sämtliche Lieder des Trobadors Giraut de Bornelh.* Halle.

Kothari, K. (1989) "Performers, gods, and heroes in the oral epics of Rajasthan," *OEI* 102–117.

Kraft, W. B. (1989) "Improvisation in Hungarian ethnic dancing: an analog to oral verse composition," *Oral Tradition* 4:273–315.

Kurke, L. (1991) *The Traffic in Praise: Pindar and the Poetics of Social Economy.* Ithaca.

Labarbe, J. (1949) *L'Homère de Platon.* Liège.

Lachmann, K., ed. (1850) *In T. Lucreti Cari de rerum natura libros commentarius.* Berlin.

Lardinois, A. P. M. H. (1995) "Wisdom in context: the use of gnomic statements in archaic Greek poetry." Ph.D. dissertation, Princeton University.

Latte, K., ed. (1953 / 1966) *Hesychius.* 2 vols., covering A-O. Copenhagen.

Laum, B. (1928) *Das alexandrinische Akzentuationssystem unter Zugrundelegung der theoretischen Lehren der Grammatiker und mit Heranziehung der praktischen Verwendung in den Papyri.* Paderborn.

Lavaud, R., ed. (1957) *Poésies complètes du troubadour Peire Cardenal (1180–1278): Texte, traduction, commentaire, analyse des travaux antérieurs, lexique.* Toulouse.

Lazar, M., ed. (1966) *Bernard de Ventadour, Chansons d'amour.* Paris.

Leach, E. (1982) "Critical introduction" to Steblin-Kamenskij 1982 (pp. 1–20).

Lefkowitz, M. R., and H. Lloyd-Jones, H. (1987) "ΛΥΚΑΙΧΜΙΑΙΣ." *Zeitschrift für Papyrologie und Epigraphik* 68:9–10.

Lehrs, K. (1882) *De Aristarchi Studiis Homericis.* 3rd ed. Leipzig.

Lincoln, B. (1981) *Emerging from the Chrysalis: Studies in Rituals of Women's Initiation.* Cambridge, Mass.

Lobeck, C. A. (1829). *Aglaophamus; sive, De theologiae mysticae Graecorum causis libri tres.* Königsberg.

Lods, J., ed. (1959) *Les lais de Marie de France.* Paris.

Lohse, G. (1964/ 1965 / 1967) "Untersuchungen über Homerzitate bei Platon," *Helikon* 4:3–28 / 5:248–295 / 7:223–231.

Loraux, N. (1987) "Le lien et la division," *Le Cahier du Collège International de Philosophie* 4:101–124.

   (1990) *Les mères en deuil.* Paris.

   (1994) Preface to Papadopoulou-Belmehdi 1994:7–17.

Lord, A. B. (1960) *The Singer of Tales.* Cambridge, Mass.

   (1995) *The Singer Resumes the Tale* (ed. M. L. Lord). Ithaca.

Lowenstam, S. (1993) "The arming of Achilleus on early Greek vases," *Classical Antiquity* 12:199–218.

Lucas, D. W., ed. (1968) *Aristotle: Poetics.* Oxford.

Lucas, H. L. (1965) "L'Edition des textes lyriques: Schéma d'ensemble ou schéma individuel?" *Actes, Xe Congrès International de Linguistique et Philologie Romanes, Strasbourg 23–28 avril 1962* (ed. G. Straka) ii, 697–703. Paris.

Bibliography

Ludwich, A. (1884/1885) *Aristarchs homerische Textkritik*. Leipzig.

(1898) *Die Homervulgata als voralexandrinisch erwiesen*. Leipzig.

Lührs, D. (1992) *Untersuchungen zu den Athetesen Aristarchs in der Ilias und zu ihrer Behandlung im Corpus der exegetischen Scholien* (Beiträge zur Altertumswissenschaft 11). Hildesheim.

Luzio, A. di. (1969) "I papiri omerici d'epoca tolemaica e la costituzione del testo dell'epica arcaica," *Rivista di Cultura Classica e Medioevale* 11:3–152.

Mâche, F.-B. (1991) *Musique, Mythe, Nature, ou les dauphins d'Arion*. Paris.

MacKendrick, P. (1954) "Demetrius of Phalerum, Cato and the *Adelphoe*," *Rivista di Filologia e d'Istruzione Classica* 32:18–35.

Maehler, H. (1981) "Problemi e prospettive della papirologia letteraria," *La critica testuale greco-latina, oggi. Metodi e problemi. Atti del Convegno Internazionale, Napoli 29–31 ottobre 1979* (ed. E. Flores) 81–90.

Malinowski, B. (1926) *Myth in Primitive Psychology*. London.

Marek, Ch. (1993) *Stadt, Ära und Territorium in Pontus-Bithynia*. Tübingen.

Marler, P. (1981) "Birdsong: the acquisition of a learned motor skill," *Trends in Neuro-Sciences* 4:88–94.

Martin, R. P. (1989) *The Language of Heroes: Speech and Performance in the Iliad*. Ithaca. Revised paperback version 1992.

Mazzucchi, C. M. (1979) "Sul sistema di accentazione dei testi greci in età romana e bizantina," *Aegyptus* 59:145–167.

McGann, J. J. (1983) *A Criticism of Modern Textual Criticism*. Chicago. Reprinted 1992. Charlottesville.

(1991) *The Textual Condition*. Princeton.

Meillet, A. (1925) *La méthode comparative en linguistique historique*. Paris.

Melia, D. F. (1975) "Parallel versions of 'The boyhood deeds of Cuchulainn'," *Oral Tradition, Seven Essays* (ed. J. J. Duggan) 25–40. Edinburgh.

Ménard, P., ed. (1970) *Les poésies de Guillaume le Vinier*. Geneva.

Menéndez Pidal, R. (1960) *La chanson de Roland et la tradition épique des Francs*. 2nd ed. Paris.

Menocal, M. (1982) "The etymology of Old Provençal *trobar, trobador*: a return to the 'third solution,'" *Romance Philology* 36:137–153.

Meyer-Lübke, W. (1935) *Romanisches etymologisches Wörterbuch*. 3rd ed. Heidelberg.

Miller, D. G. (1982a) *Homer and the Ionian Epic Tradition*. (Innsbrucker Beiträge zur Sprachwissenschaft 38). Innsbruck.

(1982b) *Improvisation, Typology, Culture, and "The New Orthodoxy": How Oral is Homer?* Washington, D.C.

Miralles, C., and Pòrtulas, J. (1983) *Archilochus and the Iambic Poetry*. Rome.

Monro, D. B., and Allen, T. W., eds. (1920) *Homeri Opera* (Iliad). 3rd ed. Oxford.

Montanari, F. (1979) *Studi di filologia omerica antica* 1. Pisa.

(1980) Review of D'Ippolito 1977. *Athenaeum* 58:511.

del Monte, A., ed. (1955) *Peire d'Alvernha, Liriche*. Torino.

Moore-Blunt, J. (1978) "Problems of accentuation in Greek papyri," *Quaderni Urbinati di Cultura Classica* 29:137–163.

Morrison, T. (1987) *Beloved*. New York.

Mossé, C. (1989) "Lycurge l'Athénien, homme du passé ou précurseur de l'avenir," *Quaderni di Storia* 15:25–36.

Mouzat, J., ed. (1965) *Les Poèmes de Gaucelm Faidit, troubadour du XIIe siècle*. Paris.

Muellner, L. (1976) *The Meaning of Homeric EYXOMAI through its Formulas*. (Innsbrucker Beiträge zur Sprachwissenschaft 13) Innsbruck.

(1990) "The simile of the cranes and pygmies: a study of Homeric metaphor," *Harvard Studies in Classical Philology* 93:59–101.

Mullen, W. (1982) *Choreia: Pindar and Dance*. Princeton.

Murray, O. (1987) "The letter of Aristeas," *Studi Ellenistici* 2:15–29.

ed. (1990) *Sympotica: A Symposium on the Symposium*. Oxford. Note especially the introduction by Murray, "Sympotic history," pp. 3–13.

N. *See* Nagy, G.

Nagy, G. (1970) *Greek Dialects and the Transformation of an Indo-European Process*. Cambridge, Mass.

(1974) *Comparative Studies in Greek and Indic Meter*. Cambridge, Mass.

(1979) *The Best of the Achaeans: Concepts of the Hero in Archaic Greek Poetry*. Baltimore.

(1985) "Theognis and Megara: a poet's vision of his city," Figueira and Nagy 1985:22–81.

(1989) "Early Greek views of poets and poetry," *Cambridge History of Literary Criticism* I (ed. G. Kennedy) 1–77. Cambridge. Revised paperback version 1993.

(1990a) *Pindar's Homer: The Lyric Possession of an Epic Past*. Baltimore. Revised paperback version 1994.

(1990b) *Greek Mythology and Poetics*. Ithaca. Revised paperback version 1992.

(1992a) "Homeric questions," *Transactions of the American Philological Association* 122:17–60.

(1992b) "Mythological exemplum in Homer," *Innovations of Antiquity* (ed. R. Hexter and D. Selden) 311–331. New York and London.

(1992c). Introduction to Homer, *The Iliad*, translated by R. Fitzgerald (Everyman's Library no. 60) v–xxi. New York.

(1992d) "Authorisation and authorship in the Hesiodic *Theogony*," *Essays on Hesiod* II (ed. A. N. Athanassakis) = *Ramus* 21:119–130.

Bibliography

(1993) "Alcaeus in sacred space," *Tradizione e innovazione nella cultura greca da Omero all' età ellenistica: Scritti in onore di Bruno Gentili* I (ed. R. Pretagostini) 221–225. Rome.

(1994a) "Copies and models in Horace *Odes* 4.1 and 4.2," *Classical World* 87:415–426.

(1994b) "The name of Apollo: etymology and essence," *Apollo: Origins and Influences* (ed. J. Solomon) 3–7. Tucson.

(1994/5) "Transformations of choral lyric traditions in the context of Athenian State Theater," *Arion* 3.2:41–55.

(1995) "An evolutionary model for the making of Homeric poetry: comparative perspectives," *The Ages of Homer: A Tribute to Emily Townsend Vermeule* (ed. J. B. Carter and S. P. Morris) 163–179. Austin.

Nagy, J. F. (1983) "Close encounters of the traditional kind in medieval Irish literature," *Celtic Folklore and Christianity: Studies in Memory of William W. Heist* (ed. P. K. Ford) 129–149. Santa Barbara.

(1985) *The Wisdom of the Outlaw: The Boyhood Deeds of Finn in Gaelic Narrative Tradition.* Berkeley and Los Angeles.

(1986) "Orality in medieval Irish narrative," *Oral Tradition* 1:272–301.

Nauck, A., ed. (1875) *Homeri Odyssea.* Berlin.

ed. (1877) *Homeri Ilias.* Berlin.

Nehamas, A. (1982) "Plato on imitation and poetry in *Republic* 10," in *Plato on Beauty, Wisdom, and the Arts* (ed. J. M. C. Moravcsik and P. Temko) 47–78. Totowa, N.J.

Neuschäfer, B. (1987) *Origenes als Philologe.* I/II (Schweizerische Beiträge zur Altertumswissenschaft 18.1/2) Basel.

Nichols, S. G., ed. (1990) "The new philology," *Speculum* 65, Special edition, including the following articles: S. G. Nichols, "Introduction: philology in a manuscript culture," 1–10; S. Wenzel, "Reflections on (new) philology," 11–18; S. Fleischman, "Philology, linguistics, and the discourse of the medieval text," 19–37; R. H. Bloch, "New philology and Old French," 38–58; G. M. Spiegel, "History, historicism, and the social logic of the text in the Middle Ages," 59–86; L. Patterson, "On the margin: postmodernism, ironic history, and medieval studies," 87–108.

Nickau, K. (1972) "Zenodotos," *Paulys Real-Encyclopädie der classischen Altertumswissenschaft* 10A columns 20–55. Stuttgart.

(1977) *Untersuchungen zur textkritischen Methode des Zenodotos von Ephesos.* Berlin and New York.

Noomen, W., and Van den Boogaard, N., eds. (1983 / 1984 / 1986) *Nouveau Recueil complet des fabliaux.* Assen.

O'Keeffe, K. O. (1990) *Visible Song: Transitional Literacy in Old English Verse.* Cambridge.

OEI. *See* Blackburn, Claus, Flueckiger, and Wadley (1989).

OLD. See Glare (1982).

Opler, M. E. (1941) *An Apache Life-Way: The Economic, Social, and Religious Institutions of the Chiricahua Indians.* Chicago.

Pack, R. A., ed. (1963) *Artemidori Daldiani Onirocriticon Libri V.* Leipzig.

Page, D. L. (1934) *Actors' Interpolations in Greek Tragedy.* Oxford.

(1955) *Sappho and Alcaeus: An Introduction to the Study of Ancient Lesbian Poetry.* Oxford.

Papadopoulou-Belmehdi, I. (1994) *Le chant de Pénélope: Poétique du tissage féminin dans l'Odyssée.* Paris.

Parca, M. G. (1982) "Sappho 1.18–19," *Zeitschrift für Papyrologie und Epigraphik* 46.47–50.

Paris, G. (1893) "Jaufré Rudel," *Revue Historique* 53:225–260.

Parry, M. (1971) *The Making of Homeric Verse: The Collected Papers of Milman Parry* (ed. A. Parry). Oxford.

Parsons, P. J., ed. (1974) *The Oxyrhynchus Papyri* XLII. London.

Pasquali, G. (1952) *Storia della tradizione e critica del testo.* 2nd ed. Florence.

Patterson, L. (1990) *See* Nichols 1990.

Patton, K. C. (1992) "When the high gods pour out wine: a paradox of Ancient Greek iconography in comparative context." Ph.D. dissertation, Harvard University.

Pavese, C. O. (1974) *Studi sulla tradizione epica rapsodica.* Rome.

Petropoulos, J. B. (1993) "Sappho the sorceress – another look at fr. 1 (LP)," *Zeitschrift für Papyrologie und Epigraphik* 97:43–56.

(1994) *Heat and Lust: Hesiod's Midsummer Festival Scene Revisited.* Lanham, Maryland.

Pfeffer, W. (1985) *The Change of Philomel: The Nightingale in Medieval Literature* (American University Studies Series III, Comparative Literature, vol. 14). New York / Berne / Frankfurt a. M.

Pfeiffer, R., ed. (1949–1953) *Callimachus.* I/II. Oxford.

(1968) *History of Classical Scholarship: From the Beginnings to the End of the Hellenistic Age.* Oxford.

Pickard-Cambridge, A. (1988) *The Dramatic Festivals of Athens.* 3rd ed., revised by J. Gould and D. M. Lewis. Cambridge.

Pickens, R. T. (1977) "Jaufré Rudel et la poétique de la mouvance," *Cahiers de Civilisation Médiévale* 20:323–337.

ed. (1978) *The Songs of Jaufré Rudel.* Toronto.

(1978b) "La Poétique de Marie de France d'après les Prologues des *Lais,*" *Les Lettres Romanes* 32:367–384.

(1994) " 'Old' philology and the crisis of the 'new'," *The Future of the Middle Ages: Medieval Literature in the 1990s* (ed. W. D. Paden) 53–86. Gainesville.

Pischinger, A. (1901) *Der Vogelgesang bei den griechischen Dichtern des klassischen Altertums*. Eichstätt.

Porter, J. I. (1992) "Hermeneutic lines and circles: Aristarchus and Crates on the exegesis of Homer," *Homer's Ancient Readers: The Hermeneutics of Greek Epic's Earliest Exegetes* (ed. R. Lamberton and J. J. Keaney) 67–114. Princeton.

Propp, V. Ja. (1961) "O russkoj narodnoj liričeskoj pesne," *Narodnye liričeskie pesni* (ed. V. Ja. Propp) 5–68. Leningrad.

(1975) "The Russian folk lyric," in *Down Along the River Volga: An Anthology of Russian Folk Lyrics, With an Introductory Essay by V. Ja. Propp* (translated from Propp 1961 by R. Reeder) 1–73. Philadelphia.

Pucci, P. (1979) "The Song of the Sirens," *Arethusa* 12:121–132.

Putnam, M. J. (1960/1) "*Throna* and Sappho 1.1," *Classical Journal* 56:79–83.

Raby, F. J. E. (1951) "Philomela praevia temporis amoeni," *Mélanges Joseph de Ghellinnck* II 435–448. Gembloux.

Raphals, L. (1992) *Knowing Words: Wisdom and Cunning in the Classical Traditions of China and Greece*. Ithaca.

Reeve, M. D. (1969) "Author's variants in Longus?" *Proceedings of the Cambridge Philological Society* 195.75–85.

(1972 / 1973) "Interpolation in Greek tragedy, I/II/III," *Greek, Roman and Byzantine Studies* 13:246–265, 451–474, 14:145–171.

(1986) "Stemmatic Method: 'Qualcosa che non funziona'?" *The Role of the Book in Medieval Culture* (ed. P. Ganz) 57–69. Turnhout.

(1989) "Eliminatio codicum descriptorum: a methodological problem," Grant 1989:1–35.

Reitzenstein, R. (1893) *Epigramm und Skolion: Ein Beitrag zur Geschichte der alexandrinischen Dichtung*. Giessen.

Rengakos, A. (1993) *Der Homertext und die hellenistischen Dichter* (Hermes Enzelschriften 64). Stuttgart.

Reynolds, L. D., and Wilson, N. G. (1991) *Scribes and Scholars: A Guide to the Transmission of Greek and Latin Literature*. 3rd ed. Oxford.

Richardson, N. J. (1975) "Homeric professors in the age of the sophists," *Proceedings of the Cambridge Philological Society* 21:65–81.

Risch, E. (1946) "Sprachliche Bemerkungen zu Alkaios," *Museum Helveticum* 3:253–256. Reprinted in Risch 1981:290–293.

(1954) "Die Sprache Alkmans," *Museum Helveticum* 11:20–37. Reprinted in Risch 1981:314–331.

(1974) *Wortbildung der homerischen Sprache*. 2nd ed. Berlin.

(1981) *Kleine Schriften* (ed. A. Etter and M. Looser). Berlin.

Ritoók, Zs. (1970) "Die Homeriden," *Acta Antiqua* 18:1–29.

(1987) "Über einige Fragen der homerischen Textgeschichte," *Acta Classica / Debrecen* 23:7–18.

Robert, J. and L. (1983) "Bulletin Epigraphique," *Revue des Etudes Grecques* 96:182–184.

Robert, L. (1936) "᾿Αρχαιολόγος," *Revue des Etudes Grecques* 1936:235–254. Reprinted in *Opera Minora Selecta* I (Amsterdam 1969) 671–690.

(1960) "Recherches épigraphiques v: inscriptions de Lesbos," *Revue des Etudes Anciennes* 62:300ff. Reprinted in Robert 1969.816ff.

(1969) *Opera Minora Selecta*. II. Amsterdam.

Roesch, P. (1982) *Etudes Béotiennes*. Paris 1982.

Rosen, R. (1988) *Old Comedy and the Iambographic Tradition*. Atlanta.

Rösler, W. (1980) *Dichter und Gruppe: Eine Untersuchung zu den Bedingungen und zur historischen Funktion früher Lyrik am Beispiel Alkaios*. Munich.

(1985) "Persona reale o persona poetica? L'interpretazione dell 'io' nella lirica greca arcaica," *Quaderni Urbinati di Cultura Classica* 19:131–144.

Rossi, L. E. (1968) "La fine alessandrina dell' *Odissea* e lo ΖΗΛΟΣ ΟΜΗΡΙΚΟΣ di Apollonio Rodio," *Rivista di filologia classica* 96:151–163.

(1971) "I generi letterari e le loro leggi scritte e non scritte nelle lettere classiche," *Bulletin of the Institute of Classical Studies* 18:69–94.

Roueché, C. (1993) *Performers and Partisans at Aphrodisias in the Roman and Late Roman Periods: A Study Based on Inscriptions from the Current Excavations at Aphrodisias in Caria* (Journal of Roman Studies Monographs no. 6). London.

Royce, A. P. (1977) *The Anthropology of Dance*. Bloomington.

Russo, J. A., and Simon, B. (1968) "Homeric psychology and the oral epic tradition," *Journal of the History of Ideas* 29:483–498.

Rychner, J., ed. (1966) *Les lais de Marie de France*. Paris.

Saussure, F. de. (1916) *Cours de linguistique générale*. Paris. Published by some of his students three years after his death.

Sax, W. S. (1991) "Ritual performance in the Pāṇḍavalīlā of Uttarakhand," *Essays on the Mahābhārata* (ed. A. Sharma) 274–295. Leiden.

Scheid, J., and Svenbro, J. (1994) *Le Métier de Zeus: Mythe du tissage et du tissu dans le monde gréco-romain*. Paris.

Schein, S. L. (1987) "Unity and meaning in Pindar's sixth Pythian Ode," *MHTIΣ: Revue d'Anthropologie du Monde Grec Ancien* 2:235–247.

Scheller, M. (1951) *Die Oxytonierung der griechischen Substantiva auf -ia*. Zurich.

Schenkeveld, D. M. (1970) "Aristarchus and ΟΜΗΡΟΣ ΦΙΛΟΤΕΧΝΟΣ," *Mnemosyne* 23:162–178.

(1992) "Prose usages of ΑΚΟΥΕΙΝ," *Classical Quarterly* 42:129–141.

Schmid, G. (1904) *De luscinia quae est apud veteres*. St. Petersburg.

Schmitt, R. (1967) *Dichtung und Dichtersprache in indogermanischer Zeit*. Wiesbaden.

Schomer, K. (1989) "Paradigms for the Kali Yuga: the heroes of the Ālhā epic and their fate," OEI 140–154

Schulze, W. (1892) *Quaestiones epicae*. Gütersloh.

Schur, D. M. (1994) "The way of oblivion: Heraclitus and Kafka." Ph.D. dissertation, Harvard University.

Seaford, R., ed. (1984) *Euripides: Cyclops*. Oxford.

(1994) *Reciprocity and Ritual: Homer and Tragedy in the Developing City-State*. Oxford.

Sealey, R. (1957) "From Phemius to Ion," *Revue des Etudes Grecques* 70:312–355.

(1990) *Women and Law in Classical Greece*. Chapel Hill.

Segal, C. P. (1982). *Dionysiac Poetics and Euripides' Bacchae*. Princeton.

(1994) "Philomela's web and the pleasures of the text: reader and violence in the *Metamorphoses* of Ovid," *Modern Critical Theory and Classical Literature* (ed. I. J. F. de Jong and J. P. Sullivan) 257–280. Leiden.

Sherratt, E. S. (1990) "'Reading the texts': archaeology and the Homeric question," *Antiquity* 64:807–824.

Slater, W., ed. (1986) *Aristophanis Byzantii Fragmenta*. Berlin and New York.

(1989) "Problems in interpreting scholia on Greek texts," Grant 1989:37–61.

Slotkin, E. M. (1977–79) "Medieval Irish scribes and fixed texts," *Éigse* 17:437–450.

Smith, J. D. (1989) "Scapegoats of the gods: the ideology of the Indian epics," OEI 176–194.

Smith, W. C. (1993) *What is Scripture? A Comparative Approach*. Minneapolis.

Speer, M. B. (1980) "Wrestling with change: Old French textual criticism and *mouvance*," *Olifant* 7:311–326.

Spiegel, G. M. (1990) *See* Nichols 1990.

Steblin-Kamenskij, M. I. (1982) *Myth* (translated by M. P. Coote). Ann Arbor.

Stephanes (Στεφανής), I. E. (1988) ΔΙΟΝΥΣΙΑΚΟΙ ΤΕΧΝΙΤΑΙ: ΣΥΜΒΟΛΕΣ ΣΤΗΝ ΠΡΟΣΩΠΟΓΡΑΦΙΑ ΤΟΥ ΘΕΑΤΡΟΥ ΚΑΙ ΤΗΣ ΜΟΥΣΙΚΗΣ ΤΩΝ ΑΡΧΑΙΩΝ ΕΛΛΗΝΩΝ. Iraklion.

Stone, L. W. (1946–1947) "Jean de Howden, poète anglo-normand du XIIIe siècle," *Romania* 69:496–519.

Svenbro, J. (1984) "La découpe du poème. Notes sur les origines sacrificielles de la poétique grecque," *Poétique* 58:215–232.

(1988) *Phrasikleia: Anthropologie de la lecture en Grèce ancienne*. Paris.

(1993) *Phrasikleia: An Anthropology of Reading in Ancient Greece*. Translation by J. Lloyd of Svenbro 1988, with additions by the author. Ithaca.

Tambiah, S. J. (1985) *Culture, Thought, and Social Action: An Anthropological Perspective.* Cambridge, Mass.

Taplin, O. (1992) *Homeric Soundings: The Shaping of the Iliad.* Oxford.

Tarrant, R. J. (1989) "The reader as author: collaborative interpolation in Latin poetry," Grant 1989:121–162.

Thiel, H. van, ed. (1991) *Homeri Odyssea.* Hildesheim.

(1992) "Zenodot, Aristarch und andere," *Zeitschrift für Papyrologie und Epigraphik* 90:1–32.

Thompson, D'Arcy W. (1936) *A Glossary of Greek Birds.* 2nd ed. Oxford.

Timpanaro, S. (1981) *La Genesi del metodo del Lachmann.* 2nd ed. Padova. Reprinted 1985, with addenda.

Todorov, Tz. (1978) *Les Genres du discours.* Paris.

(1990) *Genres in Discourse.* Translation by C. Porter of Todorov 1978. Cambridge.

Todt, D. (1971) "Äquivalente und konvalente gesangliche Reaktionen einer extrem regelmäßig singenden Nachtigall," *Zeitschrift der vergleichenden Physiologie* 71:262–285.

Traube, L. (1910) *Textgeschichte der Regula S. Benedicti.* 2nd ed. Munich.

Travis, R. M. (1990) "The descent of the goddess: ritual and difference in Sappho's prayer to Aphrodite." B.A. thesis, Harvard University.

Turner, E. G. (1987) *Greek Manuscripts of the Ancient World.* 2nd ed. by P. J. Parsons. (Institute of Classical Studies, Bulletin Supplement 46) London.

Valk, M. van der (1949) *Textual Criticism of the Odyssey.* Leiden.

(1963/1964) *Researches on the Text and Scholia of the Iliad* I/II. Leiden.

(1971) *Eustathii archiepiscopi Thessalonicensis Commentarii ad Homeri Iliadem pertinentes* I. Leiden.

Van der Werf, H. (1965) "The trouvère chansons as creations of a notationless musical culture," *Current Musicology* 2:61–68.

(1967) "Recitative melodies in trouvère chansons," *Festschrift Walter Wiora,* 231–240. Kassel.

(1972) *The Chansons of the Troubadours and Trouvères: A Study of the Melodies and their Relation to the Poems.* Utrecht.

(1993) "The raison d'être of medieval music manuscripts," *The Oldest Extant Part Music and the Origin of Western Polyphony.* 1. Appendix, pp. 173–209. Rochester.

Van Sickle, J. (1980) "The book-roll and some conventions of the poetic book," *Arethusa* 13:5–126.

Vance, E. (1986) *Mervelous Signals: Poetics and Sign Theory in the Middle Ages.* Lincoln, Nebraska.

(1987) *From Topic to Tale: Logic and Narrativity in the Middle Ages.* Minneapolis.

Ventris, M. and Chadwick, J. (1973) *Documents in Mycenaean Greek.* 2nd ed. Cambridge.

Vidal-Naquet, P. (1986) "The Black Hunter revisited," *Proceedings of the Cambridge Philological Society* 212:126–144.

Wackernagel, J. (1953) *Kleine Schriften* i–ii. Göttingen.

Wadley, S. S. (1989) "Choosing a path: performance strategies in a North Indian epic," OEI 75–101.

Wehrli, F. (1968) "Demetrios von Phaleron," *Paulys Real-Encyclopädie der classischen Altertumswissenschaft, Supplement-Band* xi 514–522. Stuttgart.

Wenzel, S. (1990). *See* Nichols 1990.

West, M. L. (1970) "Rhapsodes," in *The Oxford Classical Dictionary*, edited by N. G. L. Hammond and H. H. Scullard, 919–920. Oxford.

(1971) "Stesichorus," *Classical Quarterly* 21:302–314.

(1973) *Textual Criticism and Editorial Technique.* Stuttgart.

ed. with commentary (1978) *Hesiod: Works and Days.* Oxford.

(1981) "The singing of Homer and the modes of early Greek music," *Journal of Hellenic Studies* 101:113–129.

(1986) "The singing of hexameters: evidence from Epidaurus," *Zeitschrift für Papyrologie und Epigraphik* 63:39–46.

(1988) "The rise of the Greek epic," *Journal of Hellenic Studies* 108:151–172.

(1992) *Ancient Greek Music.* Oxford.

West, S., ed. (1967) *The Ptolemaic Papyri of Homer* (Papyrologica Coloniensia 3). Cologne and Opladen.

(1988) "The transmission of the text," in *A Commentary on Homer's Odyssey. Introduction and Books i–viii*, ed. A. Heubeck, S. West, and J. B. Hainsworth, 33–48. Oxford.

Wilamowitz-Moellendorff, U. von, ed. (1895) *Euripides' Herakles* i: *Einleitung in die griechische Tragödie* i, ii. 2nd ed. Berlin.

(1916) *Die Ilias und Homer.* Berlin.

(1924) *Hellenistische Dichtung in der Zeit des Kallimachos.* Berlin.

Wiles, D. (1984) "Menander's *Dyskolos* and Demetrius of Phaleron's dilemma," *Greece and Rome* 31:170–179.

Williams, G. (1968) *Tradition and Originality in Roman Poetry.* Oxford.

Williams, J. M. (1987) "The Peripatetic School and Demetrius of Phalerum's reforms," *Ancient World* 15:87–98.

Winkler, J. J. (1985) "The ephebes' song: *tragōidia* and *polis*," *Representations* 11:26–62. Rewritten in Winkler and Zeitlin 1990:20–62.

Winkler, J. J., and Zeitlin, F., eds. (1990) *Nothing to Do with Dionysos? Athenian Drama in its Social Context.* Princeton.

Wolf, F. A. (1795) *Prolegomena ad Homerum.* Halle. Translated 1985, with introduction and notes, by A. Grafton, G. W. Most, and J. E. G. Zetzel. Princeton.

Yatromanolakis, D. (forthcoming). "A commentary on selected fragments of Sappho." D. Phil. dissertation, University of Oxford.

Yerly, Ch. (1992) "Figures du tyran archaïque: Entre le monstre et le sage," *Etudes de Lettres: Revue de la Faculté des Lettres, Université de Lausanne* 1992:3–32.

Zeitlin, F. (1985) "The power of Aphrodite: Eros and the boundaries of the self in the *Hippolytus*," *Directions in Euripidean Criticism* (ed. P. Burian) 52–208. Durham.

   (1990) "Playing the other: theater, theatricality, and the other in Athenian drama," Winkler and Zeitlin 1990:63–96.

Zetzel, J. E. G. (1980) "The subscriptions in the manuscripts of Livy and Fronto and the meaning of *emendatio*," *Classical Philology* 75:38–59.

   (1981) *Latin Textual Criticism in Antiquity*. New York.

   (1993) "Religion, rhetoric, and editorial technique: reconstructing the classics," Bornstein and Williams 1993:99–120.

Zumthor, P. (1972) *Essai de poétique médiévale*. Paris.

   (1983) *Introduction à la poésie orale*. Paris.

   (1984) *La Poésie de la voix dans la civilisation médiévale*. Paris.

   (1987) *La Lettre et la voix: De la "littérature" médiévale*. Paris.

Zwettler, M. J. (1978) *The Oral Tradition of Classical Arabic Poetry*. Columbus.

Index

Index

Index

251

Printed in Great Britain
by Amazon.co.uk, Ltd.,
Marston Gate.